Contextuality in Translation and Interpreting

ŁÓDŹ STUDIES IN LANGUAGE

Edited by Barbara Lewandowska-Tomaszczyk and Łukasz Bogucki

VOLUME 70

PETER LANG

Michał Kornacki and Gary Massey (eds.)

Contextuality in Translation and Interpreting

Selected Papers from the Łódź-ZHAW Duo Colloquium on Translation and Meaning 2020–2021

PETER LANG

Bibliographic Information published by the Deutsche Nationalbibliothek
The Deutsche Nationalbibliothek lists this publication in the Deutsche Nationalbibliografie; detailed bibliographic data is available online at http://dnb.d-nb.de.

Library of Congress Cataloging-in-Publication Data
A CIP catalog record for this book has been applied for at the Library of Congress.

This publication was financially supported by the IUED Institute of Translation and Interpreting (ZHAW Zurich University of Applied Sciences) and by the Institute of English Studies (University of Lodz).

ISSN 1437-5281
ISBN 978-3-631-86921-5 (Print)
E-ISBN 978-3-631-88357-0 (E-PDF)
E-ISBN 978-3-631-88398-3 (EPUB)
DOI 10.3726/b19912

Peter Lang – Berlin · Bruxelles · Lausanne · New York · Oxford

This publication has been peer reviewed.

www.peterlang.com

Contents

Gary Massey, Łukasz Bogucki, Michał Kornacki

Translation, Meaning and the Duo Colloquium: Contextuality in Translation and Interpreting

The Duo Colloquium: Past and present

The first iteration of the Łódź-ZHAW Duo Colloquium on Translation and Meaning took place in 2020 and 2021. As the successor to the internationally acclaimed event organised in Maastricht and Łódź every five years between 1990 and 2015, it adopted the same format as that of its predecessors. This involved two separate but linked sessions taking place consecutively in two locations: at the University of Łódź in Poland, and at ZHAW's Institute of Translation and Interpreting in Winterthur, Switzerland. Originally conceived as in-person conferences, the restrictions imposed by the COVID-19 pandemic meant that both sessions had to be postponed and to move online: the Polish conference being staged from Łódź between the 3rd and 5th December 2020, and the Swiss session from Winterthur between the 2nd and 4th September 2021. We would like to thank the organising committees at both locations for the first-class job they did in planning and managing both conferences. We would also like to express our gratitude to the presenters of the many excellent papers delivered at the two sessions, the majority of which could not be accommodated in the present volume.

Like many other innovative initiatives, the Duo Colloquium was conceived during a conference break, 35 years ago in Berlin. Incidentally, now that online conferencing has made coffee breaks practically obsolete, one can only hope that the academic community at large will continue to come up with (and share) such spontaneous ideas. The Duo, as it is affectionately called by its participants, is the brainchild of two scholars representing the West and the East (the dichotomy was very much relevant at the time, with the iron curtain still in place). They were Professor Barbara Lewandowska-Tomaszczyk (University of Łódź, Poland) and Dr. Marcel Thelen (Maastricht School of Translation and Interpreting, subsequently Zuyd University, the Netherlands), who both participated in the said linguistics conference in Berlin in 1987. The idea bore fruit for the first time in 1990, with two events in the Netherlands and Poland, a dyad that continued in this vein every five years until 2015. At that time, Maastricht could no longer be a venue due to organisational changes; luckily, Zurich University of Applied Sciences (ZHAW) agreed to seamlessly carry on the tradition of the "Western" partner and since 2020 the conference has officially been co-organised jointly in Łódź and Winterthur. Prof. Lewandowska-Tomaszczyk and Dr. Thelen chaired the respective conference sessions in Maastricht and Łódź until their retirement, when they became Honorary Chairs; both continue in that capacity until this day.

Toutes proportions gardées, the Duo Colloquium has been a mirror of the development of Translation Studies as an academic discipline. There is hardly a famous translation scholar who has not participated in the event over the three decades of its history: Peter Newmark, Eugene A. Nida, Juliane House, Christiane Nord, Gideon Toury, Jeremy Munday, Mona Baker, Anthony Pym… the list goes on. The tangible effect of the Duo Colloquium is now 12 regular volumes of proceedings and a thirteenth special volume. The present book is the fruit of the two most recent sessions, the Lodz one and the Winterthur one, both organised in the throes of the COVID-19 pandemic. The wide scope of the conference series, covering issues pertaining to translation and meaning, has enabled a comprehensive, interdisciplinary treatment of translation from a linguistic and semantic angle, with focal points changing over the years. The diagram below, sourced from the joint keynote given by Barbara Lewandowska-Tomaszczyk, Marcel Thelen, Gary Massey and Łukasz Bogucki (2020) at the opening of the Lodz Session in December 2020, is indicative of the topics tackled by conference participants (see Figure 1).

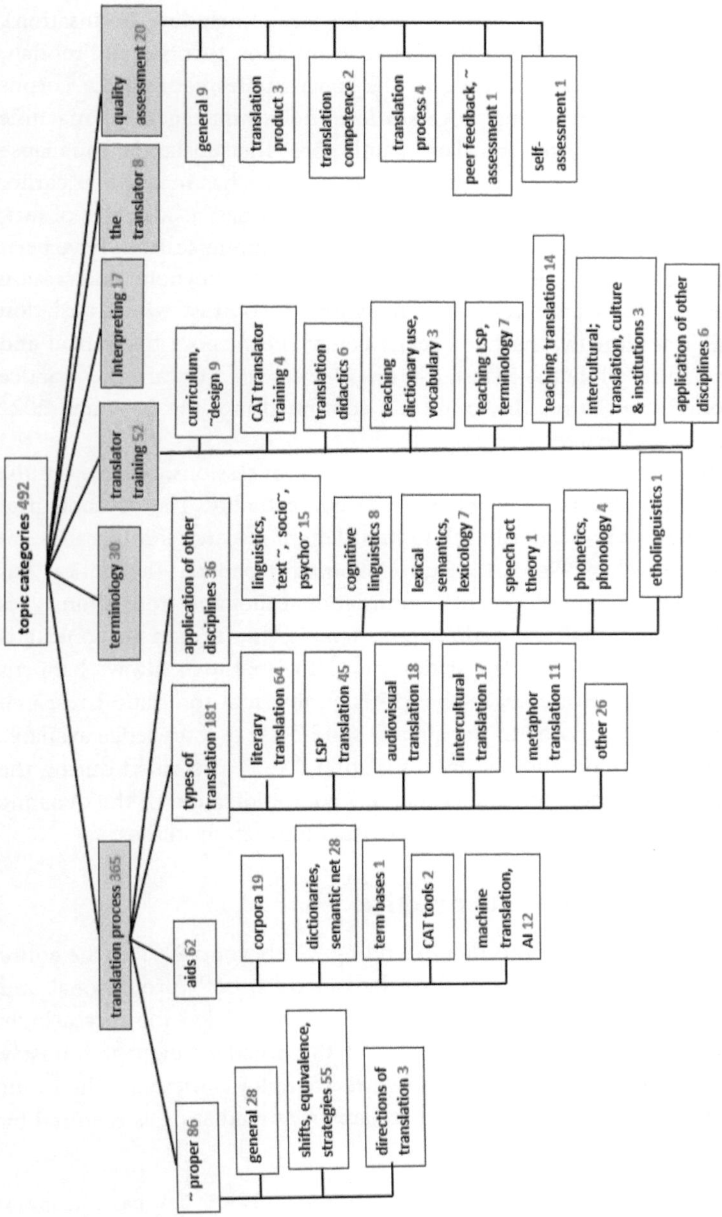

Figure 1: Range of topics covered by the Duo Colloquium conference series 1990–2015

In brief, the Duo Colloquia have witnessed discussions on all types of translation, viz. literary, specialised and audiovisual (including localisation), translator education, translation competence, translation theories and models, collaborative translation, cultural cognitive language studies, equivalence, corpus tools, translation and interpreting processes, terminology management, machine translation, computer-assisted translation and more. The substantial time lapse between the first and the latest conference in the series has meant that earlier papers have served as sources of inspiration for later ones; as a matter of fact, there are scholars for whom the respective Duo Colloquium sessions have been milestones of their entire academic careers. In general, the keynotes and session papers have explored translation as a profession in contrast with translation in academia. Traditionally, the Łódź sessions have been more theoretical and academic in nature, while the Maastricht ones have veered toward the practice of (professional) translating; this trend has continued into the 2020 and 2021 sessions in Łódź and Winterthur, respectively.

The key theme of the most recent Duo Colloquium sessions, reflected in the papers compiled in the present volume, was contextuality. The psychological notion of context has been central to translation research for decades, as evidenced also by the 1990–2015 Duo Colloquium papers. The notion has evolved along with the development of translational thought, translation types and tools. In audiovisual translation, for example, the notion of context is crucial, as – to simplify – the translation of audiovisual texts always happens in the visual context. However, in the 1990s audiovisual translation research was in its infancy, as opposed to the already solid body of knowledge available today.[1] The 18 papers on audiovisual translation (AVT) presented during the Duo Colloquium sessions over the years are a good indication of the dynamic development of the (sub)discipline of audiovisual translation studies.

Dynamic fields of study and practice

That dynamism continues to this day, extending well beyond AVT to the entire discipline of Translation Studies and to the practices, both professional and educational, which it addresses. The main drivers have been the increasingly rapid changes taking place in the contexts of the broader language industry and of the workplaces of those whose services it employs. These are the result of evolving demand in the key areas where language mediation is required by

1 The online *Bibliography of Translation and Interpreting* (BITRA) now has as many as 4226 publications on audiovisual translation.

buyers: accessing a market, complying with regulations, acquiring customers, enabling public access, managing processes and people, retaining customers, monitoring events and reactions, and discovery (see Slator, 2022: 15–17). To meet that demand efficiently, cost-effectively, and viably, the industry has witnessed an accelerating development of both the human and the technological resources it deploys.

This has been most clearly demonstrated by the qualitative leaps forward made by neural machine translation (NMT). Since 2016, research on the NMT performance has produced some very positive results. Studies already published in that year show NMT to have outperformed, or at least to have been equal to, phrase-based statistical machine translation (SMT), even when tested within specific domains, demonstrating clear improvements even in MT-challenging language pairs involving Chinese (e.g. Junczys-Dowmunt et al., 2016; Wu et al., 2016). For example, Wu et al.'s (2016: 1) human side-by-side evaluation of isolated simple sentences study suggested that Google's NMT machine reduces translation errors by an average of 60 % over Google's own phrase-based system on out-of-domain data, prompting claims by the research team that NMT was "bridging the gap between human and machine translation" quality (Wu et al., 2016: 1). Two years later, Hassan et al. (2018) asserted that Microsoft had achieved "human parity" in Chinese-English machine translation of news reports. Schmitt (2019: 209–210) sees the more recent emergence of zero-shot translation (Johnson et al., 2017) as even more significant, enabling MT to translate between arbitrary languages, including language pairs for which the system has not been trained. The closing of the quality gap between human translation and MT has prompted an increasing belief in some quarters that human language mediators will be supplanted by MT systems.

Despite the early hype and fears, however, the predictions – largely by those outside the language industry – of the disruptive effects of easily available AI technologies, and the perceived threat to language mediators working in and for the industry, have not materialised. Far from it – the latest *Slator Language Industry Market Report* (Slator, 2022: 5–6) puts the size of the global language services and technology industry in 2021 at USD 26.6 billion, a growth in market size of 11.75 % compared to the previous year. Its base scenario for project future growth stands at 6.0 % year-on-year, meaning that total market size could reach USD 30.12 billion by the end of 2026. The optimistic scenario estimates 7.5 % year-on-year growth, to USD 38.22bn by the end of 2026. Other analyses are similarly rosy. For example, Nimdzi (Hickey, 2022), whose estimates include a number of ancillary services excluded by Slator, states that "the language services market is better set up than ever before to meet the increasingly complex demands of buyers" and that "2021 was a phenomenal year," with Nimdzi's own estimate of the industry's value rising to USD 60.5 billion, a 10 % increase compared to 2020. It forecasts growth to USD 64.7 billion in 2022 and, given a predicted compound annual growth rate (CAGR) of 7 %, expects the industry to be valued at USD 84.9 billion by 2026.

By whatever measure we apply, the language industry is thus in very good health, and it continues to depend on the expert language mediators that provide its services. MT systems are making language professionals more productive than ever, but the "human-in-the-loop will *always* remain the most important link in the chain" (Way, 2020: 326). The role of language mediators is simply evolving, as it has always done, through technology (van der Meer, 2020: 308). Nowhere is this seen more clearly than in the re-profiling of translators currently underway at the Directorate General for Translation of the European Parliament (DG-TRAD) and presented in the keynote held by the European Parliament's Alison Graves and Mads Nyegaard Outzen (2021) at the Winterthur session of the Duo Colloquium. Re-branded as intercultural and language professionals, the translators are expected to translate, adapt, transcreate, mediate, subtitle, revise, post-edit, facilitate plain-language communication and assist in drafting documents, among other duties. As such, the new profile aligns well with those who, against the background of increasing MT quality, have been predicting a shift in demand for human language mediation at the higher end of the market towards the added value of adaptivity, creativity, risk management and ethical awareness (e.g. Massey & Ehrensberger-Dow, 2017), on the one hand, and towards domain expertise (e.g. Schmitt, 2019; Slator, 2022), on the other. A prerequisite is, of course, consistent top quality and full mastery of the competences – translational/mediatory, technological, personal, interpersonal, and service – set out in models and profiles such as the European Master's in Translation (EMT) competence framework (EMT Board, 2017). It is only the untrained language mediators who deliver poor quality work that language technologies will be forced out of the market (Schmitt, 2019: 206–208).

The new profile at the European Parliament is indicative of the growing diversification of tasks in the many and various working contexts of the language industry as a whole. Bond (2018) lists 600 different job titles for the industry in 2018, a figure which had increased to 700 by 2020 (Slator, 2020: 11–17). One convincing explanation lies in how the industry is progressively expanding upstream (i.e. towards multilingual content creation) and downstream (e.g. towards compliance, access and accessibility, content, data and quality management, production, publication, distribution, and consultancy work) of core translation and localisation services.

But even at the core, distinct new profiles and practices have established themselves for activities that once fell within the scope of translation. Post-editing of MT output (PEMT) is perhaps the most prominent example, with Slator (2022: 82) able to claim that "broadly speaking, the PEMT workflow is now firmly embedded across the industry as the default workflow." However, this presents its own challenge and opportunity to industry players and language mediators alike: "Access to high-quality MT is no longer a differentiator between LSPs [language service providers]. A competitive edge in the market, then, comes from how effectively LSPs can complete the last mile – the gap between MT output and enterprise / end-user-grade translation quality. A key aspect of this dynamic is that – as the size of the gap [between human and MT output] shrinks – the sophistication required to close the gap increases" (Slator, 2022: 82). Obviously, therefore, a premium accrues to identifying the specific value-adding human expertise needed for PEMT, and to finding ways of developing and implementing it effectively. Listed only seven years ago separately as a value-added service in the international translation quality standard ISO 17100 (2015: 18), PEMT has since been fully and explicitly integrated into the EMT competence framework (EMT Board, 2017), has received its own dedicated international standard complete with competence profile (ISO 18587, 2017: 6–8), and has been the subject of competence modelling in its own right (e.g. Nitzke et al., 2019: 247–252; Nitzke & Hansen-Schirra, 2021: 69–79).

Unsurprisingly, PEMT receives the attention of two contributions to the present volume, both of which adopt an educational perspective. Indeed, the training and education of language mediators is by far the strongest theme in this volume, addressed by half the number of chapters it contains. Upskilling and reskilling graduates to act as human experts in the multiple loops of the current and future language industry (Massey & Ehrensberger-Dow, 2021) will remain the crucial task of language-mediation educators in the years to come. The educators, their students and, increasingly, working language professionals themselves are faced with choices about specialising in specific domains and profiles, at the risk of longer-term obsolescence, and/or focusing on the adaptive expertise (Shreve, 2020) that will be needed to fill the diversifying roles that are proliferating within the industry.

As the language industry thrives, expands, and evolves, so, too, does the discipline of Translation Studies as it explores the multi-faceted concepts, activities processes and products of language mediation inside the industry and, in terms of investigating non-professional translation and interpreting, outside it as well. The fundamental dynamism of both the pursuit of language mediation and the study of it is amply illustrated in the current volume.

Contributions to this volume

In keeping with previous conferences, the Łódź part of the latest Duo Colloquium dealt principally with theoretical aspects of contextuality in translation and interpreting. Like the Maastricht sessions beforehand, the ZHAW session had a more applied orientation. The theme of contextuality can be understood at any level, from the geopolitical to the textual, and embraced both academic and professional considerations of translational and interpreting phenomena. It centred on context, contexts and/or decontextualisation in translation and interpreting theory and practice from a variety of disciplinary, interdisciplinary, and transdisciplinary perspectives.

In response to the calls for papers for the 2020–2021 Duo Colloquium, the array of sub-themes covered by the contributions to both sessions testifies to the diversity of academic, educational, and professional attention that language mediation currently commands. The selection of papers in the present volume reflects, inevitably only in a partial form, the range of those interests.

The collection begins by addressing translator training in the context of specialised or domain-specific translation. **Marcel Thelen** considers the place and function of term recognition in the translation process, situated principally in what ISO 17100 (2015) designates as the second stage, namely the production process. He argues that term recognition is part of a wider terminology competence and proposes a practical guide for students on how to translate terms.

In **Anna Setkowicz-Ryszka's** contribution, the focus remains on training, this time in the domain legal translation and from the perspective of PEMT. Here, the emphasis lies on raising student awareness of the various layers of context in which the translation takes place. Given the time constraints and multi-disciplinary nature of legal translation, teachers need to focus on error avoidance and problem-solving, for which PEMT presents a viable training option, though this should be balanced against the risks of introducing students to it too early in their learning. Use of post-editing exercises on context-insensitive raw MT output may speed up the learning process by enabling more text to be processed. It also allows trainees to identify the importance of context in translation, to think critically, to enhance their problem-solving and to practice PEMT, a skill that is in increasing demand on the market.

Claudia Wiesinger, **Alina Secară** and **Dragoş Ciobanu** continue the educational theme in a different working context, making the case for exposing student translators as early as possible to the use of increasingly popular speech technologies in the translation workflow. Their experimental study of undergraduate students tracked error annotation and correction performance together with evolving attitudes to speech-enabled PEMT. The results show quality and productivity benefits, though over-editing and inaccurate perceptions of productivity are also in evidence. Despite the quality improvements in some conditions, many MT errors remained uncorrected in working conditions with and without speech technology being deployed, suggesting strongly that at least one reviser should check PEMT work, especially when done by novices.

Still in the realm of translator training, **Urszula Paradowska** considers project-based teaching and learning in the context of the COVID-19 pandemic. She reports on the online delivery of authentic collaborative translation projects for undergraduates oriented on the competences set out for EMT's Master's degree programmes (EMT Board 2017), discussing the effects of the abrupt shift to online teaching and the challenges encountered in terms of interaction and engagement. Her own reflections are supplemented with the generally positive results from an anonymous course evaluation questionnaire and personal communications with the students.

The final chapter devoted to aspects of training zones in on information mining competence, again in the context of legal translation. In her second paper, **Anna Setkowicz-Ryszka** stresses the need to improve students' procedural knowledge by increasing awareness of relevant sources to consult, developing the ability to critically evaluate the usefulness of resources and cross-check information obtained, and showing how to make better decisions based on familiarity with the target language legal systems.

With **Marcel Thelen's** second paper we move from education and training *per se* to the closely related field of translation quality assessment (TQA). Arguing that existing TQA methods tend to be geared towards assessing target-text products, but not in the wider context of entrepreneurial competence in which they are embedded, he demonstrates how the personal, interpersonal and service provision competences of the EMT Competence Framework 2017 (EMT Board, 2017), and the processes described in ISO 17100 (2015) can be used to operationalise the entrepreneurial aspects of quality assessment, and makes suggestions for formalising the broader contextualisation of TQA.

A further contribution with ramifications for translator training is **Katarzyna Wiśniewska's** report on an ongoing PhD project on the retention of force-dynamics schemas in translation and dissociating linguistic and cognitive levels of translation description according to Mäkisalo and Lehtinen's (2014) cognitive retention hypothesis. The mixed quantitative and qualitative study uses trilingual bidirectional corpora of phrases with force-dynamics patterns from fragments of literary and audiovisual texts in different translation pairs. The chapter concentrates on mistranslations from Finnish into English and Polish, opening up an interesting perspective for translation training by providing evidence of embodied cognitive processes of re-conceptualisation in translation, as well as the situated dependence of meaning on the specifics of various contexts.

In the eighth chapter, **Ralph Krüger** also begins by adopting a cognitive linguistic perspective on how context and contextual meaning in human translation can be modelled – with the principal aim of exploring the extent to which machine translation architecture is able to draw on and to incorporate contextual meaning when translating. He considers the extent to which NMT processes linguistic meaning and takes account of contextual information and discusses aspects of its actual performance with regard to encoding contextually available meaning in its translation output. He ends by considering current research on document-level MT and multimodal MT, which enables an extended range of contextual information to be considered.

The technological focus continues in the contribution by **Dominik Kudła**, who looks at the phenomenon of decontextualisation in the process of localising game videos. One cause of translation errors in the localised versions of video games is sometimes referred to in the industry as "blind localisation." Such errors distort the coherence and plausibility of the in-game world and may even hinder or prevent users from completing a game. This contribution explores the factors that lead to such a situation and examines the types of errors caused by "blind localisation" in various video-game genres localised from English into Polish.

In the tenth chapter, **Martyn Gray** takes us from the act of translation to the reception of translated works in published reviews. Inspired by – and challenging – Lawrence Venuti's (1995) claim that reviewers of translated works contribute to translators' "invisibility," he presents findings from a recent study of UK-based reviews designed to address the questions of how often translations are acknowledged, how they are commented on, and by what criteria they are assessed. Proceeding from the results, which show that translators appear to have become more visible than previously imagined, he draws on the work of translation associations and organisations to determine whether the findings are connected to a broader enhancement of the status and visibility of translation in UK society.

In the next chapter, **Mehmet Yildiz's** offers a novel account of intertextuality in translated texts through the prism of what he calls "pseudo-retranslation" – the phenomenon of academic authors partially or completely using another author's translation and presenting it as a retranslation. Examining various Turkish academics' translations of Milton Rokeach's seminal assumptions about the nature of human values, he concludes that the authors in his corpus preferred to “pseudo-retranslate” from other Turkish academics’ works rather than translate directly from the respective source text as they wrote in their native language.

The focus of attention in the twelfth chapter shifts from the textual and intertextual to the extratextual. Here, **Karolina Siwek** turns to contextual factors influencing literary translation in nineteenth-century Poland. Using the example of three prominent literary translators of the time – Kazimierz Brodziński, Ignacy Hołowiński, and Józef Paszkowski –, she analyses the socio-cultural and political circumstances that shaped their translation activity and choices.

The final chapter of this collection illustrates the breadth of contexts in which language mediation operates. Taking as her subject the non-professional practice and working environment of simultaneous interpreting in Evangelical churches in Poland, **Judyta Mężyk** reports on results from an interview survey of nine churches from different Evangelical denominations, which included questions about interpreting equipment, setting and the competences of interpreters. In conclusion, the author briefly discusses the possibilities of further research on church interpreting.

The papers collected in this volume reveal the sheer range of contributions made to the 2020–2021 Łódź-ZHAW Duo Colloquium, reflecting a diverse and abiding interest in researching and reporting the principles, processes, and practices of translation, interpreting and other forms of language mediation in a variety of settings. Together, they demonstrate that the discipline of Translation Studies in all its contexts is every bit as alive and kicking as the language industry itself – and as the many non-professional forms of language mediation arrayed alongside it. It only remains for the co-editors to extend their heartfelt thanks to the many reviewers, too numerous to mention individually, who have provided such invaluable support for this publication with their expert feedback and advice.

References

Bond, E. (2018). ‘The stunning variety of job titles in the language industry.’ *Slator news*. https://slator.com/features/the-stunning-variety-of-job-titles-in-the-language-industry/.

EMT Board. (2017). *European master’s in translation. Competence framework 2017*. European Commission. https://ec.europa.eu/info/sites/info/files/emt_competence_fwk_2017_en_web.pdf

Graves, A., & Nyegaard Outzen, M. (2021, September 3). *Shaping the future – new contexts for language professionals in the European Parliament* [Keynote].

The Łódź-ZHAW Duo Colloquium on Translation and Meaning, 2nd session, ZHAW Zurich University of Applied Sciences, Winterthur, Switzerland.

Hassan, H., Aue, A., Chen, C., Chowdhary, V., Clark, J., Federmann, C., Huang, X., Junczys-Dowmunt, M., Lewis, W., Li, M., Liu, S., Liu, T.Y., Luo, R., Menezes, A., Qin, T., Seide, F., Tan, X., Tian, F., Wu, L., Wu, S., Xia, Y., Zhang, D., Zhang Z., & Zhou M. (2018). 'Achieving human parity on automatic Chinese to English news translation.' *Computing Research Repository* arXiv: 1803.05567

Hickey, S. (2022, February 24). *The 2022 Nimdzi 100*. https://www.nimdzi.com/nimdzi-100-top-lsp/

ISO 17100. (2015). *Translation services – requirements for translation services.* Geneva: International Organization for Standardization.

ISO 18587. (2017). *Translation services – post-editing of machine translation output – requirements.* Geneva: International Organization for Standardization.

Johnson, M., Schuster, M., Le, Q. V., Krikun, M., Wu, Y., Chen, Z., Thorat, N., Viégas, F., Wattenberg, M., Corrado, G., Hughes, M., & Dean, J. (2017). 'Google's multilingual neural machine translation system: Enabling zero-shot translation.' *Transactions of the Association for Computational Linguistics, 5*, 339–351. http://www.mitpressjournals.org/doi/pdf/10.1162/tacl_a_00065&hl=de&sa=X&scisig=AAGBfm21zi_TO5P_9Jk1GW5QEjWq_WaWFg&nossl=1&oi=scholarr

Junczys-Dowmunt, M., Dwojak, T., & Hoang, H. (2016). 'Is neural machine translation ready for deployment? A case study on 30 translation directions.' arXiv: 1610.01108v3 [cs.CL]. https://de.scribd.com/document/345503523/Is-Neural-Machine-Translation-Ready-for-Deployment.

Lewandowska-Tomaszczyk, B., Thelen, M., Massey G., & Bogucki, Ł. (2020, December 3). *Translation, meaning and context* [Opening keynote]. The Łódź-ZHAW Duo Colloquium on Translation and Meaning, 1st session, University of Łódź, Łódź, Poland.

Mäkisalo, J., & Lehtinen, M. (2014). 'Dissociation of linguistic and cognitive description in translation: The cognitive figure-ground alignment.' In H. Paulasto, L. Meriläinen, H. Riionheimo, & M. Kok (Eds.), *Language contacts at the crossroads of disciplines* (191–211). Cambridge Scholars.

Massey, G., & Ehrensberger-Dow, M. (2017). 'Machine learning: Implications for translator education.' *Lebende Sprachen, 62*(2), 300–312. https://doi.org/10.1515/les-2017-0021

Massey, G., & Ehrensberger-Dow M. (2021). 'Language mediation professions: Humans in multiple loops.' In ZHAW Angewandte Linguistik (Eds.), Angewandte Linguistik in Sprachberufen (157–160). De Gruyter. https://doi.org/10.1515/9783110748796-010

van der Meer, J. (2020). 'Translation technology – past, present and future.' In E. Angelone, M. Ehrensberger-Dow, & G. Massey (Eds.), *The Bloomsbury companion to language industry studies* (285–310). Bloomsbury Academic. https://doi.org/10.5040/9781350024960

Nitzke, J., Hansen-Schirra, S., & Canfora C. (2019). 'Risk management and post-editing competence.' *The Journal of Specialised Translation, 31*, 239–259. https://www.jostrans.org/issue31/art_nitzke.pdf

Nitzke, J., & Hansen-Schirra, S. (2021). *A short guide to post-editing (Translation and Multilingual Natural Language Processing 16)*. Language Science Press. https://doi.org/10.5281/zenodo.5646896.

Schmitt, P. A. (2019). 'Translation 4.0 – evolution, revolution, innovation or disruption?' *Lebende Sprachen, 64*(2), 193–229. https://doi.org/10.1515/les-2019-0013.

Shreve, G. M. (2020). 'Professional translator development from an expertise perspective.' In E. Angelone, M. Ehrensberger-Dow, & G. Massey (Eds.), *The Bloomsbury companion to language industry studies* (153–178). Bloomsbury Academic. https://doi.org/10.5040/9781350024960

Slator. (2020). *Slator 2020 language industry market report*. https://slator.com/slator-2020-language-industry-market-report/

Slator. (2022). *Slator 2022 language industry market report*. https://slator.com/slator-2022-language-industry-market-report/

Venuti, L. (1995). *The translator's invisibility: A history of translation*. Routledge.

Way, A. (2020). 'Machine translation: Where are we today?' In E. Angelone, M. Ehrensberger-Dow, & G. Massey (Eds.), *The Bloomsbury companion to language industry studies* (311–332). Bloomsbury Academic. https://doi.org/10.5040/9781350024960

Wu, Y., Schuster, M, Chen, Z., Le, Q. V., Norouzi, M., Macherey, W., Krikun, M., Cao, Y., Gao, Q., Macherey, K., Klingner, J., Shah, A., Johnson, M., Liu, X., Kaiser, L., Gouws, S., Kato, Y., Kudo, T., Kazawa, H., Stevens, K., Kurian, G., Patil, N., Wang, W., Young, C., Smith, J., Riesa, J, Rudnick, A., Vinyals, O., Corrado, G., Hughes M., & Dean J. (2016). 'Google's neural machine translation system: Bridging the gap between human and machine translation, eprint.' arXiv: 1609.08144 https://arxiv.org/ abs/1609.08144

Marcel Thelen (ret.)

Maastricht School of Translation and Interpreting, Zuyd University of Applied Sciences

Translating Terms: Towards a Practical Guide for Students of Translation

Abstract: In the context of specialised or domain-specific translation, term recognition determines to a large extent whether the translation is appropriate. As specialised texts contain both terms and words, it is of vital importance for the translator[1] to know when dealing with a term or a word. In the case of a term, there is less or no translation freedom and a standardised equivalent term must be given in the target text. In the case of a word, the translator has more translation freedom.

This paper discusses place and function of term recognition in the translation process. By analogy to ISO 17100, the translation process is roughly divided into three main stages: 1) pre-production processes and activities, 2) production processes and 3) post-production processes. Term recognition is situated in the second stage. It is, furthermore, argued that term recognition is part of a wider terminology competence. Experienced translators will probably not have problems with term recognition, but students of translation certainly do. The overall aim of this paper is to propose a practical student guide for translating terms.

Keywords: termhood, term recognition, terminology competence, translation freedom, translation competence

Introduction

"Terminology work can be carried out for different reasons, such as dictionary compilation, translation, knowledge modelling, document indexing, and standardization" (L'Homme, 2020: 59). The application discussed in this paper is translation and, therefore, the type of terminology dealt with is translation-oriented terminology.[2] It is the type of terminology that is applied in the translation of domain-specific texts: "Translation-oriented terminology work is terminology work related to the translation process and that is why

1 When in this paper "translator" is used, it refers to the translator in general, but more in particular to the student of translation.

2 Cf. Thelen (2012: 132–133).

translation-oriented terminology work is mostly bi- or multilingual." (Lušicky & Wissik, 2015: 8).

Unlike systematic terminology, which deals with such matters as term-concept relation, term creation, concept formation and standardisation, translation-oriented terminology is primarily concerned with (the process) of rendering an ST (source text) into an appropriate TT (target text) and transferring occurring terms from ST to TT and recording these and their TT equivalents for future use. This entails that translation-oriented terminology is not geared towards the terminology of translation studies as such. This may be dealt with by systematic terminology. At the most, translation-oriented terminology may be applied to texts on translation studies where the focus is on providing appropriate translations of terms relating to translation studies.[3]

Translating general language texts differs from translating domain-specific texts in that for the former the translator has more translation freedom (possibly restricted somewhat by the translation brief of the client), that is, the translator has the option of "choosing" from a number of synonyms and/or synonymous formulations the most appropriate equivalent for the TT context. When translating domain-specific texts, the translator is constrained by rules and requirements of the domain in question and possibly also by the translation brief of the client and has – *generally and to a large extent* – less "translation freedom" or less to "choose" than in the case of general language translation. *Generally and to a large extent*, because domain-specific texts contain terms as well as words, which means that the translator has both less translation freedom (for terms) and more translation freedom (for words). Less translation freedom in the case of terms entails that the translator is "almost 'forced' to give a standardised equivalent in the target text if available (depending on the translation brief of the client); if he does not do this, there is no appropriate translation"[4] (Thelen, 2002: 22), and, moreover, this standard(ised) equivalent should also be a preferred equivalent.

3 The term *translation-oriented terminology* is commonplace in the literature on terminology (cf. for example Eckman, n.d.; Bowker, 2015), but mostly it refers to terminology *management*, i,e. the recording of terms (which is stage 3 in this paper). In this paper, the focus is on the entire translation process including a pre-translation stage and a translation stage next to a post-translation stage for recording.

4 "The appropriateness of a translation is influenced by such factors as the wishes/directions of the client, the nature of the ST (both linguistically and as far as subject matter is concerned), etc." (Thelen, 2002: 1, fn. 2).

This situation requires of the translator the ability to distinguish terms from words, i.e. the ability to identify or recognise terms. And it is term recognition that may cause translation problems and inappropriate translations. If the translator does not recognise an item as a term, it will very likely be treated as a word and general resources like general dictionaries instead of specific resources will be consulted for more information (e.g. about its meaning). This will most likely lead to mistranslation, i.e., not a preferred standard terminological equivalent. Failing term recognition may take place in domain-specific texts when terms "disguised" as general language words are used – i.e. terminologised words or general language words used as terms. This happens often in such domains as psychology, art criticism, art appreciation, education, and social studies. Take for instance EN *regulation*. In an EU text, its preferred standard equivalent term in NL is *verordening*. However, when *regulation* in such a text is unfamiliar and not recognised as a term, the translator will probably consult a general EN-NL dictionary where such equivalents are given as *regeling, reglementering, (wettelijk) voorschrift, bepaling* and *overheidsbesluit*.[5] None of these is appropriate in this context. Had the translator recognised *regulation* as a term while not knowing its meaning, IATE[6] or Linguee[7] (which does not always provide enough information) should have been consulted, where *verordening* is given, which is the preferred standard equivalent term for this context. Similarly, the preferred standard NL equivalent for the term *regulation* in an EU medical (social science – health) context is *regulatie* (in IATE), and none of the above equivalents given in the general dictionary. In such cases, the translator had better consult not only a general resource but also a specialist (domain-specific) resource.

Experienced professional translators would probably not have (m)any problems with term recognition (unless perhaps when coming across "young" or new terms), but students of translation certainly will. They still have to learn how to tell terms from words in domain-specific texts. In this paper a first attempt is made at formulating a practical student guide for translating terms, which may,

5 *Van Dale Groot Woordenboek Engels-Nederlands* (2008, 4th ed.). Van Dale.

6 The EU's terminology database (Interactive Terminology for Europe).

7 Linguee is "an online bilingual concordance that provides an online dictionary for a number of language pairs, including many bilingual sentence pairs. As a translation aid, Linguee differs from machine translation services like Babelfish and is more similar in function to a translation memory. Linguee is operated by Cologne-based Linguee GmbH, which was established in Cologne in December 2008." Wikipedia.org (Accessed: 28 October 2021).

however, also be used by experienced translators as a road map to fall back on in cases of translation difficulties.

Practical student guide for translating terms[8]

Translating terms is a process with several stages rather than a single activity. Term recognition is just one stage in this process. The process of translating terms described in this paper follows to a large extent ISO 17100 (the international standard on "Translation Services – Requirements for translation services") as the basis for the proposed student guide.[9] ISO 17100 distinguishes the following stages:

1. **Resources:** human and technical/technological
2. **Pre-production processes and activities:** enquiry & feasibility, quotation, client-TSP[10] agreement, handling project-related client information, project preparation
3. **Production process:** translation service project management, translation process
4. **Post-production processes:** feedback, closing administration.

Of these, steps 2–4 function as a model for the process of translating terms. However, *quotation, translation service project management, feedback and closing administration* are not relevant for this student guide and are, therefore, left out. *Closing administration* is replaced by *recording* the terms in question and their translation in a translation memory or – together with further relevant information – in a term list or other database.

By analogy, the practical student guide proposed here is also divided into three main stages:

1. **Pre-production processes and activities:**
   a. Macroanalysis of the ST
   b. Analysis of client specifications
   c. Term extraction/term retrieval

---

8 This guide can be used by translation students for self-study or as a reference manual and by translation teachers as course material for teaching translation-oriented terminology. When it comes to teaching, this guide differs from other course proposals (e.g. Montero Martínez & Faber Benítez, 2009; Sánchez-Gijón et al., 2009) in that here the focus is on term recognition as the core of translation-oriented terminology.

9 But see also Vargas-Sierra (2011).

10 Translation Service Provider, i.e. the translation company or freelancer.

2. **Production process:**
    a. Term recognition
    b. Matching or identifying equivalence between ST term and candidate TT equivalent term(s)
    c. Applying strategies for solving equivalence issues
3. **Post-production processes:**
    a. Recording and managing results in a term base or other database

As can be seen, these main stages are further subdivided into a number of substages. Main stage 1 is standard for all types of translation and is therefore part of translation competence. The main stages 2 and 3 are specifically part of terminology competence, which is not surprising since the type of terminology for this type of translation is translation-oriented terminology.

A similar division into stages is outlined by Vargas-Sierra (2011) where present and future of terminology management for specialised translation by means of ICT is discussed and where the focus is on documentation (or data mining) and terminology management with the use of ICT. In this paper the focus is on term recognition and the overall aim is the development of a practical guide for students of translation.

Pre-production processes and activities

The pre-production stage can be schematised as shown in Figure 1:

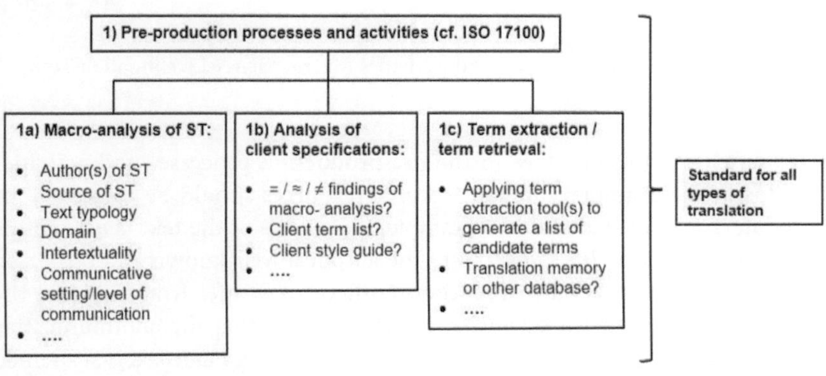

Figure 1: Pre-production processes and activities

The pre-production stage is an essential part of every translation because not only does it provide valuable clues (or signals) for likely term occurrence in the ST (which may be very helpful for term recognition), it also gives information about the client's specifications and possibly also practical documents like a term list. And finally, in this stage the application of term extraction may also provide clues for likely term occurrence in the ST. Therefore, this main stage should never be skipped.

Pre-production processes and activities: macroanalysis of the ST

The macroanalysis of the ST may provide valuable clues about the likelihood of terms occurring in the text and may make the translator alert, as shown in Table 1:

ASPECT	REALISATION IN ST	LIKELIHOOD
Author(s)	Academic (by title)	yes
Source	Scientific journal	yes
Text typology: *genre*	Research paper	yes
Text typology: *communicative function*	To report, to analyse	yes
Text typology: *register*	Academic language	yes
Domain	Psychology	yes
Intertextuality	Expectations/evidence: textual organisation, layout, tables, data, ...	yes
Communicative setting/ level of communication	Domain specialist to domain specialists	yes
		Very high: beware!

Table 1: Pre-Production Processes And Activities Macroanalysis-Likelihood of Term Occurrence, an Example

If there are sufficient clues in the pre-production processes and activities stage (as in the example), domain-specific resources should be consulted for candidate TT equivalents. If, for example, the source of the text is a scientific medical journal (e.g. *The Lancet*) and the author a well-known and respected researcher with an academic title, the translator may infer from this that the intended readers are also scientists, in other words, that the communicative setting (see below) is between scientists and that the language used is academic. On this basis it may be expected to find a high density of terms in the text. In the example all possible clues are "positive," but this need not always be the case.

Other useful clues for likely term occurrence are text typology, domain (e.g. law, medicine, economics) and intertextuality. Text typology involves genre (e.g. advertisement, obituary, contract, research paper, blog, newspaper article, travel report, etc.), communicative setting (see below) and register (formal/informal language). Text typology in combination with source, author and domain may also be a useful indicator. Intertextuality is "a global pattern which the reader compares to pre-existing cognitive templates abstracted from experience. Intertextuality is a property of 'being like other texts of this kind' which the readers attribute to texts" (Neubert & Shreve, 1992: 117).

Communicative setting refers to "The way in which they [people (MT)] refer to objects" and this way of referring varies between people and situations. It "depends 1) on the context or situation in which they find themselves, and 2) on the type of knowledge which they bring to the particular situation" (Pearson, 1998: 26). Pearson distinguishes four such settings (ibid., 36–38):

1. Expert – to – expert communication
2. Expert – to – initiates
3. Relative expert to the uninitiated
4. Teacher – pupil communication

where settings 1, 2 and 4 are reliable sources for potential term candidates (ibid., 39). Communicative settings are best accompanied by other clues, for example source and author, but also clues found in the production stage (see section 2.2.1.3 below). It is a fact, however, that "the notion of communicative setting... may be the most important factor in allowing us to decide whether words are being used as terms or words" (ibid., 28). A comparable and somewhat more refined approach is taken by Thelen (2001), named "level of communication," which is more general as it does not relate to such specific groups as teacher-pupil. In the rest of this paper *level of communication* will be used.

All in all, the macroanalysis of the ST is a very useful and possibly rich source for clues for the likelihood of term occurrence.

Pre-production processes and activities: Analysis of client specifications

Client specifications are, of course, the basis for the entire translation process. They set the translation scene as it were. Part of the specifications may be a term list and/or a style guide. If there is a term list and if this is monolingual covering the source language only, there is no longer the issue of term recognition, because a number of (or all the) terms are already given in the term list. If these terms are, however, not preferred standard terms but terms coined and used by the client, the translator will face the problem of analysing their meaning and finding the appropriate target-language equivalents. If the term list is bilingual containing also target-language equivalents, the translator may no longer need to look for target-language equivalents, i.e. at least as long as these are preferred standard equivalents. If they are not, but in-company equivalents, the translator will have to discuss this with the client and/or apply strategies for solving possible equivalence problems.

Another possible problem may occur when the client wishes a change of readership or audience for the translation. Though this may provide a translation problem for the translator, at the same time it may be considered as a clue, because the translator then knows where to look for equivalents. For example, if the ST is an academic medical text and the client wishes it to be translated for the public at large, the translator knows that it is not the expert Latin equivalent terms that should be used in the TT but their common language counterparts. Therefore, the translator should always analyse the client's specifications before stating the actual translation.

Pre-production processes and activities: Term extraction/term retrieval

The macroanalysis of the ST in the pre-production processes and activities stage can very well be paired with the application and findings of a term extraction tool. There are three main types of term extraction: 1) statistical term extraction, 2) linguistic term extraction and 3) hybrid term extraction (for more details on how these types actually analyse texts and produce results, see Pazienza, Pennacchiotti and Zanzotto, 2006; Kageura & Marshman, 2020).

A well-known term extraction tool is WordSmith (https://www.lexically.net/wordsmith/). It produces a word list or frequency list, a list of keywords and a concordance. The word list or frequency list provides frequencies of occurrence of all the items in the text under analysis and "helps find salient words… "(ibid.). The keywords list presents key items in the text "in alphabetical and frequency order" *(*ibid.*)*, and the concordance shows chunks of context of keywords. In the end, it is the translator who has to select and validate items as term candidates. Especially the keywords list and the concordance may provide clues for termhood, the keywords list because higher frequency keywords could well be term candidates, and the concordance because it may contain useful linguistic contextual signals for termhood of keywords. Frequency can also be a clue for termhood in corpora.

Of course, also translation memories or other databases may provide useful clues for termhood. Translation memories provide more than just clues, they show equivalent terms in context (usually limited to sentence, paragraph or segment level) by means of alignment. Also parallel corpora can be very useful. These are corpora containing an ST and its translation in another language with alignment at sentence level; for examples see https://en.wikipedia.org/wiki/Parallel_text, https://www.clarin.eu/resource-families/parallel-corpora, https://opus.nlpl.eu/.

Production processes

Production processes form the very heart of translation-oriented terminology; they can be visualised as shown in Figure 2:

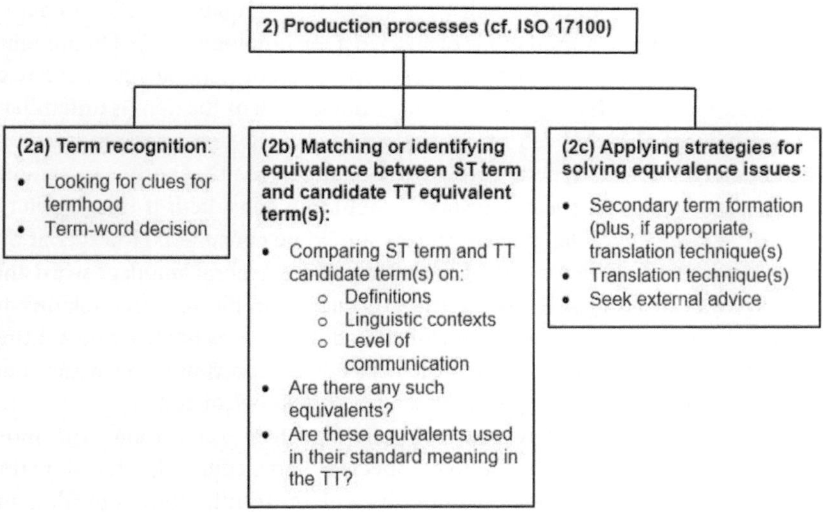

Figure 2: Production Processes.

As can be seen, the production stage is further subdivided into three substages: 1) term recognition, 2) matching or identifying equivalence between ST term and candidate TT equivalent term(s), and 3) applying strategies for solving equivalence issues. These are the most difficult substages in the entire process of translating terms.

Production processes: Term recognition

Term recognition involves deciding if an item is a term or just a general language word. This prerequires especially domain knowledge, but certainly also knowledge of what a term is (section 2.2.1.1) and what can be a term (section 2.2.1.2), but also familiarity with clues for termhood (section 2.2.1.3). Failing any of these prerequisites may lead to failing term recognition and subsequent mistranslations. Term recognition and its prerequisites are part of a wider terminology competence, for which see section 3.

Resources (e.g. dictionaries, term bases, parallel corpora, etc.) play an important role in term recognition. Successful term recognition determines the choice of resources to be used for identifying equivalence, while the choice of resources may also determine if term recognition will be successful or not. If an item has been recognised as a term and a preferred standard(ised) equivalent must be found, specialist resources (e.g. domain-specific glossaries or dictionaries, larger compilations of specialist terminology like IATE, domain-specific textbooks, etc.) should be consulted, and not general resources (e.g. general dictionaries). If an item's meaning is not known or the item is unfamiliar, and if it has not already been recognised as a term, the text in which it occurs should determine what type of resources should be consulted: if it is a domain-specific text, a domain-specific resource should be consulted; if it is a general language text, a general language resource should be consulted. However, if the unfamiliar item in a domain-specific text looks like a general language word and has not yet been recognised as a term, a domain-specific resource relating to the domain of the text should be consulted and if this does not provide a fitting equivalent, this probably means that the item in question is not a term and then a general dictionary or other general resource should be consulted.

There are several possible causes for failing term recognition. The most obvious cause is insufficient domain-specific knowledge. Greater domain-specific knowledge entails greater familiarity with the terminology of the domain in question, which will generally lead to almost flawless term recognition. New or young terms or terminologised words may, however, cause recognition problems. This is where translation experience comes in. Translation experience and domain-specific knowledge go hand in hand; the longer the experience is with translating texts of a particular domain, the greater will be the domain-specific knowledge of this domain. Professional translators specialised in translating texts of a specific domain will generally have both great domain-specific knowledge and long translation experience, and these are coupled with a strong terminology competence and an equally strong translation competence.

A student of translation or a starting translator will, obviously, not have these competences equally developed as experienced professional translators; they must still learn and train. The practical student guide presented in this paper is meant for them to learn how to translate terms. As their training progresses, they may use this guide as a reference manual in cases of difficulty or uncertainty.

What is a term?

In order to be able to tell terms from words, it is necessary to know what a term is. In the literature there are several views on what a term is. These views may be grouped under different perspectives: 1) their relation to specialist domains in general, 2) their characteristics in terms of their use, and 3) their characteristics in terms of their form. As for the first perspective (the relation to specialist domains in general), there are three views according to Hoffmann (1985: 126–127): 1) the very narrow view stating that only items belonging to a specialist domain are terms and that all other items are words, 2) the wider view in which all items used in a specialist domain are terms, and 3) the most common view according to which a specialist domain contains three types of terms, viz. domain-specific terms (used in one domain only), non-domain-specific terms (used in more domains), and general language words (e.g. *mouse* in IT). For a student of translation who has to translate terms and thus to recognise if an item is a term, these characterisations are not very helpful. What may be helpful, though, is that this third view can be interpreted in terms of expectations for domain-specific texts, i.e., about what domain-specific texts may contain. This can be 1) general lexicon (= words), terminological lexicon (e.g. *greenhouse gas*), and transdisciplinary lexicon (e.g. *model, scenario*) (L'Homme, 2020: 59, fn. 26). In other words, this tells the student that domain-specific texts may also contain general language words and that alertness is called for when coming across items that look like general language words but may well be domain-specific terms.

The second perspective (characteristics in terms of use) according to which terms are items that are used in a particular specialist domain, is not helpful either for the student of translation because it "does not tell us how to recognize terms" (Pearson, 1998: 26) and therefore "we still have no objective means of recognizing them in text" (ibid.).

The third perspective (characteristics in terms of form) is the least useful for defining terms: "formally terms are indistinguishable from words" (Sager, 1998: 41), and "Terms do not seem to be very different from words when we consider them from the formal or semantic point of view" (Cabré, 1999: 81).

All in all, these characterisations of terms seem to point at similarities between terms and words instead of differences, and therefore they are not helpful for term recognition. The similarity is endorsed in Lexical Semantics (terms are considered as lexical units – L'Homme, 2020: 46–49), but also in Terminology itself (where general characteristics of words are attributed to terms: "prototypes do have their place in linguistics, cognition and also terminology" – Weissenhofer, 1995: 46–49). And in Cognitive Semantics no difference is made either between words and terms, they are considered lexical items that "are points of access to encyclopaedic knowledge" (Evans & Green, 2006: 221). Concluding, L'Homme (2020: 66) states: "It should be obvious by now that *term* is a relative notion," as is *termhood* and Faber & Lopez-Rodriguez (2012: 16) argue that "trying to find a distinction between terms and words is no longer fruitful or even viable, and that the best way to study specialized knowledge units is by studying their behavior in texts." A similar stance is taken by Kageura (2015) who argues that usage and social recognition determine termhood:

> We can understand the contrast between a term and a word as something analogous to the contrast between a pet … and a dog or cat. This means that such extra-linguistic factors as usage and social recognition in a given domain matter when talking about terms. (Kageura, 2015: 46)

All this makes term recognition even more important and difficult. How can terms be recognised from words if there are no noticeable differences? What clues (if any) does the translator have when coming across items in a domain-specific text that are unknown and whose status is not recognised (as a term or word)? These will be discussed in section (2.2.1.3). However, for term recognition also knowledge of what can be a term is important, in other words, knowledge of possible term types. For this see the next section.

What can be a term?

Termhood need not only be sought in nouns, although this is the major category for candidate terms. Nouns can be single nouns as *biodiversity*, DE *Verkettung*. NL *ringnetwerk*, but also compound nouns like *daisy chain* (Levi, 1978: 1) and other multi-word units such as *endangered species, natural habitat* (L'Homme, 2020: 63), *front-wheel-drive* (Wright, 1997: 14), *high-vacuum electron beam fusion welding* (Cabré, 1999: 86).[11] However, also other

---

11 For a useful source of information about the interpretation of the meaning of compounds see Levi (1978).

parts of speech can provide terms such as adjectives (*viral, online* – L'Homme, 2020: 63) and verbs (*intubate*). Also larger units may be attributed termhood such as set phrases (e.g. *black and white*, NL *zwart-wit, zwart op wit* – Wright, 1997: 15), collocations (e.g. *file a patient* – Wright, 1997: 15; *forgive (someone) a debt* = "to give up all claim to" – *Longman Dictionary of Business English*, 1998), standard (chunks of) text(s) (e.g. the pre-amble to a contract[12] – Wright, 1997: 16).

Cabré (1999: 86–90) lists more examples of terms such as:

- Initialisms – "units made up of the combination of the initials of a longer expression. They often correspond to the name of an organization, document or process, and in many cases they become lexicalized in the common language: *MIT* (Massachusetts Institute of Technology), *CIA* (Central Intelligence Agency), *WHO* (World Health Organization)"
- Acronyms – "words formed by combining segments from a developed phrase which are pronounced syllabically
  - o The initial segments of the first and second elements, e.g. *Amex* (American stock Exchange), *hazmat* (hazardous material), *COMSAT* (communications satellite)
  - o The initial segment of the first element and the final segment of the second, e.g. *bit* (*binary digit*)"
- Abbreviations – "forms that are usually established by consensus. They reproduce a part of the word and practically act as a symbol for the word, e.g. *vol* (*volume*)"
- Short forms or clippings – "They are based on using the first part of a longer word, or the first word of a phrase, e.g. *super* (*superintendent*), *hypo* (*hypodermic syringe*)"
- Borrowings "(partial or full) from Greek or Latin but also other languages, e.g. *bigamy, mammography, Blitzkrieg* (DE origin)"

All the above options may raise the translator's alertness to the potential presence of termhood, and contribute to term recognition.

---

12 Standard (chunks of) texts are not suited for registration in a term bank, but more suitable for a translation memory. It is almost impossible to formulate a solid definition for such chunks of text.

Looking for clues for termhood

Clues for termhood may help the translator decide whether an element should be treated as a term or a word, and may determine to a large extent the strategy to be followed. There are several types of clue:

1. Clues found in the pre-production processes and activities stage (see section 2.1):
   a. Clues emerging from the macroanalysis of the ST, for example Information about the author, source, domain, and level of communication of the ST as well as a text typology of the ST
   b. Clues emerging from the analysis of client specifications
   c. Clues emerging from the application of a term extraction tool, a translation memory or other database
2. Clues found in the production processes stage:
   a. Formal clues
   b. Contextual clues
   c. Textual clues
   d. Miscellaneous clues

Formal clues

Formal clues relate to the form of a lexical item (for examples of such clues see section 2.2.1.2 above).

Contextual clues

Contextual clues are formulations in the immediate context of a lexical item under consideration. Pearson (1998: 130–134) gives the following examples: "*i.e.*, e.g. *denotes, called, known as,* "" (where a lexical item is placed between quotation marks), "*the term.*" The clues "*called*" and "*known as*" may have various realisations:

- "*called:*" *is/are called, is/are often called, usually called, generally called, sometimes called, (usually called), (often called)*
- "*known as:*" *also known as, sometimes known as, generally known as, commonly known as.*

Pearson derived the examples from a number of corpora. There may be many more such clues. L'Homme (2020: 58, fn. 25), for example, gives *defined as* and *means*. More clues may be found through studying linguistic corpora. If none of these clues is helpful, the student may return to the pre-production processes and activities stage in order to check if any clues have been overlooked in this stage.

Textual clues

Textual clues are clues in the wider context of the ST. They relate to "the frequency with which the same terminological phrase[13] occurs in texts of a particular special field" (Cabré, 1999: 137). An example is *generalists* as opposed to *specialists* (Fischer, 2020: 71). As both occurred frequently in the same text under consideration, they should be treated as terms, i.e. they should be attributed termhood, which means that the translator should not for stylistic reasons vary their translation by means of synonyms. In the text in question, both referred to special groups of staff in a company. The text had to be translated into Hungarian; had it been into Dutch, their equivalent terms should have been *generalisten* and *specialisten*, respectively.

Miscellaneous clues

Finally, there is a rag-bag category of clues that cannot easily be classified in one of the previous groups. For examples see Cabré (1999: 137).

It may be clear from this section that there are quite a few clues for termhood that may make term recognition somewhat easier. Term extraction (see section 2.1.3 before) may provide additional clues. If there are no clues at all, the translator may return to the pre-production stage or consult the client and/or a domain expert or a colleague specialist translator.

Production-processes: Matching or identifying equivalence

Matching or identifying equivalence between an ST term (if it is decided that this is a term and not a word) with one or more possible candidate TT terms involves in the first place finding out if the ST term is a preferred standard term and if there is a preferred standard TT candidate. It may well be that there are several standard TT equivalent terms; in that case, the preferred standard equivalent has

13 The use of *terminological phrase* in this context is confusing. It implies that the phrase has already been recognised as a term, which is not the case. As this refers to a clue indicating that the phrase still has to be recognised as a term, it would have been better to use just *phrase* instead of *terminological phrase*.

to be used.[14] Then the preferred candidate TT term should be compared with the ST term in question. This should be done on at least the following points: 1) their definitions as found in authoritative sources, 2) the linguistic context of the ST term and the linguistic context of the candidate TT term as found in a term base or other database, and 3) their levels of communication. In the ideal case the level of communication should be the same for ST term and candidate TT term(s) and is to a large extent determined by the source of the definitions and contexts. If there is correspondence on the above basic aspects, there is equivalence between ST term and preferred TT candidate term and the preferred TT equivalent may be used in the translation. If, however, there appear to be equivalence issues, the translator is forced to apply strategies in order to solve them (see next section).

Production processes: Applying strategies for solving equivalence issues

The most common equivalence issues between ST term and candidate TT term(s) are:

1. There is no TL equivalent term:
   a. e.g. EN *WYSIWYG* →FR *WYSIWYG* ("ce q'on voit est ce que l'on obtient à l'impression"): [FR "has no adequate equivalent to express the meaning conveyed by" the ST term (cf. L'Homme, 2020: 235)]. Translation techniques applied: direct borrowing + explanatory paraphrase
   b. other options: EN *lockdown* →NL *lockdown*, "EN: *hashtag* – FR: *hashtag* (direct borrowing), *mot-clic* (term creation), EN: *deep learning* – FR: *apprentissage profond* (literal translation)" (L'Homme, 2020: 235)
   c. NL *Elfstedentocht* →EN *Elfstedentocht, Elfstedentocht (Dutch 200 km skating race between 11 Frisian cities), Eleven Cities tour.* Translation techniques applied: direct borrowing, direct borrowing + explanatory paraphrase, or literal translation

14 Equivalence comes in a number of varieties, e.g. SL [= Source Language (MT)] one lexical item *vs.* TL [= Target Language (MT)] more lexical items: EN *cognitive* – PL *poznawczy / kognitywny* (Lewandowska-Tomaszczyk, 2008: 303). For a more exhaustive survey of the various types of equivalence see Lewandowska-Tomaszczyk, 2008 and 2015).

2. There is a TL equivalent term, but denoting a (partially) different concept:
   a. (e.g. politics) EN *parliament* (= "House of Commons" + "House of Lords") vs. NL *parlement* (= "Tweede Kamer")
   b. EN *to farm* ("raise animals" or "cultivate land for food")→ FR *éléver* ("raise animals") and *cultiver* ("grow and harvest vegetables or plants") (L'Homme, 2020: 236)
3. The ST term is not used in its standard meaning, i.e. there may be a difference between the definition of the term in isolation as found in a term bank or other database and the contextually determined meaning (cf. also Rogers, 1999). Here the translator must first try to solve the inaccurateness in the ST before starting to look for TT candidate equivalent terms; if none is found, one or more translation techniques must be applied
4. There is terminological variation in the candidate TT term. Terminological variation may, for example, take the form of a variation of word order in compound medical terms such as *cardiovascular – vasculocardiac* (Bowker & Hawkins, 2006: 88)

These complicating factors require terminology competence where needed or appropriate, combined with translation competence, i.e. the application of translation techniques. In the case of absence of candidate TT equivalent terms, for example, the translator has a few options: (1) try to fill the terminological gap by creating a term (if possible) – i.e. applying secondary term formation (cf. Sager, 1990: 80),[15] (if appropriate) in combination with translation techniques, (2) apply translation techniques only, or (3) seek external advice (e.g. the client, a colleague translator or a domain expert). For example, EN *Excise Contact Group* ("an expert group advising about excise taxation and regulations") or EN *Contact Group Firearms* ("an expert group advising about firearms") used in an

15 Sager (1990) distinguishes between two types of term formation or creation: 1) primary term formation and 2) secondary term formation: "Primary term formation accompanies concept formation and is therefore monolingual; it may be provisional, i.e. accompanied by a stipulative or otherwise temporary definition or it may be seen as definitive. Secondary term formation occurs when a new term is created for a known concept … in primary term formation there is no linguistic precedent, though there may be more or less strict rules for the formation of appropriate terms, whereas in secondary term formation there always is the precedent of an existent term with its own motivation. The new term to be created must then be justified in some way and this justification may include reference to the form of existent terms. Secondary term formation is more often subject to guidelines than primary formation" (Sager, 1990: 80–81).

EU context does not have an NL equivalent according to IATE (cf. Buysschaert & Thelen, 2020: 37), but *Contact Group* does (*contact groep/Contact Groep*). By analogy to the existing NL term *Contactgroep mensenrechten* the translator may decide to create *Contactgroep accijnzen*. Applying secondary term formation requires terminological knowledge.

For a useful survey of various term formation methods see Cabré (1998: 92–95).

Post-production processes: recording and managing results

Post-production processes form the last stage in the process of translating terms, but by no means the least important (as visualised in Figure 3):

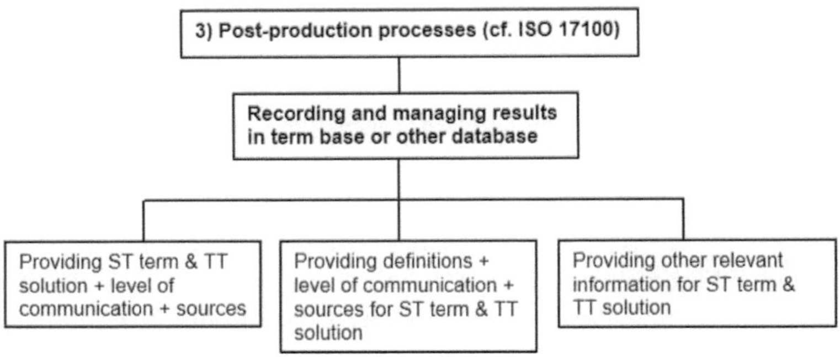

Figure 3: Post-production Processes.

For efficiency reasons, i.e. for efficient later use, the translator should record the problem term in question together with the translation solution(s) in a term base.[16] Recording remains an absolute must:

> As part of any translation project, translators must identify appropriate equivalents for the specialized terms that they encounter in the SLT [= Source Language text (MT)]. … Researching the specific terminology needed to complete any given translation can be a time-consuming and labour-intensive task, and it has long been recognized that it does not make sense to repeat this research when a new text needs to be translated. … In today's era of information overload and intense time-to-market pressures, translators recognize

16 See e.g. MultiTerm 2021, https://www.trados.com/products/multiterm-desktop/ or https://www.rws.com/localization/products/multiterm or a different database.

> more than ever the importance of keeping track of pertinent terminological information in order to avoid repeating time-consuming research. (Bowker, 2015: 304–305)

For completeness and clearest information a term base or other database is to be preferred over a translation memory, as in the latter only aligned translations are given, whereas a term base, for example, also contains such information as level of communication, related terms, etc.

In principle there are three recording options:

1) When the solution is a preferred standard TT equivalent term, the term base should preferably contain all the information that one would expect to see in a term base:
   a) **For the ST term:**
      - ST term + source
      - ST context + level of communication
      - ST definition + authoritative source
      - Synonym term(s) (if existent)
      - Related term(s) (if existent)
      - Additional information (if available)
   b) **For the TT preferred standard equivalent term:**
      - TT preferred standard equivalent term + authoritative source
      - Reliability of TT equivalent term (if possible)
      - TT context + level of communication
      - TT definition + authoritative source
      - synonym term(s) (if existent)
      - related term(s) (if existent)
      - additional information (if available).
2) When the solution is a newly created term (by means of secondary term creation), the term base should preferably contain:
   a) **For the ST term:**
      - See (1a)
   b) **For the created TT equivalent term:**
      - Created TT equivalent term
      - Authoritative source(s) consulted for created TT equivalent term
      - Term(s) the created TT equivalent term was/were compared with
      - Definition of terms of comparison
      - Context(s) + level(s) of communication of terms of comparison
      - Definition of created TT equivalent term
      - Translation technique (if applied).

3) When the solution is the result of just a translation technique, the term base should preferably contain:

   a) **For the ST term:**
      - See (1a)

   b) **For the solution by means of a translation technique in the TT:**
      - Translation
      - Translation technique applied.

Recording definitions requires knowing what types of definition there are, and which definition is the most informative (cf. Sager, 1990: 42–51), but also knowing how to formulate ST/TT context-based definitions if no definitions can be found. And last but not least, knowing about terminological relations between terms (cf. Sager, 1990: 51–54) and between definition and term. Similarly, recording contexts requires knowing how to decide on the most informative and relevant context out of more contexts (cf. Dubuc & Lauriston, 1997: 80–87).

The above list is exhaustive, but the translator may, of course, (have to) decide not to follow it completely and decide to pick out only elements depending on needs and time. The more elements are included, the more precise the information will be for later use.

Terminology competence

Terminology competence (cf. Thelen, 2002; 2007: 137; Fischer, 2020: 67) is a crucial competence for specialised translation (cf. Montero Martínez & Faber Benítez, 2009) and is the essence of translation-oriented terminology. It encompasses the production processes and the post-production processes, i.e. it involves not only term recognition, but also matching (or equivalence identification), applying strategies for solving equivalence issues (including secondary term formation) and recording results in a term base (or a different database). Figure 4 illustrates the various components of terminology competence:

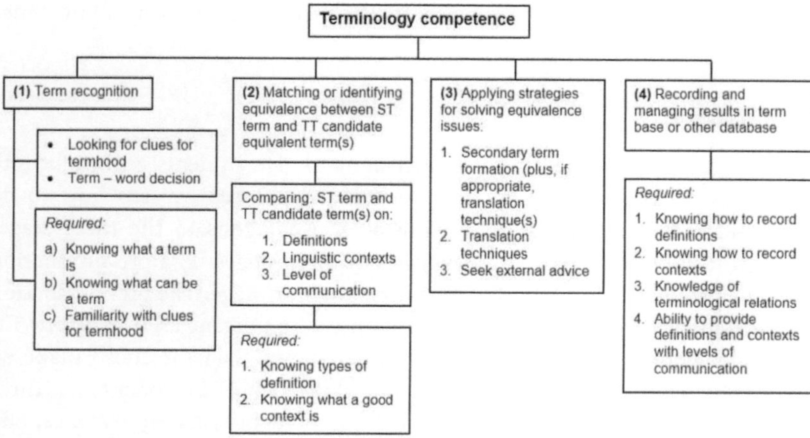

Figure 4: Terminology Competence

Because terminology competence involves competences that differ from those involved in translation competence (e.g. term recognition and secondary term formation are not present in translation competence) and because of the importance of the constraint on translation freedom in particular, it is a separate competence (cf. Thelen, 2007: 138). Terminology competence requires knowledge about the principles of terminology and the skills to apply these to the translation job at hand.[17] Translation competence requires knowledge about the principles of translation and the skills to apply these to the translation job at hand. Very often both terminology competence and translation competence (have to) go hand in hand and (have to) complement one another. Terminological knowledge and skills are indispensable for specialised translation:

> It is translators who need an understanding of terminology … because they have to work as terminologists when they are faced with decisions concerning the right choice among several alternatives of expression forms or the choice of creating a neologism, a neonym or a paraphrase… Translators have to change roles during the complex decision-making process of translation and work in the analytical mode of terminologists before switching back to text production. (Sager, 1992: 112–113)

17 For a discussion of how much theory (i.e. what principles) should be included in a translation and terminology course and what the relation between theory and practice should be see Korkas & Rogers (2010).

Therefore, terminology competence should be included in existing competence frameworks.

Conclusions

The student guide outlined in this paper aims to give students an insight into the process of translating terms and to guide them step by step how to do this in order to prevent translation mistakes. Analogous to the three stages described in ISO 17100, the guide consists of three stages: 1) a pre-production stage, 2) a production stage and 3) a post-production stage. The pre-production stage is standard for all translation work and is important as it may provide useful information that may impact the other stages. Stages 2 and 3 make up terminology competence. The production stage (stage 2) consists of three substages: 2a) term recognition, 2b) matching or identifying equivalence, and 2c) applying strategies for equivalence issues. Term recognition is fed by clues or signals found in the pre-production stage and clues for termhood of lexical items encountered in the ST and determines the freedom of translation. If the item is recognised as a term, a preferred standard equivalent must be found for the translation. Term recognition is a crucial step in the whole translation process. Substage 2b (matching) is equally important as it paves the way for an appropriate translation. In case of an equivalence issue substage 2c should be applied with secondary term formation as one of the options. The results of stage 2 should then be recorded in a term base or other database in stage 3. Especially stages 2 and 3, could also serve as a characterisation of translation-oriented terminology.

Finally, although terminology competence is such an important competence in the whole process of specialised translation, it is not mentioned explicitly or detailed enough in existing competence frameworks such as the EMT Competence Framework 2017 or its 2009 predecessor (*Competences for professional translators, experts in multilingual and multimedia communication*). However, the 2017 edition admits that "The framework does not claim to provide a comprehensive description or model of all the competences, skills and knowledge that translation graduates should acquire" (*EMT Competence Framework 2017*, 4). In other words, there is still room for addition and more precision. Hopefully, this will be undertaken sometime in the future. This practical guide may provide an impetus for this.

References

Bowker, L., & Hawkins, S. (2006). 'Variation in the organization of medical terms. Exploring some motivations for term choice.' *Terminology, 12*(1), 79–110.

Bowker, L. (2015). 'Terminology and translation.' In H. Kockaert, & F. Steurs, *Handbook of Terminology*, Vol, 1 (304–323). John Benjamins.

Buysschaert, J., & Thelen, M. (2020). 'Termbepaling: bestaat hier wel een Nederlandse term voor?' In Wermuth, C., E. Ruysendaal, I. van Gent & J. Buysschaert (Eds.), *TiNT-dag 2019.* Nieuwe Reeks Terminologie in het Nederlandse Taalgebied – 1 (36–41). NL-Term. https://nlterm.eu/tint2019webpublicatie.html.

Cabré, M.T. (1999). *Terminology. Theory, Methods and Applications.* John Benjamins.

Dubuc, R., & Lauriston, A. (1997). 'Terms and Contexts.' In S.E. Wright & G. Budin (Eds.), *Handbook of Terminology Management*, Vol. 1. (80–87). John Benjamins.

EMT Expert Group (2009). *Competences for professional translators, experts in multilingual and multimedia communication.* https://ec.europa.eu/info/sites/info/files/emt_competences_translators_en.pdf.

EMT Competence Framework 2017. https://ec.europa.eu/info/sites/default/files/emt_competence_fwk_2017_en_web.pdf.

Evans, V., & Green, M. (2006). *Cognitive Linguistics. An Introduction.* Edinburgh University Press.

Faber, P., & Lopez-Rodriguez, C.I. (2012). 'Terminology and Specialized Language.' In Faber, P. (Ed.), *A Cognitive Linguistics View of Terminology and Specialized Language* (9–32). De Gruyter Mouton. https://www.researchgate.net/publication/235424403_Terminology_and_Specialized_Language.

Fischer, M. (2020). 'Developing terminology competence, with special focus on recognising terms.' In R. Besznyák, M. Fischer and C. Szabó (Eds.), *Fit-For-Market Translator and Interpreter Training in a Digital Age* (65–83). Vernon Press.

ISO 17100. (2015). *Translation services – requirements for translation services.* International Organization for Standardization.

Kageura, K. (2015). 'Terminology and Lexicography'. In Kockaert, H. & F. Steurs, *Handbook of Terminology*, Vol. 1 (45–59). John Benjamins.

Kageura, K. & Marshman, E. (2020). 'Terminology Extraction and Management.' In O'Hagan, Minako (Ed.), *The Routledge Handbook of Translation and Technology* (61–77). Routledge.

Korkas, V., & Rogers, M. (2010). 'How much terminological theory do we need for practice? An old pedagogical dilemma in a new field.' In M. Thelen & F. Steurs (Eds.), *Terminology in Everyday Life* (123–136). John Benjamins,

Levi, J. (1978). *The Syntax and Semantics of Complex Nominals*. Academic Press.

Lewandowska-Tomaszczyk, B. (2008). 'Notes on Lexicology and Terminology.' In B. & M. Thelen (Eds.), *Translation and Meaning, Part 8* (297–307). Zuyd University of Applied Sciences. Maastricht School of Translation and Interpreting, .

Lewandowska-Tomaszczyk, B. (2015). 'Equivalence.' In Ł. Bogucki, St. Goźdź-Roszkowski, & P. Stalmaszczyk (Eds.), *Ways to Translation* (11–54). Łódź University Press,

L'Homme M-C. (2020). *Lexical Semantics for Terminology. An introduction*. John Benjamins.

Longman Dictionary of Business English (1982). Longman.

Lušicky, V., & Wissik, T. (2015). *Procedural Manual on Terminology. Translation-Oriented Terminology Work*. https://www.sep.gov.mk/data/file/Preveduvanje/Procedural_Manual_on_Terminology_final_version.pdf

Montero Martínez, S., & Faber Benítez, P. (2009). 'Terminological competence in translation.' *Terminology, 15*(1), 88–104.

Neubert, A., & Shreve, G. (1992). *Translation as Text*. Kent State University Press.

Newmark, P. (1988). *A Textbook of Translation*. Prentice Hall.

Pazienzia, M. T., Pennacchiotti, M., & Zanzotto, M. (2006). 'Terminology extraction: an analysis of linguistic and statistical approaches.' https://www.researchgate.net/publication/226335889_Terminology_Extraction_An_Analysis_of_Linguistic_and_Statistical_Approaches.

Pearson, J. (1999). *Terms in Context*. John Benjamins.

Rogers, M. (1999). 'Translating Terms in Text: Holding on to Some Slippery Customers.' In Anderman, G. & M. Rogers (Eds.), *Word, Text,* Translation (104–116). Multilingual Matters.

Sager, J. (1990). *A Practical Course in Terminology Processing*. John Benjamins.

Sager, J. (1992), 'The translator as terminologist.' In Dollerup, C. & A, Loddegaard (Eds.), *Teaching Translation and Interpreting. Training, Talent and* Experience (107–122). John Benjamins.

Sager, J. (1998). 'In search of a foundation: Towards a theory of the term.' *Terminology, 5*(1).

Sánchez-Gijón, P., Aguilar-Amat, A., Mesa-Lao, B., & Pahisa Solé, M. (2009). 'Applying terminology knowledge to translation: Problem-based learning for a degree in translation and interpreting.' *Terminology, 15*(1), 105–118.

Thelen, M. (2001). 'Present Issues in Teaching Specialised Translation: a practice-oriented MA programme.' In Desblache, L. (Ed.), *Aspects of specialised translation*. La Mason du Dictionnaire.

Thelen, M. (2004). 'Competence in recognition and production in the translation of Subject Field Specific Language (SSL).' In E. Fleischmann, A. Schmitt, & G. Wotjak (Eds.), *Translationskompetenz. Tagungsakten der LICTRA 2001, VII. Leipziger Internationale Konferenz zu Grundfragen der Translationswissenschaft. Studien zur Translation*, Vol. 14 (563–581). Stauffenburg.

Thelen, M. (2007). 'Is there such a thing as terminology competence?' In M. Thelen, & B. Lewandowska-Tomaszczyk (Eds.), *Translation and Meaning*, Part 7 (129–139). Zuyd University of Applied Sciences. Maastricht School of Translation and Interpreting. https://www.academia.edu/23959330/Translation_and_Meaning_Part_7.

Thelen, M. (2010). 'Terminology in Theory and Practice.' In B. Lewandowska-Tomaszczyk, & M. Thelen (Eds.), *Meaning in Translation* (31–39). Peter Lang.

Thelen, M. (2012). *The structure of the lexicon. Incorporating a cognitive approach in the TCM lexicon, with applications to lexicography, terminology and translation*. Academia Press.

Thelen, M. (2015). 'The Interaction between Terminology and Translation or Where Terminology and Translation Meet.' *Trans-kom*, *8*(2), 347–381. http://www.trans-kom.eu.

Vargas-Sierra, C. (2011). 'Translation-oriented Terminology Management and ICTs: Present and Future.' In F. Suau Jiménez, & B. Pennock (Eds.), *Interdisciplinarity and Languages: Current Issues in Research, Teaching, Professional Applications and ICT* (45–64). Peter Lang.

Weissenhofer, P. (1995). *Conceptology in Terminology Theory: Semantics and Word-Formation*. TermNet.

Woordenboek van de Psychologie (1989). ed. A.S. Reber, trans. A. van der Wurff and W. Zeegers. Uitgeverij Bert Bakker.

Wright, S. E. (1997). 'Term Selection: The Initial Phase of Terminology Management.' In S.E. Wright, & G. Budin (Eds.), *Handbook of Terminology Management*, Vol. 1 (13–23). John Benjamins.

Anna Setkowicz-Ryszka

University of Lodz

Raising Legal Translator Trainees' Awareness of Context through Post-Editing: Reflections of a Practitioner Delivering a Contract Translation Module at Postgraduate Level (EN/PL, PL/EN)[1]

Abstract: In training legal translators considerable effort should be geared towards raising their awareness of the various layers of context in which the translation takes place. Translators of contracts need some knowledge about the general, extra-linguistic context, i.e. legal systems in which contracts are used and the role of contracts in common- and civil-law countries. This influences the understanding of the source text and potential problems experienced by target text recipients, as well as the choice of sources to be consulted. In terms of the linguistic context, trainees need to know the contract-related terminology in both source and target languages, which affects their strategies of dealing with varying degrees of equivalence. They should also know the linguistic conventions, including syntactic particularities, of the language of contracts. Considering time constraints and multi-disciplinary nature of legal translation, the trainer cannot impart all necessary knowledge to trainees and instead should teach them how to avoid errors and deal with problems. With samples of boilerplate contract provisions and free machine translation available online, post-editing may be a viable training option. Raw machine-translated output can be viewed as a translation made by an entity without much sensitivity to extra-linguistic or linguistic context. Use of post-editing exercises may speed up learning process by enabling more text to be processed, though the risks of introducing it too early should be taken into account. MT output enables trainees to identify areas where a human translator can make errors too and see that a feasible translation can be wrong in a certain context. They practice critical thinking and problem solving. Post-editing as such is increasingly in demand on the market, so there is potential for immediate application. In the context

1 I would like to thank the anonymous reviewer for their great help in making this text clearer and for pointing out an interesting resource. I am the only one to blame for any remaining shortcomings.

of the Polish education paradigm, where errors are still to be avoided rather than used as learning opportunities, trainees avoid having their errors discussed in class.

Keywords: legal translation, post-editing, linguistic context, extra-linguistic context, error management, andragogy

1. Introduction

This paper reflects on the use of post-editing (PE) exercises in training legal translators, especially in developing their awareness of context through correcting errors in raw machine translation (MT) output. It is based on the author's experience delivering a contract translation module in EN/PL, PL/EN pair as part of the Interdisciplinary Postgraduate Studies in Translation and Interpreting at the Institute of Applied Linguistics, University of Warsaw. Following this introduction, section 2 argues that an important part of translation/translator competence is knowing how to take into account the general linguistic and extra-linguistic context of both the source text (ST) and the target text (TT), as well as the particular communicative context of a given translation. Section 3 presents in more detail the various layers of context a legal translator should be aware of. Section 4 presents information about the module and the programme of which it is part, as well as general remarks about the Polish education paradigm and the approach to errors in Poland's educational system. Section 5 offers a classification of errors found in MT output from the perspective of a lack of knowledge of or sensitivity to context (i.e. what could be seen as insensitivity to context of a human translator), providing examples of such errors. It also briefly discusses the trainees' success in PE tasks, as well as their responses to questions about their perception of difficulty of PE vs. translation from scratch or usefulness of PE for the acquisition of translation/translator competence. Finally, section 6 concludes with the author's perception of the benefits and risks of using elements of PE in training legal translators.

2. Context in translation competence models

Tellingly, questions about context are among the first reactions that less experienced translators receive when they ask for help with translating a specific term or expression.[2] However, context or sensitivity to it are not usually

2 My personal observations from a large Facebook (over 25,000 users) group for Polish translators.

expressly mentioned in numerous existing translation/translator[3] competence models, where the focus is mainly on sub-competences that can be summarised as the linguistic sub-competence, the cultural sub-competence, subject-matter knowledge, the ability to transfer (translate) the message, and assorted additional skills required of a translator.[4]

Among the more recent models, the model of translation competence proposed by the Process in the Acquisition of Translation Competence and Evaluation (PACTE) Group and the translation competence framework created by the European Master's in Translation (EMT) Expert Group merit attention since both were developed in the context of translator training. The PACTE model specifies the following elements: language sub-competence, extra-linguistic sub-competence, instrumental/professional sub-competence, psycho-physiological sub-competence, transfer sub-competence and strategic sub-competence. Of these, the transfer sub-competence is considered central, where all the others come together, and refers to: "the ability to complete the transfer process from the source text to the target text, that is, to understand the source text and re-express it in the target language, *taking into account the purpose of the translation and the characteristics of the receptor*" [my emphasis] (PACTE Group, 2003: 48). It therefore implies sensitivity to context in which all the other sub-competences are put to use, including the purpose for which a text is translated, as well as the recipients' needs and expectations, which could also be seen as part of the broader context.

A number of the learning outcomes mentioned in the EMT competence framework in the translation area of competence (the other four areas being language and culture, technology, personal and interpersonal skills, as well as service provision) also confirm that context – even without that word actually being used – matters in the training of future translators. Students should be able, for instance, to: "[a]nalyse a source document, identify potential textual and cognitive difficulties and assess the strategies and resources needed for appropriate reformulation *in line with communicative needs*;" "[i]mplement the instructions, style guides, or *conventions relevant to a particular translation*;"

3 As for the distinction between translation competence, understood as the hard skills, mainly the linguistic skills needed to produce an acceptable translation, and translator competence, seen as a set of soft skills, including interacting with clients and searching for/critically evaluating information (Pym, 2012: 482), I believe the module should develop both, since they are inseparable at this level.

4 For a comprehensive review of translation/translator competence models see Pietrzak (2015) or Kościałkowska-Okońska (2013).

"[t]ranslate general and domain-specific material … producing a *'fit for purpose'* translation" or "[d]raft texts for specific purposes … *taking into account specific situations, recipients and constraints*" [my emphasis] (Outcomes 1, 5, 6 and 9, EMT Competence Framework – 2017: 8). It can be said that the service provision cluster also relates to context: "[c]larify the requirements, objectives and purposes of the client, recipients of the language service and other stakeholders and offer the appropriate services to meet those requirements" (Outcome 29, EMT Competence Framework – 2017: 11).

The minimalist definition of functional competence put forward by Pym (2004) also seems to imply taking context into account. He defines functional competence as: "[t]he ability to generate a series of more than one viable target text (TTI, TT2… TTn) for a pertinent source text (ST)" and "[t]he ability to select only one viable TT from this series, quickly and with justified confidence" (Pym, 2004: 489). In legal translation, bearing in mind the differences between common law and civil law systems, which are reflected in the terminology of contracts and in their very contents, it is actually the "justified confidence" in selecting one viable translation that the teacher/trainer wants the trainees to demonstrate. The confidence in the selection should be justified by trainees' awareness of the various layers of context in which legal translation takes place, which will be discussed in more detail in the following section.

3. Layers of context affecting contract translation

According to Scott (2017: 37, 42–43), legal translation is "a multi-dimensional endeavour," which differs from other kinds of specialised translation in that not only is the translator required to use the legal language in a specific genre in both languages, but also in that the solutions have to be negotiated between two legal systems. As is the case with common and civil law, the systems may be very different, resulting in various degrees of terminological non-equivalence or partial equivalence, but first and foremost in non-correspondence or partial correspondence between concepts uses in the legal discourse in both languages (Scott, 2017: 49–52). I believe the extra-linguistic reality to be the main source of difficulty in legal translation, which I will elaborate on slightly in the following subsection.

3.1. Extra-linguistic context

To successfully translate contracts, one should have considerable knowledge about the general, extra-linguistic context: the legal systems in which contracts are made, including the role of contracts in common- and civil-law countries.

This knowledge influences the understanding of the meaning of STs and the potential problems experienced by TT recipients, as well as the familiarity with the sources that can and should be consulted in terminological searches. When there are legislative instruments (such as the Polish Civil Code) that regulate contracts in general or specific types of contracts (referred to as named contracts in Polish legal scholarship), they can be consulted as the first port of call. However, there are named contracts in the Polish law that do not have equivalents among common law contract types (and there are no parallel texts to consult, only other translations from Polish that can be used as models) or popular contract types which are not regulated by any Polish statute (so-called unnamed contracts), such as franchise agreements or factoring agreements, but which are used in practice (so only parallel texts exist in both languages). There is, for instance, a peculiar case of *lease* with three possible equivalent Polish contracts (*umowa najmu, umowa dzierżawy, umowa leasingu*), where only an analysis of the contract's contents and knowledge of the differences between the three Polish contract types can help decide on the correct Polish equivalent of *lease*. Hence subject-matter knowledge influences the linguistic choices.

One of the most salient features of common law contracts is their extensive boilerplate section. A translator needs to know why it is so important in common law contracts, which have to be mostly self-contained and deal with all eventualities, and less so in civil law contracts, where matters not regulated in the contract will be determined by the applicable statutory provisions. As far as boilerplate clauses are concerned, there are three main scenarios relating to the presence or absence of equivalent clauses in Polish legal texts. Firstly, some clauses (e.g. arbitration or amendment clauses) do have corresponding Polish contractual clauses. Secondly, for some boilerplate clauses (e.g. severance or assignment clauses) it is possible to find Polish statutory provisions that correspond to their contents or at least can provide relevant terminology. Thirdly, there are also completely "exotic" provisions, such as waiver/no waiver clauses, whose objective is unclear to a Polish lawyer unless they have already been exposed to common law contracts.[5] All this shows that even in the case of relatively simple texts, such as contracts, a translator needs to deploy some legal

5 On the other hand, some Polish lawyers do draft contracts containing a boilerplate section in the style of common law, but governed by the Polish law, where certain provisions become unnecessary, counterproductive or ineffective (Szewczyk, 2014).

knowledge,[6] preferably in the field of comparative law (Doczekalska, 2013), and to be able to supplement such existing knowledge by doing research when faced with new challenges.

3.2. Linguistic context

In terms of the linguistic context, though closely linked with the extra-linguistic context, the translator needs to know the contract-related terminology in both the source language (SL) and the target language (TL), which will affect the strategies of dealing with varying degrees of non-equivalence, as well as the linguistic conventions of the legal language (Jopek-Bosiacka, 2010: 112), including the syntactic particularities of legal discourse (Kościałkowska-Okońska, 2013: 138–139). Among other things, legal translators need to be aware that certain terms, such as the English term *waiver*, need to be explained in translation or that certain terms carry a high risk of misunderstanding, such as the literally translated Polish term *kara umowna.*[7]

It is worth stressing that it is not only long and complex sentences with many subordinate clauses that constitute a problems for translators, though the dense syntax of legal language, including contracts, is rightly identified as challenging (e.g. Alcaraz Varó and Hughes, 2014: 18–20, Berezowski, 2012: 23–32). My experience, including in the classroom, is that contracts written in plain English can also prove quite difficult to translate, because a corresponding register in Polish contracts is only beginning to emerge. If the translator tries to recreate this register in Polish, due to the readers' expectations, the result can be perceived as bad, i.e. displaying low textual fit or departing from generic conventions (Biel, 2014, discusses similar phenomena leading to low textual fit of early translations of EU law into Polish). Otherwise it becomes an act of balancing between more formal and more colloquial style, requiring the knowledge as to when the necessary terminology has to be retained and when certain expressions can be replaced with more everyday language.

---

6 Polish law and common law lectures are also offered as part of our postgraduate programme, though the comparative approach is missing (Polish law is taught in the first semester, common law in the second semester).

7 When *kara umowna* is translated literally as *contractual penalty*, English-speaking lawyers can perceive it as an unenforceable provision, therefore *liquidated damages* is a better equivalent, as it suggests that the given sum is a faithful estimate of the loss incurred by one party if the other party fails to perform is obligations.

3.3. Communicative context

Finally, translator's choices are affected by communicative context, i.e. the situation in which a a contract is translated. For instance, the recipient of the translation may be a business entity ordering goods from a Polish supplier (or that Polish supplier itself), an individual buying property in Poland, but the translation can also be used as evidence in court. Each of these situations will require slightly different strategies, determined by the aforementioned levels of context and by the familiarity of the translation recipient with the SL legal system, to make sure that either the parties to the contract do actually understand each other, which will help them avoid future legal disputes, or that the judge knows what the contract used as evidence says, which will help the latter decide the case fairly.

I hope the contents of this section show sufficiently clearly that in the field of legal translation subject knowledge, knowledge of linguistic conventions and particularities of a given communicative situation must all be taken into account simultaneously, requiring the translator to use their judgement to select what will work best in a given context.

4. Setting the scene: translator training and the Polish education paradigm

4.1. The contract translation module

The original context for these reflections is that in Poland state examinations are held for sworn translators/court interpreters. The Act on the Profession of Sworn Translator requires that candidates hold a graduate degree in philology or linguistics, or complete a postgraduate course in legal translation and interpreting. Many candidates enrol in such courses anyway because graduate courses for translators in Poland are not sufficiently specialised (legal translation is just one of several modules offered as part of the programme). I belong to a group of practitioners, i.e. sworn translators, who deliver practical legal translation classes on one such course at the Interdisciplinary Postgraduate Studies in Translation and Interpreting (IPSKT) at the Institute of Applied Linguistics, University of Warsaw. For the past three years I have taught a contract translation module, in both the English-Polish and Polish-English directions.

Considering the complex nature of legal translation (Scott, 2017) and the time constraints of the postgraduate programme,[8] one has to accept that it is impossible

8 The whole programme only lasts two semesters, and the contract translation module comprises just 13 meetings of 90 minutes each. The number rose to 17 in the academic year 2020/2021.

to provide the trainees with all the information and background knowledge they need to translate any contract. In the time available, one can discuss and practice the types of contracts they are most likely to encounter as translators (e.g. contracts of sale, including sale of real property, contracts of supply or leases) in considerable detail. It also makes sense to devote more attention to the boilerplate section of common law contracts, as most legal translators will inevitably deal with standard provisions over and over. Otherwise, one has to make do with teaching trainees how to solve problems (e.g. in cases of a lack of equivalent terms or diverging conventions of legal language) rather than providing them with ready-made model solutions. Problem-solving includes efficient use of resources such as legislative instruments, parallel texts, translators' online fora or encyclopaedias, efficient web searching skills (Paradowska, 2014) and, finally, the ability to critically evaluate information.

The time constraints are even more acute when one considers that the programme is delivered on weekends and almost all trainees are in employment. They often fail to do the assignments that the trainer might want to build the next lesson on (peer review, group work, comparing the different solutions and discussing reasons behind their choices), which can be an unpleasant surprise if you allocated plenty of time for such activities. With the exception of those who are more experienced translators, trainees are not yet able to quickly offer sight translations that might be evaluated by peers. In a mixed group with more experienced translators and complete beginners, the former are often happy to take the floor, but there is risk of the latter just becoming passive listeners. Still, I strongly believe that one cannot become a translator without practising translation and reflecting on their own or others' translations. As Pym (2012: 475) puts it, the value of experience cannot be underestimated: "[a] great deal is learnt on the job, from superiors, colleagues, reviewers and clients, or otherwise through trial and error." My response was to introduce PE activities, which I had previously used only with experienced translators. With the availability of contract templates online and generic MT engines, this seemed a viable option when the trainees' initial enthusiasm waned or their overall workload became excessive, roughly halfway through the module.[9] I also hoped that students would find correcting errors made by artificial intelligence easier than correcting errors made by other group members who were present. In the

9 Another condition is that the trainees must have been exposed to some authentic parallel texts and the language of contracts before being asked to post-edit.

next subsection I briefly describe the Polish education paradigm and why I think it makes trainees reluctant to use the trial and error method.

4.2. The Polish education paradigm

The Polish education paradigm is still very much teacher-centered. The admired Polish educator Przemysław Staroń[10] put it bluntly: "[t]he aim of Polish education has for years been to 'memorise-get grade-forget,' and in the case of homework: 'copy and forget.' Neither us, nor our parents, nor our children were taught in school to solve problems, to search for information in reliable sources, to reflect on issues. What mattered – and still does – is the correct answer, not independent thinking" [my translation from Polish] (Łygas, 2020). This quote, which appeared in the spring of 2020, when the first Polish lockdown forced schools to move to remote teaching almost overnight and many parents were suddenly faced with the requirements of something akin to home schooling and struggled to help their children with homework, aptly describes what I had been grappling with well before the COVID-19 pandemic. Most of my trainees – having spent 17 or more years in the system – were reluctant to make errors in front of their peers or myself. Repeated requests for the "correct translation" (i.e. a model) or glossaries confirm the lasting impact of the paradigm, while the initial heavy reliance on bilingual dictionaries is a sign that the authority of a source is not questioned (or, rather, critically evaluated) and that the net is not cast wide enough in the search for information relevant to the translation task. Yet, it is impossible to learn how to translate without actually translating, i.e. practicing the skill, including trial and error and solving problems more or less successfully.

There are basically two approaches to dealing with errors in any organisation: error prevention and error management (Keith & Frese, 2011: 139–140). In her analysis of Polish schools, Domagała-Kręcioch (2019) confirms that error prevention is the dominant paradigm in Poland, while advocating for the second approach as more constructive. Error management facilitates learning from errors. She describes conditions in which such an error culture can develop, including openness to (acceptance of) errors, the use of errors for building negative knowledge (meta-cognition), and the readiness to learn from one's own and others' errors (Domagała-Kręcioch, 2019: 100). Moreover, the principles of andragogy, i.e. the discipline concerned with adult learning – and

10 Polish Teacher of the Year 2018, nominated to the Global Teacher Prize, known for his critical comments about the Polish education system.

at the postgraduate level the trainees are professionally active adults – tell us that "experience (*including mistakes*) provides the basis for learning activities" [my emphasis] and that "[a]dult learning is problem-centered rather than content-oriented"[11] (Conlan, Grabowski and Smith, 2003: 116).

Errors in trainees' translations have considerable diagnostic potential and can be used to identify problem areas in a relatively safe environment. This opportunity is sadly missed when few trainees volunteer for their translations to be discussed or reviewed in class. Errors also offer an opportunity to reflect on their causes as well as ways to avoid and correct them. Finally, the fact that trainees in many postgraduate translation programmes and particularly those at my institution come from different backgrounds (mainly applied linguistics, English philology or law) should enable gathering different contributions and comparing different feasible – even though not yet error-free – translations of the same piece. Unfortunately, usually only a few of them prepare a rough copy of the translation and the others, when asked for a sight translation, take a long time to produce one. To avoid working with the handful of persons who come to class prepared, one of the options is to use MT output and ask trainees to post-edit it. Their translation skills may not yet be sufficiently advanced for such an exercise, since it is argued that PE should not be taught before a person is relatively experienced and confident in their own translation work, but also that PE should not be taught to non-translators (O'Brien, 2002). In terms of cognitive effort, translation from scratch and PE are not identical either.[12] Still, Vanroy at al. argue that these activities are at least related. Crucially, there is some overlap between the text features (such as lexical or structural ambiguity, very long sentences, etc.) that lead to errors in MT output and those that cause difficulties for human translators (Vanroy, De Clercq and Macken, 2019). More recently, do Carmo and Moorkens (2020) argued that PE should be seen more as a form of translation than revision.

5. What can raw MT output teach us about context?

Raw MT output clearly displays what would be perceived in humans as a lack of sensitivity to the various layers of context mentioned above, compounded by the

11 Another principle is that adults are more willing to learn about subjects that have 'immediate relevance to their job,' so the growing demand for PE can be a motivating factor.

12 O'Brien (2002) mentions different cognitive processes, more linear processing in PE, and two source texts instead of one.

usual problems of lack of textual coherence or lexical cohesion beyond sentence level in MT (Voita, Sennrich and Titov, 2019). Despite the recent advances in MT technology and the constantly improving quality of the output, generic MT engines (like DeepL or Google Translate) still produce output in the field of legal translation which is rather challenging and time-consuming to post-edit. This may partly be due to market participants' reluctance to risk disclosure of confidential information contained in contracts, hence there being not enough material available for training generally available MT engines. With trainees, however, MT output can be used to discuss why a certain translation solution is right or wrong and the repertoire of mistranslations to draw on is quite rich, as subsection 5.2 illustrates.

In order to properly introduce PE, trainees need to be made aware of the kinds of errors they can expect in MT output. It may be a somewhat controversial statement, but I believe that, in terms of quality, errors in MT output do not differ greatly from errors made by less experienced translators, though the quantity is usually greater and additional types of errors can be found. For the purposes of the present paper, I am mainly interested in errors that would result from a disregard for the extra-linguistic, linguistic, or communicative context if made by human translators. In the following subsections I present a typology of errors from this perspective (5.1) and examples from contracts used during the contract translation module taught by myself (5.2).

5.1. Categories of MT errors

MT output offers ample evidence that an otherwise feasible translation can be wrong in a particular context, for instance when the whole document is considered (Voita, Sennrich, & Titov, 2019). In legal translation this can be aggravated when words from the general lexicon are used as legal terms or have different meanings (multiple equivalents) depending on the branch of law. Legal terms being system-bound (Jopek-Bosiacka, 2013), the meaning may also have to be explained even if an appropriate equivalent is used, but the notion is unfamiliar in TL legal system.

Considering that PE exercises in a training module are meant to enhance translation/translator competence, it is useful to view MT errors from an anthropomorphic perspective (when would a human translator make such an error?), taking into account different kinds of context. The first group includes errors resulting from disregard for extralinguistic context, which could demonstrate: poor knowledge of SL or TL legal system, including failure to explain concepts unknown to TL recipients, and insufficient general knowledge/

life experience. The second group, errors relating to linguistic context, can stem from: misunderstanding the ST, failure to recognise terms from the SL legal system or failure to use proper TL legal terms, problems with processing the syntax of legal language, failure to apply TL conventions (legal or general language). Thirdly, MT output will often contain errors caused by the impossibility of the MT system to consider the perspective of the recipient and the purpose of the translation (communicative context).

Naturally, such expertise can hardly be expected of any MT engine, though identifying and correcting these errors can raise trainees' awareness of the complexity of the tasks they are expected to take up in their professional life and the degree to which context influences translation strategies. Even simple errors, like inconsistent use of terms in texts where consistency and precision are desirable, might be explained with the help of immediate context, i.e. internal document level cohesion.

5.2. Examples of errors in MT output

This section provides examples of errors found in the machine-translated texts used during the contract translation module under study, which illustrate the categories mentioned in the previous section. Examples come from contracts which were machine-translated in both directions (EN-PL and PL-EN); each example starts with the ST sentence, followed by MT output and the post-edited target version (PEMT). I provide my own PEMT as the versions discussed in class were not recorded. Sentences in Polish are translated into English fairly literally to show differences between MT and PEMT, with the problematic passages in italics. When Polish is the source language, the post-edited English version should be seen as the preferred translation.

5.2.1. Errors relating to extralinguistic context

Poor knowledge of SL or TL legal system (property sale contracts are executed before a notary in Poland):

PL: AKT NOTARIALNY [document title]
MT: NOTIFIED ACT
PEMT: NOTARIAL DEED/NOTARISED AGREEMENT

Failure to explain a concept that may be unknown to TL recipients:

EN: This Agreement may be *executed in counterpart.*
MT: Niniejsza Umowa może być *zawarta w formie ekwiwalentu.* [This Agreement may be executed *in the form of an equivalent.*]

PEMT: Niniejsza Umowa może zostać zawarta *w taki sposób, że każda strona podpisze swój egzemplarz.* [This Agreement can be *executed by means of each party signing his/her copy.*]

Insufficient general knowledge/life experience:

EN: Repair of walls due to plugs, large nails, or any unreasonable number of holes...
MT: Naprawa ścian za pomocą kołków rozporowych, dużych gwoździ lub dowolnej nieracjonalnej ilości otworów... [Repair of walls *by means of* plugs, large nails, or any unreasonable number of holes...]
PEMT: Naprawa ścian w związku z użyciem [przez Najemcę] kołków rozporowych, dużych gwoździ lub wykonaniem nadmiernej ilości otworów... [Repair of walls *because of* [the Tenant] having used plugs, large nails, or having made an unreasonable number of holes...]

Insufficient knowledge/experience leading to overreliance on the literal wording of ST:

EN: The Tenant has inspected the Premises and has found it satisfactory.
MT: Najemca przeprowadził kontrolę lokalu i uznał ją za zadowalającą. [The Tenant has inspected the Premises and has found it (= the inspection) satisfactory.]
PEMT: Najemca przeprowadził oględziny lokalu i uznał jego stan za zadowalający. [The Tenant has inspected the Premises and has found their condition satisfactory.]

5.2.2. Errors relating to linguistic context

Problems with processing the complex syntax of SL legal text (word order is not fixed in Polish):

PL: Tożsamość stawających notariusz ustaliła na podstawie:
MT: The identity of the standing notary was established on the basis of:
PEMT: The notary established the identity of the appearing persons on the basis of:

Poor knowledge of TL legal terminology (even though the message is conveyed):

EN: This Lease *binds and benefits* both the *Landlord* and *Tenant* and any successors.
MT: Umowa ta jest *wiążąca i korzystna* zarówno dla *Właściciela* i *Najemcy*, jak i jego następców. [This Agreement is *binding and beneficial* both for the *Owner* and *Tenant*, and their successors.]
PEMT: Niniejsza Umowa *ustanawia obowiązki i prawa* zarówno dla *Wynajmującego*, jak i *Najemcy*, jak i ich następców. [This Agreement *establishes rights and obligations* both for the *Lessor* and *Lessee*, and their successors.]

Inconsistent use of TL legal terms (though all the equivalents used are feasible):

PL: Sprzedający oświadcza, że: 1) jest właścicielem nieruchomości stanowiącej *lokal mieszkalny*…2) *lokal mieszkalny* oznaczony jest numerem…3) opisany wyżej *lokal mieszkalny* wyposażony jest w… 4) z własnością opisanego wyżej *lokalu mieszkalnego* związany jest udział…

MT: The seller declares that: 1) is the owner of real estate constituting *residential premises*…2) the *apartment* is marked with…3) the *dwelling* described above is equipped with…4) ownership of the *residential unit* described above is connected with a share…

PEMT: The seller represents that: (1) he/she owns the property in the form of an *apartment*… (2) the *apartment* is marked with number… (3) the apartment *described* above is equipped with… (4) ownership of the *apartment* described above is connected with a share…

Failure to apply the conventions of TL legal texts, where doublets or triplets such as those below are not used (poor textual fit):

EN: The Landlord covenants that on paying the Rent and performing the covenants contained in this Lease, the Tenant will peacefully and quietly have, hold, and enjoy the Premises for the agreed term.

MT: Wynajmujący zobowiązuje się, że płacąc czynsz i wykonując przymierza zawarte w niniejszej Umowie Najmu, Najemca będzie *spokojnie i cicho posiadał, utrzymywał i korzystał* z Lokalu przez uzgodniony okres. [The Landlord covenants that while paying the rent and performing the covenants contained in this Lease, the Tenant will *peacefully and silently have, maintain, and use* the Premises for the agreed term.]

PEMT: Wynajmujący zobowiązuje się, że w zamian za zapłatę czynszu i przestrzeganie zobowiązań określonych w niniejszej Umowie Najmu umożliwi Najemcy *korzystanie z* Lokalu *w sposób niezakłócony* przez uzgodniony okres. [The Landlord covenants that in exchange for paying the rent and discharging the obligations hereunder he/she will let the Tenant *peacefully enjoy* the Premises.]

Poor knowledge of general TL conventions (leaving a participle that is redundant in English):

PL: …(pomimo braku takiej umowy zawartej między Polską a Liechtensteinem)… […(despite lack of such agreement *concluded* between Poland and Liechtenstein)…]

MT: …(despite the absence of such an agreement *concluded* between Poland and Liechtenstein)…

PEMT: …(despite there being no such agreement between Poland and Liechtenstein)…

5.2.3. Errors relating to communicative context

Failure to take into consideration the perspective of the recipient (here the buyer), who should know that his/her obligations are set out in Polish law:

PL: Z datą podpisania niniejszej umowy Kupujący przejmuje wszystkie obowiązki właściciela wynikające z *przepisów prawa powszechnie obowiązującego*. [see PEMT below]

MT: As of the date of signing this Agreement, the Buyer shall assume all obligations of the owner *under common law*.

PEMT: As of the day of signature hereof, the Buyer shall assume all obligations of the owner provided for *in generally applicable Polish laws (and regulations)*.

Failure to warn a party to the contract about the consequences of failing to meet a deadline:

EN: Time is *of the essence* of this Agreement.

MT: Istotą tej umowy jest czas. [Time is the essence of this Agreement]

PEMT: W niniejszej umowie terminy mają istotne znaczenie. [Time limits are essential terms of this Agreement.]

5.3. Trainees' performance as post-editors

In the three years in which I included PE exercises in the module I could observe that some trainees post-edited MT output to an insufficient extent, leaving text of clearly unacceptable quality even in their mother tongue. This was so regardless of whether frequent categories of MT errors were first presented to trainees or whether they were asked to identify such errors themselves. For the trainees who under-edited, the use of PE exercises might have posed more risks than it offered benefits. There were also trainees who were much more successful at PE, but these were usually the persons who were also able to prepare good translations from scratch. Generally, the marks trainees got for translation assignments and PE assignments did not differ greatly. This seems to confirm the view that PE should only be taught as a skill once a person can translate with relative confidence (O'Brien, 2002), especially considering the additional knowledge a legal translator needs. Still, it would be interesting to see any research that would help determine the precise minimum threshold beyond which teaching through PE would be safe or answer the question whether exposure to MT output too early indeed poses any risks.

On the other hand, in terms of developing trainees' meta-cognition and awareness of various layers of context, I was delighted to see interesting exchanges of views between them when a PE exercise was done in the form of an asynchronous online discussion forum. Each person was asked to post-edit a short passage from a contract and post it on the forum. They were also asked to comment on at least two persons' solutions. In their comments, the trainees quoted sources, provided links and even referred to what other teachers from the programme had said to justify their choices, which seems to confirm that the resources tapped into both during from-scratch translation and post-editing do not differ much. However, a more in-depth analysis of the trainees' PE process, e.g. with the use of think-aloud protocols, verbal recollection protocols, or screen recordings might be interesting and reveal more about the process.

5.4. Trainees' responses to a questionnaire about post-editing

In the 2019/2020 academic year, seven out of around thirty trainees took a short optional questionnaire after the module. None of them had tried PE before the module. Three had no prior translation experience, three had up to 2 years of experience, and only one person had between 2 and 5 years. The majority said they would be willing to use PE as a time-saving device (five out of seven) or to make their work easier (four respondents). But considering the small size of the sample, no general picture can be extrapolated from these responses.

More telling are the answers to an open question about the level of difficulty in PE and from-scratch translation. One person who perceived PE as more difficult mentioned that being a visual learner, when they look at an incorrectly written text, they start to like it and get confused. This person had to prepare a translation before post-editing the text. Another person commented that from-scratch translation was easier, because with an already existing structure thinking "outside the box" was more difficult, whereas in some situations non-standard solutions were needed.

Another open question concerned the awareness of potential pitfalls of PE. Five persons mentioned the risk of a post-editor's attention being dulled by the grammatically correct sentences or the risk of trusting MT output too much, while there could be terminological, syntactic or grammatical errors. In all responses to this question trainees appreciated that there were more problems in MT output than they had realised previously, especially relating to terminology, lack of cohesion, and bridging the differences between the respective legal cultures.

The number of trainees who were willing to fill an updated questionnaire in the 2020/2021 academic year was even smaller: four out of a total of 21. Two of them admitted they had tried PE before the module, but for the other two it was new. When asked if PE was useful for acquiring elements of translation/translator competence (ST analysis, translation, terminology, correct expression of ideas in TL, revision, and context awareness) all four respondents strongly agreed or agreed that PE was useful for learning to analyse STs. Three people agreed that it was useful for context awareness, though one strongly disagreed.

In the remaining categories the answers were more dispersed, so no regularities could be determined.

Again, interesting insights came from answers to open questions, one of which concerned the benefits and risks of PE in the process of learning to translate contracts in PL-EN/EN-PL pair. One person was enthusiastic about the fact that MT output sometimes prompted new ideas for translating a given sentence and claimed that the more versions there were the quicker the pace of learning could be. This person believed that combining the best of both machine and human translation was the optimum solution and perceived PE to be a skill transferable to revising. Other respondents were less enthusiastic, expressing views about PE 'unfortunately' gaining popularity or being an important or even indispensable skill *per se*. All four expressed awareness of the dangers of MT, especially those errors that are less visible, but can change the sense of the whole sentence and thus require more effort and time to correct.

6. Conclusion: benefits and risks of teaching legal translation with the help of post-editing

As can be seen from the comments discussed in the previous section, inclusion of PE tasks can speed up the learning process for some translator trainees or in some respects, particularly ST analysis or becoming aware of context (as well as learning yet another, separate skill), though the immediate beneficiary is the teacher/trainer, who is quickly provided with some material to work with. First of all, analysing MT output enables translator trainees to identify areas where human translators might (and do) make errors too and reflect on the resources that would help to avoid them (knowledge of legal systems, familiarity with the relevant register), though the risk that they will remember the bad translations they looked at should not be underestimated.

The second benefit is a chance to practice critical evaluation and problem solving by spotting and correcting errors, which might be skills transferable to revising or even translation, especially considering that the boundary between PE and revision is becoming increasingly blurred nowadays, with the increased use of both translation memory matches and MT suggestions in CAT tools and with MT being trained on human-translated or human-edited texts (O'Brien, 2012: 117). But it can also be argued on the basis of studies carried out outside of labs that PE is more similar to translation than to revision (do Carmo and Moorkens, 2020). Trainees' attempts at PE showed that not all of them were at such a level in their professional development that they could post-edit a text to acceptable quality, though their instructive exchanges of information in the online forum (including evidence of research they did) were already a success from the perspective of moving towards a less teacher-centred approach. Whether or not they are conducive to translation/translator competence acquisition should be the object of further research.

Thirdly, when attempting PE, trainees practice a skill which is increasingly in demand on the market, so there is potential for immediate application of the acquired knowledge. There is no doubt that trainees need to first be exposed to good quality legal texts in TL, and given the chance to practise translating themselves. As pointed out in Massey and Kiraly (2019: 23), "I do not see how PE is going to work … without the posteditors having acquired a strong ability to translate themselves. … I do not think you can post-edit unless you can translate." There is a risk that, for the trainees with no or little professional experience, PE is simply too demanding a task, but as mentioned above, some errors found in trainees' translations do resemble those that appear in MT output.

Finally, but importantly in the context of the Polish education system, with its focus on error prevention, trainees are spared the embarrassment of making their own errors in front of their peers and/or the teacher if they work with MT output. As mentioned above, the Polish education system does not generally welcome errors as learning opportunities, so by the time trainees are at postgraduate level they may have internalised the strategy of staying silent lest they make an error. This attitude seems difficult to change in the short time available during a single module, while errors are in fact desirable, because they permit externalising the processes which should take place in the translator's "black box" and provide an opportunity to turn trainees' focus away from the equivalence of small translation units towards the capacity to recognise problems of translation and resolve them effectively, a feature associated with increasing expertise (Shreve, 2009).

References

Alcaraz Varó, E., & Hughes, B. (2014). *Legal translation explained.* Routledge.

Berezowski, L. (2012). *Jak czytać i rozumieć angielskie umowy?* (4th ed.). C. H. Beck.

Biel, Ł. (2014). 'The textual fit of translated EU law: A corpus-based study of deontic modality.' *The Translator, 20*(3), 332–355. https://doi.org/10.1080/13556509.2014.909675

Conlan, J., Grabowski, S., & Smith, K. (2003). 'Adult Learning.' In M. Orey (Ed.), *Emerging perspectives on learning, teaching, and technology* (115–126). Association for Educational Communications and Technology. http://epltt.coe.uga.edu/index.php?title=Adult_Learning.

Doczekalska, A. (2013). 'Comparative law and legal translation. In the search for functional equivalents – intertwined or separate domains?' *Comparative Legilinguistics, 16*, 63–76. https://doi.org/10.14746/cl.2013.16.5

Do Carmo, F., & Moorkens. J. (2020). 'Differentiating editing, post-editing, and revision.' In M. Koponen, B. Mossop, I. Robert, & G. Scocchera (Eds.), *Translation revision and post-editing: Industry practices and cognitive processes* (35–49). Routledge.

Domagała-Kręcioch, A. (2019). 'Refleksje wokół szkolnej kultury błędu.' *Kultura i Wychowanie, 15*(1), 97–110. https://doi.org/10.25312/2083-2923.15/2019_05adk

EMT Competence Framework 2017. https://ec.europa.eu/info/sites/default/files/emt_competence_fwk_2017_en_web.pdf

Jopek-Bosiacka, A. (2010). *Przekład prawny i sądowy*. PWN.

Jopek-Bosiacka, A. (2013). 'Comparative law and equivalence assessment of system-bound terms.' In Ł. Biel, & J. Engberg (Eds.) *Linguistica Antverpiensia, New Series – Themes in Translation Studies*, (12), 110–146. https://doi.org/10.52034/lanstts.v12i.237

Keith, N., & Frese, M. (2011). 'Enhancing firm performance and innovativeness through error management culture.' In N. M. Ashkanasy, C. P. Wilderom, & M. F. Peterson (Eds.), *The handbook of organizational culture and climate* (137–157). Thousand Oaks: SAGE Publications.

Kościałkowska-Okońska, E. (2013). 'Dydaktyka przekładu tekstów specjalistycznych w kontekście rozwoju kompetencji tłumaczeniowej.' *Rocznik Przekładoznawczy*, (8), 138–155.

Łygas, H. (2020). '"Tępak po mamusi." Rodziców przerasta program nauczania dla IV klasy.' https://kobieta.onet.pl/tepak-po-mamusi-rodzicow-przerasta-program-nauczania-dla-iv-klasy

Massey, G., & Kiraly, D. (2019). 'The future of translator education: A dialogue.' *Cultus: The Intercultural Journal of Mediation and Communication*, (12), 15–34. https://www.cultusjournal.com/files/Archives/Cultus_2019_12_002_Kiraly_Massey.pdf

O'Brien, S. (2002). 'Teaching post-editing: A proposal for course content.' In *Proceedings of the 6th EAMT Workshop on "Teaching Machine Translation"* (99–106). European Association for Machine Translation.

O'Brien, S. (2012). 'Translation as human–computer interaction.' *Translation Spaces, 1*(1), 101–122.

PACTE Group. (2003). 'Building a translation competence model.' In F. Alves (Ed.), *Triangulating translation: Perspectives in process oriented research* (43–66). John Benjamins.

Paradowska, U. (2014, November 28–29). *Expert web searching skills for translators – A multiple case study.* Teaching Translation and Interpreting 4.

Pietrzak, P. (2015). 'Translation competence.' In Ł. Bogucki, S. Góźdź-Roszkowski, & P. Stalmaszczyk (Eds.), *Ways to translation* (317–338). Łódź University Press & Jagiellonian University Press.

Pym, A. (2004). 'Redefining translation competence in an electronic age. In defence of a minimalist approach.' *Meta: Translators' Journal*, *48*(4), 481–497. https://doi.org/10.7202/008533ar

Pym, A. (2012). 'Training Translators.' In K. Malmkjær, & K. Windle (Eds.), *The Oxford handbook of translation studies* (475–489). OUP.

Scott, J. (2017). 'Legal translation – A multidimensional endeavour.' *Comparative Legilinguistics,* (32), 37–66. http://dx.doi.org/10.14746/cl.2017.32.1

Shreve, G. (2009). 'Recipient-orientation and metacognition in the translation process.' In R. Dimitriu, & M. Shlesinger (Eds.), *Translators and Their Readers* (255–270). Les Editions du Hazard.

Szewczyk, M. (2014, January 10). *Standardowe klauzule umowne (tzw. boilerplate clauses) w umowach transakcyjnych poddanych prawu polskiemu*, codozasady.pl. https://codozasady.pl/p/standardowe-klauzule-umowne-tzw-boilerplate-clauses-w-umowach-transakcyjnych-poddanych-prawu-polskie.

Vanroy, B., De Clercq, O., & Macken, L. (2019). 'Correlating process and product data to get an insight into translation difficulty.' *Perspectives, 27*(6), 924–941.

Voita, E., Sennrich, R., & Titov, I. (2019). 'When a good translation is wrong in context: Context-aware machine translation improves on deixis, ellipsis, and lexical cohesion.' In *Proceedings of the 57th Annual Meeting of the Association for Computational Linguistics* (1198–1212). Association for Computational Linguistics.

Claudia Wiesinger, Justus Brockmann, Alina Secară, Dragoş Ciobanu

Centre for Translation Studies (ZTW), University of Vienna

Speech-Enabled Post-Editing Machine Translation (PEMT) in the Context of Translator Training

Abstract: Speech technologies are becoming increasingly popular among professional translators and several studies have already highlighted the benefits of automatic speech recognition (ASR, also known as speech-to-text (S2T)) and speech synthesis (text-to-speech (T2S)) for translation and revision. Consequently, several mainstream and experimental computer-assisted translation tools now support ASR/T2S to various degrees. This drive towards making established workflows more effective and ergonomic by integrating speech technologies into translation/revision/post-editing machine translation (PEMT) tasks, combined with the growing adoption of machine translation (MT) and PEMT by language service providers (LSPs), makes the case for exposing trainee translators to such technologies as early as possible. Improved workflows may also reduce and even counterbalance some of the reticence towards PEMT felt in the industry. However, higher-education programmes currently introduce PEMT mainly at postgraduate level. Such limited exposure to PEMT during translator training fuels the spread of MT/PEMT myths and misunderstandings.

As part of an initiative to introduce novel translation technologies and professional practices starting from the undergraduate level, we conducted a study with 17 University of Vienna students using speech-enabled PEMT – i.e., a combination of speech synthesis and PEMT. In this paper, we report on the students' error annotation and correction performance alongside their evolving attitudes during the English into German PEMT experiment, which was carried out in four different working conditions (in silence; with speech synthesis for the source text segments; with speech synthesis for the target text segments; and with speech synthesis for both source and target text segments).

We find that PEMT with both source and target speech synthesis has benefits both in terms of quality and productivity compared to PEMT in silence, justifying our call for neural synthetic voices to be included for both source and target segments in all PEMT environments – which includes all CAT tools. Performing error annotation during PEMT also proves beneficial, despite being viewed as inefficient. On the other hand, there is evidence of over-editing and inaccurate self-perceptions regarding productivity. Moreover, despite the quality improvements in some conditions, many MT errors remain uncorrected in all working conditions, which proves the need for at least one reviser to check the work of post-editors, especially novice ones.

Keywords: speech synthesis, text-to-speech, post-editing machine translation (PEMT), speech-enabled PEMT, translator training

1. Introduction

Recent academic and industry debates about machine translation (MT) have revolved around the impact of the increasingly popular practice of post-editing machine translation (PEMT) on the translation profession, and have addressed issues such as automation anxiety, the human-in-the-loop and MT literacy (see Translating and the Computer TC43,[1] or Translating Europe Forum 2021 – Collaboration in Times of Automation[2]). These debates arise from a number of concerns, including the impact on rates, translators' fear of being replaced, and the constraints to creativity (Alvarez-Vidal, Oliver and Badia, 2020: 55). What has been talked about to a lesser degree, however, is the impact of this narrative on translator training – both on the ways in which novel translation technologies and professional practices are being introduced into the curriculum, and on the attitudes that are being conveyed to the future generation of translators.

In the context of translator training, it has been suggested that undergraduate students should be exposed to PEMT only at a later stage of their degree given the specific skill-set that this task requires (O'Brien, 2002) (e.g. knowledge of source and target languages, cultures, and audiences; knowledge of translation strategies; knowledge of translation technologies – including, but not limited to MT –, attention to detail, etc.). However, a study of European Master's in Translation (EMT) and related programmes has shown that there is not enough hands-on PEMT practice even at a post-graduate level (Ginovart Cid and Colominas Ventura, 2020). This limited exposure to PEMT during translator training courses, combined with the spread of MT/PEMT myths and misunderstandings, is in stark contrast with the fact that PEMT has become standard practice for many translators.

The growing adoption of MT in the translation services industry has coincided with an increased availability and use of speech technologies for translation, revision and PEMT. The possibility of dictating using automatic

1 https://www.asling.org/tc43/.
2 https://ec.europa.eu/info/events/2021TEF_en.

speech recognition technology (ASR, also known as speech-to-text (S2T)) has motivated a number of researchers to investigate its benefits for translation, as well as PEMT (Dragsted, Mees and Hansen, 2011; Ciobanu, 2014, 2016; Mesa-Lao, 2014; Zapata, Castilho and Moorkens, 2017; Liyanapathirana, 2021). The use of automatic speech synthesis (text-to-speech (T2S)) has received comparatively much less attention, although its impact on revision quality and processes has not escaped researchers' attention altogether (Ciobanu, Ragni and Secară, 2019; Secară and Ciobanu, forthcoming). Nevertheless, to our knowledge there are no studies to date looking at the impact of T2S on PEMT product quality or on post-editors' productivity and attitudes towards this mode of working.

We set out to investigate four research questions, looking at the impact of PEMT with T2S on: MT error correction (RQ1), MT error annotation (RQ2), PEMT productivity (RQ3), and post-editors' attitudes (RQ4).

Our hypothesis that T2S-enabled PEMT is a viable mode of working is based on Ciobanu, Ragni and Secară's (2019) encouraging findings in relation to T2S-enabled *revision* which led to better performance especially in terms of Accuracy error correction without having a negative impact on productivity. We hypothesise that the use of T2S will continue to serve as an attention-raising technology that adds value to the PEMT process, as well, and will support emerging and professional translators in their work not just during revision tasks, but also during PEMT ones.

This article will focus on the benefits and challenges of exposing students to novel technologies and practices such as PEMT performed with synthetic voices early on in their training. To that end, we first discuss relevant previous literature in relation to the growing integration of MT and speech technologies into different translation workflows. We then introduce our research questions and methodology, and present the data collected during our study in relation to each research question. This is followed by the discussion and conclusion sections, in which we highlight the observed consequences of the interactions between students and such novel technologies and practices. We find that PEMT with both source and target speech synthesis has benefits both in terms of quality and productivity compared to PEMT in silence. Error annotation during PEMT also proves beneficial, despite being viewed as inefficient. Nevertheless, there is evidence of over-editing and inaccurate self-perceptions regarding productivity. Moreover, despite the quality improvements in some conditions, many errors remain uncorrected in all working conditions, which proves the need for at least one additional workflow step in which at least one reviser checks the work of post-editors, especially novice ones.

2. Previous research

Since the integration of data-driven MT into commercial translation workflows in the 2000s (Kenny, 2020), a growing body of language service providers (LSPs) have added it to their service offering (ELIA et al., 2020: 44) by asking translators to carry out more PEMT tasks (Vieira, 2020). PEMT aims at improving the quality of the machine-translated target language content while leveraging the productivity benefits which MT can offer translators (Hu and Cadwell, 2016). Prior research suggests that MT output can enable translators to achieve quality and productivity gains comparable to levels achieved with high-percentage translation memory (TM) matches (Guerberof Arenas, 2014) while recording similar editing times and distances (Sánchez-Gijón, Moorkens and Way, 2019).

However, there is evidence of a lack of hands-on PEMT training in European university Translation Studies programmes both at postgraduate and undergraduate levels (Ginovart Cid and Colominas Ventura, 2020). This may be caused by slow institutional course update cycles, the trainers' own apprehension regarding MT, the tendency to segregate translation technologies to individual, isolated courses, or a combination of all these and other realities. Nevertheless, the fact that PEMT is increasingly adopted in the industry should encourage educators to challenge local traditions and introduce students to MT and PEMT as early as possible in their training. After all, not doing so does not prevent our students from using MT; it simply contributes to their using it inappropriately due to knowledge gaps, unrealistic expectations, and missing reflective practice, just like other MT users do outside of Translation Studies (TS). The ironic difference is that, while at least such non-TS users are seeing a growing number of TS academics working to improve their MT literacy (Bowker and Ciro, 2019), we are missing the opportunity to train our current students fully and also address the reticence of some translators to engage with PEMT (ELIA et al., 2020: 51).

When investigating PEMT, an important aspect to consider is the type of text to be processed by MT. Studies have been conducted on domain-specific and general language content from a wide range of text types, including IT-domain texts (Guerberof Arenas, 2014), user manuals, patient information leaflets, promotional brochures (Jia, Carl and Wang, 2019), or clinical study results (Alves et al., 2016). In a survey of professional post-editors, Alvarez-Vidal et al. (2020) found that it is the technical domain where PEMT is most commonly applied, followed by the medical domain. The vast majority of PEMT studies are concerned with functional texts, with less attention paid so far to applications in literary or creative translation.

While literary translation is often seen as the biggest challenge for MT, the rise of neural machine translation (NMT), as well as the growing availability of training data, have led to significant improvements in translation quality (Toral and Way, 2018). In light of these improvements, the viability of using NMT in literary translation is emerging as a new research area (Tezcan, Daems and Macken, 2019; Vieira, 2020). Similar to Toral and Way (2018), Webster et al. (2020) studied the performance of NMT on the translation of classic novels. While they found that the MT output has significant shortcomings compared to human translations, the authors suggest that "NMT systems can definitely be employed in the field of literary translation, but perhaps more as an aid during translation" (ibid., 18). In a review of recent studies that address the use of MT for literary texts, Youdale (2019) notes that, while "there appears to be an almost wholesale rejection by literary translators of the use of CAT tools and MT in their craft" (ibid., 15), the picture that emerges from research is more nuanced in terms of applicability of MT in literary translation. Potential benefits include time savings, as well as the ability of MT to achieve near-human quality depending on training resources and language pair (ibid., 23).

While the use of technologies like MT is growing in the industry, Moorkens and O'Brien (2017) highlight a lack of human-computer interaction (HCI) input in the development of translation tools, leading to dissatisfaction among users. Several projects have been carried out with an aim to create enhanced tools that add functionalities to assist PEMT (ibid.), some of which also include the use of ASR (Teixeira et al., 2019; Herbig et al., 2020).

In the 2020 European Language Industry Survey (ELIA et al., 2020), over 80 % of respondents stated that they use dictation tools at least occasionally, which indicates an uptake of speech technology in the industry. A general positive attitude towards the use of ASR in the translation workflow was also reported among translators working in international organisations (Liyanapathirana, Bouillon and Mesa-Lao, 2019), as well as among student translators (Mesa-Lao, 2014).

In addition to user preferences and attitudes, experimental studies also indicate possible advantages to using ASR. A recent study (Liyanapathirana, 2021) found post-editing with dictation to be faster and achieve better BLEU (Papineni et al., 2002) and TER (Snover et al., 2006) scores when compared to post-editing with typing or dictating the translation from scratch using MT as inspiration only. It is useful to note that the analysis methods in this study rely either on automatically-generated scores comparing the output to a reference translation (BLEU) or mechanical measures (number of edits made), which do not provide insights into the linguistic quality of the outputs.

While the findings above encourage the integration of speech recognition technology into the PEMT process, little research has so far been published on the use of speech synthesis technology (or text-to-speech (T2S)) as a text-reception method for translators, revisers, or post-editors. A recent study (Ciobanu, Ragni and Secară, 2019) delivered promising results on the integration of source text sound into the translation *revision* process. The authors concluded that "linguists are open to such speech-enabled revision environments, produce higher-quality output using them, and need enhanced training specifically for revision with sound" (ibid., 16). Ciobanu and Secară (2020) further identified a need for more research on the effects of T2S technology on translators' work, with Ciobanu (2016) suggesting that T2S has potential to add value to the PEMT task, as well.

Although current technologies endorsed by the language services industry do not routinely support translation, revision or PEMT in another mode except in silence, professionals do seek ways around this (see Ciobanu, 2016). Another example is the 2013 survey of professional translators and revisers working in the Italian publishing market which indicated that 36.4 % of self-revising translators and 20 % of revisers regularly read aloud the translation during revision (Scocchera, 2017). This points to an intuitively perceived benefit of aurally processing a translated text during revision. This mode of working can be implemented individually or in pairs, the latter being known as the practice of *relecture croisée/cross-reading* (Allain, 2010).

The findings by Ciobanu, Ragni and Secară (2019) suggest that the presence of sound while revising is generally conducive to identifying and correcting more errors – above all, accuracy errors – compared to working in silence. The application of T2S to PEMT processes is encouraged by the fact that it is precisely accuracy errors like mistranslations that have repeatedly been identified as one of the most frequent error categories in output produced by MT engines belonging to the currently dominant NMT paradigm (Vardaro, Schaeffer and Hansen-Schirra, 2019). We therefore hope that translation, revision and PEMT tools producers will be more willing to make speech technologies – especially T2S, but also ASR – available to the users of their interfaces.

3. The study

Participants

We report on a study conducted at the University of Vienna with 16 undergraduate students of Transcultural Communication and 1 postgraduate student of Translation. Using the results from a pre-experiment questionnaire, we quasi-randomly allocated the participants to two groups, G1 and G2, while ensuring that the groups were roughly balanced in terms of participants' language skills and translation experience. Most of the students in both groups were native speakers of German with an English language level of C1 and had very limited translation experience. Due to the COVID-19 pandemic, the study was conducted fully online. For this reason, control mechanisms were put in place: the participants were asked to work in front of their active webcams and observe strict time limits. The students were all part of a compulsory module on Machine Translation and took part in this task voluntarily.

Source text selection and target text production

The source text used in the study was a 1,800-word excerpt from the 2019 stage adaptation of Hanif Kureishi's *My Beautiful Laundrette* (1985), which was translated from English into German using Google Translate. This text type was chosen due to emerging research on the use of NMT for literary translation, as well as the assumption that a synthetic voice reading out a text that was written to be spoken (i.e., in the form of a dialogue) would be particularly beneficial to the PEMT process. In the preparation stage, the text was translated with the freely available MT engines DeepL,[3] Microsoft Translator[4] and Google Translate,[5] and the resulting target texts were annotated by a member of the research team using the harmonised DQF-MQM error typology. Google Translate was chosen because its output contained fewer errors than Microsoft Translator and more errors than DeepL, thus qualifying as a moderate PEMT challenge for our participants. The source text was split into four equal parts of roughly 450 source words each.

Task details

After attending an introductory workshop in which they practised PEMT and error annotation on a 124-word excerpt from the play, the students were asked to both annotate and post-edit the four target text parts during two separate experiment sessions (two parts per session). Students received instructions both during the introductory workshop and in writing on how to use T2S in the PEMT task, as well as how to change the synthetic voices if they wanted to. In addition to the short sequence of steps needed to activate and change the

3 https://www.deepl.com/; translation retrieval date: 7/04/2021.
4 https://www.bing.com/translator; translation retrieval date: 7/04/2021.
5 https://translate.google.com/; translation retrieval date: 7/04/2021.

synthetic voices, the written instructions also included the relevant Windows and MacOS keyboard shortcuts necessary to increase productivity when using synthetic voices: play/pause/skip back/skip forward/increase or decrease reading speed.

The two experiment sessions took place on different days within a two-week interval. In the sessions, the participants were allocated 45 minutes per part, and each part was tackled in a different working condition: 1. in silence for both groups; 2. with source text sound (STS) **or** target text sound (TTS), depending on the group; 3. with TTS **or** STS; and 4. with STS **and** TTS for both groups. In each sound condition, the students were instructed to use synthetic voices for each segment they were working on at least once – i.e. each student would start post-editing each segment by first listening to the source, the target, or both the source and the target segment, as required by each sound condition; however, students could activate the synthetic voice(s) again during or after finishing post-editing each segment. Although the remote experiment set-up did not allow the recording of time lost switching between the two synthetic voices for the two languages present in the final condition, we believe this time to be minimal due to three factors: the students' growing familiarity with T2S operation after completing the previous two PEMT tasks; the point-and-click implementation of the T2S technology used; and the availability of keyboard shortcuts to increase productivity.

The order in which the two groups were confronted with the first sound condition was reversed to counteract the influence of growing familiarity with the text on the results (Table 1). The students used Microsoft Word's built-in Read Aloud function for the synthetic voices because they needed to access both source and target text synthesis seamlessly during the final condition regardless of their computers' operating systems and without making major changes to their previous work environment.

Table 1: Distribution of experimental groups, parts, and sound conditions

	Part 1	**Part 2**	**Part 3**	**Part 4**
G1 (n=9)	Silence	STS	TTS	STS+TTS
G2 (n=8)	Silence	TTS	STS	STS+TTS

After the final experiment session, the students participated in a feedback meeting during which they could ask questions and compare their performance. In order to collect data on the students' prior experience and evolving attitudes, we asked them to fill in an initial questionnaire during recruitment, as well as one short questionnaire after each experiment session and one questionnaire after the feedback meeting (6 questionnaires in total).

Error annotation

The text that the participants worked on was presented to them in a three-column table format in Microsoft Word. The first column contained the source text, each cell representing one segment of an excerpt of the aforementioned stage play in English. The second and third columns contained identical copies of the German output produced by Google Translate for each segment. This way of presenting the text was chosen to enable the participants to carry out both error annotation and post-editing of the MT output without having to combine the annotations and edits in a single cell.

For the annotation part of the task, the participants were introduced to the harmonised DQF-MQM error typology to enable them to classify the errors they found in the MT output. This typology and the encompassing framework were created during the EU-funded QT21 project by the German Research Centre for Artificial Intelligence (DFKI) and the Translation Automation User Society (TAUS). DFKI and TAUS brought together their respective translation quality frameworks to advance standardisation in translation quality assessment. The error typology contained in the harmonised framework is available online,[6] and has since its release in 2015 become the preferred way of applying the MQM framework, including adoption by major companies for their localisation needs (Lommel, 2018).

The typology used in the experiment features eight high-level error types, namely 'Accuracy,' 'Fluency,' 'Terminology,' 'Style,' 'Design,' 'Locale convention,' 'Verity,' and 'Other.' All these high-level error types – except for the 'Other' type – are branched into granular error types that allow for more precise error annotation. There are 33 granular error types in total. Each error type has a numerical identifier, with the high-level types numbered one to eight, and the granular error types having a double-digit identifier starting with the figure that corresponds to the appropriate high-level type. The error typology also features five severity levels that can be assigned to the errors. They range from 'Critical' to 'Neutral,' complemented by a 'Kudos' option to praise exceptional performance. These severity levels are numbered one to five from highest to lowest severity.

To reduce typing effort for our participants and to simplify data collection, the participants were asked to annotate the MT errors using the numerical

6 https://www.taus.net/qt21-project#harmonized-error-typology.

identifiers in the following format: High-level error type – Granular error type – Severity level. They did so using the comment function in Microsoft Word, working on the second column in their documents. For instance, the comment for a 'Mistranslation' error with 'Major' severity would be: 1–13 – 2 (corresponding to Accuracy – Mistranslation – Major). The 'Other' error type is meant to accommodate issues not covered by the rest of the typology, so this is the only error type for which actual text had to be entered in a comment by the participants. An example would look like this: 8 – Word order – 3.

Post-editing

For the post-editing part of the task, the participants were asked to correct errors present in the MT output by making changes to the text in the third column of their respective documents. To facilitate data collection, they were asked to use the Track Changes feature in Microsoft Word, which displays and highlights any changes made to the document. The error annotation and correction tasks were sequential: for each segment, students were instructed to first annotate the errors in the raw MT output displayed in the second column, and then to correct them in the third column. Then they would proceed to the next segment, and so on. Without eye-tracking and screen recording data, however, we do not know to what extent students blended the annotation and correction tasks. Some of their questionnaire answers suggest that, while post-editing, they referred back to their annotations. Whether they changed their initial annotations while post-editing, however, we cannot tell.

Prior to the experiment sessions, the participants were provided with an instruction document which contained a task brief with information on the text they would process and the tasks they would perform. This contained instructions from a fictitious client to perform full post-editing to achieve publishable quality. In this case, publishable quality meant that the post-edited target text should be fit for the purpose of presenting the play to an Austrian audience as a stage performance.

Creating a gold standard

In order to establish a reference against which the participants' annotations and edits could be compared, two members of the research team each carried out the same task of annotating and post-editing the MT output. Both researchers are experienced in translation, post-editing, and revision tasks, holding postgraduate degrees in translation, and having worked for more than four years in the language services industry. Both are German native speakers. In contrast to the participants, the researchers carried out the annotation and post-editing without time constraints, to prevent the factor of time from impacting on the number of errors found and corrected. Furthermore, no sound was present during their work.

The annotations made by the researchers were then merged by mutual agreement into a 'gold standard' version which, for the purpose of this study, was assumed to contain all of the errors that needed to be corrected in the MT output. According to this gold standard, there were 91 errors in Part 1, 75 errors in Part 2, 62 errors in Part 3, and 45 errors in Part 4.

Only the annotations were merged into a gold standard, since the aim was to identify the number, location, and types of errors present in the MT output. No gold standard post-edited target text was created since this would not have helped to facilitate data collection and evaluation.

Research questions

In this study, we set out to answer the following research questions using a variety of methods, measures, and types of analysis (see Table 2):

- (RQ1) Which of the four conditions (silence, STS, TTS, or STS+TTS) is conducive to correcting more MT errors in line with the Gold Standard?
- (RQ2) What is the effect of sound (STS, TTS, or STS+TTS) on MT error annotation?
- (RQ3) In which of the four conditions (silence, STS, TTS, or STS+TTS) are the participants the most productive?
- (RQ4) What are the participants' attitudes towards the integration of speech synthesis into the PEMT process?

Table 2: Research questions, measure/method and type of analysis used

Research Question	Method/ measure	Type of Analysis
RQ1	Error counts	Error correction rate (based on the TAUS DQF-MQM error typology)
RQ2	Error annotation	Error annotation rate (based on the TAUS DQF-MQM error typology)
RQ3	Productivity	Annotated and post-edited Target text/Time ratio (target words per hour)
RQ4	Questionnaires	Qualitative and quantitative analysis of responses

5. Results

Each participant in each experiment condition submitted a separate file containing their error annotation and PEMT work. These individual files were subsequently evaluated, and the resulting data stored: the number of post-edited target text words per task time; the number of MT errors annotated; the number of MT errors corrected; and the number of MT errors corrected in line with the gold standard.

This last measure, divided by the number of gold standard MT errors present in the portions of text edited by the participants, resulted in an individual MT error correction rate for each participant, which was used as a measure of how successful participants were in correcting MT errors that genuinely needed to be corrected in the portion of text they worked on – RQ1. Figure 1 shows the individual MT error correction rates in each sound condition, for each group participant. Blue indicates the PEMT-in-silence condition, orange – PEMT with STS –, grey – PEMT with TTS –, and yellow – PEMT with both STS and TTS.

The edits made by the participants were compared against the annotations in the gold standard. For each edit, we judged whether it was an attempt to correct an MT error marked up in the gold standard.

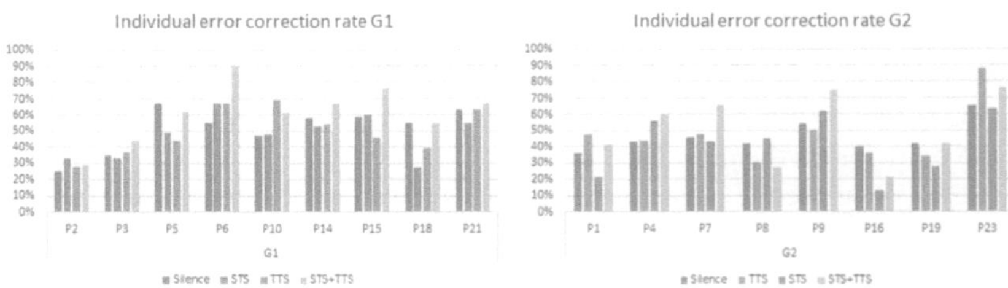

Figure 1: Individual error correction rates for each group member

Table 3 presents the average error correction rates for each group and each experiment condition. The highest scores were obtained by both groups when post-editing with both source and target speech synthesis (STS+TTS) in the fourth experiment condition. On the other hand, the lowest scores were observed for the first condition in which participants worked with speech synthesis – for G1 this was the STS condition, while for G2 this was the TTS condition.

Table 3: Average group error correction rates (in line with the gold standard) in all four experiment conditions

	Silence	**STS**	**TTS**	**STS+TTS**
G1	52 %	47 %	50 %	**61 %**
G2	46 %	47 %	41 %	**51 %**

Data was also collected on the error types annotated by participants – RQ2. This included the high-level error type, the granular error type, and the severity level. However, for the purpose of gaining an overview of the general types of errors that were annotated, and to draw conclusions regarding a possible impact of speech synthesis use, our current analysis is done on the high-level error types. Figure 2 shows these error types annotated in each experiment condition, averaged per group.

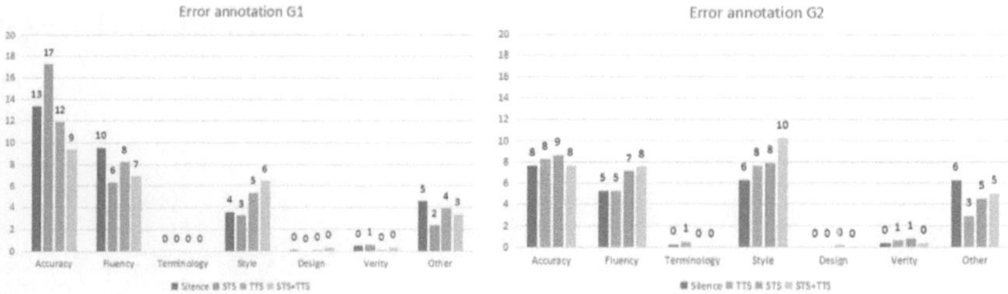

Figure 2: Average high-level error types annotated by each group

Moreover, combining the data collected when investigating RQ1 and RQ2 enabled us to look for trends in error annotation and correction – Figure 3 illustrates, for instance, the different average performances of the two groups in conditions 1 and 4 of our experiment, while Figure 4 presents this information for each participant. In Figure 3, the first two bars for each Part are of different sizes because they represent the average number of MT errors present in the gold standard for the amount of text each group managed to work on in each of the two experiment conditions presented; given that each participant in each group finished a different number of sentences, the resulting averages are different, as well.

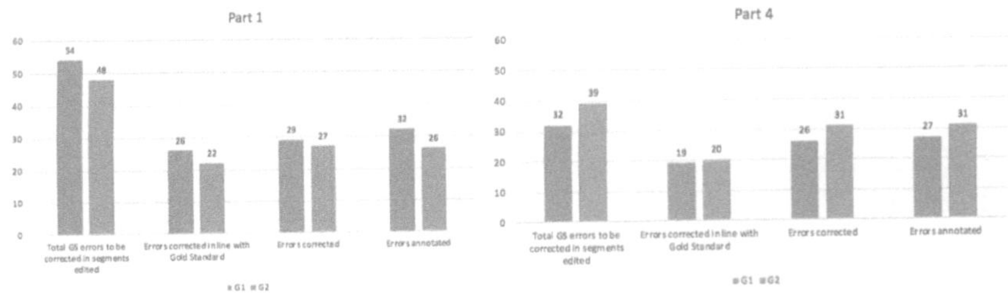

Figure 3: Average group error annotation and correction performance in experiment conditions 1 (PEMT in silence) and 4 (PEMT with STS+TTS)

In Figure 4, the first blue bar indicates the number of errors present in the gold standard for the amount of text each participant managed to work on in conditions 1 and 4; some participants' productivity was high, resulting in a tall blue bar, but their accuracy in annotating and correcting errors was much lower (at least in the first condition), resulting in several visual discrepancies between the blue bar and the orange, grey and yellow ones.

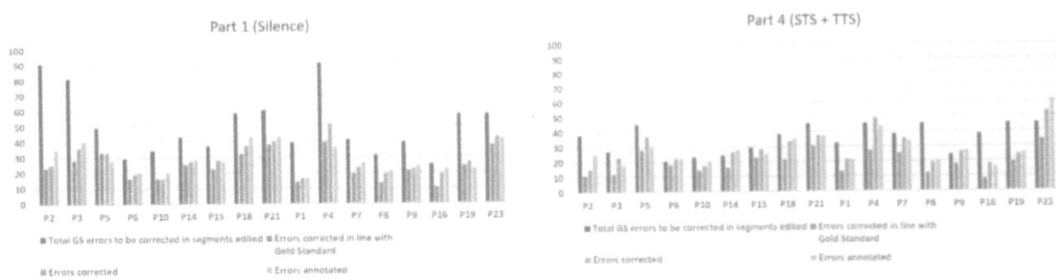

Figure 4: Individual error annotation and correction performance in experiment conditions 1 (PEMT in silence) and 4 (PEMT with STS+TTS)

Productivity – RQ3 – was measured as post-edited and annotated target text words per time. The number of post-edited words was counted from the beginning of each text to the last segment where an edit was made within the allocated 45 minutes. For better generalisability, the values obtained as post-edited words per 45 minutes were normalised to per-hour values, since this is a more common unit of measure for productivity in the industry. Figure 5 shows the productivity for each participant in each experiment condition, split per groups, and Table 4 presents the averages for each group, highlighting the condition in which the highest average productivity was achieved for each group.

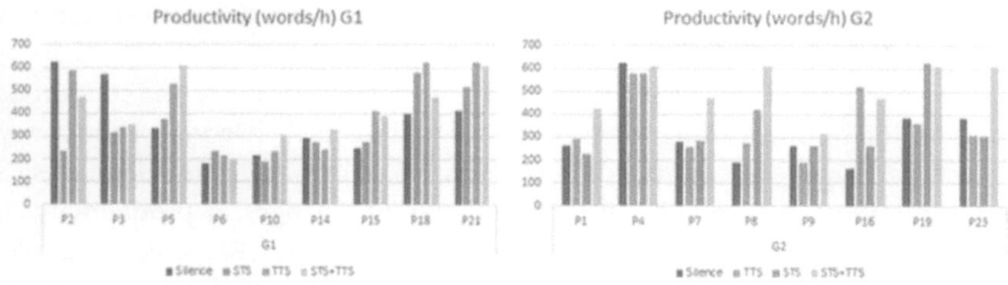

Figure 5: Productivity (in words/h) for each participant in all four experiment conditions

Table 4: Average group productivity (in words/h) in all four experiment conditions

	Silence	**STS**	**TTS**	**STS+TTS**
G1	363	332	**424**	415
G2	319	370	348	**515**

The attitudes of the participants towards the integration of T2S in the PEMT process – RQ4 – ranged from very positive – "exciting" – to very negative – "annoying"–, and also included "cool," "interesting," "helpful," "new," "distracting," "confusing," and "difficult." The most frequently used qualifier for the experience, though, was "time-consuming."

When asked whether they felt their attitude to PEMT with T2S had changed by the end of the experiment, the participants' answers provided more useful context for the qualifiers mentioned above and indicated that these may have simply referred to the current implementation of T2S in MS Word: "I think I answered 'no' the first time [to the question whether I would consider using speech synthesis for PEMT], but now I can see some benefits. I am indeed more focused and caught some errors I would have overlooked otherwise, but it is also more time consuming and a bit awkward [in Word]." "The biggest hindrance/annoyance was manually starting/stopping the speech synthesis – with an integrated tool, it could be way more productive. Especially in the 3rd part, when I didn't have to start/stop that often."

The need for high-quality multilingual T2S was mentioned, and the technology itself was considered useful: "I now think that it will probably be part of a translator's routine to use speech synthesis, because although the tool doesn't work that [well] in other languages apart from English, I think this will change in the future." "I don't exactly remember my first answer but after the study (especially after the last part), I understand that speech synthesis can sometimes be very helpful for PEMT."

The self-reported impact of T2S on PEMT productivity in the sound conditions made for interesting reading when compared to the actual observed productivity of each participant in each condition – Figure 6 illustrates these differences (S represents the self-reported 'same productivity/no changes in productivity,' L represents 'less productive' and M represents 'more productive'). For example, P1's self-reported productivity was SMM. However, the actual productivity for P1, as indicated by the bars in the chart, was LMM (Lower in STS, More in TTS and More in STS+TTS compared to Silence).

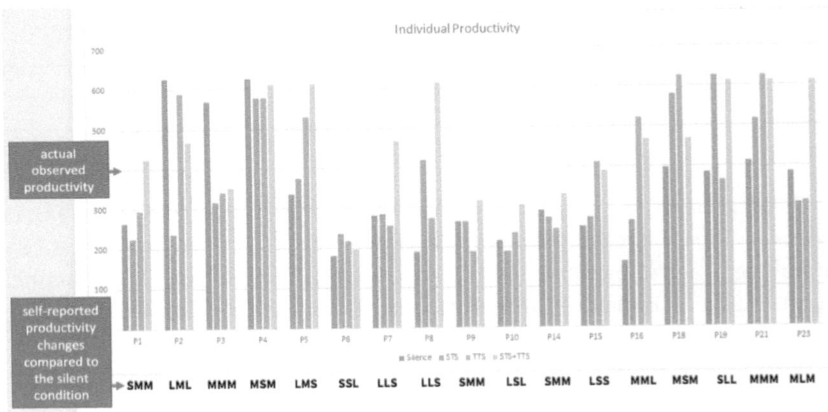

Figure 6: Observed v Self-reported productivity in all four experiment conditions

6. Discussion

Industry advocates of PEMT – especially since the advent of NMT – have been active in their portrayal of this task as a simple one which can be performed with limited or even no training, by non-experts, and even without the need for the source text. However, our data shows that, with limited PEMT experience and despite some PEMT training in the beginning of our project, our participants missed close to, and at times even more than, half of the errors present in the NMT output they were asked to post-edit.

In response to RQ1, our data shows that, on average and for each group, the final experiment condition (STS+TTS) resulted in the highest proportion of MT errors corrected in line with our gold standard – henceforth called *performance*.

While qualitative data analysed for our RQ4 mentions the perceived benefit of post-editing with speech synthesis, especially for improved attention and sensitivity to subtle errors, we cannot discard the possibility that some of the recorded improvement in PEMT performance will also be due to participants getting used to the task content. This hypothesis is also supported by an observed increase in productivity (RQ3) for most participants by the end of the experiment, although not always along the same pattern as error correction performance.

The first time our participants were exposed to PEMT with speech synthesis (in condition 2: STS for G1 and TTS for G2), their performance decreased compared to their PEMT in silence level, but only G1 experienced a drop in productivity. Nevertheless, both groups improved their performance in the subsequent two conditions, although for G1 the third condition performance was still below their PEMT in silence level and only the fourth condition surpassed it.

Looking beyond group averages, we observe major variations between the performance of individual participants: four participants did not benefit from any of the sound conditions; three performed better than in silence only in one sound condition (two in the final STS+TTS condition, and one in STS); six performed better in two (all six in STS+TTS, as well as four in TTS and two in STS), and four participants performed better than in silence in all three sound conditions. These findings highlight the importance of both source and target speech synthesis being available to post-editors for achieving better-quality PEMT. From a training perspective, these findings also highlight the importance of exposing trainee translators to a variety of modes of working as early as possible, so that they are better equipped to choose their ideal technology set-up when they join the profession.

In our experiment, we asked participants not only to correct errors, but first to annotate them using the TAUS DQF-MQM error typology, and we trained them accordingly. The analysis of their results (RQ2) showed that G1 was much more sensitive to Accuracy and Fluency errors, while G2 identified more Style errors. At the same time, while G1 tended to annotate fewer Accuracy and Fluency errors and more Style errors as the experiment progressed, G2 tended to annotate increasingly more errors in all three categories. Specifically, the STS condition was conducive to the annotation of the highest number of Accuracy errors in both groups. This finding mirrors Ciobanu, Ragni and Secară's (2019) findings for *revision*.

Predictably, there was great disparity in the participants' annotations, which is visible even if we only consider the high-level error types. For instance, P2 annotated 28 'Accuracy' errors and zero 'Other' errors in Part 1, while P4 only annotated 14 'Accuracy' errors, but 10 'Other' errors for the same part.

Productivity was 625 words/h for both P2 and P4. The granular error types and severity levels further amplify this disparity. For instance, one and the same error identified as 'Accuracy – Untranslated – Minor' in the gold standard was annotated by different participants as 'Accuracy – Untranslated – Minor/Major,' 'Accuracy – Mistranslation – Minor/Major,' 'Fluency – Grammar – Minor,' 'Verity – Culture-specific reference – Major,' or not identified as an error at all. Further work will investigate these disparities in more detail.

However, for the time being, an interesting picture still develops when analysing the data through the lenses of RQ2 combined with RQ1 and the regular participant surveys (RQ4) which offer useful insights regarding causality. As already stated, both groups corrected far fewer MT errors than they should have done in line with the gold standard – even though this gap almost halved by the fourth experiment condition. However, both groups consistently corrected more errors than they needed to – a situation particularly visible in the case of condition 4, when G1 corrected on average 26 errors while only 19 were in the gold standard, and G2 corrected 31 while only 20 were in the gold standard. This phenomenon of over-correction is known to alarm advocates of efficiency in PEMT, but they need to remember that translation, revision or PEMT work is not comparable to a conveyor-belt process in which defects are clearly visible. Translation, revision and PEMT remain expert tasks firmly anchored in the area of knowledge work which benefit from a certain amount of standardisation and efficiency gains brought about by a combination of relevant technologies, but cannot become routine, mindless activities. At least not in all text types and all language pairs.

What was also interesting to notice in our data was the difference in the number of errors annotated versus the number of errors corrected by our participants. This was clearly explained in their survey submissions, though: at times participants identified an error in the MT output but could not come up with or source a solution at the time, while in other situations they saw an error which they corrected but could not find a suitable label to annotate it with. Nevertheless, data collected for RQ4 shows that, although participants reported an initial level of impatience and viewed the error annotation task as time-consuming, as the experiment progressed, they came to see it as a useful step: being able to attach a label to most of the errors they identified in the MT output gave them a sense of confidence that they were demonstratively improving the target text. The benefit of using such industry-approved error typologies is therefore obvious: they represent learning tools with which students can benchmark their progress during a training course. They are far more useful than a grade and a general comment provided without further guidance by trainers. They also serve as a solid basis for students to learn to give each other constructive feedback, an important skill they will use extensively in their professional careers. Our participants received our gold standard for all experiment texts at the end of the experiment, and a feedback meeting was provided to them to discuss their performance.

In terms of productivity (RQ3), as already mentioned, our groups' productivity improved – sometimes drastically – during the experiment. However, when viewed in combination with RQ1 results, we see that the highest improvement in PEMT quality (G1 increased its 52 % MT error correction performance in condition 1 to 61 % in condition 4) came with the lowest improvement in productivity (from 363 words/h to 415 words/h). By comparison, G2's error correction grew from 46 % to 51 %, but their productivity rocketed from 319 words/h to 515 words/h. This data rings a cautionary bell, therefore, especially when participants are investigated separately. We can identify a majority of participants whose quality of PEMT went up using speech synthesis, alongside their productivity, but there are also cases in which quality went down and productivity up, or the other way around.

Our participant surveys showed the evolution of both our participants' confidence in offering PEMT as a service, and their growing appreciation for using speech synthesis during PEMT (RQ4). On the other hand, the surveys also offered an interesting insight into the reliability of self-reported data when combined with RQ3 findings. The comparison of self-reported productivity information against observed data (presented in Figure 6) shows that only one participant – P21 – estimated correctly whether their productivity in each of the three PEMT conditions with speech synthesis was more (M), less (L) or the same (S) as PEMT in silence. All the other 16 participants estimated wrongly how productive they were in one, two, or all three conditions.

The idea of participant perception contradicting empirical data when working with MT and speech technologies is not exclusive to our study, though. When asking translators about their subjectively experienced productivity, Zapata, Castilho and Moorkens (2017) report that three out of four participants reported that translating from scratch and dictation using speech recognition was faster than post editing with speech recognition, when in fact the reverse was true. This highlights the importance of triangulation methods and non-reliance on one type of data collection and investigation method.

7. Conclusion

PEMT is frequently promoted as being very similar to a revision task, based in large part on the claim that a further reviser to check the work of the post-editor is not required. Our data shows that this approach has inherent risks, especially when working with novice post-editors, who missed close to 50 % of MT errors in several of our experiment conditions. It is reasonable to expect a similar level of risk even with experienced post-editors working in an unfamiliar domain, so LSPs need to be proactive to mitigate this risk and the community needs to have more realistic and nuanced NMT expectations.

Moreover, relying on self-reported information to inform technology adoption also proves problematic, thus strengthening the call for mixed-methods research which supplements user questionnaires with practical tasks. We also recommend going beyond group average scores and include participant-level observations to gain more in-depth insights into the effects of the research intervention.

Based on our experiment data, we recommend that PEMT environments (which include CAT tools) make available speech synthesis at the segment level for both source and target segments to enable post-editors to benefit from this technology. In doing so, we recommend they implement the latest neural synthetic voices whose features increasingly resemble authentic human speech. We are looking forward to the introduction of high-quality multilingual voices into PEMT environments to redo our experiments without the confounding factor of PEMT environment user-friendliness.

Finally, we encourage translation trainers to include PEMT tasks early and often in their training programmes to familiarise students with this activity and demonstrate how new technologies (including speech synthesis) can help produce higher-quality PEMT work, with possible productivity gains alongside it, as well. We support the use of industry-validated error typologies during training programmes at all levels to build both translation competences and feedback giving and taking skills.

References

Allain, J.-F. (2010). 'Repenser la revision.' *Traduire. Revue française de la traduction*, (223), 114–120. https://doi.org/10.4000/traduire.316

Alvarez-Vidal, S., Oliver, A., & Badia, T. (2020). 'Post-editing for Professional Translators: Cheer or Fear?' *Tradumàtica: tecnologies de la traducció*, 0(18), 49–69. https://doi.org/10.5565/rev/tradumatica.275

Alves, F., et al. (2016). 'Investigating cognitive effort in post-editing: A relevance-theoretical approach.' In Hansen-Schirra, S. and Grucza, S. (Eds.), *Eyetracking and Applied Linguistics*. Language Science Press.

Bowker, L., & Ciro, J. B. (2019). *Machine Translation and Global Research: Towards Improved Machine Translation Literacy in the Scholarly Community*. Emerald. doi: https://doi.org 10.1108/9781787567214

Ciobanu, D. (2014). 'Of Dragons and Speech Recognition Wizards and Apprentices.' *Tradumàtica: tecnologies de la traducció*, 12, 524–538.

Ciobanu, D. (2016). 'Automatic Speech Recognition in the professional translation process.' *Translation Spaces, 5*(1), 124–144.

Ciobanu, D., Ragni, V., & Secară, A. (2019). 'Speech Synthesis in the Translation Revision Process: Evidence from Error Analysis, Questionnaire, and Eye-Tracking.' *Informatics, 6*(4), 51. 10.3390/informatics6040051

Ciobanu, D., & Secară, A. (2020). 'Speech recognition and synthesis technologies in the translation workflow.' In O'Hagan, M. (Ed.), *The Routledge Handbook of Translation and Technology* (91–106). Routledge. doi: 10.4324/9781315311258-6.

Dragsted, B., Mees, I. M., & Hansen, I. G. (2011). 'Speaking your translation: students' first encounter with speech recognition technology.' *The International Journal for Translation & Interpreting Research, 3*(1), 10–43.

ELIA, et al. (2020). *2020 European Language Industry Survey. Before and after COVID-19.* https://ec.europa.eu/info/sites/default/files/2020_language_industry_survey_report.pdf

Ginovart Cid, C., & Colominas Ventura, C. (2020). 'The MT Post-Editing Skill Set. Course descriptions and educators' thoughts.' In Koponen, M. et al. (Eds.), *Translation Revision and Post-editing: Industry Practices and Cognitive Processes*. Routledge. https://www.routledge.com/Translation-Revision-and-Post-editing-Industry-Practices-and-Cognitive/Koponen-Mossop-Robert-Scocchera/p/book/9781138549715.

Guerberof Arenas, A. (2014). 'Correlations between productivity and quality when post-editing in a professional context.' *Machine Translation, 28*, 165–186.

Herbig, N., et al. (2020). 'MMPE: A Multi-Modal Interface for Post-Editing Machine Translation.' In *Proceedings of the 58th Annual Meeting of the Association for Computational Linguistics. ACL 2020* (1691–1702). Association for Computational Linguistics. 10.18653/v1/2020.acl-main.155.

Hu, K., & Cadwell, P. (2016). 'A Comparative Study of Post-editing Guidelines.' https://www.researchgate.net/publication/303564681_A_Comparative_Study_of_Post-editing_Guidelines.

Jia, Y., Carl, M., & Wang, X. (2019). 'How does the post-editing of neural machine translation compare with from-scratch translation? A product and process study.' *The Journal of Specialised Translation, 31*. https://www.jostrans.org/issue31/art_jia.php

Kenny, D. (2020). 'Machine Translation.' In Baker, M. and Saldanha, G. (Eds.), *Routledge Encyclopedia of Translation Studies*. 3rd ed. (305–310). Routledge.

Liyanapathirana, J. (2021). 'Integrating post-editing with Dragon speech recognizer: a use case at international organizations.' *Asling 43*, online, 17 November. https://www.asling.org/tc43/videos/Liyanapathirana.mp4.

Liyanapathirana, J., Bouillon, P., & Mesa-Lao, B. (2019). 'Surveying the potential of using speech technologies for post-editing purposes in the context of international organizations: What do professional translators think?' In *Proceedings of Machine Translation Summit XVII: Translator, Project and User Tracks. Machine Translation Summit, Dublin, Ireland* (149–158). European Association for Machine Translation. https://aclanthology.org/W19-6728.

Lommel, A. (2018). 'Metrics for Translation Quality Assessment: A Case for Standardising Error Typologies.' In Moorkens, J., et al. (Eds.), *Translation Quality Assessment: From Principles to Practice* (109–127). Springer International. https://doi.org/10.1007/978-3-319-91241-7_6

Mesa-Lao, B. (2014). 'Speech-Enabled Computer-Aided Translation: A Satisfaction Survey with Post-Editor Trainees.' In *Proceedings of the EACL 2014 Workshop on Humans and Computer-assisted Translation, Gothenburg, Sweden* (99–103). Association for Computational Linguistics.

Moorkens, J., & O'Brien, S. (2017). 'Assessing user interface needs of post-editors of machine translation.' In Kenny, D. (Ed.), *Human Issues in Translation Technology* (109–130). Routledge. https://www-taylorfrancis-com.uaccess.univie.ac.at/books/edit/10.4324/9781315648934/human-issues-translation-technology-dorothy-kenny

O'Brien, S. (2002). 'Teaching post-editing: a proposal for course content.' In *Proceedings of the 6th EAMT Workshop: Teaching Machine Translation. EAMT 2002, Manchester, England* (99–106). European Association for Machine Translation. https://aclanthology.org/2002.eamt-1.11

Papineni, K., et al. (2002). 'BLEU: A Method for Automatic Evaluation of Machine Translation.' In *Proceedings of the 40th Annual Meeting on Association for Computational Linguistics*. Stroudsburg, PA, USA: Association for Computational Linguistics (ACL'02), 311–318. https://doi.org/10.3115/1073083.1073135

Sánchez-Gijón, P., Moorkens, J., & Way, A. (2019). 'Post-editing neural machine translation versus translation memory segments.' *Machine Translation, 33*, 31–59.

Scocchera, G. (2017). 'Translation Revision as Rereading: Different Aspects of the Translator's and Reviser's Approach to the Revision Process.' *Mémoires du livre / Studies in Book Culture*, *9*(1).

Secară, A., & Ciobanu, D. (forthcoming). 'Benefits of speech technologies for translators and revisers.' In *#AFFUMT2021: « Former aux métiers de la* *traduction aujourd'hui et demain » | "Translator Training: From the present to the future,"* Grenoble, France.

Snover, M., et al. (2006). 'A Study of Translation Edit Rate with Targeted Human Annotation.' In *Proceedings of the 7th Conference of the Association for Machine Translation in the Americas: Technical Papers. AMTA 2006, Cambridge, Massachusetts, USA* (223–231). Association for Machine Translation in the Americas. https://aclanthology.org/2006.amta-papers.25

Teixeira, C. S. C., et al. (2019). 'Creating a Multimodal Translation Tool and Testing Machine Translation Integration Using Touch and Voice.' *Informatics*, *6*(1), 13. 10.3390/informatics6010013

Tezcan, A., Daems, J., & Macken, L. (2019). 'When a 'sport' is a person and other issues for NMT of novels.' In Hadley, J. et al. (Eds.), *Proceedings of the Qualities of Literary Machine Translation* (40–49). European Association for Machine Translation. https://www.aclweb.org/anthology/W19-7306

Toral, A. and Way, A. (2018). 'What Level of Quality Can Neural Machine Translation Attain on Literary Text?' In Moorkens, J. et al. (Eds.), *Translation Quality Assessment: From Principles to Practice*. Cham: Springer International Publishing, 263–287. 10.1007/978-3-319-91241-7_12.

Vardaro, J., Schaeffer, M. and Hansen-Schirra, S. (2019). 'Translation Quality and Error Recognition in Professional Neural Machine Translation Post-Editing.' *Informatics*, *6*(3).

Vieira, L.N. (2020). 'Post-editing of machine translation.' In O'Hagan, M. (Ed.), *The Routledge Handbook of Translation and Technology*. Routledge, 319–335. 10.4324/9781315311258-6.

Webster, R. et al. (2020). 'Gutenberg Goes Neural: Comparing Features of Dutch Human Translations with Raw Neural Machine Translation Outputs in a Corpus of English Literary Classics.' *Informatics*, *7*(3). 10.3390/informatics7030032

Youdale, R. (2019). *Using computers in the translation of literary style: challenges and opportunities*. Routledge.

Zapata, J., Castilho, S., & Moorkens, J. (2017). 'Translation Dictation vs. Post-editing with Cloud-based Voice Recognition: A Pilot Experiment.' In *MT Summit XVI, Nagoya, Japan*. https://www.researchgate.net/publication/319853140_Translation_Dictation_vs_Post-editing_with_Cloud-based_Voice_Recognition_A_Pilot_Experiment

Urszula Paradowska

The Jacob of Paradies University, Gorzów Wielkopolski, Poland

Expect the Unexpected and Still Be Surprised: Teaching Translation through Projects during the COVID-19 Pandemic

Abstract: Declared by the WHO in March 2020, the COVID-19 pandemic took the world by surprise, providing quite a unique context for teaching and learning translation. As online and blended approaches had been adopted at translator education institutions around the world before the coronavirus locked the world down, translator educators did not start working in the online mode totally unprepared. This paper reports on the implementation of an undergraduate Translation Project course offered to 3rd-year translation and interpreting students at the Jacob of Paradies University, Poland. The course, designed around the areas of competence set out for EMT's Master's degree programmes (2009; EMT Board 2017), aimed to develop the students' service provision competence, information mining competence, technological competence, and interpersonal skills by engaging them in authentic, individual and collaborative Polish-English translation projects. The first part of the paper focuses on the aspects of the course which were either unaffected or even improved by the abrupt shift to online teaching mode. These areas include course design, the use of cloud-based translation tools, authentic project work, and assessment. The second part discusses the challenges encountered during the online delivery of the course, focusing in particular on interaction and engagement. The teacher's reflections on the course are supplemented with findings from an anonymous course evaluation questionnaire and personal communication with the students, offering insight into the effectiveness of the Translation Project course delivered online due to the pandemic. The results indicate that students were generally satisfied with online learning.

Keywords: COVID-19, translator education, virtual learning environment, authentic project work, simulated translation bureaus

1. Introduction

We are now in the third year of the COVID-19 pandemic, which has reshaped education, changing the working environments of university teachers and students. Quite understandably, when the first lockdown was announced in March 2020, those who struggled the most, when they were told to switch to remote instruction, were teachers who had avoided modern technologies in their classrooms before the pandemic, as it became impossible to continue with the status quo. One could expect, though, that the transition from in-person classes to remote instruction would be particularly smooth for those who had already incorporated an online component into face-to-face teaching.

Translator educators should be the ones accustomed to technology and innovation as the market requires translation professionals to use digital technologies and communicate online with their clients and collaborators. University programmes worldwide have been incorporating diverse forms of teaching and learning translation supported on the Web. Also, blended learning approaches have been used for years to educate new generations of translators. When the pandemic hit, what came as a surprise, though, was the fact that moving away from the face-to-face classroom into a virtual learning environment was not as easy as it seemed despite the apparent advantages of previous experience with online translation, communication, and collaboration tools.

2. Online Learning Environments

Previous developments in the field of translator education helped translation teachers to prepare for the unexpected. Although translator education is typically delivered face-to-face, information and communication technologies (ICT) have made it possible to introduce online teaching and learning as well as a 'blended' mode, which integrates online and face-to-face teaching and learning activities. Singh and Thurman (2019), who conducted a systematic literature review of the concept, collecting 46 definitions from 37 resources published between 1988 and 2018, conclude that all the definitions of online learning share the following elements: (1) the use of technology; (2) synchronous or asynchronous time; and (3) the use of synonymous terms such as 'web-based education' or 'e-learning.' In addition, most of the definitions mention interactivity and physical distance among the participants, and compare the online learning mode with a traditional classroom.

Due to the fact that online learning is first and foremost a form of learning in general, before looking at the examples of the use of remote instruction in translator education, let us see the general attributes of efficient learning. In their book "How People Learn," Bransford et al. (2000) posit that effective learning environments are (1) learner-centred, (2) knowledge-centred, (3) assessment-centred, and (4) community-centred. To begin with, *learner-centredness* means that teachers must be sensitive to the beliefs, opinions, cultural practices, and conceptual knowledge that their students bring into the classroom. Secondly, *knowledge-centred* environments enable students to develop metacognitive strategies in the context of a specific domain of knowledge. This is because learning involves making connections with facts, ideas, etc. *Assessment-centredness* is yet another essential component of successful learning environments. Quite importantly, the term does not refer to summative assessment, but highlights the need to provide students and teachers with feedback on the learning process. Last but not least, the authors argue that learning must be *community-centred*, which means that members of the same learning community should support one another. More recently, Zajda (2021) highlights the importance of the student's cultural identity, self-concept, self-esteem, self-efficacy, motivation to learn, and active engagement, which contribute to the quality of learning, affecting the students' overall academic achievement.

In Translation Studies, much has been written about a student-centred approach to translator education. The principles of social constructivism, a pedagogical theory proposed by Vygotsky in the 1930s were first applied to translator education by Kiraly (2000). Social constructivists argue that learning is a social activity and knowledge is constructed through social interaction. The entire learning process is highly contextualised, with educators working as facilitators who assist their students during authentic and semi-authentic projects.

Anderson (2008) analyses the four criteria proposed by Bransford et al. (2000) for efficient learning environments from the perspective of the online learning context. He notes that at the start of online classes learner-centred teachers must provide their students with an opportunity to share their opinions and preconceptions due to the fact that interactions during online instruction are less transparent. As for knowledge-centredness, the author emphasises that, during remote instruction, the teacher should help their students navigate the Web, which provides an easy access to unlimited knowledge resources, which may be daunting. It must be noted that nearly 14 years after the publication of Anderson's analysis, the term 'navigating the Web' is now less concerned with showing students how to interact with the Web, as most translation students are digital natives. Instead, the teacher's role in this respect is to show their students how to assess the reliability of web-based resources. The third element of efficient learning, as specified by Anderson (2008) is assessment-centredness. Online learning contexts offer multiple tools to provide feedback, including automatically marked assessments, simulation exercises, peer feedback via questionnaires and monitoring each other's work. In Anderson's view, the last attribute of an efficient learning environment, community-centredness, poses a challenge when classes are held online. Despite the obvious advantage of sharing a learning space across a distance, participants in online communities may experience problems with commitment, a sense of belonging, and the lack of physical presence. As a result, creating a learning community online may be challenging. Xu and Jaggars (2013), who analysed data from 40,000 American students attending community college courses, found that students engaged in online learning typically face the following problems: technical issues, insufficient computer skills, self-motivation, adaptability and time management. All of these constraints must be considered when designing an online course or switching the mode of teaching from physical classes to the online mode.

Over the last 20 years, technologies used in online learning and teaching have evolved from email correspondence, the Internet and videos, through learning management systems (LMS), wikis, Massive Open Online Courses (MOOCs), mobile and smart devices, to cloud-based applications and virtual reality technologies (Chang et al. 2018). The benefits of online learning can be summarised as follows:

> For learners, online learning knows no time zones, and location and distance are not issues. In asynchronous online learning, students can access the online materials anytime, while synchronous online learning allows for real-time interaction between students and instructors. Learners can use the Internet to access up-to-date and relevant learning materials, and can communicate with experts in the field which they are studying. Situated learning, or the application of knowledge and skills in specific contexts, is facilitated, since learners can complete online courses while working on the job or in their own space, and can contextualize the learning. (Ally 2008: 17)

In higher education, online learning is used both to provide distance learning opportunities and to supplement in-person classes. To facilitate remote instruction, teachers use web-based systems which integrate a number of tools for course administration, communication, accessing learning materials, submissions and testing. Such web-based software packages are known in literature as both a Learning Management System (LMS) and a Virtual Learning Environment (VLE). Pinner (2014) argues that both terms refer to two distinct learning paradigms. In his view, while LMSs are limited to passive consumption of online information hosted in the system, VLEs are used to interact with members of the same learning community. One prominent example of such a system is the open-source Moodle platform (i.e. Modular Object-Oriented Dynamic Learning Environment). The importance of social interaction is highlighted by Moodle developers, who specifically mention the social constructivist approach underpinning the development of the software in the About page at moodle.org (2020). Both (passive) LMSs and (interactive) VLEs have become important tools for university students and teachers alike.

3. Online and Blended Learning in Translator Education

In the world of Translation Studies, the first fully online translation courses and degrees emerged at the turn of the 21st century. More and more universities around the globe are offering online translation degrees, e.g. the Universitat Jaume I and the Universitat Autónoma of Barcelona in Spain, the University of Bristol, the University of Birmingham, and The Open University in the UK, the University of Rennes 2 in France, and New York University and the University of Texas Rio Grande Valley in the USA. Jiménez-Crespo (2015) points out two reasons for introducing e-learning at European universities: high demand for translation courses among students and the need to develop translation competence in an environment which resembles the workplace of professional translators. The money factor may also be the reason for switching to the online mode. To illustrate, the establishment of the E-Learning Centre at the Moscow State Linguistic University was motivated by the need to lower the costs of professional translator education, which was regarded as expensive and unnecessary (Gorozhanov et al. 2018). The authors describe the implementation of an online translation course from English into Russian (Moodle combined with video conferences), naming a number of reasons for closing translator education institutions in Russia which, in turn, has led to the creation of a VLE alternative. They are: the use of English as lingua franca, the view that people with linguistic competence at B2 level or the introduction of Machine Translation solutions can replace translators.

In addition to fully online translator education, blended learning approaches have been applied for a number of years. The blended learning mode integrates online and face-to-face instruction in order to meet specific teaching and learning needs. It is crucial to remember, though, that both modes should complement one another, allowing participants to benefit from its flexibility, self-paced learning a wide access to resources and face-to-face interaction. Before the pandemic, online learning platforms were used in translator education for a number of reasons: cost-cutting, large student groups, the need to create collaborative learning environments (stemming from social constructivism), and the need to train students in the use of translation tools and develop their information competence.

Let us now take a look at some examples of blended learning environments in translator education from Europe, Asia, and Australia. Secară et al. (2009) report on two European collaborative projects, eCoLoTrain (2005–2007) and eCoLoMedia (2007–2009), which aimed to support blended learning in translation and localisation. The created materials were used by students for self-study or incorporated into translation and localisation courses by translator educators. Galán-Mañas and Hurtado Albir (2010) describe the implementation of two courses in Spain, technical scientific translation and introduction to translation, delivered in a blended mode. In their case study, two units were completed online in a virtual learning environment, called Virtual Campus. The authors concluded that the blend allowed for greater timetable flexibility and promoted collaborative learning and student autonomy, but also required greater workload on the part of the teacher. They found that both courses were well received by the students, who "[were] better able to argue, justifying their opinions as they [had] more time to reflect on the subject, resulting in richer debates" (Galán-Mañas and Albir 2010: 218).

Another example of adopting a blended learning approach is the case of a non-degree programme, called the Business Interpreting and Translation (BIT) Certificate Program, reported by Lee and Huh (2018). Since 2015, the 120-hour programme has been available in a blended format to cater for the needs of full-time workers. On weekdays, the classes are held online and on Saturdays on-campus classes are arranged. The authors found that self-paced learning, flexibility, and in-depth feedback were considered by the trainees to be the main advantages of the adopted approach. The survey showed that the students were not unanimous regarding the disadvantages of the blended learning mode. Among others, the perceived drawbacks included the inconvenience of asynchronous communication with the teacher and limited interaction with other students. The last example of blended learning in translator education is that of Gerber et al. (2020), who report on a MA programme in Australia, where face-to-face lectures were replaced with pre-recorded online seminars (a video presentation, worksheets and PowerPoint slides). The authors followed a flipped classroom learning sequence: *watch-read-think-do*. So, the content presented online was used as a pre-class activity. They found that the students were satisfied with this blended mode, praising its interactive and user-oriented approach.

The above are just a few examples of the many translation courses and translator education programmes which integrate web-based technologies with face-to-face instruction. In most cases, off-the-shelf LMSs or VLEs, such as Moodle or Google Classroom, are used. It should be noted that attempts have been made to develop e-learning environments to meet the specific needs of translation students and teachers. The Erasmus+ DigiLing e-learning hub and the TransShare platform are good examples of solutions designed specifically for the translator education context. DigiLing is a 3-year project (2016–2019), funded by the Erasmus+ programme, aiming to develop a model curriculum for digital linguistics, train teachers in the use of digital technologies, and design open-access online courses for core modules. It was designed to prepare translators and other language service providers for the job market (Nitzke et al. 2019). The e-learning platform[1] contains a set of interactive online courses, which are available free of charge. Another translation-specific e-learning environment created for translator education purposes is the TransShare platform developed in Jordan following consultations with translation students, educators, translators, and e-learning experts (Al-Batineh et al. 2020). It is a specialised Web-based Collaborative Learning Tool (WCLT), which enables interaction between the different persons involved in the translation process and serves as a repository of shared translation memories and term bases. The main functionalities of the system are divided into five categories: (1) project information and materials as well as a tool for holding virtual meetings; (2) project execution; (3) CAT tool functionalities such as TM, TB, concordance search, machine translation, etc.; (4) web search and corpus search tools; and (5) email. Al-Batineh et al. (2020) found that the students who tested the platform considered it to be very useful and user-friendly.

Having discussed how online and blended learning approaches were employed before translator education institutions were forced into lockdown in March 2020, the final section of this literature review looks at the approaches to deliver translation courses during the COVID-19 pandemic.

4. Problems with Teaching Translation Online during the COVID-19 Pandemic

Since the beginning of the global pandemic, there has been a surge in interest in online teaching and learning. Due to the speed of the transition, it should be noted, however, that the forced shift to the online format cannot be compared to well-planned online learning experiences (Hodges et al. 2020). At the time of writing, the pandemic has lasted for 18 months. So, instead of describing how individual translator educators have approached the change, let us focus on the problems arising from the shift to the online class format.

In their introduction to the special issue of *The Journal of Specialised Translation*, Hubscher-Davidson and Devaux (2021) note that the primary obstacles encountered by translator educators were linked to adequate forms of assessment, keeping learner motivation and engagement, and encouraging interaction and peer cooperation. Bordet (2021) looks at lockdown-related

1 https://learn.digiling.eu/.

issues from the student's perspective. She points at the digital divide among students, i.e. problems with Internet connection and equipment, no access to reference materials on-campus, as well as stress linked to their unfavourable housing conditions and social environment.

Wu and Wei (2021) examine the impact of moving all teaching activities online on translator educators, focusing on their self-efficacy beliefs about online teaching. As regards the problems encountered in online instruction, the participants in their study, 49 translation teachers from Australia and New Zealand, felt they lacked previous online teaching experience and had insufficient technological literacy, including the use of digital tools and the ability to solve technical problems. The authors of the study rightly observe that many teachers would not choose to teach online if this decision was up to them. So, to teach online effectively, translator educators need to re-evaluate their teaching approaches and adapt them to the new situation, which requires, for instance, a higher level of learner autonomy and different communication and interaction patterns (no eye contact or non-verbal cues when the majority of students close their webcams).

This section has described online learning and blended learning environments in education and translator education and has discussed major issues related to teaching online during the pandemic. The next part of this paper will focus on the implementation of an undergraduate Translation Project course, looking at the aspects of the course which were unaffected or even improved when the classes went online as well as the challenges encountered during the online delivery of the course.

5. Teaching and Learning Context

The course, Translation Project 3.2, was taught in Spring 2020. It was last part of a three-semester course, which starts in Year 2 and covers 15 weekly 90-minute meetings per semester (90 contact hours in total, 9 ECTS credits).[2] It is a core course, which is offered to undergraduate translation and interpreting students working with Polish and English. The whole Translation Project course is designed around the EMT framework for translator and translation competence (2009, 2017). It focuses in particular on service provision competence, information

2 For an overview of the Translation Project course objectives, content and task design, see Paradowska (2020). See Paradowska (2021) for a discussion of the students' collaboration in simulated translation bureaus, which focuses on the benefits and challenges connected with the implementation of authentic translation projects for clients sourced from within the university.

mining competence, technological competence, and interpersonal skills. In Semester 1, the students are engaged in individual work, developing information competence, and getting acquainted with CAT tools. In Semester 2, they set up simulated translation bureaus and carry out collaborative projects commissioned by the teacher, who is acting as the client. In Semester 3, the learning process is organised around translation projects. Students are engaged in individual and collaborative tasks, including translation assignments commissioned by an external client. Authentic collaborative projects are considered to be an extremely important part of the course as they enable students to develop translation service provision competence by engaging them in real-life interactions with an external client.

Unlike in the first edition of the course, in Spring 2020, only the first two classes were held in a computer lab at university, with the remaining 13 classes being delivered remotely. At first, the transition seemed to be seamless. With previous experience and technological tools at hand, the author, who taught this course, felt ready to take up the challenge. The next section presents the course components which were unchanged when in-person classes were moved online. It is followed by a discussion of course modifications introduced in response to the shift to a virtual environment.

6. Shift to Online Instruction: What Remained the Same?

This section describes the aspects of the course which were either unaffected or even improved by the abrupt shift to the online teaching mode. These areas include: the use of cloud-based translation and communication tools, course design, assessment criteria, and authentic translation assignments.

6.1. The Tools

The shift to distance learning did not require a change of the tools used for student-teacher communication or computer-assisted translation tools. As was the case in previous years, all course-related links and materials were provided on the Moodle platform and students were encouraged to contact the teacher via email. For student-student communication, Facebook Messenger and Discord were used. The choice of the platform was left entirely at the discretion of the students, who chose the network to be used in their teams. All course-related questionnaires were administered via Google Forms. Both CAT tools used during individual and collaborative translation projects, Memsource and Smartcat, remained the same as they were cloud-based. The Memsource Academic Edition was used as the main CAT tool due to the fact the university is provided with an academic licence free of charge. At the same time, Smartcat was selected for one translation project because this CAT tool is free to use and available online. Due to the fact that the students were familiar with these online tools, the transition from in-person classes to a virtual environment was smooth. The only tool-related change involved the use of the Zoom platform for weekly online live classes.

6.2. Course Design and Assessment Criteria

As far as the course design and assessment criteria are concerned, only minor adjustments were required when the classes were moved online. Before the start of the semester, the author planned five graded assignments, including:

1. Project Management Task
2. Short Story Project
3. In-class New CAT Project
4. Subtitling Project
5. Corpus Analysis Project

Each assignment was worth 20 % of the course grade. Projects 1–4 were carried out as originally planned. This means that the 14 students managed a translation project in a simulated translation bureau, translated a short story, completed a translation assignment using an unfamiliar CAT tool, and translated subtitles using an online subtitle editor. Only one graded task, i.e. the Corpus Analysis Project, which required downloading the AntConc software, was replaced with an online task, i.e. translating a Wikipedia page using its content translation tool. Table 1 shows that only two learning objectives were not achieved due to the coronavirus lockdown.

Table 1: Course learning objectives

During this course, you will:	
- develop service provision competence (working with an external client)	✓
- manage a translation project	✓
- analyse translation problems	✓
- develop a term base	✓
- develop information competence	✓
- translate a short story (working with Polish philology students)	✓
- translate, review and proofread texts	✓
- learn how to build a corpus	✖
- translate subtitles	✓
- attend a mock job interview	✖

It should be noted that while the decision to drop the Corpus Analysis Project was made arbitrarily by the teacher, who anticipated technical issues, it was the students who decided against attending a mock job interview despite the fact that it could be easily arranged online.

6.3. The Project Management Task

As previously stated, authentic translation projects, both individual and collaborative, are considered to be the most important part of the Translation Project course. In the first two semesters, the students were provided with scaffolding, which allowed them to move gradually from teacher-led activities, through guided practice, towards more situated practice and collaborative learning. One such project was the Project Management Task, which involved completing an authentic translation project for a real client. In Spring 2020, this assignment was carried out with minimum teacher intervention. For this edition of the course, the teacher decided to cooperate with a local women's basketball club, AZS AJP Gorzów, which belongs to her university. Even though the club plays in EuroCup games and Poland's first league, their website had not been translated into English. It was agreed that the club's representative will act as the client.

The students worked in three simulated translation bureaus, called KAMP Project (5 members), FADA (4 members), and Translation (5 members). A cloud-based CAT tool, Memsource, was used to translate content to be published on the club's website. The students were familiar with the tool, as they worked in it in Semester 1. Also, the student teams remained the same, as the simulated bureaus had been set up in October 2019, in Semester 2. The Project Management Task had all the features of a real translation assignment, including a client, a brief, deadlines, publication, and incentives. The students were not paid for their work, but the club agreed to include their names on the website. As shown in Figure 1, the project was divided into 5 rounds.

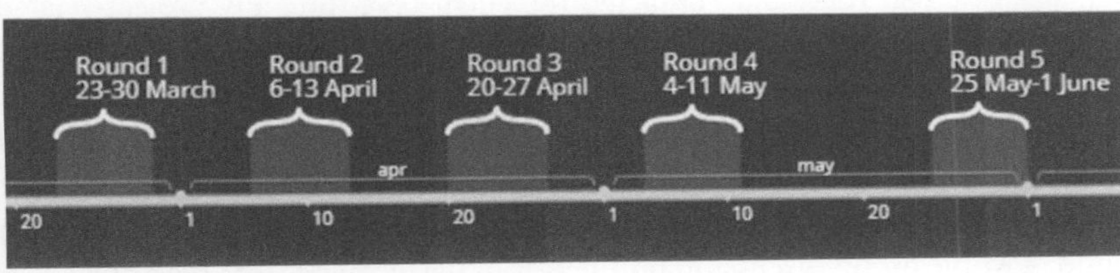

Figure 1: Timeline of the Project Management Task

The group consisted of 14 students, so it was agreed that there would be five project rounds, with three students (two in the fifth round), each representing a different translation bureau, acting as Project Manager. At the start of the course, a set of step-by-step procedures for accomplishing the task was presented (see Table 2 below).

Table 2: The Project Management Task procedures

Monday (Round 1 starts on 23 March)	**Procedures to be followed in Rounds 1–5**
	The client emails a source text to each of the 3 PMs and asks for the price. The email correspondence is between the club and the PM.
	The PM replies including a cost estimate and confirms the due date; she may ask for a deadline extension (1–2 days).
	The client confirms the price and date.
	Upon confirmation, the PM creates a Memsource project and assigns roles. Use the following project name format: date – round number – your company name – PM initials e.g. 2020.03.25 Round 1 FADA FL – Add the same term base (AZS AJP TB) and translation memory (AZS AJP TM) in all projects. – Terminologists should check the terms in the TB before adding new ones. – Please remember to assign me to the Client Review stage.
	Team members perform their tasks.
Agreed date	The PM emails the translation to the client.
	The client confirms the receipt.
	The PM saves the email correspondence with the client as a PDF and uploads the PDF along with a Project Management Report via Moodle.
	The client provides feedback via Google Forms.

At the start of each round, the club's representative emailed translation assignments to three students who were appointed project managers. The other team members were translators, terminologists, and revisers. The team's project manager assigned roles and contacted the client regarding any project-related issues. As soon as the project was completed, the project manager emailed the translation product to the client and uploaded his or her PM report to Moodle. The client filled in a feedback form in Google Forms and uploaded the translated content. To make sure that the translations were market-ready, the teacher was added to the translation workflow at the Client Review stage. After each round, a whole group discussion on the teams' performance was held during an online meeting. The students reported on their problem-solving strategies, and I provided feedback on their email correspondence with the client, deadlines, terminology, and target text quality. The final grade was based on five information sources: (1) PM report and (2) correspondence with the client, (3) Memsource setup/editor, (4) feedback from the client, and (5) the teacher's feedback after each round. The points were allocated as follows:

1. Professionalism (deadlines, email address, signatures, language) – 6 points
2. Memsource setup (project, TM, term base, reference files) – 6 points
3. Target text (file name, quality) – 4 points
4. PM report (detailed/superficial) – 4 points

The total number of points for the Project Management Task was 20 points, i.e. 20 % of the total course grade.

6.4. The Subtitling Project

The next project completed, as planned, despite the lockdown involved translating subtitles. This individual project was inspired by a workshop on audiovisual translation attended by the students in the previous year. As they had no experience with this translation mode or the tool, this project was much supervised than the Project Management Task. As shown in Figure 2, the Subtitling Project lasted seven weeks.

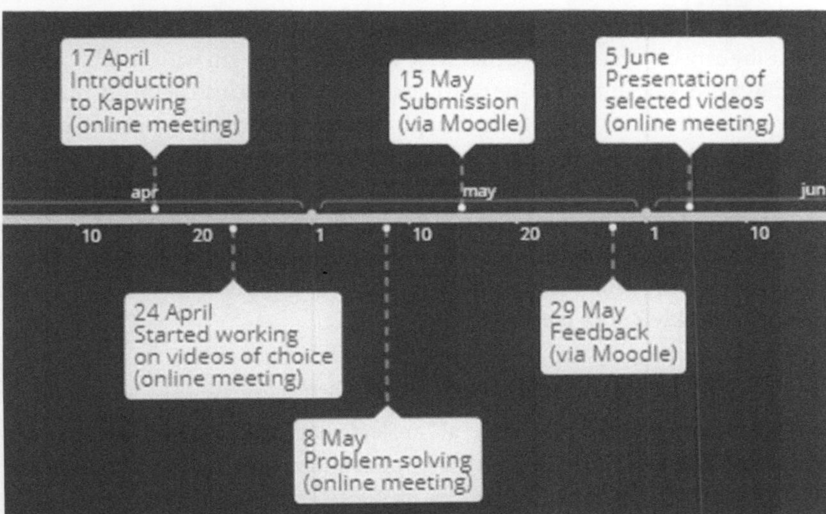

Figure 2: Timeline of the Subtitling Project

Three online meetings were devoted to the presentation of subtitling guidelines, controlled practice in the use of the Kapwing subtitling tool,[3] and addressing any problems encountered by the students when they started working on their own videos. When the projects were graded, the students received feedback, and the teacher asked the students' permission to share their recordings with the rest of the group. Finally, at the end of the semester, five subtitled videos were presented during an online class. The selected projects were either the highest graded or the most challenging ones.

6.5. The New CAT Project

The last project that was not affected by the transition to online instruction was an in-class translation assignment which required students to learn how to use a new CAT tool and deliver their translations in 90 minutes. The task was inspired by a 2015 talk given by Anthony Pym,[4] who argued that translation students must be prepared to deal with new tools and resources and need to be able to learn quickly. The CAT tool selected for the project, i.e. Smartcat,[5] may be accessed in a web browser, so there was no need to download the software.

7. Shift to Online Instruction: What Changed?

So far, this paper has focused on the aspects of the course that were not influenced by the shift from in-person classes to the remote teaching mode. So let us now look at the aspects of the course that were different. To begin with, weekly online meetings were shorter than in-person classes (60 minutes instead of 90 minutes). The workload remained the same though. Before each class, a meeting agenda was posted on Moodle, so that students could prepare to discuss the projects they were currently working on. Next, two out of five projects planned for the semester were modified: one was replaced and the other one was extended. These two changes were not problematic. What was difficult during the online delivery of the course, though, was the level of student engagement and interaction during the weekly Zoom meetings.

7.1 The Short Story Project

The fact that during the pandemic all projects had to be carried out remotely encouraged the author to create more opportunities for online collaboration.

3 https://www.kapwing.com/subtitles.
4 https://www.youtube.com/watch?v=gVJ_Aj60i3Q&ab_channel=AnthonyPym.
5 https://www.smartcat.com/.

The Short Story Project is a good example of a successful project expansion, which included collaboration with the Polish philology department and local secondary schools. At first, the author was planning to ask her students to translate a children's story, "What-a-Mess and the Birthday Present" by Frank Muir, adopting one translation strategy: either foreignisation or domestication. But what was meant as a simple pair work translation assignment focusing on domestication and foreignisation strategies expanded into a larger venture.

Table 3 shows the individual stages of the Short Story Project, which is based on the project described by Maria González Davies (2004) in her book "Multiple Voices in the Translation Classroom." The project was introduced in the second meeting of the semester, which was also the last in-person class. The students received a PDF of the story and could also read the book. In the following week, when the class moved online, the students were put into 7 pairs and read their translation briefs. Then, the students identified and translated culture-bound items such as names of the main characters, food, and other references to British culture. Throughout the project, the teams worked together, outside the class, using their preferred communication tools. During online meetings, the project was discussed briefly, and only upon the students' request.

Table 3. Timeline of the extended Short Story Project

Project stages	
6 March	Introduction (in-person class)
13 March	Pairs/strategies randomly assigned
20 March	Pairs propose equivalents for culture-bound items
27 March	1st draft uploaded + written feedback
10 April	Final version uploaded
Project extension	
20 April	Polish philology students review the translations
8 May	Pairs submit improved translations
20 May	Secondary school students select the best translations
5 June	Written and oral feedback
June	Proofreading, graphic design, printing

The project was then extended so as to involve local educational institutions. When the students completed their translations, the texts were reviewed by Polish philology students from the same university. Then, the teacher approached local secondary schools, and asked the students to analyse the source text and the 7 Polish exoticised/domesticated translations. All the documents (instructions, the source text, anonymised translations) were included in a Google Form, so that secondary school teachers could use them during their online lessons. In addition to selecting the most successful translation products (one exoticised and one domesticated), secondary students provide feedback, which was passed on to the student translators. At the end of the semester, the two winning texts were published in a booklet. So, the project ended with a tangible product. The Short Story Project was followed up in the next academic year, when pupils from local primary schools were asked to read both translations and fill in a questionnaire. This part of the project was also carried out online as the coronavirus lockdown continued in 2021.

7.2. The Wikipedia Project

The Wikipedia Project was introduced as a replacement for the Corpus Analysis Project, which was planned for the end of the semester. The teacher decided against working with the AntConc software in a virtual learning environment because she was expecting technological problems on the part of the students if they would have to download it. Another argument against introducing a corpus analysis task was the inability to monitor the students' performance during the process of learning how to use the tool. Screen sharing seemed to be the only option, and the teacher wanted to avoid lengthy presentations, and teacher-frontedness in the limited time she had during online meetings. So instead, the students learnt how to use a less complicated cloud-based tool, i.e. the Wikipedia content translation tool. Translating a Wikipedia entry was a short individual project, which comprised the milestones presented in Figure 3 below.

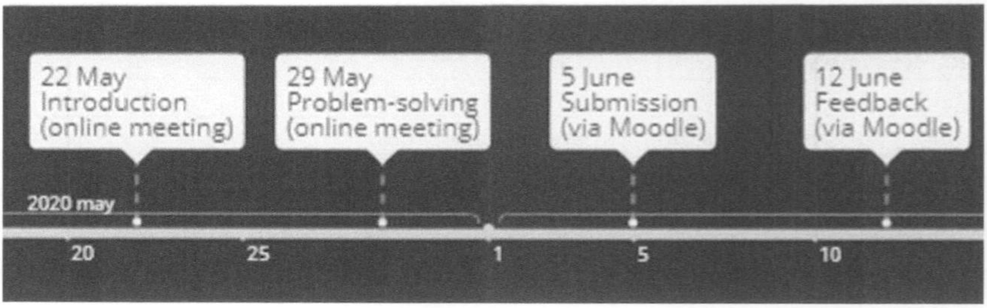

Figure 3: Timeline of the Wikipedia Project

The author had implemented a similar project before and she was aware of the limitations of the tool. This previous experience was used to stimulate discussion on the potential shortcomings of various proprietary tools, which are reported by professional translators. Another reason for going ahead with the Wikipedia Project was that the students could translate a Wikipedia entry of their choice and share their translations on the Internet, which – it was hoped – would boost their motivation.

7.3. Student Interaction and Engagement

The challenges arising from the forced transition to remote instruction included reluctance to interact with the other students and/or the teacher demonstrated by some students. The weekly online classes via Zoom were too teacher-fronted, with too many students choosing to switch off their webcams. This could be due to stress and low mood reported by some students in personal communication and confidentiality issues related to using Zoom voiced by others. Waiting for the students' responses was frustrating and it was much easier for the online participants to hide and engage in other activities which were not related to the class work.

The interaction problem during online classes was not solved until October 2020, when the teacher started using breakout rooms (with the next group of translation students). Typically, students complete a task in groups and the teacher visits each room for a while to provide assistance. This is followed by a summary of results in the common room. It is not an ideal solution, but I must say the student engagement and interaction have improved. Unlike in Spring 2020, both teachers and students are more used to online meetings and have more experience in this form of communication. Unfortunately, one thing has not changed: students are still reluctant to switch on their web cams.

8. Feedback from Students

In spite of the unexpected difficulties, the author was quite satisfied with the implementation of the course. The 9 responses to a post-course questionnaire designed and administered by the teacher in June 2020 via Google Forms as well as personal communication both indicate that her students thought likewise. The survey (included as Appendix 1) consisted of 13 questions in the English language, of which 6 were open-ended and 7 were closed-ended. The first part of the questionnaire (4 items) focused on the course content, measuring the extent to which the students found the projects useful. Q1–Q4 were closed-ended question with ten single-choice answer options. The second part contained 5 questions related to the Project Management Task, of which two were closed-ended (Q5–Q6) and four (Q7–Q10) were open-ended. The third part of the questionnaire (Q11–Q13) aimed at collecting feedback on other aspects of the course, i.e. the use of Moodle and Zoom platforms, and general comments on the course content and organisation.

The results indicate that the Short Story Project and the Subtitling Project were the most enjoyable, with mean ratings of 8.1 (Q1) and 8.3 (Q2) respectively. When asked which topics and activities completed in class the students liked the most (Q12), 5 respondents mentioned the Short Story Project while 6 admitted they enjoyed the Subtitling Project the most. At the same time, collaborating with the external client in simulated translation bureaus was considered to be the most useful in terms of their preparation for the translation market. The students enjoyed working in their teams (Q5: mean rating of 8.6) and their answers to open-ended questions (Q7–Q10) seem to suggest that they developed service provision competence by interacting with the client and improved interpersonal skills. In their responses to Q7 (What do you think of the Project Management task you have completed this semester? To what extent are you going to use the skills developed in class in the future?), the students emphasised that they could experience what "working as a translator really looks like and it teaches us how to act as a real translator" and thought the simulation could be useful in the future "in the least expected moment." The comment below shows that that despite the lockdown the students managed to raise their awareness of the translation profession,

> Practical experience seems to be the best teacher, this task certainly gave me an idea of how it is to work on a translation with other people. I think that everything I've learnt is very useful and I'll be trying to gain even more knowledge. I liked my group and we got on well with each other so that was additionally pleasant.

Q8 asked the participants to provide feedback on the cooperation with the external client. Three students appreciated the opportunity to practise working with a real client ("It was a fun way to show us how in the near future we may have to cooperate with clients"). Two students found the experience stressful ("I wanted my client to think of me as of a professional so I was considering using more proper words"). And three voiced their dissatisfaction with the client's reluctance to interact with the Project Manager ("The client was not responsive at all, after getting the completed work he didn't confirm getting it or even saying thank you.").

In response to Q9 (What did you learn from being a PM in your simulated translation bureau?), 7 out of 9 students mentioned the ability to manage a team. They learnt to "monitor progress and [be] ready to step in if necessary" and "advise people on what they should do" on the one hand, and acknowledged they sometimes had to be "more harsh in order to fit with the deadlines." Similarly, the responses to Q10 (What did you learn from being a terminologist/linguist/reviser in your simulated translation bureau?) indicate that the students learnt to be team members ("[I learnt to] always check twice whether everything is done properly so my teammates would not have to work longer due to my mistakes") who are responsible for the final result ("Working in a team and being responsible not only for my own work, but for the final results as well").

The authentic project was a good way to develop interpersonal skills, which are increasingly important for language service providers. Present-day translators rarely resemble lone individuals "hammering away on a word processor" (Konttinen et al. 2019: 1). More often than not, they collaborate with other people engaged in the translation process. The majority of participants emphasised that being a Project Manager helped them to learn how to communicate effectively, coordinate tasks and supervise their teams. They felt that they were responsible for their teams.

Opinions differed as to the usefulness of the Wikipedia Project (Q3: mean rating of 6.1). Two participants reported they had had technical issues with the content translation tool. Although the New CAT Project was not very well received by the students (Q4: mean rating of 6.2), most of them wrote that were comfortable using CAT tools (Q6: mean score of 8.9). Overall, these results indicate that the students were quite satisfied with the way the course was organised after the sudden shift from in-person to online classes.

9. Conclusion

Based on a case study of the Translation Project 3.2 course, this paper examined the various aspects of the course which were modified or left unchanged in response to the emergency shift to online learning. A reflection on teaching translation during the COVID-19 pandemic leads to a conclusion that prior experience with online technologies as well as adopting a project-based methodology made the unexpected transition easier. Despite the challenges faced while working in a virtual learning environment, the course objectives were met. The students were able to communicate effectively and deal with unexpected problems. They seem to have increased service provision competence and information competence. They also developed their organisational, interpersonal and ICT skills, which are highly desirable in future translators. The improvement in these areas was acknowledged by the students in their responses to the questionnaire, observed by the teacher and reflected in their grades.

The sudden transition to remote instruction can hardly be compared to online courses which are planned well in advance (Hodges et al. 2020). But, as Hubscher-Davidson and Devaux (2021) aptly observe, "[w]hile emergency remote teaching in T&I may not be able to take full advantage of the affordances and possibilities of the online format, it nonetheless presents an opportunity to rethink and enhance our teaching practices." The coronavirus pandemic has created yet another opportunity for learning, both for the students and the teacher.

References

Al-Batineh, M., Muhaisen, B. and Al-Ramadan, R. (2020). 'Towards an e-learning platform for translator training: Getting stakeholders involved.' *The Arab Journal For Arts, 17*(1), 321–344.

Ally, M. (2008). 'Foundations of educational theory for online learning.' In T. Anderson (Ed.), *The theory and practice of online learning* (15–44). AU Press.

Anderson, T. (2008). 'Toward a theory of online learning.' In T. Anderson (Ed.), *The theory and practice of online* learning (45–74). AU Press.

Bordet, G. (2021). 'Teaching online in translation studies: A teacher-researcher's feedback from France.' In N. Radić, A. Atabekova, M. Freddi, & J. Schmied (Eds.), *The world universities' response to COVID-19: remote online language teaching* (235–248). Research-publishing.net. https://research-publishing.net/publication/978-2-490057-92-4.pdf

Bransford, J., Brown, A., & Cocking, R. (Eds.). (2000). *How People Learn: Brain, Mind, Experience, and School: Expanded Edition*. National Academies Press.

Chang, V., Gütl, C., & Ebner, M. (2018). 'Trends and Opportunities in Online Learning, MOOCs, and Cloud-Based Tools.' In Rosalind Latiner Raby and Edward J. Valeau (Eds.), *Handbook of Comparative Studies on Community Colleges and Global* Counterparts (1–19). Springer International. http://link.springer.com/10.1007/978-3-319-53803-7_64-1

EMT Board. (2017). *European Master's in Translation. Competence Framework 2017.* https://ec.europa.eu/info/sites/info/files/emt_competence_fwk_2017_en_web.pdf

EMT Expert Group. (2009). *Competences for professional translators, experts in multilingual and multimedia communication.* https://ec.europa.eu/info/sites/info/files/emt_competences_translators_en.pdf

Galán-Mañas, A., & Hurtado Albir, A. (2010). 'Blended learning in translator training: Methodology and results of an empirical validation.' *The Interpreter and Translator Trainer, 4*(2), 197–231.

Gerber, L., Orlando, M., & Tobias, S. (2020). '"Blended learning" in the training of professional translators.' *Translatologia, 1*, 1–26.

González Davies, M. (2004). *Multiple voices in the translation classroom: activities, tasks, and projects*. John Benjamins.

Gorozhanov, A. I., Kosichenko, E. F., & Guseynova, I. A. (2018). 'Teaching written translation online: Theoretical model, software development, interim results.' *SHS Web of Conferences* 50: 01062.

Hodges, C., Moore, S., Barb, L, Trust, T., & Bond, A. (2020). 'The difference between emergency remote teaching and online learning.' *Educause Review*. https://er.educause.edu/articles/2020/3/the-difference-between-emergency-remote-teaching-and-online-learning

Hubscher-Davidson, S., & Devaux, J. (2021). 'Teaching translation and interpreting in virtual environments.' *Special Issue of The Journal of Specialised Translation, 36b*, 184–192.

Jiménez-Crespo, M. A. (2015). 'The Internet in translation education: Two decades later.' *Translation and Interpreting Studies, 10*(1), 33–57.

Kiraly, D. (2000). *A social constructivist approach to translator education: empowerment from theory to practice*. St. Jerome.

Konttinen, K., Veivo, O., & Salo, P. (2019). 'Translation students' conceptions of translation workflow in a simulated translation company environment.' *The Interpreter and Translator Trainer, 14*(1), 79–94.

Lee, J., & Huh, J. (2018). 'Why not go online?: A case study of blended mode business interpreting and translation certificate program.' *The Interpreter and Translator Trainer, 12*(4), 444–466.

Moodle.org. (2020). *About Moodle*. https://docs.moodle.org/311/en/About_Moodle.

Nitzke, J., Tardel, A., & Hansen-Schirra, S. (2019). 'Training the modern translator – the acquisition of digital competencies through blended learning.' *The Interpreter and Translator Trainer, 13*(3), 292–306.

Paradowska, U. (2020). 'Helping undergraduate students to prepare for the translation market: The case of a translation project course.' In B. Tichoniuk, J. Bobin, & P. Kłos-Czerwińska (Eds.), *Język. Literatura. Komunikacja* (123–138). Wydawnictwo Naukowe Akademii im. Jakuba z Paradyża. http://cwn.ajp.edu.pl/2020/39/

Paradowska, U. (2021). 'Benefits and challenges of an intra-university authentic collaborative translation project.' *Special Issue of New Voices in Translation Studies, 24*, 23–45.

Pinner, R. (2014). *What is the difference between an LMS and a VLE?* http://elearningindustry.com/difference-between-lms-and-vle

Secară, A., Merten, P., & Ramírez, Y. (2009). 'What's in Your Blend?: Creating Blended Resources for Translator Training.' *The Interpreter and Translator Trainer, 3*(2), 275–294.

Singh, V., & Thurman, A. (2019). 'How Many Ways Can We Define Online Learning? A Systematic Literature Review of Definitions of Online Learning (1988–2018).' *American Journal of Distance Education, 33*(4), 289–306.

Wu, D., & Wei, L. (2021). 'Teaching translation and interpreting in virtual environments.' *Special Issue of The Journal of Specialised Translation, 36b,* 301–326.

Xu, D., & Smith Jaggars, S. (2013). 'Adaptability to online learning: Differences across types of students and academic subject areas.' *CCRC Working Paper 54.* https://files.eric.ed.gov/fulltext/ED539911.pdf

Zajda, J. (2021). *Globalisation and Education Reforms: Creating Effective Learning Environments.* Springer International.

Appendix 1

Post-course questionnaire

<u>*Course Content*</u>

1. What do you think of the Short Story Project (What-a-Mess)?

	1	2	3	4	5	6	7	8	9	10	
useless	○	○	○	○	○	○	○	○	○	○	useful

2. What do you think of the Subtitling Project?

	1	2	3	4	5	6	7	8	9	10	
useless	○	○	○	○	○	○	○	○	○	○	useful

3. What do you think of the Wikipedia Project?

	1	2	3	4	5	6	7	8	9	10	
useless	○	○	○	○	○	○	○	○	○	○	useful

4. What do you think of the task which required you to learn a new CAT tool (SmartCat)?

	1	2	3	4	5	6	7	8	9	10	
useless	○	○	○	○	○	○	○	○	○	○	useful

<u>Project Management Task (AZS AJP website translation)</u>

5. Did enjoy working for Kamp Project/FADA/Translatio?

	1	2	3	4	5	6	7	8	9	10	
Never again!	○	○	○	○	○	○	○	○	○	○	It was fantastic!

6. Are you comfortable using CAT tools (Memsource, SmartCat)?

	1	2	3	4	5	6	7	8	9	10	
not at all	○	○	○	○	○	○	○	○	○	○	sure!

7. What do you think of the Project Management task you have completed this semester? To what extent are you going to use the skills developed in class in the future?
8. What do you think of working with an external client? Comment on your cooperation with the AZS AJP Basketball Club.
9. What did you learn from being a PM in your simulated translation bureau?
10. What did you learn from being a terminologist/linguist/reviser in your simulated translation bureau?

<u>General feedback</u>

11. What do you think of using a combination of Zoom and Moodle during remote classes? Do you feel you have developed your skills? What could have been better?
12. Which topics and activities we did in class did you like the most?
13. What was missing in the course? Would you add anything?

Anna Setkowicz-Ryszka

University of Lodz

Teaching Trainees the Importance of Research beyond Word Level: Reflections on How Extra-Linguistic Context Determines Translator's Research

Abstract: Information mining competence (or equivalent skills) is part of translation competence models, including their versions adapted to legal translation. However, translator trainers do not find much advice on how to develop this element of competence. Many legal translation trainees initially rely mainly on bilingual dictionaries, trust unreservedly translators' fora or the Internet, ask for glossaries or model translations. During a contract translation module (EN-PL/PL-EN) the trainer's tasks include introducing the broader extra-linguistic context, i.e. the legal system(s) in which contracts are used, and encouraging trainees to use other information sources: legislation, parallel texts, legal literature, online bilingual concordancers, corpora, etc. For greater efficiency, the various sources should be used to solve actual terminological problems in the classroom, of which this paper provides many examples, and particular information sources should be matched to terminological challenges found in particular types of contracts or in particular standard clauses. Cross-checking, critical evaluation and using multiple sources should be encouraged. Such activities, which develop the trainees' information mining competence, should accompany practical translation tasks. It is impossible to cover all contract types in the syllabus, yet the activities should prepare trainees for tackling future translation challenges (procedural knowledge) by increasing their (1) awareness of what sources are available and which ones to consult when; (2) ability to critically evaluate their usefulness and cross-check information or equivalents they find, (3) ability to take into account the recipient's perspective, thanks to better knowledge of the target language's legal system, all of which should lead to better translation decisions.

Keywords: legal translation, translator training, information mining competence (instrumental sub-competence), information sources, translator's research

1. Introduction

Legal translation is notoriously difficult. It is not my aim to discuss theories of legal translation here, but in a book on translating English judgments in criminal cases Gościński (2019) discusses as many as fourteen theories of legal translation, arriving at a fairly optimistic conclusion that legal translation is not impossible, as demonstrated by the rich body of theoretical literature and the long practice. He also warns that it is a rather taxing task, which requires translators to employ broad subject knowledge, intellectual capacity, analytical skills, linguistic creativity, effort and humility, certain translation loss being inevitable (2019: 141). Scott neatly sums up the difficulties involved under the headings of, firstly, dealing with legal discourse with its linguistic particularities; secondly, negotiating solutions between legal systems and their – often very different – concepts; thirdly, using correctly a given target genre, including sublanguage, and finally, making sure that the target text correctly reflects the purpose of the source one if the client so wishes (2017: 39). Many authors stress the comparative law aspect of legal translation, particularly in the process of choosing appropriate legal terminology (de Groot, 1987a; de Groot, 1987b; Sandrini, 1999; Prieto Ramos, 2011; Doczekalska, 2013; Jopek-Bosiacka, 2013).

When I was first invited to conduct practical legal translation workshops at postgraduate level, I expected probing questions about fine points of legal translation, mainly discussions about (lack of) terminological equivalence. These happened, too, but, regardless of the subject I taught (texts on human rights, accounting and banking documents or contracts), what would invariably come up was syntax or, rather, how to reshuffle the elements of the original sentence to create a natural-sounding sentence in translation. Other similarly basic issues needed to be discussed too, often in response to questions asked by trainees or to problems that appeared in their assignments.

Among my experiences from these practical classes, three stand out from the perspective of identifying the need for information sources to be "taught" along with other translation activities. The first one was a sincere question from a rather irritated student: "But why is it so illogical? Why can't *loan* always be the equivalent of *pożyczka* and *credit* the equivalent of *kredyt*?" Then someone copied a fellow student's translation and changed some terms. All the replacements must have come from a bilingual dictionary, but they were so out of place in the auditor's opinion about financial statements that the person got caught. Finally, I once refused to mark an assignment which read like raw machine translation output, to which the trainee replied with indignation: "But I found it on Linguee." All three memories show clearly that information sources – which enable the translator to see how the terms and phrases are used in context or how notions function in the broader context of a legal system – deserve more attention from the trainer than just listing the sources and encouraging the trainees to use them. And even when multiple sources are consulted, there remains the question of cross-checking and critically evaluating them. Therefore, I now try to show how useful various sources are for solving real problems posed by the texts used in class.

The next section discusses the place of information mining competence in multi-componential models of translation competence developed by EMT network and PACTE group, both subsequently adapted to legal translation. Section 3 briefly presents online information sources that are available to legal translators. The next two sections present specific information needs relating to contracts and suggest ways of meeting these needs without using bilingual dictionaries. More specifically, section 4 describes some terminological problems posed by translation of particular contract types (sale, supply, lease and two Polish contracts) and the matching information sources (legislation, parallel texts, legal websites, translator's fora, etc.). Section 5 discusses three scenarios of availability of information sources when English standard contractual provisions are translated into Polish. Finally, section 6 contains general remarks about teaching digital natives to use online information sources.

2. Information mining competence in translation competence models

2.1. Definitions

Information mining competence is one of six areas of competence identified in the European Master's in Translation (EMT) network model of translation competence. In this model, competence is defined in accordance with the European Qualifications Framework as "proven ability to use knowledge, skills and personal, social and/or methodological abilities, in work or study situations and in professional and personal development" (European Commission, 2008: 11). More specifically, information mining competence includes knowing how to "identify one's information … requirements," "extract and process relevant information," "evaluate the reliability of documentary sources (critical mind)" and "use tools and search engines effectively" (EMT Expert Group, 2009: 6). This model was subsequently developed in QUALETRA project[1] (JUST/2011/JPEN/AG/2975) to identify elements of translation competence pertinent to legal

1 The project was implemented by a number of universities from EMT network, with the participation of European Legal Interpreters and Translators Association (EULITA), Council of Bars and Law Societies of Europe (CCBE) and European Criminal Bar Association (ECBA). The focus was on the right to translation and interpretation in criminal proceedings, guaranteed by Directive 2010/64/EU.

translation, including in particular the following elements of information mining competence: "[i]dentifying specific *legal sources* … and evaluating their reliability," "differentiat[ing] between legal sources with reference to national, international and EU systems and jurisdictions" and "[e]xtracting relevant information (documentary, terminological, phraseological) from *parallel and comparable documents*" [*my emphasis*] (Scarpa & Orlando, 2017: 30). QUALETRA survey of legal translation trainers confirmed the importance of "ability to use information retrieval and text data mining resources," rated as an "essential" skill (Scarpa & Orlando, 2017: 35). Considering that EMT model is one of main "reference standards for translator training" (EMT Competence Framework – 2017: 2), from the next section on I will use the term *information mining competence*.

In another well-known translation competence model developed by PACTE (Process in the Acquisition of Translation Competence and Evaluation) group, the above skills form part of the *instrumental/professional sub-competence*, one of the six sub-competences. In the original 1998 model, this sub-competence concerned "the knowledge and abilities associated with the practice of professional translation," including "knowledge and use of all kinds of documentation sources" (PACTE Group, 2003: 48). When the model was subsequently refined, it became simply *instrumental sub-competence*, defined as "[p]redominantly procedural knowledge related to the use of documentation sources and information and communication technologies applied to translation: dictionaries of all kinds, encyclopaedias, grammars, style books, parallel texts, electronic corpora, searchers, etc." (PACTE Group, 2003: 59). Importantly, as group members observe, procedural knowledge, or knowing how, is difficult to talk about, because it comprises strategies and processes that are acquired through practice and largely automatised (PACTE Group, 2003: 45). For me, this aptly explains the cause of difficulty for the trainer, who has to describe their automatised processes in words and demonstrate them to trainees, including elements they no longer need to repeat. The PACTE model was adapted to the legal translation reality by Prieto Ramos (2011), who defines instrumental competence as "knowledge of specialized sources, information and terminology management, use of parallel documents, application of computer tools to translation," at the same time stressing that comparative law belongs to the thematic sub-competence (12–13).

From an employer-oriented perspective and in the context of increasing use of translation memories (TM) and machine translation (MT) in translation work, Pym (2013) suggests adding new skills to the models based on the "negative competence," revealed by Lafeber's (2012) list of shortcomings noticed by revisers of translations of new recruits in international institutions. Pym (2013) challenges the very existence of information mining as a separate set of skills, much of the information being already provided by the translation tools, but stresses that knowing what sources to trust is as important for selecting TM fuzzy matches or MT suggestions as for evaluating parallel texts (490–491). One of these skills to add is directly related to information sources: "[a]bility to reduce learning curves (i.e. learn fast) by locating and processing online resources" under the "learning to learn" heading (494). On Lafeber's list of skills frequently lacking in new recruits, four seem relevant in the context of use of information sources (all in the top 20 skills in her questionnaire): judging the reliability of information sources occupies 11th place, tracking down sources to check facts and to understand the topic are in 17th and 18th place, respectively, followed by mining reference material for phrasing in 19th place (2012: 118). In terms of impact ratings, these skills are around the middle of the list, with tracking down sources to check facts and mining reference material for phrasing in 16th and 17th places, while judging the reliability of information sources and tracking down sources to understand the topic in 23rd and 24th places (2012: 114–115).

Finally, in a relatively recent re-run of OPTIMALE survey concerning European universities' Master's programmes in translation, data mining was among the top 3 compulsory items, after translation memories and term bases, the percentage of programmes where it is compulsory having gone up from 62 % in 2012, when the first survey was run, to 78 % in 2017 (Rothwell & Svoboda, 2019: 36). It remains to be seen what the results of EFFORT[2] project will be in terms of the proposed descriptors of specialist (including legal) translator competence and common educational framework. The part focusing on descriptors of the specialised translator profile will be addressed to trainers of specialised translation, specialised translators and professional translation associations and employers, therefore it will be of interest from the perspective of the subject of this paper.

2.2. Acquisition of information mining competence during translator training

Though competence models do mention various information mining skills, I have not found much about how to develop them in trainees, save for González Davies (2004) mentioning the aim of "practicing resourcing skills" in a number

2 Towards a European framework of reference for translation. The project term is 2020–2023. So far only an overview is available: https://portalrecerca.uab.cat/en/projects/towards-a-european-framework-of-reference-for-translation.

of activities, but without any specific steps. Despite the generally high level of computer literacy among translator trainees nowadays, the range of sources would-be legal translators consult requires the trainer's attention. It is still often the case that at the start of a specialised programme in legal translation trainees rely mainly on bilingual dictionaries (Paradowska, 2021: 123), trust the Internet unreservedly or wish to see one-to-one equivalence, as confirmed by the three memories mentioned in section 1. I have had repeated requests for glossaries or model translations. On the other hand, it has been discussed in literature that one of the markers of progression from a novice translator to an expert is greater problem awareness, along with more procedures or strategies for solving them (Shreve, 2006: 35). The comparative aspect of legal translation requires comparing multiple sources to establish the terms' definitions, places in the legal systems or patterns of use. Due to the differences between common and civil law systems, especially different degrees of terminological equivalence (Doczekalska, 2013; Scott, 2017), which is never perfect in case of system-bound terms (Jopek-Bosiacka, 2013: 122), a trainer frequently has to show that legal translation presents more problems than trainees might have anticipated.

My experience led me to believe that the tasks of a trainer teaching contract translation include familiarising trainees with broader extra-linguistic context, i.e. some elements of the legal system(s), in which contracts are used, countering some trainees' excessive reliance on dictionaries and offering other information sources, be it to solve translation problems or simply check the equivalents provided in dictionaries. Some sources help understand the source text, others – produce a translation that meets recipients' expectations. Research has shown that freelance translators may spend as much as 30 % of their working time on research (Gough, 2018: 10), so part of a legal translator's skillset is knowing what sources are available and how to narrow down the search for solutions to particular problems, which I will try to illustrate in sections 4 and 5. Before that, the next section briefly presents individual types of sources.

3. Information sources used in legal translation

Below is a non-exhaustive list of information sources that a legal translator might find useful in their work. It is more detailed than the one suggested in QUALETRA, but it excludes experts[3] (all sources are available online, most of them for free).

---

3 There usually are some trainees with a legal background, who can act as subject-matter experts.

- **Bilingual and monolingual legal dictionaries** are an improvement compared to general bilingual dictionaries as they focus on the legal meaning of words. A number of Polish-English/English-Polish legal dictionaries can be found on ling.pl website, which saves time as a single search term can yield results from many dictionaries aggregated by the website. As for monolingual English dictionaries, it is worthwhile to mention *Black's Law Dictionary*, according to the publisher, Thomson Reuters, "the most widely cited law book in the world," however, unavailable online.[4] Still, there are other legal dictionaries that are available online and free to use, such as FindLaw Legal Dictionary[5] or Duhaime's Law Dictionary.[6] Term bases, such as IATE, can be mentioned here, because for the language pair of interest here they can be used much like bilingual dictionaries.
- **Legislation.** Many types of contracts are regulated in the Polish Civil Code, though this is not the only Polish statute that a translator can consult: the Banking Law, the Copyright Law or the Industrial Property Law will be useful in translating other contract types. As for the Polish Civil Code, there exist multiple English translations (Gwiazdowski, 1992; Kierzkowska & Miler, 2000; The Civil Code. Kodeks cywilny, 2019). It is important to point out that civil codes in English are rare, with except for the Louisiana Civil Code[7] or the Civil Code of Quebec,[8] so a translator should not waste time searching for such statutes, though less comprehensive ones, such as the Third Parties Rights Act in the UK, do exist. EU legislation is a different case with all directives and regulations available in English and Polish on EUR-Lex website.[9]
- **Parallel texts.** One can easily find model contracts for download, contract templates that can be filled online or samples of contractual provisions. It would be difficult to list all websites that provide models or templates. However, trainees should be warned that not all contract types are equally popular (it is easier to find contracts that are likely to be executed between individuals or between small businesses) and that certain contract types cannot be found in one language or the other because they are not used in that legal culture (see section 4.5). As for samples of contractual provisions,

4 Only the 4th edition, from 1968, is available in full: https://www.latestlaws.com/wp-content/uploads/2015/04/Blacks-Law-Dictionery.pdf.

5 https://dictionary.findlaw.com/.

6 https://www.duhaime.org/.

7 https://lcco.law.lsu.edu/?uid=1&ver=en#1.

8 http://legisquebec.gouv.qc.ca/en/document/cs/ccq-1991.

9 https://eur-lex.europa.eu/homepage.html?locale=en.

websites such as lawinsider.com, upcounsel.com or contractscounsel.com can be mentioned; there is no shortage of samples of contractual provisions, with or without explanations or contract drafting tips.

- **Legal websites.** Websites with legal advice, including contract drafting, and websites for expats can be mentioned here. As for the first category, it has already been mentioned briefly in the context of sample contract provisions or legal dictionaries, because these websites often serve as reference websites for law students and lawyers. As for the second category, these websites provide insights on what foreigners who, for instance, buy property struggle within the local law applicable such transactions (naturally, advice on other subjects can also be found). Even if translators do not find solutions to terminology problems on these websites, they enable them to "walk a mile in the client's shoes" and prepare a more recipient-oriented translation. An example is provided in section 4.3.
- **Online bilingual concordancers** (Linguee, Glosbe, Reverso Context) may be defined as "non-automatic bilingual online tools which retrieve pre-existing and manual sentence pairs from the Web used as a corpus" (Genette, 2016: 22). They enable users to quickly collect a number of existing translations of a particular word or phrase as if from a parallel corpus or translation memory. Linguee and Glosbe also provide information about the website the given example comes from. These websites refer to themselves as dictionaries. EU legislation tends to be overrepresented in online bilingual concordaners due to its availability in multiple languages.
- **Translators' fora or Facebook groups**. These sites can be treasure troves, but one can also find rather rubbish advice there. But they should certainly be on a translator's list of sources, because the advice from other practitioners cannot be underestimated. The arguments for or against a certain equivalent can be quite elaborate. I particularly recommend ProZ.com as the starting point and when several suggestions can be found there, cross-checking can be practised, as discussed in subsection 4.5.
- **Corpora or Web-as-corpus approach**. Corpora seem to be among sources translators do not consult very often (at least this was the case at a course for practising translator I delivered in 2019). Using corpora may be more time-consuming and there are not many legal corpora in general,[10] the situation

10 There are corpora of judgments, such as the monolingual BLaRC – British Law Reports Corpus , the trilingual COSPE Corpus de Sentencias Penales or the multilingual corpus of EU case law EUCLCORP

being even worse for Polish.[11] Moreover, contracts are unlikely to be included in corpora for reasons of confidentiality and data protection. Still, looking at many instances of a key word in context can help make a translation decision. In the context of contracts, Web-as corpus (Kilgariff & Grefenstette, 2003) approach can certainly be used, with operators such as quotation marks, asterisk, plus/minus signs, domain restriction, etc. (Paradowska, 2021: 163).

- **Latin expressions** which appear in dictionary definitions or legal commentaries. Reliance on Latin may be seen as the last resort, but as the example of *lease* in subsection 4.4 shows, sometimes a third language can help arrive at a translation solution. From my own experience, it is not only Latin – the once *lingua franca* of Europe and the language of Roman law – that proves helpful for tackling terminological problems, but also certain large languages used in other civil law countries, such as German.

4. Examples of contracts and available information sources

As mentioned earlier, I am not aware of any specific guidelines for translator trainers to help with the introduction of information sources, so the following part is a result of my trial-and-error efforts. The aims of many activities suggested by Gonzáles Davies (2004) include "practicing/developing resourcing skills" or "using parallel texts." But however tempting it might be to let trainees discover themselves which information sources help them solve particular problems, this might be also too time consuming to squeeze in a syllabus which is already quite full. I believe it is more appealing when information sources are shown to help in solving real terminological problems and when they are matched to terminological challenges posed by individual types of contracts or individual standard clauses from common law contracts. Such activities, which are aimed at developing the trainees' information mining competence, can accompany practical translation tasks. I introduce these sources in a piecemeal fashion and briefly demonstrate the practical usefulness of e.g. parallel or legislative texts in the search for specific terms or expressions, as well as in evaluating the equivalents found in dictionaries or suggested by fellow translators on the Internet. In the following subsections I describe my approach, which crystallised in the academic year 2020–2021.

11 The only large corpus of Polish, NKJP, contains seven Polish codes, including the Civil Code and the Labour Code (http://www.nkjp.pl/settings/Ksiazki_pl.html). I do not know any generally accessible legal corpora in Polish.

4.1. Contract of sale. Legislation

Contracts of sale are a good choice as the first translation task: they are fairly easy to understand and very frequent. It is also likely that trainees have some personal experience of entering into contracts of sale. The whole range of sources could be presented in this context but in order to avoid information overload and enable trainees to focus on the translation task, I prefer to introduce statutory law at this stage. More specifically, when one translates a contract of sale from English into Polish, it is possible to find certain terms and expressions in the relevant part of the Polish Civil Code (Articles 535–555). This is an opportunity to introduce trainees without legal background to statutory law, mention the distinction between nominate and innominate contracts in Polish law[12] and the different roles of contracts in common and civil law systems.[13]

Comparing the operative part of the translated contract with the relevant provisions of the Polish Civil Code we can find a correct term for one of the contract parties, which is commonly mistaken in Polish: the Code equivalent of *vendor/seller* is *sprzedawca*, although it is often rendered as *sprzedający* (e.g. in model contracts available on the Internet), probably due to its similarity to *kupujący* – the equivalent of *purchaser/buyer*. A number of other terms and expressions from the contract I use in class that can be found in the very first Civil Code articles that regulate contracts of sale: *conveyance of title/transfer of title* (*przeniesienie własności*), *passing of risk* (*przejście niebezpieczeństwa utraty/uszkodzenia*), *delivery* (*wydanie*), *to take/accept possession* (*odebrać [rzecz]*), *upon [delivery]* (*z chwilą*).

When the translation is done in the reverse direction (which the trainees will invariably have to do as legal translators), the available sources include contract templates, legal drafting websites or websites with legal advice for the general public (as sources of encyclopaedic knowledge), as well as civil codes in English, such as the Louisiana Civil Code or the Civil Code of Quebec.

---

12 Nominate contracts are those that are regulated in statutory law, such as the contract of sale, supply, loan, employment, while innominate contracts are those that are not, like the contract of franchise or forfaiting. The table of contents of the Polish Civil Code lists the types of contracts regulated in it. The distinction is used in Art. 1914 of the Louisiana Civil Code.

13 The main difference is that under common law a contract should regulate all aspects of the parties' legal relationship, while under civil law certain missing provisions can be replaced with the "default" legal solutions from the Civil Code. This does not apply if any essential provisions are missing but explains why the final provisions or boilerplate section is often much shorter in Polish contracts (Berezowski, 2012: 263–264).

4.2. Contract of supply. Parallel texts

When translating the operative part of a contract of supply into Polish, one can rely on parallel texts and the relevant title of the Civil Code, which contains only eight articles and provisions on sale apply *mutatis mutandis* in matters not regulated in this title. Both these sources can help trainees identify the names of parties: *dostawca – supplier* and *odbiorca* – literally *recipient*. The latter is an interesting case, because an analysis of English parallel texts shows that rather than *recipient*, this party to the contract is referred to as *client*, *customer*, by the proper name or simply *you*. This last solution appears the model contract I use in class, which gives an opportunity to mention plain legal language (Zych, 2018).

As a fairly more recent phenomenon, plain Polish is not yet as advanced as plain English and has only begun to affect the language of Polish contracts. However, in the last decade, plain Polish has been embraced by more and more local and central authorities, including the Social Insurance Institution, as well as various companies, including insurers and banks (Piekot, Zarzeczny, & Moroń, 2018). It is precisely in banks that the first plain Polish contracts have appeared,[14] so it is already possible to show trainees a contract (another parallel text, though not a contract of supply) where the parties are referred to by pronouns *my* (*us*) and *ty* (*you*). Considering the scarcity of contracts written in plain Polish I do not yet recommend trainees to start using these pronouns in their translations of plain English contracts, though the use of pronouns may soon become more widespread in contracts with consumers in Polish. The current standard is to use the names of parties from the Civil Code (or other statutes), so in this case *you* is replaced with *odbiorca*.

Another terminological problem that can be solved by analysing the Polish parallel text is the relatively difficult distinction between the terms *supply* (*dostawa*) and *delivery* (*dostarczenie*). When translating into Polish it is easy to render both *supply* and *delivery* as *dostawa* – they are confused in everyday language, but both the Polish parallel text and Article 605 of the Civil Code mention *wytworzenie* (*manufacturing*) and *dostarczenie* (*delivering*) goods among the supplier's obligations, making it clear that these two terms should be differentiated in Polish. Disappointingly, in one of the English translations of the

---

14 The first examples of bank account agreements written in plain Polish can be found on banks' websites: https://static.credit-agricole.pl/asset/u/m/o/umowa-konta-wzorzec_20390.pdf or https://www.mbank.pl/pdf/przydatne-dokumenty/rachunki-indywidualne/wzor-umowy-o-prowadzenie-bankowych-rachunkow-oszczednosciowo-rozliczeniowych.pdf (Accessed: 14 December 2021).

Polish Civil Code (Kierzkowska & Miler, 2000) this distinction is lost, and the contract is referred to as one of delivery.

4.3. Contract of sale of property. Websites for expats

Contracts of sale of property are a special type of contracts of sale. They are important for Polish sworn translators[15] in that they can expect to be requested to do sight translations of such contracts when foreigners purchase or sell real estate in Poland. This service is usually provided at a notary's office, with both parties and their agents present, the translator does not always get the draft in advance. These contracts are usually lengthy, with exceptionally long sentences even for a Polish contract, and contain plenty of terms connected with real estate.

They also provide a good opportunity to consider the recipient's perspective: not only does the foreigner-purchaser listen to the translation instead of reading it, in which case the translator should consider simplifying the syntax or using more repetitions, but they may also be under considerable stress due to the usually high sums involved and the fact that the transaction is concluded under unfamiliar law. The translator's choice of terminology might to some extent depend on the foreigner's country of origin if such information is provided. It is also helpful to read some advice on websites for expats, where problematic terms are explained by persons who have been through the process. This can help a translator make the contract easier to understand for the foreigner.

The following passage from a website called "Just Landed"[16] deals with two easily confused Polish terms for *advance payment* or *deposit*. Since in a single property purchase transaction both can be paid and different rules apply to either of them, it is important not only to distinguish between them by using different terms, but also to make the distinction meaningful to the foreigner listening to the sight translation:

> There is a very important thing you should know. There are two types of advance payments. A **deposit "Zaliczka"** makes it possible that each party can easily withdraw from the preliminary agreement as it is fully refundable. On the other hand **"Zadatek"** makes you more bound to the agreement as if you wished to cancel it you lose paid money. If seller wish to withdraw from the preliminary agreement he should pay you

---

15 The whole programme is designed to provide trainees with knowledge and skills they need to pass the state exam for sworn translators (also referred to as certified translators or court interpreters).

16 https://polassets.com/en/how-to-buy-an-apartment-in-poland/.

double the amount of "Zadatek" you have paid. Zadatek is in the common use in such case in Poland. [*original spelling and punctuation*]

Finally, it is worthwhile to make the trainees aware of the importance of having at least a short conversation with the foreigner to probe what terms they are already using in conversations with their real estate agent or partner. It is likely that the process of searching for the house or apartment they have developed a mini glossary, which the translator might follow in the sight translation or at least explain the differences in the terminology that they will use.

4.4. Lease. The Louisiana Civil Code, legal websites, translations of Polish statutes and Latin expressions

A lease is a type of contract which enables (or indeed forces) the trainer to show a plethora of new information sources. Hopefully, by this time the trainees have become familiar with a few types of such sources. In this context, it is the contract name that poses a problem, since three Polish equivalents of *lease* are possible, depending on the terms of the contract: *umowa najmu, umowa dzierżawy, umowa leasingu*. All three are regulated in the Polish Civil Code[17] and in all three the parties' names are different: the landlord/lessor can be rendered as *wynajmujący*, *wydzierżawiający* or *finansujący*, respectively, while the tenant/lessee as *najemca*, *dzierżawca* or *korzystający*, respectively. Once the hurdle of the title is overcome, the remainder of the contract is often fairly easy to translate. However, a certain amount of legal knowledge is required of the translator to decide which Polish title to use.

According to the Polish Civil Code, the main difference between the first two types of contracts is that in the case of *najem* the lessee can only use the leased thing (including premises), while in the case of *dzierżawa* the lessee can also collect *pożytki* (translated into English as *fruits/benefits*, see the discussion below in this subsection). Hence, a residential lease will most likely be *umowa najmu*, while a land lease or lease of intellectual property rights are likely to correspond to *umowa dzierżawy*. On the other hand, *umowa leasingu* must be made between a professional lessor and after its term the lessee has the option to buy the leased vehicle or machine, which makes it slightly easier to decide whether a lease corresponds to this kind of Polish contract. However, in practice it may be difficult for a translator to distinguish between these three contract types with

17 The relevant provisions are: for *umowa najmu* – Art. 659–692; for *umowa dzierżawy* – Art. 693–709 and for *umowa leasingu* – Art. 709^1–709^{19}.

confidence, therefore it is important to confirm the selected title by referring to Polish legal information websites where the differences between these contracts are discussed.[18]

The upside of this situation is that in most cases when translating *najem*, *dzierżawa* or *leasing* into English, a translator can dispense with legal research and translate all three as *lease*, except for cases when it is necessary to come up with two English equivalents for *najem* and *dzierżawa* if a comparison is made between them. They are notoriously difficult to distinguish even though other terms apart from *lease* exist in English: *rental* and *tenancy*. Still, the definitions found on various English legal information websites confirm that these terms are in fact synonyms, while the definitions are rather circular: "[r]eal estate *leases* are also commonly known as *rental agreements*"[19] and "[a] written *tenancy* is known as a *lease*"[20] [*my emphasis*]. According to another definition rental agreements, unlike leases, are usually made on a month-to-month basis but can be even shorter.[21] Even the Louisiana Civil Code only mentions *lease,* without making any such distinction, whereas the Civil Code of Quebec has only distinguished *leasing* and *lease*. In two of the published English translations of the Polish Civil Code, *lease* is used as the equivalent of *najem*, while *tenancy* as the equivalent of *dzierżawa*, and in one the reverse is the case. Other documents found on the Internet tend to confirm that pairs of equivalents *lease-najem* and *tenancy-dzierżawa* are more frequent, so it might be a good idea to follow suit. It is, however, worthwhile to show that a translator can and indeed should check such information, bearing in mind the fact that definitions of *lease* and *tenancy* might suggest little or no difference between the two types.

Cross-checking can include reading Polish legal commentaries on the difference between *najem* and *dzierżawa*, which consists in the fact that in the latter case the lessee is not only entitled to use the property, but also to derive *pożytki,* defined in Article 53 of the Polish Civil Code. This term is explained by some commentators (Szewc, Zioło, & Grzesiczak, 2011: 97) with the help of

---

18 In this context it is also possible to show how to formulate complex Google queries using search operators (Paradowska 2021: 163) if this has not been done before.

19 https://www.diffen.com/difference/Lease_vs_Rent.

20 https://www.askaboutmoney.com/threads/tenant-moved-in-boyfriend-without-asking-landlord.149314/.

21 https://www.apartments.com/rental-manager/resources/article/lease-vs-rental-agreement-which-to-choose.

Latin expressions *fructus naturales* and *fructus civiles*. Luckily, both these Latin expressions feature in Black's Law Dictionary,[22] so a number of terms can be selected to explain *pożytki* (fruits, produce, income, depending on context) and thus the difference between the two contracts. Finally, in the context of this distinction, which is not completely clear to the target text recipient, who knows *lease*, *rental* and *tenancy* to be (quasi-)synonymous, it is also worthwhile to mention the technique of providing the original terms in square brackets. Lease and its three Polish counterparts are a reminder, despite diligent and thorough research, there may not be a good equivalent because of the differences between legal systems.

4.5. *Umowa zlecenia* and *umowa o dzieło*. Translators' fora, dictionaries and more cross-checking

The last two types of contracts are typical system-bound terms: both are regulated in the Polish Civil Code and have no corresponding contracts in the common law area. In this context it might be important to know what other translators working in the Polish-English pair use as equivalents of these two contract names. One of the popular fora where translators have asked other translators for help with translation problems since 1999 is ProZ.com with its KudoZ™ network.[23]

On ProZ.com forum one can find a number of equivalents suggested by forum users:

- contract of mandate, order contract, commission contract, contract for services, fee-for-task agreement, contract for freelance services, freelance assignment, mandatory contract (*umowa zlecenia*);
- contract of/for specific work, work made for hire, contract for performing a specified task or work, project contract, service contract, work performance contract, specific task contract (*umowa o dzieło*).

22 The definitions are as follows: *fructus naturales* [Latin "natural fruits"] The natural produce of land or plants and the offspring of animals. Fructus naturales are considered part of the real property; and *fructus civiles* [Latin "civil fruits"] Roman & civil law. Income (such as rent or interest) that one receives from another for the use or enjoyment of a thing, esp. real property or loaned money.

23 https://www.proz.com/about.

Some suggested terms are backed by links to sources, quotes, or explanations, some not (or the translator simply says they think so, using hedging devices like IMHO). Some forum users use their real names, which permits their identification as e.g. authors of dictionaries or experienced translators, but the majority are only known by their nicknames. The suggested equivalents show that advice found on the forum can be rather conflicting. When one only has other translators' word and analyses to rely on, it is time to apply critical thinking and use the cross-checking techniques, such as the ones introduced in the case of *lease* (subsection 4.3), or consult expats doing business in Poland, like in the context of property transactions (subsection 4.4). This is also a reminder that translators should always check the accuracy of information they find, because in the end it is them who are responsible for the final product, i.e. the translation.

5. Standard contractual provisions: three scenarios of availability of sources

5.1. 'Boilerplate' clauses in common law contracts

Once all the above information sources have been introduced in the context of operative provisions of various types of contracts, it is possible to group the standard provisions of common law contracts, the so-called boilerplate section, according to how familiar or exotic they can sound to a Polish lawyer. I believe it is important to analyse the boilerplate provisions because they will appear in every common law contract, and some are even likely to be found in civil law contracts. Research reveals a growing trend of drafting common-law-style standard provisions in civil law contracts, which also produces "undesired legal effects" (Cordero-Moss, 2011: 344) resulting from interaction with the law governing the contract. "[F]undamental principles of the governing law, such as good faith in the performance of the contract and the prohibition of abuse of a right, may still correct and limit the contractual regulation" (Cordero-Moss, 2011: 354). In particular, under Polish law, imitating some boilerplate provisions can be counterproductive, i.e. the opposite of the desired outcome is achieved (Szewczyk, 2014). If a certain aspect of a contractual relationship is not regulated in the contract governed by Polish law, this means that the relevant provisions of statutory law regulate this aspect and the parties do not wish to exercise their freedom of contract to change it. From my professional experience, the most frequent Polish final provision is precisely the one stating that in matter not regulated in the contract, the Civil Code (or another statute) applies *mutatis mutandis*.

5.2. Boilerplate clauses with equivalents in Polish contracts

There is a fairly large group of standard contractual provisions that have some sort of counterpart provisions in Polish contracts, which means that parallel texts may be used to look for terminology or phraseology. This group includes clauses that concern: amendments, jurisdiction, governing law, arbitration, indemnity, survival, notices confidentiality, force majeure or term and termination (the list is not exhaustive). Of course, there still exist some differences between the terminology used in common law contracts and Polish ones, but the purpose of these clauses is fairly similar in both legal cultures and the parallel texts can be very useful for a translator.

Two noteworthy cases can be singled out here. Firstly, somewhat surprisingly, Polish legislation does not contain a list of events which are treated as events of force majeure. Article 495 of the Civil Code only mentions impossibility to perform the contract due to circumstances beyond the party's control. The consequence is that the equivalent Polish clauses enumerate such events in a way which resembles the common law approach. The second interesting case might be placed on the other end of the spectrum of similarity between contractual provisions in both legal cultures: the translator will look in vain in a Polish contract for insolvency-related terms, which are frequently found in the clause on term and termination. The reason is that Polish law, namely Article 83 of the Bankruptcy Law, provides for invalidity of contractual provisions on contract termination due to declaration of bankruptcy or filing a bankruptcy petition (Szewczyk, 2014).

5.3. Boilerplate clauses corresponding to provisions of Polish statutory law

The second group of standard contractual provisions do not usually appear in Polish contracts, because they are simply not needed. Either a similar provision exists in statutory law, which is the case with e.g. severability clause, which more or less repeats Article 58(3) of the Civil Code (Szewczyk, 2014), confidentiality clause in contracts with certain professionals, headings clause, or statutory provisions can help in their translation, as is the with liquidated damages (regulated in Articles 483–485 of the Civil Code), attorney's fees (which it is for the court to award) and assignment clauses. Unless a translator has a legal background, they may be unaware of the similarities between common law contractual provisions and individual articles in the Polish Civil Code or other statutes, so I believe trainees need to be provided with the relevant statutory provisions to be able to translate these contractual provisions correctly.

5.4. "Exotic" boilerplate clauses

The last group of boilerplate clauses are ones that may seem completely exotic to a Polish lawyer who has not studied English or US law or who is not familiar with common law contracts. This group includes: waiver, entire agreement, representations and warranties, relationship (no employment, no agency etc.) clauses. As stated in subsection 5.2, the part of the term and termination clause that makes bankruptcy one of the grounds for termination of the contract cannot be found in any Polish contracts because it is illegal under Polish law. Again, as in the case of contracts without equivalent contract types in the target language legal culture (discussed in section 4.5), translation research is done in legal literature or on websites, including by comparing definitions in monolingual dictionaries.

6. Conclusions

It is impossible to cover all contract types in the syllabus, yet the classroom activities should prepare trainees for tackling future translation challenges by helping them acquire procedural knowledge. The activities described in the preceding sections are aimed to increase trainees': (1) awareness of what sources are available and which ones to consult when faced with certain problems; (2) ability to critically evaluate the usefulness of such sources and cross-check information or equivalents they find; (3) ability to take into account the recipient's perspective, thanks to better knowledge of the target language's legal system, all of which should lead to better translation decisions. I hope that this approach can be adapted by other trainers of contract translation between English and any of the languages used in civil law countries.

Importantly, as a legal translator trainer, one cannot assume that trainees know how to do research just because they grew up with computers and the Internet around. They may be used to asking Google full questions ("What is the Polish equivalent of X?") rather than formulating queries using operators, and go for speed of the search rather than depth (e.g. by stopping at a Wikipedia entry and not going any further). It is also important to realise that when trainees are used to having the world at their fingertips, they do not expect to find evidence of partial or non-equivalence, to have to compare definitions, let alone use Latin – all in order to choose the right (or the least wrong) term in the target language or to find out there is no right term.

All that means, in my view, that during practical workshops trainers cannot just request trainees to do research or tell them where they might look for solutions to translation problems. We need to display the options and show

how various sources and methods help us solve translation problems (and detect them first!). Also, we should emphasise that a combination of sources is the preferred option. Finally, in order to practice critical thinking, I keep reminding my class I do not know everything and have to check the sources before answering their questions. And when I check the sources, the computer I use in class is always in projector mode (or in remote mode I am showing all screen activity), so I can show them how I make sure that what I said is correct, or rather, likely to be correct. Of course, this does not guarantee they will follow suit (and certainly not immediately), but the more exposure they get to this kind of translator research, the more likely they are to do it in the future.

References

Berezowski, L. (2012). *Jak czytać i rozumieć angielskie umowy?* (4 ed.). Warsaw: C. H. Beck.

Cordero-Moss, G. (2011). *Boilerplate Clauses, International Commercial Contracts and the Applicable Law.* Cambridge University Press.

de Groot, G.-R. (1987a). 'Problems of legal translation from the point of view of a comparative lawyer: Seven theses for the XIth World Conference of Federation Internationale des Traducteurs.' *Van taal tot taal, 31*(4), 189.

de Groot, G.-R. (1987b). 'The point of view of a comparative lawyer.' *Les Cahiers de droit, 28*(4), 793–812. https://doi.org/10.7202/042842ar

Doczekalska, A. (2013). 'Comparative Law and Legal Translation in the Search for Functional Equivalents – Intertwined or Separate Domains?' *Comparative Legilinguistics, 16*, 63–76.

EMT Competence Framework 2017. https://ec.europa.eu/info/sites/default/files/emt_competence_fwk_2017_en_web.pdf

EMT Expert Group. (2009). *Competences for professional translators, experts in multilingual and multimedia communication.* Brussels. https://ec.europa.eu/info/sites/default/files/emt_competences_translators_en.pdf

European Commission. (2008). *The European Qualifications Framework for Lifelong Learning (EQF).*

Genette, M. (2016). *How reliable are online bilingual concordancers? An investigation of Linguee, TradooIT, WeBiText and ReversoContext and their reliability through a contrastive analysis of complex prepositions from French to English* [MA thesis].

González Davies, M. (2004). *Multiple voices in the translation classroom: Activities, tasks and projects.* John Benjamins.

Gościński, J. (2019). *Egzamin na tłumacza przysięgłego. Angielskie orzeczenia w sprawach karnych.* C. H. Beck.

Gough, J. (2018). 'Investigating the use of resources in the translation process.' In *Trends in e-tools and resources for translators and interpreters* (9–36). Brill.

Gwiazdowski, R. (Ed.). (1992). *The Polish Commercial Code & The Polish Civil Code.* (M. Witkowski, Trans.) AP Consulting S.A.

Jopek-Bosiacka, A. (2013). 'Comparative law and equivalence assessment of system-bound terms.' In Ł. Biel, & J. Engberg (Eds.), *Linguistica Antverpiensia, New Series – Themes in Translation Studies, 12*, 110–146.

Kierzkowska, D., & Miler, J. (Eds.). (2000). *The Polish civil code: the law is stated as at 15 August 2000: full text without commentary.* (O. Wojtasiewicz, Trans.) TEPIS.

Kilgariff, A., & Grefenstette, G. (2003). 'Web as Corpus.' *Computational Linguistics, V*(N), 1–15.

Lafeber, A. (2012). 'Translation skills and knowledge – Preliminary findings of a survey of translators and revisers working at inter-governmental organizations.' *Meta, 57*(1), 108–131. https://doi.org/10.7202/1012744ar.

Marín, M. J. (2018). 'Legalese as seen through the lens of corpus linguistics – An introduction to software tools for terminological analysis.' *International Journal of Language and the Law,* 6, 18–45.

PACTE Group. (2003). 'Building a translation competence model.' In F. Alves (Ed.), *Triangulating Translation: Perspectives in Process Oriented Research* (43–66). Amsterdam: John Benjamins.

Paradowska, U. (2021). *Developing Information Competence in Translator Training.* Peter Lang.

Piekot, T., Zarzeczny, G., & Moroń, E. (2018). 'Upraszczanie tekstu użytkowego jako (współ)działanie. Perspektywa prostej polszczyzny.' In S. Niebrzegowska-Bartmińska, M. Nowosad-Bakalarczyk, & T. Piekot (Eds.), *Działania na tekście. Przekład – redagowanie – ilustrowanie* (99–116). Wydawnictwo UMCS.

Pontrandolfo, G. (2015). 'Investigating judicial phraseology with COSPE: A contrastive corpus-based study.' In C. Fantuoli, & F. Zanettin (Eds.), *New directions in corpus-based translation studies* (137–160). Language Science Press. https://arts.units.it/retrieve/handle/11368/2840765/150164/Investigating%20Judicial%20Phraseology%20with%20COSPE-%20A%20contrastive%20Corpus-based%20Study.pdf

Prieto Ramos, F. (2011). 'Developing legal translation competence: an integrative process-oriented approach.' *Comparative Legilinguistics, 5*, 7–22. https://doi.org/10.14746/cl.2011.5.01

Pym, A. (2013). 'Translation skill-sets in a machine-translation age.' *Meta, 58*(3), 487–503. https://doi.org/10.7202/1025047ar

Rothwell, A., & Svoboda, T. (2019). 'Tracking translator training in tools and technologies: findings of the EMT survey 2017.' *The Journal of Specialised Translation, 32*, 26–60.

Sandrini, P. (1999). 'Legal terminology: Some aspects for a new methodology.' *Hermes, 28*, 101–112. https://doi.org/10.7146/hjlcb.v12i22.25496

Scarpa, F., & Orlando, D. (2017). 'Extracting terminology from relevant documents.' *The Journal of Specialised Translation, 27,* 21–42.

Scott, J. (2017). 'Legal translation – A multidimensional endeavour.' *Comparative Legilinguistics, 32,* 37–66.

Shreve, G. M. (2006). 'The deliberate practice: Translation and expertise.' *Journal of Translation Studies, 9*(1), 27–42.

Szewc, A., Zioło, K., & Grzesiczak, M. (2011). *Umowy jako prawne narzędzie transferu innowacji,* http://tu.kielce.pl/wp-content/uploads/2017/12/patenty_umowy-jako-prawne-narz%C4%99dzie-transferu-innowacji.pdf

Szewczyk, M. (2014, January 10). *Standardowe klauzule umowne (tzw. boilerplate clauses) w umowach transakcyjnych poddanych prawu polskiemu.* https://codozasady.pl/p/standardowe-klauzule-umowne-tzw-boilerplate-clauses-w-umowach-transakcyjnych-poddanych-prawu-polskie.

The Civil Code. Kodeks cywilny (4th ed.). (2019). (E. Kucharska, Trans.) C. H. Beck.

Trklja, A., & McAuliffe, K. (2018). 'The European Union Case Law Corpus (EUCLCORP): A multilingual parallel and comparative corpus of EU court judgments.' In A. U. Frank, C. Ivanovic, F. Mambrini, M. Passarotti, & C. Sporleder (Eds.), *Proceedings of the Second Workshop on Corpus-Based Research in the Humanities: CRH-2.* (217–226). https://papers.ssrn.com/sol3/papers.cfm?abstract_id=3134457

Zych, N. (2018). 'Plain-language approach in legislative drafting: A perspective from Poland.' *Comparative Legilinguistics, 38*, 117–130. doi:http://dx.doi.org/10.14746/cl.2018.33.5

Marcel Thelen (ret.)

Maastricht School of Translation and Interpreting,
Zuyd University of Applied Sciences

Translation Quality Assessment Contextualised

Abstract: Existing translation quality assessment methods are mostly and specifically geared towards assessing the quality of translation[1] as a product. Generally, they are not geared towards assessing the quality of the wider context of the translation product, i.e., entrepreneurial competence. If at all, entrepreneurial activities are considered to be integrated in the translation delivered and their assessment forms an integral part of the assessment of the translation. This is generally done by such means as for example questionnaires or reflective papers (viz. in an indirect way), but not by assessing the performance itself on these activities. The descriptions of the personal and interpersonal competence area and the service provision competence area given in the EMT Competence Framework 2017, but also many of the stages described in ISO 17100, the international standard on "Translation Services – Requirements for translation services," lend themselves well as a basis for contextualised translation quality assessment, i.e. the quality assessment of entrepreneurial competence. In this paper, an attempt will be made to operationalise its assessment (cf. Thelen 2019) and suggestions will be given for further formalisation.

Keywords: collaborative translation, contextualised translation quality assessment, didactic methods and activities, employability, EMT Competence Framework 2017, entrepreneurial competence, INSTB, ISO 17100, skills lab, student translation company

Introduction

Since the start of the Bologna process, Quality Assessment has become one of the core principles educational institutes have to adhere to and bring into practice. For educational institutes, a sound quality assessment system relates directly to their position and raison d'être and makes them eligible for government subsidies. For students, a sound quality system co-determines their study success in particular and their future in general. It gives them an insight into their own abilities and chances for post-graduate employment. Equally important is what it is that is to be assessed on quality, what quality is at all, and how quality is assessed. All these three aspects should be geared towards the

1 The focus in this paper is on translation, not on interpreting.

objectives of the educational institute and the requirements of the professional field the institute educates/trains students for. For translation, this means that the quality assessment system should not only address the process of translating and the products delivered, but also all those factors that make a good translator who is fit for employment in a professional market. Thus, employability has become a key objective. Consequently, the education/training of students to become professional translators should not only involve *translation* education/training, but also *translator* education/training. In other words, not only the translation process and product as such should be assessed on quality, but also their context, i.e. (1) everything related to the provision of the translation, (2) the translator delivering the translation and (3) the relation of the translator with his commissioner or client, in short, the entrepreneurial competence of the translator.[2]

Many institutes offering translation programmes[3] have taken/are taking measures to incorporate employability in their curricula. These measures include not only the expansion of the set of competences with a personal and interpersonal competence and a service provision competence (as in e.g., the EMT Competence Framework 2017), but also the introduction of new didactic methods and activities for these competences, for example group or collaborative translation (see e.g. O'Brien 2013). I will come back to this in section 4.

Contextualised translation quality assessment: the EMT Competence Framework 2017

A basis for contextualised translation quality assessment, i.e., the quality assessment of entrepreneurial competence, can be found in the EMT Competence Framework 2017 which has the following competences for the European Master's in Translation:[4]

2 In terms of the traditional dichotomy between academic and vocational conceptions of translator training the ideal situation is a combination of the two (cf. for example Kiraly, 1995; Thelen, 2005b; Kearns, 2006, and Calvo, 2011). In terms of the dichotomy between theory and practice, both are needed and support one another (cf. Thelen, 2005b, and Di Mango, 2018).

3 Henceforth called translator training institutes without making a distinction between education and training (see also Thelen, 2016a).

4 This Framework applies explicitly to master programmes, but the competences mentioned are also very well applicable to bachelor programmes. At the most it may be a difference in degree of mastering the competences mentioned that sets master programmes apart from bachelor programmes.

1. Language and culture
2. Translation
3. Technology
4. Personal and interpersonal
5. Service provision

Of these, Personal and interpersonal as well as Service provision are typically entrepreneurial competence areas. The Personal and interpersonal competence "includes all the generic skills, often referred to as 'soft skills,' that enhance graduate adaptability and employability." (EMT Competence Framework 2017, 10), and the Service provision competence "covers all the skills relating to the implementation of translation and, more generally, to language services in a professional context – from client awareness and negotiating through to project management and quality assurance" (ibid., 11). Both competences contribute to employability. These personal/interpersonal and service provision competences cover entrepreneurial skills (Klimkowski, 2016) and together they are also called entrepreneurial competence (van Egdom et al., 2020).

The EMT Competence Framework 2017 distinguishes the following skills or sub-competences for these competences (numbering as in the Framework; preceding numbers are for other competences):

Personal and Interpersonal

21. Plan and manage time, stress, and workload
22. Comply with deadlines, instructions, and specifications
23. Work in a team, including, where appropriate, in virtual, multicultural and multilingual environments, using current communication technologies
24. Use social media responsibly for professional purposes
25. Take account of and adapt the organisational and physical ergonomics of the working environment
26. Continuously self-evaluate, update, and develop competences and skills through personal strategies and collaborative learning

Service provision

27. Monitor and take account of new societal and language industry demands, new market requirements and emerging job profiles
28. Approach existing clients and find new clients through prospecting and marketing strategies using the appropriate written and oral communication techniques

Personal and Interpersonal
29. Clarify the requirements, objectives and purposes of the client, recipients of the language service and other stakeholders and offer the appropriate services to meet those requirements
30. Negotiate with the client (to define deadlines, rates/invoicing, working conditions, access to information, contracts, rights, responsibilities, language service specifications, tender specifications etc.)
31. Organise, budget, and manage translation projects involving single or multiple translators and/or other service providers
32. Understand and implement the standards applicable to the provision of a language service
33. Apply the quality management and quality assurance procedures required to meet pre-defined quality standards
34. Comply with professional ethical codes and standards (confidentiality, fair competition etc.) and network with other translators and language providers via social media and professional associations
35. Analyse and critically review language services and policies and suggest improvement strategies

The Language and culture, Translation and Technology competences lend themselves perfectly well for direct quality assessment of individual translations and make up the core of prevailing quality assessment systems. These competences are, however, only applied/applicable to the translation process from SLT to TLT and the resulting translation product. Personal/interpersonal competence as well as service provision competence are more difficult to assess on quality and need other ways of assessment. These can be indirect through reflective comments and papers, but more direct assessment ways would be more effective and challenging. Moreover, training these competences would increase employability. And for this, other didactic methods and activities are needed.

Contextualised translation quality assessment: ISO 17100

Another basis for contextualised translation quality assessment, i.e., the quality assessment of entrepreneurial competence, is provided by the translation industry in terms of ISO 17100 (preceded by EN 15038: 2006). This standard is meant for professional translation companies but also for freelance translators, albeit that for the latter not all parts apply. Whereas the focus of the EMT competences

2017 is on the competences a student of translation should master in the course of and at the end of his study in order to be prepared for employment in the profession, ISO 17100 describes all the requirements for a translation company/freelancer to act professionally and to deliver quality products and services: "This International Standard provides requirements for the core processes, resources, and other aspects necessary for the delivery of a quality translation service that meets applicable specifications." (ISO 17100, 1).

The requirements for translation services comprise:

5. **Resources:** human and technical/technological
6. **Pre-production processes and activities:** enquiry & feasibility, quotation, client-TSP[5] agreement, handling project-related client information, project preparation
7. **Production process:** translation service project management, translation process
8. **Post-production process:** feedback, closing administration.

Under human resources the professional competences are listed for translators, revisers, reviewers,[6] and translation project managers, as well as the required qualifications of translators. Overall, the competences listed in the EMT competence framework and ISO 17100 are more or less similar, though the EMT set is more detailed.

As a quality standard geared towards assessing quality, ISO 17100 provides useful assessment criteria for implementation in curricula. Combined, the EMT Competence Framework 2017 and ISO 17100 provide an ideal basic set of criteria for contextualised translation quality assessment. The question is how both can be materialised in curricula and what didactic method(s) would be most appropriate for this.

Didactic methods and activities for contextualised translation quality assessment

True, at least sub-competence 22 of personal/interpersonal competence ("Comply with deadlines, instructions and specifications") can well be trained and assessed for traditional individual translation assignments, but other sub-competences

5 Translation Service Provider, i.e. the translation company of freelancer.
6 Domain specialists who check the translation product on the quality of the domain-specific language and the correctness of terminology used as well as whether the content is in accordance with the domain.

would be problematic, and their assessment would be rather "artificial." For other entrepreneurial sub-competences other didactic methods and activities are called for and other assessment methods and criteria are needed for these new didactic methods and activities, i.e., quality assessment must be widened or contextualised to apply to other stages in the translation delivery process than translation sec.

Torres and Pym (2017), in comparing the MA programmes of the EMT member institutes, mention two types of didactic method for these entrepreneurial sub-competences, viz. "courses on the translation profession" including "accounting, client-professional relationships, etc."[7] (Torres and Pym, 2017, 3) and "professional internships" (*ibid.*, 11).[8] For more suggestions for these courses on the translation profession see e.g., Muñoz-Miquel (2020).

Thelen (2016) proposes group or collaborative translation. It is conceived of as a cover term for a number of different methods of translation that can be implemented in various ways in translator training. At the Maastricht School of Translation and Interpreting of Zuyd University of Applied Sciences, for example, three types are used: (1) sub-group translations (i.e. written translations done by 3 to 4 students), (2) oral in-class on sight translations by 15–20 students on average, and (3) translations for the in-house simulated translation bureau (called *skills lab*) (cf. Thelen 2005, 2013, 2015, 2016a, 2016b, 2016c, 2019; Buysschaert et al., 2017, and van Egdom et al. 2020).[9] Of these, the in-house simulated translation bureau or skills lab is best suitable for assessing entrepreneurial competence based on the combination of EMT competences and ISO 17100. It has been in use in Maastricht for more than 30 years now and has proven to be a solid didactic method for training and practising entrepreneurial competence.

---

7 It is a pity that "etc." is not further specified.

8 The "strict philosophy" of the EMT programme is "training professionals for the market" (Pym, 2017, 16) where both methods should be part of the curriculum, but this is not the case for each member institution: "When at least 85 percent of the programs offer theory courses and 90 percent include research work of some kind, one must recognize that these remain academic curricula within academic institutions, despite the absence of these elements from the main competences in the EMT model." (Ibid., 16).

9 The skills lab concept resembles the OCTC Tradutech project with "fictitious translation companies" set up by students. Tradutech was initiated by Daniel Gouadec (Rennes University) and Hugo Marquant (Institut Marie-Haps Brussels) at the end of the 1990s. The project deals with technical texts only (see https://otct.huma-num.fr/about/project-background-and-objectives/; accessed: 14 June 2021). The skills lab is older: it dates back to 1984. Both are forms of collaborative learning.

Until now, 16 universities in Europe (in Netherlands, Belgium, France, United Kingdom, Spain, Ireland, Finland, and Germany) have embraced the skills lab concept and have adapted it to their local needs and possibilities.[10] Together they form the International Network of Simulated Translation Bureaus (INSTB, https://www.INSTB.eu) that was officially launched in Maastricht in 2015. The members of INSTB have a number of basic ISO 17100 elements in common:

- client contact (e.g., with discussion of specifications, etc., final registration of arrangements, quotation);
- project preparation (e.g., analysis of project and availability of required staff and equipment, allocation of job to translator(s) and reviser(s), registration in workflow management system);
- translation process (e.g., translation, self-check by translator, revision by other translator, if needed check of target language text by domain specialist, final check, filling in and registering quality forms, registration of all steps in workflow management system);
- delivering the end product (e.g., check of client satisfaction, complaint procedure if required).

Skills labs may vary in set-up and internal organisation, as well as in number of students depending on the local situation.

A skills lab is a form of situated learning (e.g. Kurt, 2021), collaborative learning (cf. Thelen, 2016) or authentic experiential or emergentist learning (cf. Kiraly, 2016), or simply learning in a community of practice by doing and applying what one already knows and is able to do. Kiraly (2016: 137) visualised authentic experiential or emergentist learning in the form of a "Multi-Vortex Model of Translator Competence Development" (see Figure 1):

10 Also, the names may vary among locations. Turku University, for example, has *Multilingual Translation Workshop (MTW)* and Ghent University *student company*.

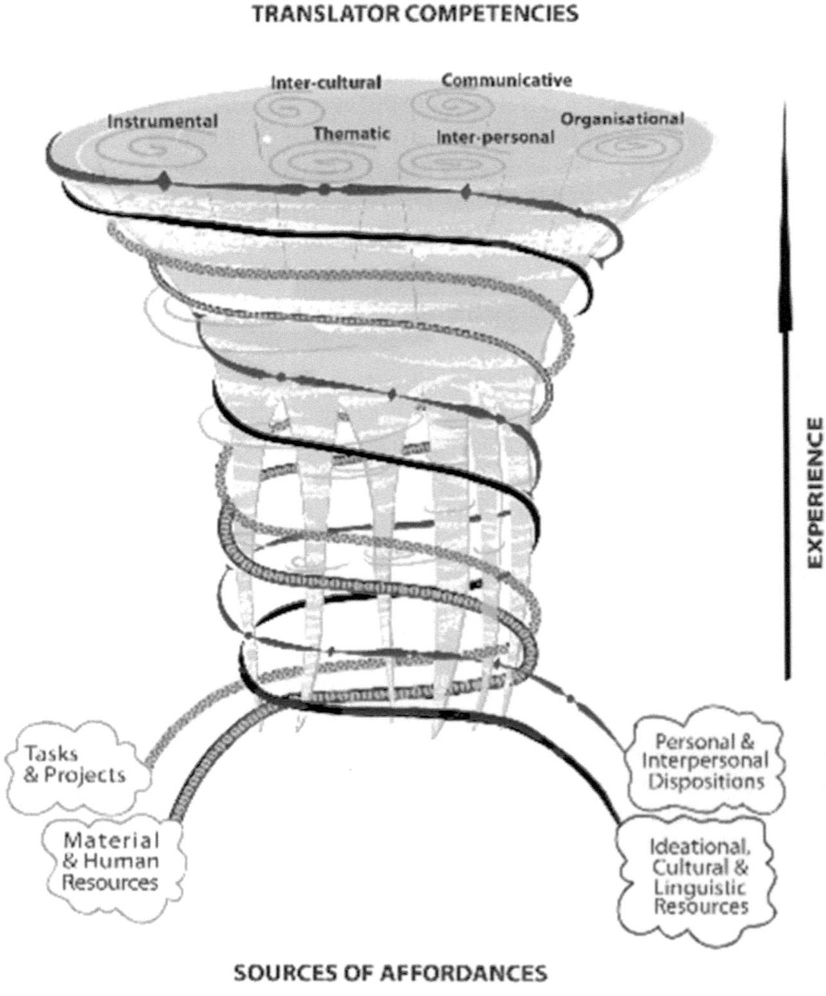

Figure 1: "Multi-Vortex Model of Translator Competence Development" (Kiraly, 2016: 137)

In a skills lab all competences come together and are practised and trained in a professional environment. It is a simulated translation bureau that is set up, staffed and run by students under the supervision of a lecturer-director, and earns credit points. It operates as a real translation bureau with as many stages mentioned in ISO

17100 as possible. The management of the bureau (in Maastricht at least) is made up of a number of students with various functions and tasks and is responsible for running and managing the bureau, making profit (avoiding losses/bankruptcy), complaints handling, workflow, bookkeeping, HR, client liaison, quality management and assurance, permanent education, PR (incl. website), etc., in short, for the stages mentioned in ISO 17100. Management students should, of course, be good team players. Translators/revisers are responsible for delivering translation/revision quality, working professionally (comply with deadlines, instructions, and specifications, and be good team players), permanent education, etc. And it is on these criteria that they are assessed. Assignments/jobs may come from lecturers, external translation bureaus, other departments of the university where the skills lab operates or from partner skills labs in the INSB network. For more details on the skills lab see Thelen (2005a, 2013 and 2016a).

In the context of INSTB five member institutes carried out a study among students. One of its aims was "To formulate and test specific hypotheses: e.g. soft skills, and more specifically interpersonal skills, are cultivated through authentic experiential learning." In this study, they compared the situation before and after the skills lab by presenting the students with self-assessment questions on the various skills. The data showed an overall improvement in skills, but in particular service provision skills and managerial skills. Another study by van Egdom et al. (2020) measured "student progress in translation company simulations" and to do this, "a survey instrument was developed to gauge the factors of Perceived entrepreneurial competence and Self-efficacy for planning, setting up, and managing a translating organisation." (ibid. 92). The results showed that participating in a skills lab indeed gives a boost to entrepreneurial self-efficacy[11] and perceived competence.

The skills lab is, by its very nature, an ideal place in the curriculum to train, practise and assess entrepreneurial competence. Besides, it increases motivation among students and provides students with hands-on experience, which will eventually contribute to their post-graduate employability.

Right from the beginning in 1984, the skills lab in Maastricht was an alternative for a professional placement/internship with a translation bureau.

11 Self-efficacy is, according to psychologist Albert Bandura who originally proposed the concept, a personal judgment of how well or poorly a person is able to cope with a given situation based on the skills they have and the circumstances they face (https://en.wikipedia.org/wiki/Self-efficacy; accessed: 20 May 2021), or as De Noble et al. (1999) put it, a "can-do attitude" which is a combination of competence and self-confidence.

Assessment methods and criteria for contextualised translation quality assessment

Here a distinction should be made between *assessment types* and *assessment criteria*. Since in a skills lab environment several actors participate with differing authority, there are also several assessment types as shown in Figure 2 (cf. Thelen, 2019: 11–12):[12]

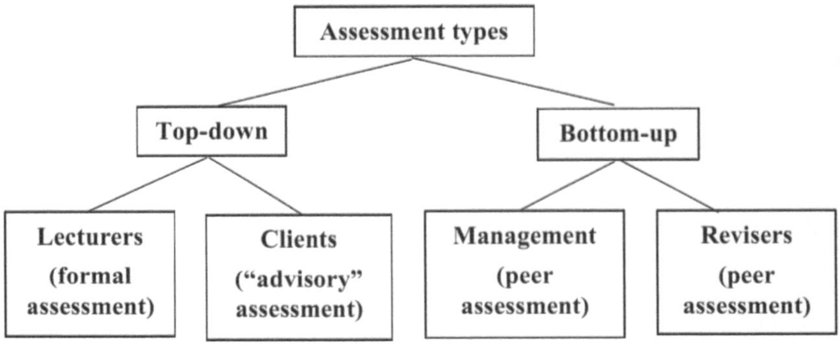

Figure 2: Assessment types

The actors include the management (with various functions and tasks), translators/revisers, one or more lecturers and (school internal and external) clients. All these actors function as assessors at some point. The management, for example, is accountable for the successful running of the skills lab and assesses continually all aspects of the skills lab, including all the translations and other services provided as well as the functioning of translators and revisers. Translators and revisers, on the other hand, assess/check their own work, and revisers also the work done by translators. Clients assess the products and services delivered by the skills lab. The lecturer-director, finally, is responsible for the final and overall assessment of all the students involved in the skills lab and their assessment is directly related to credits and study success. These assessment types go not only for translations and other services, but also for everything else that is related to the skills lab.

12 For "top-down" and "bottom-up" see Drugan 2013.

The *assessment criteria* for translations and other services delivered can obviously not be the same for all the other factors, deliverables, activities and actions at the basis of and surrounding these translations and other services delivered. Putting it differently, there is a difference in assessment criteria between the language and culture ~, translation ~ and technology competences on the one hand, and the personal/interpersonal and service provision competences (i.e. entrepreneurial competence) on the other.

The following two tables represent a number of suggestions for criteria for the assessment of entrepreneurial competence, viz. EMT 2017 personal/interpersonal competence and service competence. In the formulation of these criteria, also aspects of ISO 17100 are included. It should be noted that these criteria do not apply to the first three EMT competences (language and culture, translation and technology); these suggested criteria complement the criteria that are already available and in use for the quality assessment of translation as a product. These suggestions are by no means exhaustive. It should also be noted that the assessment criteria suggested here focus on and start from the assessment of entrepreneurial competence, whereas the focus of the criteria suggested in Thelen (2019) is more on the performance in various functions present in a skills lab with these functions as points of departure. Inevitably, there may be a certain degree of overlap.

Table 1: Assessment criteria for EMT 2017 Personal and Interpersonal competence

EMT competence framework 2017: Personal and Interpersonal competence ***with input from ISO 17100***	
(sub-)competence	*Assessment criteria*
21: Plan and manage time, stress and workload	**Management:** [a] • is there a workflow management system/document and is this traceable, complete? • have targets been set and have they been met? • was the planning realistic and feasible? • have there been any planning problems? If yes, were these due to inadequate time management, stress, workload, …? • Have there been any client complaints about the planning? • was the workload well divided among the management itself and among translators/revisers? • have there been any burnouts or absences due to sickness or complaints about workload among the management or translators/revisers? • have there been any problems related to the allocation of assignments/jobs to translators/revisers? • have problems been solved adequately and satisfactorily? **Translators/revisers:** have the deadlines given by the managementz[b] been kept? If not, what was the cause of the excession: inadequate time management, stress, workload, …?
22: Comply with deadlines, instructions and specifications	**Management:** • Have there been any client complaints related to deadlines, instructions of specifications? • have translators/revisers been given clear instructions about clients' specifications and wishes? • are these deadlines, instructions and specifications documented and traceable in a workflow management system? **Translators/revisers:** • has the translator/reviser complied with the deadlines, specifications and wishes given by the management? • Have there been any management complaints related to deadlines, instructions of specifications? • Have there been any translator/reviser complaints to the management related to deadlines, instructions of specifications?

Table 1: Continued

EMT competence framework 2017: Personal and Interpersonal competence ***with input from ISO 17100***	
23: Work in a team, including, where appropriate, in virtual, multicultural and multilingual environments, using current communication technologies	**Management:** • Has the management functioned as a team? • Has the management used the available technical and communication tools well? • Has the management communicated professionally and enough among themselves and with the translators / revisers? **Translators/revisers:** • Has the translator/reviser been a good team player and colleague? • Has the translator/reviser communicated professionally with the management and his revisers making use of the available communication technologies?
24: Use social media responsibly for professional purposes	**Management:** Has the management – when appropriate for the situation at hand – used social media and done this responsibly and professionally? **Translators/revisers:** Has the translator/reviser – when appropriate for the situation at hand – used social media and done this responsibly and professionally?
25: Take account of and adapt the organisational and physical ergonomics of the working environment	**Management:** • Has the management made available the devices, tools, computer programs and technologies that are required for the organisation of the skills lab and the work to be done by translators/revisers? • Have there been any problems related to this and has the management taken action to solve these problems? • Has the management refused any jobs/assignments in the client contact because these were not feasible for lack of appropriate resources (human, technical or technological)? **Translators/revisers:** Has the translator/reviser refused any jobs/assignments given by the management because these were not feasible for lack of appropriate resources (human, technical or technological)?

(*Continued*)

Table 1: Continued

EMT competence framework 2017: Personal and Interpersonal competence ***with input from ISO 17100***	
26: Continuously self-evaluate, update and develop competences and skills through personal strategies, and collaborative learning	**Management:** • Has the management implemented a professional development scheme by which "disfunctioning" staff (management or translators/revisers) are helped to improve by getting a second chance and/or a coach? • Has the management implemented a scheme for permanent education and made it possible for all skills lab members to participate? • Has the management participated in the permanent education scheme? **Translators/revisers:** • Has the translator/reviser participated in the permanent education scheme?

[a] From this formulation one might conclude that the criteria mentioned apply to the management as a whole. Depending on the local set-up and internal organisation of the skills lab this may, however, be specified further by mentioning the functions within the management such as liaison officer, office manager, quality manager, HR officer, etc. (cf. Thelen, 2019: 14–20). Clearly, this would involve a more detailed and "bespoke" formulation of the assessment criteria for the various functions.
[b] There are two types of deadlines: deadlines for the management set by the client and deadlines the management sets for translators/revisers. This distinction is necessary because management needs to have time for review, proofreading, final verification and release (cf. ISO 17100: 11).

Management functions and the function of translator/reviser may rotate between all students participating in the skills lab, depending on the particular setup of the skills lab.

The criteria in the following table for the assessment of the EMT 2017 service provision competence as part of entrepreneurial competence are very much in line with and based on the quality requirements mentioned in ISO 17100. Most of these criteria typically apply to the management in a skills lab environment where translators/revisers are employed as in-house members of staff. If, however, the translators/revisers act as freelancers to the bureau, not all of these criteria will apply. Again, this depends on the setup of the skills lab. In the case of freelancers, the simulated translation bureau will act as client.

The assessment criteria suggested have been formulated in question form. In general, the answers in terms of YES/NO to the questions posed have to be evidenced by traceable and complete documents such as workflow, books, client feedback forms, management records, etc. This seemed the most efficient way

Table 2: Assessment criteria for EMT 2017 Service Provision competence

EMT competence framework 2017: Service provision competence[a] ***with input from ISO 17100***	
(sub-)competence	*Assessment criteria*
27: Monitor and take account of new societal and language industry demands, new market requirements and emerging job profiles	**Management and translators/revisers**: • Has the management/translator/reviser complied with the requirements of ISO 17100 wherever possible and feasible? • Has the management/translator/reviser taken part in a permanent education scheme to update his skills and knowledge and learn about new developments and demands/requirements?
28: Approach existing clients and find new clients through prospecting and marketing strategies using the appropriate written and oral communication techniques	**Management and/or translators/revisers:** • Has the management/translator/reviser set up a professional website and/or created an account on relevant social media for PR? • Has management/translator/reviser used any other means for PR? • Has management/translator/reviser used the appropriate means of communication to contact existing clients?
29: Clarify the requirements, objectives and purposes of the client, recipients of the language service and other stakeholders and offer the appropriate services to meet those requirements	**Management and/or translators/revisers:** Has the management/translator/reviser clarified the requirements, objectives and purposes of the client and taken the necessary measures and made the appropriate offer to find a balance between these, the recipients and all other stakeholders and the service(s) to be provided on the basis of available (human/technical/technological) resources and feasibility?
30: Negotiate with the client (to define deadlines, rates/invoicing, working conditions, access to information, contracts, rights, responsibilities, language service specifications, tender specifications etc.)	**Management and/or translators/revisers:** Has the management/translator/reviser negotiated with the client about all the practical details of the service required (incl. quotation/tender and contract)?

(*Continued*)

Table 2: Continued

31: Organise, budget, and manage translation projects involving single or multiple translators and/or other service providers	**Management (and/or translators/revisers** but only if these act as primary contractors with a number of sub-contractors): • is there a workflow management system/document and is this traceable, complete? • have targets been set and have they been met? • was the planning realistic and feasible? • have there been any planning problems? If yes, were these due to inadequate time management, stress, workload, …? • Have there been any client complaints about the planning? • have problems been solved adequately and satisfactorily?
32: Understand and implement the standards applicable to the provision of a language service	**Management and/or translators/revisers:** • Has the management/translator/reviser implemented ISO 17100 and acted in line with it? • Has ISO 17100 been applied correctly?
33: Apply the quality management and quality assurance procedures required to meet pre-defined quality standards	**Management and/or translators/revisers:** Have the quality requirements of ISO 17100 been complied with?
34: Comply with professional ethical codes and standards (confidentiality, fair competition etc.) and network with other translators and language providers via social media and professional associations	**Management and/or translators/revisers:** Has the management/translator/reviser complied with available and prevailing professional ethical codes (for confidentiality, fair competition, security of client information, etc.)?
35: Analyse and critically review language services and policies and suggest improvement strategies	**Management and/or translators/revisers:** Has the management/translator/reviser critically analysed their own work and that by others and suggested/applied improvements?

[a] Not all of the sub-competences mentioned necessarily apply to individual or freelance translators/revisers in a skills lab setting, but to management only; but this depends, of course on the local implementation of the concept of skills lab. In the form of skills lab described here, negotiating with the client, for example, is done by the management only.

to operationalise the (sub-)competences described. There are, of course, other ways, e.g. weighting or giving marks. It would, for example, be rather difficult, if not impossible, to assess sub-competence 26 ("Continuously self-evaluate, update and develop competences and skills through personal strategies, and collaborative learning") of the Personal and interpersonal competence in terms of marks from 1 to 10. The number of YES and NO answers would determine the final score for a given (sub-) competence in terms of PASS (more YES answers) or FAIL (more NO answers). And the calculation of the final score may even vary. One option is simply counting the number of YES answers and NO answers and assigning PASS or FAIL to the highest number (more YES than NO = PASS, more NO than YES = FAIL). Another option would be to set a minimum of required YES answers as a threshold for assigning PASS. I will not dwell on this further.

Conclusion

Generally, existing translation quality assessment methods are primarily designed for the quality assessment of translation as a product and not as a service, or, in terms of EMT 2017 competences, for the assessment of student's mastering of translation competence, cultural competence and technology competence, but not entrepreneurial competence (i.e. personal and interpersonal competence and service provision competence). However, entrepreneurial competence has been introduced as a key competence for post-graduate employability and as a factor of importance to help reduce the perceived skills gap between training/education and life as a professional market player. Meanwhile, ISO 17100 introduced a quality standard for translation service provision in the market. As such, it can contribute to the implementation of entrepreneurial competence in translator training and provide clues for its assessment. The EMT 2017 competences provide a formulation of competences and ISO 171100 gives a set of requirements for professional translation provision service. Together they form a valuable basis for developing new ways of quality assessment, called contextualised translation quality assessment. For this to be possible, new training methods should be introduced in the curriculum.

A skills lab or in-house simulated translation bureau has proven to be a good candidate for this as it encompasses all aspects of translation provision, not only translation as a product, but also its "surrounding" stages. It gives students the opportunity to train and practise entrepreneurial competence. For its assessment a number of criteria have been suggested based on the EMT 2017 competence framework and ISO 17100 requirements.

The suggested assessment criteria for the assessment of entrepreneurial competence are meant for and work well in a skills lab setting; therefore, the question is whether they could also be fruitfully applied to other training methods like individual translations. Although the assessment criteria are suggestions, they may be a good step in the direction of the formulation of assessment criteria for entrepreneurial competence.

References

Buysschaert, J., Fernández-Parra, M., & van Egdom, G.W. (2017). 'Professionalising the Curriculum and Increasing Employability Through Authentic Experiential Learning: The Cases of INSTB.' In *Current Trends in Translation Teaching and Learning E, 4*, 78–111. http://www.cttl.org/uploads/5/2/4/3/5243866/cttl_e_2017_3.pdf

Calvo, E. (2011). 'Translation and/or translator skills as organising principles for curriculum development practice.' *The Journal of Specialised Translation, 16*.

De Noble, A., Jung, D., & S. Ehrlich. (1999). 'Entrepreneurial Self-Efficacy: The Development of a Measure and Its Relationship to Entrepreneurial Action.' In P. Reynolds, W. Bygrave, S. Manigart, C. Mason, D. Meyer, H. Sapienza, & K. Shaver (Eds.), *Frontiers of Entrepreneurship Research 1999: Proceedings of the 19th Annual Entrepreneurship Research Conference* (73–87). Babson College.

Di Mango, D. (2018). *The Role of Theory in Translator Training*. Narr Francke Attempto.

Drugan, J. (2013). *Quality in Professional Translation. Assessment and Improvement*. Bloomsbury.

EMT Board (2017). *European Master's in Translation: Competence Framework 2017*. Available at: https://ec.europa.eu/info/sites/info/files/emt_competence_fwk_2017_en_web.pdf.

EN 15038 (2006). *Translation services—Service requirements*. CEN.

Fernandez-Parra, M., K. Kerremans, K. Kontinen, R. Loock, S. Vandepitte, I. van der Lek-Ciudin, & G-W. van Egdom (2018). 'Assessing interpersonal skills in translator training: the cases of INSTB.' Ppt presented at the Fourth International Conference on Research into the Didactics of Translation. 20–22 June 2018 at Universitat Autònoma de Barcelona. https://grupsderecerca.uab.cat/pacte/en/didtrad_2018

ISO 17100. (2015). *Translation Services – Requirements for translation services*. ISO.

Kearns, J. (2006). *Curriculum Renewal in Translator Training: Vocational challenges in academic environments with reference to needs and situation analysis and skills transferability from the contemporary experience of Polish translator training culture*. John_Kearns_20121129165721.pdf

Kiraly, D. (1995). *Pathways to Translation: Pedagogy and Process*. Kent State University Press.

Kiraly, D. (2016). 'Beyond the Static Impasse in Translator Education.' In M. Thelen, G-W. van Egdom, D. Verbeeck, Ł. Bogucki, & B. Lewandowska-Tomaszczyk (Eds.), *Translation and Meaning, New Series*, Vol. 1, (129–142). Peter Lang.

Klimkowski, K. (2016). 'Entrepreneurial Aspects of Translation Competence in Didactic Reflection and Practice.' In Ł. Bogucki, B. Lewandowska-Tomaszczyk and M. Thelen (Eds.) (2016), *Translation and Meaning*, New series, Vol. 2, Pt. 2 (143–155). Peter Lang.

Kurt, S. (2021). 'Situated Learning Theory.' *Educational Technology*, February 17, 2021. https://educationaltechnology.net/situated-learning-theory/

Muñoz-Miquel, A. (2020). 'Translation and Interpreting as a Profession: Some Proposals to Boost Entrepreneurial Competence.' *Hermes – Journal of Language and Communication in Business, 60*, 29–46.

O'Brien, S. (2013). 'Collaborative translation.' In Y. Gambier, & L. van Doorslaer (Eds.), *Handbook of Translation Studies*, Vol 2 (17–20). John Benjamins.

Torres-Simón, E., & Pym, A. (2017). 'European Masters in Translation. A comparative study.' https://usuaris.tinet.cat/apym/on-line/training/2016_EMT_masters.pdf

Thelen, M. (2005a). 'Going European: A Plea for Building a Network of Simulated Translation Bureaus.' In M. Forstner, & H. Lee-Jahnke (Eds.), *CIUTI-Forum Paris 2005. Regards sur les aspects culturels de la communication* (219–236). Peter Lang.

Thelen, M, (2005b). 'Theory and Practice in Translation: Co-operation or Mere Co-existence?' In J. Peeters (Ed.), *On the relationships between translation theory and translation practice* (41–50). Peter Lang.

Thelen, M. (2013). 'Facing New Challenges: Updating the Training Curriculum.' In M. Forstner, & H. Lee-Jahnke (Eds.), *CIUTI-Forum 2013. Facing the World's New Challenges. The Role of T&I in Providing Integrated Efficient and Sustainable Solutions* (227–254). Peter Lang.

Thelen, M. (2015). 'Cooperation between universities and the profession in the translator training curriculum: Issues of testing, assessing and quality assurance.' In M. Forstner, H. Lee-Jahnke, & M. Chai (Eds.), *CIUTI-Forum 2014. Pooling Academic Excellence with Entrepreneurship for New Partnerships* (293–312). Peter Lang.

Thelen, M. (2016a). 'Professionalisation in the translator training curriculum.' In Ł. Bogucki, B. Lewandowska-Tomaszczyk, & M. Thelen (Eds.), *Translation and Meaning*. New Series, Vol. 2, Pt. 2 (117–142). Peter Lang, .

Thelen, M. (2016b). 'The Practice-oriented Translator Training Curriculum: An Example' *Current Trends in Translation Teaching and Learning E, 3,* 163–200. http://www.cttl.org/uploads/5/2/4/3/5243866/cttl_e_3_thelen_m.pd

Thelen, M. (2016c). 'Collaborative translation in translator training.' *Konin Language Studies, KSJ, 4*(3), 253–269.

Thelen, M. (2019). 'Quality and Quality Assessment in Translation: Paradigms in Perspective.' In E. Huertas-Barros, S. Vandepitte, & E. Iglesias-Fernández (Eds.), *Quality Assurance and Assessment Practices in Translation and Interpreting* (1–25). IGI Global.

Van Egdom, G-W., K. Konttinen, S. Vandepitte, M. Fernández-Parra, R. Loock, & J. Bindels. (2020). 'Empowering Translators through Entrepreneurship in Simulated Translation Bureaus.' *Hermes – Journal of Language and Communication in Business, 60,* 81–95.

Katarzyna Wiśniewska

University of Eastern Finland

Mistranslations in the Context of Cognitive Retention of Force Dynamics in Translation

Abstract: This paper reports on part of ongoing PhD research,[1] which concentrates on the retention of Talmy's (2000) force-dynamics schemas in translation and on the existing evidence on dissociating linguistic and cognitive levels of translation description (cognitive retention hypothesis put forward by Mäkisalo and Lehtinen, 2014). The matter is studied quantitatively and qualitatively on trilingual bidirectional corpora of phrases containing simple and complex verb phrases with force-dynamics patterns from fragments of literary and audiovisual texts in different translation pairs combining English, Polish and Finnish; with translations from Finnish into English and Polish being in the very focus of this paper.

Interesting cases of mistranslations found in the verb phrases from the self-compiled literary corpora triggered the need for a separate analysis of such inadequate translation cases that would account for their specific cognitive nature, but also their impact and consequences on distorting the force-dynamics event scenarios found in the studied texts. The issue raised in this paper complements Mäkisalo and Lehtinen's cognitive retention hypothesis, since mistranslations were not considered in the methodological assumptions of their framework.

The analysis of mistranslations in the context of cognitive retention of force-dynamics structural patterns constitutes an interesting perspective for translation training (not translation-quality assessment), by providing evidence for embodied cognitive processes of re-conceptualisation in translation, as well as the dependence of meaning (situatedness) on the specifics of various contexts. The analysis of selected mistranslations in this paper refers

1 The PhD project, *Description of force dynamics and cognitive retention in literary and audiovisual translation*, is supported by Kone Foundation, a Helsinki-based independent non-profit organisation with a mission to make the world a better place by advancing bold initiatives in research and the arts. The PhD project constitutes part of larger innovative research, *Cognitive description of translation*, carried out at the University of Eastern Finland together with Jukka Mäkisalo and Esa Penttilä, seeking international recognition by constructing a systematic description of translation at sentence level, following the four conceptual schematic systems proposed by Leonard Talmy. The reason behind this collaboration is the current lack of means and tools necessary for a cognitive description of translation. The goal is to elaborate and present a broad and comprehensive body of knowledge and empirical findings to an international audience that would serve translation training.

to experiential information processing and the notion of cognitive economy (Hietaranta, 2017), which is a way of processing information based on intuition, often leading translators to subconsciously overlook details based on their individual and cultural experiences.

Keywords: cognitive economy, cognitive retention, force dynamics, mistranslations, translation training

Background

The idea for this paper emerged out of an ongoing PhD work, which is concerned with the notion of force dynamics in the context of cognitive retention in translation. This paper goes into the qualitative (case study) part of the whole dissertation and looks into two instances of mistranslations identified in the collected data. The main aim of the overall PhD work, however, is to find out whether and how force-dynamics event structures are retained in translation and subtitling based on three different languages, English, Finnish and Polish, combined into various translation pairs. This section is meant to provide background information necessary to understand the connection of mistranslations, constituting a separate cognitive phenomenon to cognitive retention, to the rest of the project.

The ongoing research constitutes part of a bigger innovative project aiming at constructing a systematic description of translation at sentence level, following the conceptual schematic systems, elaborated by Talmy (2000), harking back to the principles of Gestalt psychology and attempting to understand the laws behind the ability of the human mind to acquire and maintain meaningful perception from fragmented sensations. The project is implemented in the vein of cognitive semantics, the study of linguistic meaning, which holds that language is part of a more general human cognitive ability. The Talmyan schematic systems in focus include: the 'configurational structure system,' the 'attentional system,' the 'perspective system' and the 'force-dynamics system.' The scaffolding of any work carried out under this long-term project is the Talmyan framework, but also the schema coined by Mäkisalo and Lehtinen (2014), who demonstrate useful outlines for contrastive studies exploring the interface between cognitive linguistics and translation studies from the perspective of the dissociation of the linguistic and cognitive description and information mediation in translation.

As a methodological approach in translation studies, cognitive linguistics supports the cognitive nature of the translation process in which two different conceptual worlds are linked (Rojo and Ibarretxe-Antuñano, 2013). Cognitive linguistics provides answers to questions regarding cognitive processes underlying translation, e.g. how translators make decisions about what is decoded from the original they process, and what should be encoded in a brand-new text they produce. For example, the motivation underlying translators' decision-making derives from political, cultural, social, personal, or ideological norms they want to conform to (Chesterman, 2016). It is also the intuition that is viewed as a subconsciously operating psychological construct that is inherent to translator behaviour (Hubscher-Davidson, 2015). These examples are connected to embodiment. Embodied and situated approaches presently constitute the extended view on cognition (Clark, 2014). According to Zlatev (2005: 315), it is the use of the body for representational purposes he calls 'bodily mimesis' that helps embodiment to be mapped onto language structures, enabling the language to be used as a communicative tool. During translation, the same 'bodily mimesis' helps translators to extract and transfer embodied conceptual structures from semantic structures (Wang, 2015).

Based on English-Finnish informative prose translation (2014) and subtitling corpora (2017), Mäkisalo and Lehtinen investigate the phenomenon of the semantic structure of figure and ground. The figure-ground alignment is included in the Talmyan 'attentional system' (Talmy, 2000). In short, the phenomenon has to do with how we perceive our environment, so that certain elements stand out as more prominent or salient (the figure) from the rest of the environment (the ground). It is a construal operation instantiating a general cognitive process in which smaller and movable objects (being in the focus of attention) are a natural choice for the figure, and larger and non-movable objects are the ground. According to Mäkisalo and Lehtinen, texts contain information at the linguistic and cognitive level. In their empirical approach, they formulate the so-called cognitive retention hypothesis, which assumes that in translation the information is retained more accurately at the cognitive level than at the linguistic level. This hypothesis put forward in 2014 based on a pilot study is validated again in 2017, reconfirming that a dissociation between linguistic and cognitive levels does exist in translation: "When describing translation from a source text (ST) to a target text (TT), it is possible to distinguish linguistic and cognitive levels, and it is the cognitive level (cognitive model of the state of affairs) that is primarily retained in translation" (Mäkisalo and Lehtinen, 2017: 49).

The notions of force dynamics and causation in language, constituting the last schematic system of Talmy, is studied by Mäkisalo and Lehtinen as well (2019). The 'force-dynamics system' relates to the way in which entities interact with respect to force. However, pervading language and discourse on several levels, it does not only apply to expressions in the physical domain, but it also plays an important role in expressions involving psychological and abstract forces. Force dynamics functions structurally in visual perception of events. However, because of its metaphorical extension from physical to abstract domains, it is also an important concept in accounting for modality in various languages. According to Mäkisalo and Lehtinen's (2019) results on the retention of force dynamics in translation, this cognitive construal tends to be retained more often than the linguistic realisation (the verb form), just like in the case of figure and ground, but there seem to be no strict distinction as to what should be considered as a retention of the verb form in constructions that carry force-dynamics patterns. In addition, since the hypothesis has so far been tested only on one language combination, it is not possible to know how it applies to other language pairs and translation directions.

The objective of the overall study is to contribute to the research initiated by Mäkisalo and Lehtinen to test their cognitive retention hypothesis against the following language combinations: English-Finnish, English-Polish, Finnish-English, Finnish-Polish, as well as Polish-English and Polish-Finnish. Each of the three languages is being examined both as a source language (SL) and as a target language (TL) to check the commonness of force dynamics in both original and translated language. The rationale behind these particular languages is the fact that they belong to different language families and/or branches (Germanic, Slavic, and Finnic). To gain more evidence on information retention at the cognitive level, the study strives to answer the following research questions: *What does the study of cognitive retention with force dynamics in focus tell us about cognitive processes related to translation?* and *In what way studying cognitive retention on various categories like force dynamics may contribute to the translation process research?* These two global questions are divided into the following subquestions: *Are force-dynamics structural patterns retained in translation more than linguistic patterns? How do force-dynamics patterns behave in translation?* and *What elements of force-dynamics structures are retained in translation?* As a side observation, based on comparative linguistics and motivated by the fact that the Talmyan framework is focused on English only, the study explores the following additional question: *What kind of differences are there between typologically different languages when it comes to expressing force dynamics in language?*

Since the work involves a multilingual context of translation, it helps to investigate the relationship between language and thinking from a more complex perspective than mainstream cognitive linguistics, which is typically placed in a monolingual context (here, particularly in the context of cognitive semantics and the theory of embodiment).[2] Moreover, the study aims to report on a

2 Many key publications in cognitive linguistics (e.g. Evans and Green, 2006; Kristiansen et al., 2006; Gibbs, 2008, and Dancygier, 2017) do not include translation in their

product-oriented study, dealing with two different modes of communication, i.e. literary and audiovisual translation materials. Thus, not only because of the multiple languages being used, but also because of the two channels being explored, the work contributes to the description of the human cognitive system from a wider perspective than most cognitive theories and can be used to develop these theories further. Moreover, the phenomenon of dissociation of cognitive and linguistic levels in translation constitutes an interesting tool that could be used in translation training. By providing necessary tools to describe translation from the cognitive perspective, the research also adds to the establishment of the immense impact of cognitive aspects on the process and product of translation, solving problems faced by translation trainers and scholars, as well as providing solutions in translation training.

To explore the nature of the interlingual retention of force-dynamics patterns, self-compiled, small-scale parallel literary and subtitling corpora has been used. The corpus work has resulted into six bi-directional sets of data with a bit over 3,000 ST entries (with around 500 entries for each language pair and direction): 1. English > Finnish/Polish literary data set; 2. Finnish > English/Polish literary data set; 3. Polish > English/Finnish literary data set; 4. English > Finnish/Polish audiovisual data set; 5. Finnish > English/Polish audiovisual data set; and 6. Polish > English/Finnish audiovisual data set. Having collected the necessary data, the quantitative analysis was conducted in the first place. Instances of TT retention and non-retention of the cognitive structure present in the STs are counted to verify the statistical significance of the numerical results obtained and to validate or discredit the adopted cognitive retention hypothesis. The later qualitative analysis consists of an extensive, intuitive, distributional linguistic analysis of cases in which force-dynamics elements are retained in translation and in which cognitive information is not transferred to the TT. In the former case, the idea is to see what happens to the cognitive structure when it is retained and how it is expressed in the TT. In the latter case, however, the objective is to check what happens in the TT when the cognitive structure is abandoned, getting an insight into possible reasons behind modification or non-retention.

What comes as no surprise, when collecting translation data, cases of various mistranslations were encountered. Some also appeared in the verb phrases of interest, affecting the identified force-dynamics structures undergoing analysis.

---

indexes. Croft and Cruse (2004) and Geeraerts and Cuyckens (2007) list translation in theirs, but the discussion of the phenomenon is sparse.

Soon, it was decided that mistranslations should be included in the analysis, but that they should be given a separate treatment. They deserve special considerations because they represent a separate cognitive phenomenon as such, but also because they have turned out to constitute a new concept in the cognitive retention theorisation, as mistranslations (i.e. situations in which some lexical and/or syntactic structures are retained, but the cognitive structure in question is changed) did not occupy any place in the analyses offered by the proponents of the cognitive retention hypothesis. Translations and real-life corpus data offer a great insight into this phenomenon because in monolingual material mistranslations are rare, if not non-existent, and very difficult, or even impossible, to detect.

Objectives

Mistranslations in this paper are mistakes and shortcomings in translating, i.e. faulty, incorrect or inadequate translations or wrong translation choices. Mistranslations that were found to have an impact on distorting the force-dynamics event structures included in the corpora have been judged to consist in overlooking details. The identified mistranslations do not distort the original substantially, and there is no intention to stigmatise the translators involved or to discredit their overall work. These minor translation shortcomings do not change the original plot in any major way that would mean putting the quality of the translations under question. The translations have been also positively received by their respective TL audiences. Generally speaking, to know about any translation mistakes requires text comparison. Most likely, audiences of translations have no way of even knowing that there are any mistakes, since the texts they read are usually still coherent.

The nature of the identified mistranslations has to do with cognitive economy, discussed in the context of translation by Hietaranta (2017). Cognitive economy constitutes the tendency for cognitive processes to minimise processing effort and necessary resources. Humans store facts as general default assumptions for concepts and have a separate memory only for exceptional cases in which the default options do not apply. Given such an experiential mode of information processing, it is self-explanatory that mistranslations might occur, among other scenarios, when the translator interprets the ST in some ways differently from the intentions of the author of the original. This paper aims at taking a detailed look at cases where the wrong translation choices were made and to offer cognition-based explanations (related to embodiment) as for how the miscommunications that occurred distorted the force-dynamics structures. As a scientific field and a profession, translation has always played a highly important role in bilingual or even multilingual transfer of culture and information by attempting to interpret concepts as faithfully and accurately as possible. Therefore, looking specifically at mistranslations in the context of cognitive description provides a specific perspective for translation training, rather than translation quality assessment. This is because translation evaluation depends on too many aspects, which do not necessarily have to be of linguistic or even cognitive nature.

To understand the way mistranslations can affect the retention of force dynamics in translation, it is important to elaborate a bit more on this schematic system itself. Different verbs, voice forms and argument-linking constructions reflect different conceptualisations of a force-dynamics event structure. Language expressions can be force-dynamically neutral (e.g. *the bowl was on the table* as a static situation, Croft and Cruse, 2004: 66) or exhibit a force-dynamic pattern (e.g. *the bowl stayed on the table* (ibid.) as a situation with a force-dynamics value of resisting the effects of an unspecified force-applying process). Two force-exerting elements are distinguished in a prototypical force-dynamic expression. There is no strength balance between the two elements; they are not equally strong. In the example above, the bowl is the agonist and the force making the bowl stay on the table is the antagonist.

Although it is mostly the case, force dynamics does not necessarily always remain stable in translation. A modification in force dynamics during translation process can be illustrated with the following example from Mäkisalo and Lehtinen's (2018 and 2019) data: *I can try to help you* in English translated into Finnish as *Antaisit minun yrittää auttaa* (back-translated as "You should let me try to help"). This example clearly shows that force dynamics present in the ST is retained, but, at the same time, also modified in the TT. There is some sort of psychological force that appears as an activity between the two participants. What is also happening is a change of force direction. The focus is shifted from the addresser (*I can try …*) to the addressee (*You should let me …*). There might also be cases when the force-dynamics of the original phrase is completely missing in the translation, as in the following example from the Finnish > English/Polish data set of the present study: *He wouldn't be able to find you* translated as *Hän ei tiedä, missä olet* ("He doesn't know where you are"). However, the lack of force dynamics in the translation does not mean it is incorrect. It does not only have a different linguistic realisation but is also differently conceptualised. Nevertheless, the message is similar, and when possibly put in a wider context, it could be communicatively the same. In this paper, the objective is to show what happens to the cognitive (covert) structure of translation in terms of the construal of force dynamics, as well as to its linguistic (overt) structure, in the least possible scenario in the context of professional translation. That is to say, when minor communication and comprehension errors, visible only when the two corresponding texts are juxtaposed for a detailed analysis, come into play.

Materials and methods

The overall project is empirical in nature, lending itself to corpus-based research combining quantitative and qualitative methods. The study follows a mixed-methods design in which quantitative and qualitative methods complement each other. This design is combined with a case-study research approach.[3] To explore the nature of the interlingual retention of force-dynamics patterns, small-scale parallel literary and subtitling data sets (corpora) were compiled. The STs consist of English, Finnish and Polish literary prose publications, and film materials (dialogues), and the TTs consist of their two official translations and subtitles, again, from each SL to the other two TLs.

The literary part of the corpora consists exclusively of published written material which falls under the category of literary fiction of prestigious status, i.e. bestsellers, sales of which are among the highest of their class, or works by well-known authors (assuming a top translation quality). To acquire materials in contemporary standard varieties of the selected languages, the texts were supposed to be originally written in and translated into the languages of the study in the 2000s. Although the study deals with products of subconscious conceptualisation processes that are understood as being more or less conceptually and cognitively universal, to assure theoretical significance, the texts were supposed to be professional translations prepared into the translator's first language and received by wide audiences.

Just as with literary texts, recent (released in the 2000s) and prestigious (awarded) film productions were selected. In the case of both literature and audiovisual materials, it was essential to select materials directly translated into desired languages without no (or at least very little) interference from any pivot language. This is also essential because the project deals with smaller, rarer, and less popular languages and translation pairs than the dominant English which often serves as a pivot language in the translation industry. This requirement was more easily met by the literary texts because translators of literature are usually

3 This paper presents only the case-study approach of the PhD dissertation, and no quantitative analysis is included.

publicly credited in the professional environment in all the countries in which the languages of the study are spoken.

Due to space constraints, only Finnish literary ST examples and their respective TTs in English and Polish are brought into focus in this paper. This is because relatively more mistranslations were found in literature in these particular language combinations. The reason might be the exotic status of the Finnish language. It is not a popular foreign language to study in general, with limited learning and teaching resources available, and translation training offered for this language outside Finland is also rarely available.

The literary examples discussed for the purpose of this paper come from the 2008 award-winning novel, *Puhdistus*, by Sofi Oksanen, a Finnish novelist and playwright of Estonian origin on her mother's side. Her overall literary work is widely recognised, with her novels translated into more than 40 languages. *Puhdistus*, set in Estonia and originally conceived as a play, is a story of two women, Aliide and Zara, connected by blood relationship, who are forced to confront their own dark pasts of collusion and resistance, as well as of rape and sexual slavery, set against the backdrop of the occupation of Estonia by the Soviet Union. The book was translated into English (*Purge*) and Polish (*Oczyszczenie*) in 2010 by acclaimed literary translators, Lola Rogers and Sebastian Musielak respectively, both former translation interns at FILI Finnish Literature Exchange in Helsinki.

The paper presents two representative cases of mistranslations: one leading to the original force dynamics not being retained in the translation, and one leading to a modification of the force-dynamics structure. Other mistranslations identified in the corpus are in fact of similar nature. Mistranslations outside the studied phrases and verb forms are not considered and might have been even unnoticed during data elicitation and limitation. To understand the non-retention and modification of force dynamics in the presented examples, it is essential to define what makes force dynamics retained and what procedures can cause it modification or loss. Basic elements used to represent force-dynamics patterns are presented in Table 1 below. Any force-dynamics expression needs the two already mentioned force entities of different strength intensity (balance of strength). The agonist is in focus of a force-dynamics expression, and it can have a tendency either toward action or toward rest (intrinsic force tendency). In its interaction with the antagonist, the agonist either keeps its tendency or is forced to change it to the opposing one (resultant).

Table 1: The Talmyan force-dynamics diagrammatic system (adapted from Talmy, 2000)

FORCE ENTITIES		**INTRINSIC FORCE TENDENCY**	
Agonist (Ago):	◯	toward action:	›
Antagonist (Ant):	⊐	toward rest:	•
BALANCE OF STRENGTH		**RESULTANT**	
stronger entity:	+	action:	——›——
weaker entity:	–	rest:	——•——

The theorisation of force dynamics targets verbs and verb phrases that express force-dynamics relationships. Linguistic features of the verb complex constitute the surface (overt) realisations of the cognitive (covert) structure of force dynamics. When it comes to the degree of retention of linguistic structures (encompassing syntax and lexis) and cognitive structures in translation, four categories can be distinguished:

1. both the linguistic structure and the cognitive structure are retained;
2. both the linguistic structure and the cognitive structure are changed;
3. the linguistic structure is changed, but the cognitive structure is retained; and
4. the linguistic structure is retained, but the cognitive structure is changed.

The last category concerns cases of mistranslations, and particular mechanisms connected to this phenomenon in the context of cognitive retention will be shown later in the following section dedicated to the discussion of the selected cases. However, to see first how force dynamics behaves in translation according to the other three categories, i.e. when texts are translated without comprehension errors, the easiest is to see it based on specific examples. The example below (1) shows a sentence from the Finnish ST translated into both English (TT1) and Polish (TT2). Both Finnish and Polish are back-translated (BT for back translation), observing the English language rules as much as possible, and glossed in as much detail as necessary to demonstrate the structural (overt) differences between the three languages. Both marked and unmarked (basic forms) nominal and verbal classes are indicated in the glossing annotation. Markings are attached to their items with hyphens (-), and different markings attached to the same item are separated with dots (.). Neither stem forms nor morphemes are marked in the glossing annotation. The list of glossing abbreviations is to be found at the end of this paper.

(1)

ST: Aliide rapsutti kultahammastaan, hampaiden väliin *oli jäänyt* jotain. (*Puhdistus*, 14)

Aliide rapsutti kulta-hammasta-an,

Aliide-PN.NOM.SG scratch-V.PAST.ACT.3SG gold-N.NOM.SG-tooth-N.PTV.SG-her-PX.3SG

hampaiden väliin

tooth-N.GEN.PL gap-N.ILL.SG

oli *jäänyt* jotain.

be-V.PAST.ACT.3SG *remain*-PAST.ACT.PCP.SG something-NDEF.PRON.PTV.SG

BT: Aliide scratched her golden tooth, something *had remained* between the teeth. (my translation)

TT1: She scratched at her gold tooth, … – there *was* something *stuck* there … (*Purge*, 7)

TT2: Potarła swój złoty ząb, coś jej *weszło* w szparę. (*Oczyszczenie*, 13)

Potarła swój

Rub-V.PAST.ACT.PFV.3SG.FEM own-REFL.POSS.PRON.ACC.SG.MSC

złoty ząb,

golden-ADJ.ACC.SG.MSC tooth-N.ACC.SG.MSC

coś jej *weszło*

something-NDEF.PRON.NOM.SG.NEUT she-PERS.PRON.DAT.SG.FEM *enter*-V.PAST.ACT.PFV.3SG.NEUT

w szparę.

in-PREP crack-N.ACC.SG.FEM

BT: She rubbed her golden tooth, something entered into the crack. (my translation)

Figure 1 shows a force-dynamics diagram for the Finnish ST described in (1). The food is conceptualised and linguistically expressed as a weaker agonist with force tendency towards action made by a stronger antagonist to rest. It is important to emphasise at this stage that force dynamics reflected in language represents human conceptualisation of force and causation and does not describe the actual state of affairs. According to Talmy (2000), conceptual models embedded within linguistic organisation are strikingly similar to those evident in our naïve world conceptions (naïve physics). We all know that no food stuck between our teeth is ever trying to get out of its trap on its own, and that our teeth are neither consciously nor unconsciously holding anything back. In the very sentence, the antagonist opposing the agonist is actually unknown. In reality, we know that teeth often stand so close to each other that it is simply difficult to remove some food from between them. Just because it says the food is stuck between the teeth, it does not mean the teeth are the opposing force. It is unknown. Again, in real life it is very unlikely to even assume that something or someone would place any food between the teeth on purpose, so this distinction between conceptualisation and world knowledge is crucial to consider.

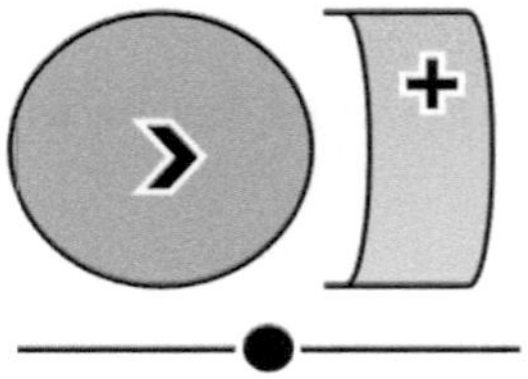

Figure 1: "..., hampaiden väliin *oli jäänyt* jotain" [..., something *had remained* between the teeth]

Despite major differences in its linguistic realisation, the English translation contains exactly the same force-dynamics scenario and can be represented by exactly the same force-dynamics diagram, as in Figure 1 above. The linguistic differences of the italicised verb forms, i.e. the use of passive voice in the translation as opposed to active voice in the original (syntax), as well as different word choices (lexis) when comparing the two, do not affect the force-dynamics patterns of the utterance. The English translation is a clear example of the third category listed above: the linguistic structure is changed, but the cognitive structure is retained.

When we look at the Polish translation, however, we see that these patterns disappear. The something does not have any force opposing it, as it makes its way into the crack between the tooth on its own, again as per mere conceptualisation. Since there is no opposing force implied, this scenario cannot be represented with a force-dynamics diagram. Here, it is important to mention that the lack of force-dynamics patterns of the original does not make the Polish translation invalid or incorrect. Conceptualising food as something that can literally (thus, linguistically) stay or get stuck between the teeth is not common. However, personifying food as something that can make its entry between the teeth is very widespread. The Polish translation falls under the second category, in which both the linguistic structure and the cognitive structure are changed.

Case discussion

This section is meant to discuss similar examples, with the difference that it treats the mistranslations occurring in the translations of phrases containing force-dynamics patterns. The example in (2) presents an English TT of a sentence in Finnish, in which the mistranslation of the verb form does not allow for the retention of some of its force-dynamics characteristics, whereas the example in (3) shows a modification of the force-dynamics scenario of the original string, introduced by a mistranslation of the agonist entity. Note that the examples include more than just one element with force dynamics. Only the verb strings or verb phrases in focus (mistranslations) are considered and stand in italics.

(2)

ST: Sille pitäisikin soittaa ja sanoa, että *säätäisivät* sellaisen lain, että maalta ei pääsisi lähtemään ihan noin vain. (*Puhdistus*, 28)

Sille	pitäisi-kin	soittaa	ja	sanoa,
It-PERS.PRON.ALL	should-V. COND.ACT.3SG-also-CL	call-V.1INF	and-CONJ	say-V.1INF

että	*säätäisivät*	sellaisen	lain,
that-CONJ	*enact*-V.COND.ACT.3PL	such-ADJ.GEN.SG	law-N.GEN.SG

että	maalta	ei	pääsisi
that-CONJ	countryside-N.ABL.SG	no-NE.G.PTCL.3SG	get-V.COND.ACT.3SG

lähtemään	ihan	noin	vain.
leave-V.3INF	quite-ADV	SO-ADV	just-ADV

BT: He should be called and told that they *should pass* such a law that people would not get to leave the countryside just so. (my translation)

TT: Someone should call them and tell them that they *passed* a law that says you cannot just up and leave the countryside. (*Purge*, 21)

The broader context of the utterance includes the son of a family living in the same village as one of the novel's protagonists. The son got interested in politics and settled in Tallinn, leaving the village and his family behind. It is suggested that he should be persuaded to make the authorities he works for pass a countryside-friendlier law. In the original, the law does not exist yet. In the force-dynamics context, a stronger, unknown antagonist (though obviously the son) makes a weaker agonist (the authorities), with an intrinsic tendency towards rest, to actually act (see Figure 2 on the next page). However, the English translation suggests that the law has been passed already. The lexical meaning of the verb *säätää* is present in the translation, but its essential grammatical element *-isi-* was overlooked. This small element introduces conditional mood to the verb. Finnish often uses conditional forms to render polite modality.

What is also worth noting is that it is not clear enough who *they* in the English actually are. What is meant might be that the authorities should be contacted directly, not through the son. Another possibility is that these are the parents of the son in question or maybe all other young people who left the village for the bigger world. The exact actors in the scene were not identified correctly. The Finnish passage is written in a spoken language in which the pronoun *se* 'it' commonly refers to people, not only objects, so the *se* actually stands for the son. It could be that this has not been recognised by the translator, and this confusion led to a misleading assumption of what the correct verb form is.

This mistranslation does not allow for the modality to be retained. It is, however, interesting to notice, that the translation does introduce another force-dynamics scenario because the verb *säätää* has force dynamics embedded in its meaning by default. If the authorities pass a law, they cause it to exist, and, although the scenario's diagram would look exactly the same, it is the law that becomes the new agonist in the translation. As this is rather a lexical pattern, and the structural grammatical one is missing, it is considered that the force dynamics is not retained in this translation.

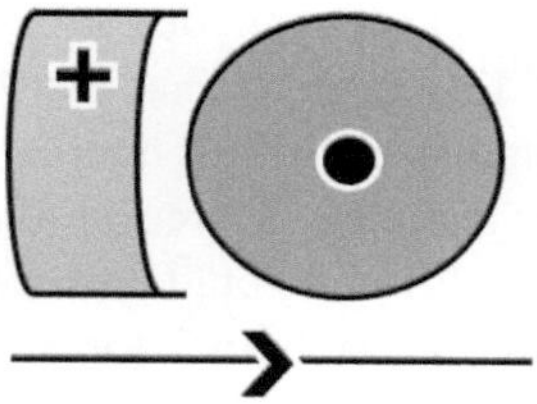

Figure 2: "(…), että *säätäisivät* sellaisen lain, (…)" [(…) that they *should pass* such a law (…)] "(…), *siirsi kangen* ulko-oven edestä pois, (…)" [(…), *moved the latch* out of the front door, (…)]

Figure 2 above constitutes the diagram for the example in (3) as well. It contains a stronger antagonist (a human character in the plot) that causes a weaker agonist (a bar) with (cognitively not logically perceived) force tendency towards rest to move.

The problem with this translation starts with the Finnish word (and agonist) *kanki* (here, a self-standing iron bar, used as a lever),[4] which in the genitive case takes the form *kangen*. Possibly because of its standing in the genitive case, it could have been taken for another word: *kangas* (genitive *kankaan*). *Kangas* means material or cloth, which somehow explains why in the translation we read about a curtain. Apart from this trap when word forms look similar to other words, *kangas* is a more frequently occurring word than *kanki*, and this makes even more sense when we consider that it is a non-native speaker of Finnish who is decoding Finnish for translation purposes. The word itself is also very rare in everyday language of modern Finland. In addition, there is a conceptual trap as well. In many Polish countryside households, there is a curtain often hanging right behind the entrance door, and most likely this is nothing exclusively specific to Polish villages. The curtain serves to protect the household from insects flying

4 Note that in fact, this Finnish word is mistranslated in both English (*curtain*) and Polish (*kotara*) versions. This might suggest that one of the translations could affect the other one, and probably a likely scenario is that it was English affecting Polish. However, both translations were prepared in the same year, and the scenario has not been verified in any way. Thus, the same mistranslation might also be a mere coincidence. In the project, it has been attempted to assure the directedness of translation to its possible maximum by selecting prestigious novels translated by professionals. Nevertheless, lack of influences of other translations cannot be fully assured, and this is a topic for another study.

into the house when the door is kept open for a longer while, for example during summer's warmer weather. This suggests that the Polish translator took it for granted that it must be a curtain because he is familiar with the concept described above, and, in fact, so is his audience. Moreover, the use of a bar in front of a door is culture-specific, so omitting it could have been a conscious procedure. It is a custom in Finland, and probably in Estonia, but it is not one in Poland. Therefore, the translation still looks credible with the curtain instead of the bar.

(3)

ST: Hän pisti sen vielä hetkeksi nojaamaan seinään, silotteli hiuksensa, kiinnitti hiusneulan paremmin, vuoli otsahiukset tarkasti korvien taakse, tarttui viikatteeseen uudelleen, *siirsi kangen* ulko-oven edestä pois, avasi lukon ja astui pihalle. (*Puhdistus*, 15)

Hän pisti sen vielä hetkeksi

She-PERS.PRON.NOM put-V.PAST.3SG it-DEF.PRON.GEN.SG still-ADV moment-N.TRANSL

nojaamaan seinään,

lean-V.3INF wall-N.INE.3SG

silotteli hiukse-nsa,

smooth-V.PAST.ACT.3SG hair-GEN.SG-her-PX.3SG

kiinnitti hius-neulan paremmin,

fasten-V.PAST.ACT.3SG hair-N.NOM.SG-needle-N.GEN.SG well-ADV.CMPR

vuoli otsa-hiukset tarkasti korvien taakse,

move-V.PAST.ACT.3SG forehead-N.NOM.SG-hair-N.ACC.PL accurately-ADV ear-N.GEN.PL behind-ADV

tarttui viikatteeseen uudelleen,

grab-V.PAST.ACT.3SG scythe-N.INE.SG again-ADV

siirsi *kangen* ulkooven edestä pois

move-V.PAST.ACT.3SG *bar*-N.GEN.SG outside-ADJ-door-N.GEN.SG from-POST.ELA away-ADV

avasi lukon ja astui pihalle.

open- V.PAST.ACT.3SG lock-N.GEN.SG and-CNJ step-V.PAST.3SG yard-N.ALL.SG

BT: She put it again against the wall for a moment, smoothed her hair, fixed the hairpin better, pulled her fringe finely behind her ears, grabbed the scythe again, *moved the bar* off the front door, opened the lock and stepped into the yard. (my translation)

TT: Oparła ją jeszcze o ścianę, przygładziła włosy, poprawiła wsuwkę, założyła luźne kosmyki starannie za uszy, po czym ujęła kosę w garść, *odsunęła kotarę*, przekręciła zamek drzwi wejściowych i wyszła na podwórze. (*Oczyszczenie*, 13)

Oparła ją jeszcze o ścianę,

Lean-V.PAST.ACT.PFV.3SG.FEM she-DEF.PRON.ACC.3SG.FEM still-PTCL against-PREP wall-N.ACC.SG.FEM

przygładziła włosy,

smooth-V.PAST.ACT.PFV.3SG.FEM hair-N.ACC.PL.NMSC

poprawiła wsuwkę,

adjust-V.PAST.ACT.PFV.3SG.FEM hairgrip-N.ACC.SG.FEM

założyła luźne kosmyki

put-V.PAST.ACT.PFV.3SG.FEM loose-ADJ.ACC.PL.NMSC strand-N.ACC.PL.NMSC

starannie za uszy,

carefully-ADV behind-PREP ear-N.ACC.PL.NMSC

po czym

after-PREP what-REL.PRON.LOC.SG

ujęła kosę w garść,

grab-V.PAST.ACT.PFV.3SG.FEM scythe-N.ACC.SG.FEM in-PREP handful-N.ACC.SG.FEM

odsunęła kotarę,

shift-V.PAST.ACT.PFV.3SG.FEM curtain-N.ACC.SG.FEM

przekręciła zamek drzwi wejściowych

turn-V.PAST.ACT.PFV.3SG.FEM lock-N.ACC.SG.MASC door-N.GEN.PL.NMSC front-ADJ.GEN.PL.NMSC

i wyszła na podwórze.

and-CNJ exit-V.PAST.ACT.PFV.3SG.FEM on-PREP yard-N.ACC.SG.NEUT

BT: She leaned it against the wall again, smoothed her hair, adjusted the hairgrip, put loose strands neatly behind her ears, then took the scythe in her hand, *pulled the curtain away*, turned the lock of the entrance door and went out into the yard. (my translation)

From the perspective the force-dynamics description, the Polish translation can be assigned the same diagram as in Figure 2. However, the proposed retention model assumes that the agonists and antagonists in both original and translated scenarios should match. Since the translation of the verb string keeps its force-dynamics patterns, but the agonist is changed, it is considered that the force dynamics is not fully lost in the scenario, but modified instead.

Conclusion

When studying cognitive retention in translation, mistranslations need to be treated separately from other analysed samples. In fact, mistranslations deserve a separate treatment no matter what cognitive aspect of translation is under study because they present a cognitive phenomenon in its own right. Force dynamics might be modified or not retained in the TT because the ST evoked conceptualisations in the head of the translator that do not match the conceptualisations originally meant by the author.

Translation is communication. As seen from the analysis of the translation product above, the translation process opens interesting possibilities to account for faulty translations from various cognitive retention perspectives. Let us take Hejwowski's (2004) model of cognitive and communicative translation process as an example. In this process, the translator activates his or her knowledge about the topic of the original, trying to reconstruct the cognitive base of the author and assessing how the text would be understood by its S: recipients. Having established his or her own interpretation of the ST, the translator builds the TT with its TL recipients in mind. Knowledge about the two audiences guides the translator into particular translation choices. However, the choices might be misled by various factors as the interpretation of the peculiarities of the two worlds is cognitively automated and subconscious.

The mistranslation cases presented in this paper support the claim that the translation process involves a re-conceptualisation of a SL message into a TL message (Lewandowska-Tomaszczyk, 2010). Furthermore, translation is also proven to be not only about context and semantics as such, but about references to the real world, about situatedness, i.e. dependence of meaning, that is based on knowledge, beliefs, attitudes, and spatiotemporal location (Croft and Cruse, 2004). Situatedness is about embodiment and the real world being perceived and interpreted by language users (here, translators who are cognisers), and it is also dependent on their own personal perspectives.

Cognitive economy plays an important explanatory role in miscommunication in translation. As the two mistranslations analysed in this paper show, cognitive economy seems to be occasionally manifested during translation as a subconscious decision of the translator to switch to experiential information processing (Hietaranta, 2017). Such information processing is not analytical, but rather based on individual experiences, making the translator susceptible to overlooking details that eventually leads to inadequate translations.

As the cognitive description of translation based on various semantic structures is meant to constitute a useful tool for translation training, looking at force dynamics and other Talmyan (2000) cognitive construals is a worthy endeavour for the sake of an intellectual exercise. Although in the context of mistranslations the presented cognitive tool might seem to provide a specific perspective for translation quality assessment as well, it is important to emphasise that retaining the ST cognitive structures in the TT is far from enough for translation quality to be considered acceptable. It is difficult to establish how cognitive retention could possibly interact with many other aspects of translation quality, not necessarily linguistic or cognitive in nature. After all, the faulty translations presented in this paper resulted from complex re-conceptualisations, and the distortions in the force-dynamics structures were only the product of these re-conceptualisation processes. Still, in the context of translation training, the tool can help to describe translation errors more precisely, and this description is better grounded than relying on mere intuition.

List of glossing abbreviations

ABL	ablative case
ACC	accusative case
ACT	active voice
ADJ	adjective
ADV	adverb
ALL	allative case
CL	clitic
CMPR	comparative
COND	conditional mood
CONJ	conjunction
DAT	dative case
DEF	definite
DET	determiner
ELA	elative case
FEM	feminine gender
GEN	genitive case
ILL	illative case
INE	inessive case
1INF	1st infinitive verb form

3INF	3rd infinitive verb form
LOC	locative case
MSC	masculine gender
N	noun
NDEF	indefinite
NEG	negation
NEUT	neutral gender
NMSC	non-masculine gender
NOM	nominative case
PAST	past tense
PERS	personal
PL	plural
3PL	3rd person plural person marking
POST	postposition
PRON	pronoun
PTCL	particle
PTV	partitive case
PX	possessive suffix
REL	relative
REFL	reflexive
SG	singular
3SG	3rd person singular person marking
TRANSL	translative case
V	verb

References

Primary sources

Oksanen, S. (2008). *Puhdistus*. WSOY.

Oksanen, S. (2010). *Oczyszczenie* (S. Musielak, Trans.). Świat Książki.

Oksanen, S. (2010) *Purge* (L. Rogers, Trans). Black Cat.

Secondary sources

Chesterman, A. (2016). *Memes of Translation: The Spread of Ideas in Translation Theory*. John Benjamins.

Clark, A. (2014). *Mindware: An Introduction to the Philosophy of Cognitive Science*. Oxford University Press.

Croft, W., & Cruse, A. (2004). *Cognitive Linguistics*. Cambridge University Press.

Dancygier, B. (Ed.). (2017). *The Cambridge Handbook of Cognitive Linguistics*. Cambridge University Press.

Evans, V., & Green, M. (2006). *Cognitive Linguistics: An Introduction*. Edinburgh University Press.

Geeraerts, D., & Cuyckens, H. (Eds.). (2007). *The Oxford Handbook of Cognitive Linguistics*. Oxford University Press.

Gibbs, R. W. (Ed.). (2006). *The Cambridge Handbook of Metaphor and Thought*. Cambridge University Press.

Hejwowski, K. (2004). *Kognitywno-komunikacyjna teoria przekładu* [The cognitive and communicative theory of translation]. Wydawnictwo Naukowe PWN.

Hietaranta, P. (2017). 'Cognitive economy and mental worlds: Accounting for translation mistakes and other communication errors.' In S. Hansen-Shirra, O. Czulo, & S. Hofmann (Eds.), *Empirical Modelling of Translation and Interpreting* (441–463). Language Science Press.

Hubscher-Davidson, S. (2015). 'The role of intuition in the translation process: A case study.' In M. Ehrensberger-Dow, B. Englund Dimitrova, S. Hubscher-Davidson, & U. Norberg (Eds.), *Describing Cognitive Processes in Translation: Acts and Events* (63–84). John Benjamins.

Kristiansen, G., Archard, M., Dirven, R., & Ruiz de Mendoza Ibáñez, F. J. (Eds.). (2006). *Cognitive Linguistics: Current Applications and Future Perspectives*. Berlin / New York, NY: Mouton de Gruyter.

Lewandowska-Tomaszczyk, B. (2010). 'Re-conceptualization and the emergence of discourse-meaning as a theory of translation.' In Barbara Lewandowska-Tomaszczyk, and Marcel Thelen (Eds.), *Meaning in Translation* (105–148). Peter Lang.

Mäkisalo, J., & Lehtinen, M. (2014). 'Dissociation of linguistic and cognitive description in translation: The cognitive figure-ground alignment.' In H. Paulasto, H. Riionheimo, L. Meriläinen, & M. Kok (Eds.), *Language Contacts at the Crossroads of Disciplines* (191–211). Cambridge Scholars.

Mäkisalo, J., & Lehtinen, M. (2017). 'Changes in figure-ground alignment in translation: Condensing information in subtitling.' In M. Luodonpää-Manni, E. Penttilä, & J. Viimaranta (Eds.), *Empirical approaches to cognitive linguistics: Analysing Real-Life Data* (49–74). Cambridge Scholars.

Mäkisalo, J., & Lehtinen, M. (2019). 'Voimadynamiikan kognitiivinen rakenne ja sen säilyminen käännettäessä' [The cognitive structure of force dynamics and its retention in translation], in *MikaEL*, 12, 63–74.

Rojo, A., & Ibarretxe-Antuñano, I. (Eds.). (2013). *Cognitive Linguistics and Translation: Advances in Some Theoretical Models of Application*. Mouton de Gruyter.

Talmy, L. (2000). *Toward a Cognitive Semantics: Vol. 1. Concept Structuring Systems*. MIT Press.

Wang, B. (2015). 'Embodied cognition anchors translating.' In *Linguistics and Literature Studies, 3*(2), 58–65.

Zlatev, J. (2005). 'What's in a schema? Bodily mimesis and the grounding of language.' In Beate Hampe and Joseph E. Grady (Eds.), *From Perception to Meaning: Image Schemas in Cognitive Linguistics*. (313–342). Mouton de Gruyter..

Ralph Krüger

TH Köln (University of Applied Sciences)

Contextual Meaning in Neural Machine Translation

Abstract: Against the backdrop of the current debate on (super)human performance of neural machine translation, this paper discusses the extent to which this machine translation architecture is able to draw on and incorporate contextual meaning when translating, which is assumed to be an important added value of competent human translators. First of all, the paper takes a cognitive linguistic perspective and investigates how context and (contextual) meaning in human translation can be modelled. Then, the paper illustrates how neural machine translation processes linguistic meaning and to what extent contextual information are considered in this process. In the next step, the actual performance of the generic neural machine translation system DeepL with regard to encoding contextually available meaning in its translation output is discussed. In this context, the paper analyses several English-German translation examples where DeepL either performed an explicitation shift in translation or failed to perform such a shift when a human translator of the same text did so. Finally, the paper discusses current research on document-level machine translation and multimodal machine translation, which aims to extend the range of contextual information which neural machine translation systems can take into account.

Keywords: Neural machine translation, human translation, contextual meaning, document-level machine translation, multimodal machine translation

1. Introduction

Recently, developers in the field of neural machine translation (NMT) have made increasingly strong claims concerning the level of quality achieved by their machine translation (MT) systems. For example, in 2018, a research team at Microsoft stated that their latest NMT system for the language combination English-Chinese had reached "a new state-of-the-art, and that the translation quality is at human parity when compared to professional human translations" (Hassan et al., 2018, 1). Two years later, another research team claimed that their CUBBIT system (Charles University Block-Backtranslation-Improved Transformer Translation) "significantly outperformed professional-agency English-to-Czech news translation in preserving text meaning" (Popel et al., 2020,

1), leading the authors to conclude that "human translation is not necessarily an upper bound of translation quality, which was a long-standing dogma in the field" (Popel et al., 2020, 10). These claims are far from uncontroversial and have been challenged by various papers (see, for example, Läubli et al., 2018, Toral et al., 2018, Läubli et al., 2020, Freitag et al., 2021), which highlight several structural shortcomings of the respective methodologies employed to measure MT quality. The present paper would like to contribute to the debate on (super) human performance of neural machine translation by discussing – both from a theoretical and a practical point of view – the role of contextual meaning in professional human translation (HT) and the extent to which current NMT systems are able to draw on and integrate such contextual meaning in their translation output. Incorporating such contextual meaning seems to be a tall order for NMT. However, there are two reasons which may warrant placing such high demands on this current MT paradigm: The first reason is that, as the quotes above show, more and more voices are emerging which claim that modern NMT systems are on par with or potentially superior to professional human translation. A technology receiving that much (premature?) praise should certainly also be measured according to performance criteria to be fulfilled by professional human translators, one of these criteria being the ability to draw on contextually available information in translation. Secondly, the significant increase in quality of NMT over its predecessor paradigms of rule-based machine translation (RBMT) and phrase-based statistical machine translation (PBSMT) is evident (see, for example, Jia et al., 2019, 60) and it is therefore hardly surprising that NMT has come to play an important role in the professional translation process (see, for example, ELIS, 2021). Consequently, it becomes more and more important to highlight the added value of professional human translators and the potential edge that human translators still have over machine translation. Ultimately, this somewhat unfortunate dichotomy of human vs. machine translation (which is, to some extent, fuelled by strong claims on MT performance such as those quoted above) should be abandoned in favour of a holistic *human-in-the-loop* (HITL) conceptualisation of the MT-assisted translation process (see, for example, Vashee, 2021). From such a HITL perspective, competent human translators work in tandem with high-performing MT systems in order to provide high-quality translation at a higher throughput than was previously possible. However, in order to move away from a human vs. machine translation dichotomy and to arrive at a sound HITL perspective, the relative strengths and weaknesses of both HT and MT should be outlined very clearly, so that the contributions of both 'actors' to the MT-assisted translation process are made transparent. The present paper intends to contribute to this endeavour.

2. Representation of Context and (Contextual) Meaning in Human Translation

Context is an inherently difficult concept to define. The reason may be that context is potentially unbounded, i.e., it is often difficult to predict which part of the world may become relevant for interpreting a particular text. Consequently, von Hahn (1998, 383, referring to Pinkal, 1985, 36, original quote in German) defines context as potentially 'the whole world relative to the speech event.' However, for analytical purposes, a distinction is often made between *discourse context*, *knowledge context* and *situational context*. According to Aschenberg (1999, 9) these contexts can be regarded as the three elementary context types necessary for the emergence of textual meaning. The discourse context is also known as *co-text* (Catford, 1965) and refers to the textual environment of a given linguistic unit.[1] The knowledge context refers to the discourse participants' knowledge available to them when interpreting a specific text. The intersection of the knowledge contexts of the author(s) and the reader(s) of a particular text could be conceptualised as the *common ground* (Clark, 1996) of the discourse participants. Finally, the situational context is often understood in its functional linguistic triad consisting of *field* (subject matter of the text), *tenor* (relationship between discourse participants) and *mode* (channel of communication) (Halliday, 1985). For the purpose of this paper, the situational context is understood in the wider sense of *situated translation* (Risku, 2004), covering a wide range of artefacts and factors (such as translation briefs, client instructions, standards, cooperation partners, context of source text production and target text production, etc.) that could potentially influence a translator's translational action when working on a specific text.[2]

How the representation of context and (contextual) meaning is to be described depends primarily on the theoretical framework underpinning this effort. This paper draws on concepts from cognitive linguistics (e.g., Langacker, 1987, 2008), a usage-based linguistic theory which has proven useful for modelling knowledge organisation and representation in translation (see, for example, Krüger, 2015). Unlike other linguistic theories, cognitive linguistics makes no principled distinction between linguistic/semantic/dictionary meaning (*essentialia* in Aristotle's terms) and extra-linguistic/pragmatic/encyclopaedic

1 In MT research, this discourse context/co-text is often called *document(-level) context* (see section 5.1 below).

2 For a more detailed discussion of discourse context, knowledge context and situational context from a translation studies perspective, see Krüger (2015: 189–199). For a more detailed discussion of situational factors with relevance to specialised translation, see, for example, Krüger (2016).

meaning (*accidentialia*) (see, for example, Marmaridou, 2000: 45). Cognitive linguistics claims that all meaning is encyclopaedic in nature and that lexical units are merely "partial and impoverished prompts upon which highly complex cognitive processes work giving rise to rich and detailed conceptualisation" (Evans & Green, 2006: 368). According to *frame semantics* (Fillmore, 1982), a well-known cognitive semantic theory belonging to the overall framework of cognitive linguistics, the potentially vast amount of encyclopaedic meaning associated with a given linguistic unit is structured and organised in the form of *frames*. These are understood as "any system of concepts related in such a way that to understand any of them you have to understand the whole structure in which it fits" (Fillmore, 1982: 111). A more detailed definition by Busse (2009: 85) stipulates that a frame is an abstract, complex structure of knowledge elements, which is activated by linguistic expressions and/or chains of expressions, the result of this process being linguistic meanings. These linguistic meanings consist of a network of knowledge elements, which is inferred in the process of language comprehension (or, in the present case, translation) by drawing on background knowledge. A frame could be depicted as shown in figure 1 below.

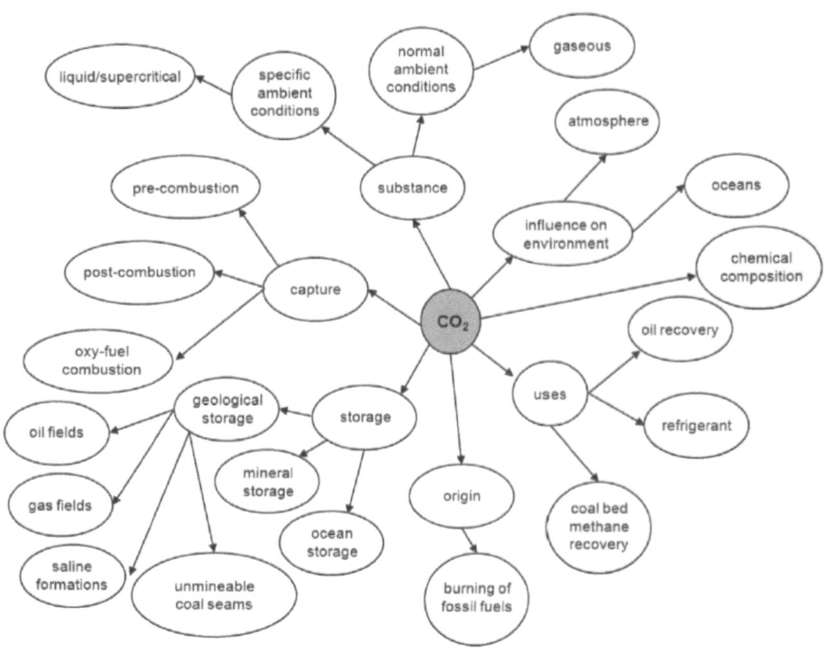

Figure 1: A graphical depiction of the CO_2 frame (figure taken from Krüger, 2016, 305)

The representation of the CO_2 frame in figure 1 is based on Busse (2012: 744). It should be pointed out that this frame captures merely a small subset of the whole body of encyclopaedic knowledge which may be relevant for understanding the concept of CO_2 in a given context. One of the central tenets of frame semantics and other cognitive semantic theories is that the encyclopaedic knowledge associated with a given lexical concept is potentially unlimited (see, for example, Langacker, 2008: 47; Busse, 2012: 611; and the discussion at the beginning of this section). At the same time, a distinction should be made between *general social* and *individual cognitive* frames (Busse, 2012: 563, 619). The frame depicted here is a social construct, i.e., an idealised theoretical frame in which the domain knowledge of a certain community (e.g., climate scientists) concerning a particular concept is organised. Individual cognitive frames such as those stored in a translator's long-term memory will probably be less specified and exhibit certain knowledge gaps, which may be filled by using external artefacts such as reference books, translation memories or terminology databases.

From a frame-semantic perspective, contextual meaning would then be the saliency of a given aspect of encyclopaedic meaning in a specific usage context, saliency here being understood as the "likelihood of activation" (Langacker, 2008, 57) of such linguistic meaning in a given context. For example, in a sentence such as *CO_2 is generated from a primary fossil fuel*, the *origin* dimension of the CO_2 frame will be activated (where the encyclopaedic information that CO_2 is generated by *burning* a primary fossil fuel will be particularly salient), whereas a sentence such as *CO_2 emissions into the atmosphere have to be reduced* will highlight the influence of CO_2 on the environment, particularly on earth's atmosphere. A more detailed discussion of how cognitive linguistics and frame semantics can be used to model knowledge organisation and representation and to explain textual and contextual aspects of specialised translation can be found in Krüger (2015).

3. Representation of Context and (Contextual) Meaning in Neural Machine Translation

Having illustrated how aspects of context and (contextual) meaning in human translation can be modelled using the framework of cognitive linguistics, the paper will now investigate how neural machine translation processes linguistic meaning and to which extent NMT draws on contextual information in doing so. First, some sign-theoretic considerations. While, according to cognitive linguistics, human language is based on symbols consisting of form-meaning pairings[3] (Langacker, 1987, 76), the basic building blocks of 'meaning' processed by NMT systems are sub-symbolic in nature (Carl, 2020, 505). These building blocks are so-called *word embeddings* (Mikolov et al., 2013). Word embeddings are high-dimensional vector representations of words, which are mapped to (or *embedded* in) a high-dimensional vector space. Figure 2 below depicts the process of converting natural-language words into high-dimensional word vectors/embeddings.

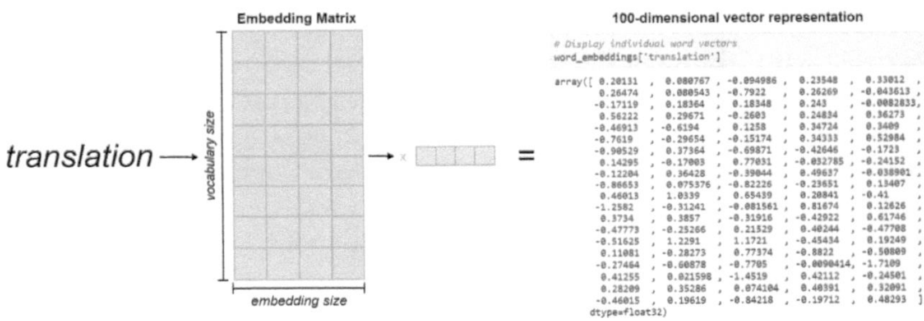

Figure 2: Converting natural-language words into word embeddings (figure adapted from Krüger, 2021b, 286)

Before natural-language words are fed into an NMT system for further processing, a so-called embedding matrix looks up the word embeddings of these words. An embedding matrix is the hidden layer of a shallow neural network trained specifically for converting words into word embeddings. The size of this matrix is defined by the size of the training vocabulary times the embedding size. The embedding size is a configurable hyperparameter, which equals the dimensionality of the word embeddings. In figure 2 above, the embedding size is 100, resulting in a 100-dimensional vector representation of the word *translation*.[4] As can be seen on the right side of figure 2, these 100

3 These symbolic form-meaning pairings propagated by cognitive linguistics are not unlike the linguistic sign as envisaged by Saussurean structural linguistics. For a detailed discussion of the differences between the linguistic sign as conceptualised by de Saussure and the symbolic form-meaning pairings as conceptualised by cognitive linguistics, see Taylor (2002, 38 ff.).

4 The word embedding depicted in figure 2 was calculated using the *glove-wiki-gigaword-100* model made available as part of the *Gensim* library. *Glove-wiki-gigaword-100* is an embedding model with a vocabulary size of 400,000 words and an embedding size/

vector dimensions are simply 100 floating-point numbers. Intuitively, these 100 numerical values can be interpreted as 100 'meaning components' of the word *translation.*[5] If two words are semantically similar, the vector representations of these words will share many similar dimensions, as depicted in figure 3 below.

```
# Create the visual representations
plt.figure(figsize=(30,3))
sns.heatmap([word_embeddings["father"], word_embeddings["son"], word_embeddings["translation"]], xticklabels=True, yticklabels=True, cbar=True,
            vmin=-1, vmax=1, linewidths=0.7)
plt.show()
```

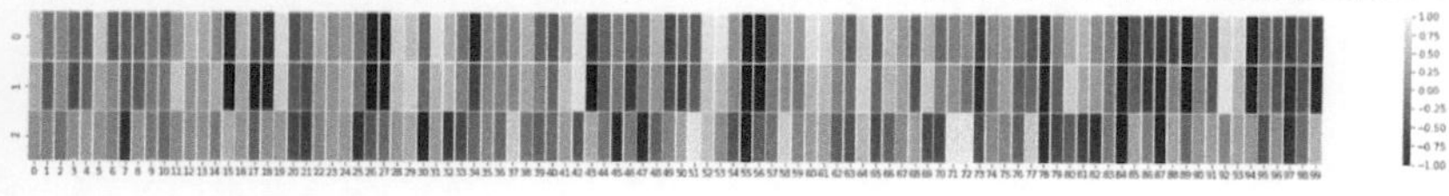

Figure 3: Colour-coded vector dimensions of the words *father*, *son* and *translation*

Figure 3 shows three lines of 100 vertical bars in different colours. The 100 bars in each line represent the 100 vector dimensions (i.e. 100 floating-point numbers) of the word vector of a particular word. The floating-point numbers were scaled to a range of -1 to 1, with the values close to -1 being coloured darkly and the values close to 1 being coloured lightly (see the colour scale at the right side of figure 3). As can be seen, the first two lines, representing the word vectors of the semantically similar words *father* and *son*, share many similarly coloured dimensions, while many dimensions of the vector representing the semantically dissimilar word *translation* (line 3) differ in colour from the dimensions in line 1 and 2. This serves to illustrate the basic principle of word embeddings: semantic similarity of the words represented by particular word vectors is expressed by similar numerical values of the individual dimensions of these word vectors.

vector dimensionality of 100 (for more information see Krüger, 2021a and Řehůřek, 2021). Current NMT systems based on the transformer architecture (Vaswani et al., 2017) use 512-dimensional embeddings.

5 However, the individual vector dimensions of a word embedding cannot be equated in any straightforward way with meaning components as postulated in structural linguistics. While, from a structural linguistic perspective, the meaning of the lexical unit *Man* could be decomposed into the meaning components *+Human*, *+Adult* and *+Male*, the individual vector dimensions of word embeddings elude such simple interpretations (Carl, 2020: 505). How word vectors and their individual dimensions are to be interpreted depends, among other things, on the rotation of the vector space these word vectors are embedded in (Park et al., 2017).

When converting natural-language words into word vectors, these vectors are embedded in a vector space with a dimensionality equal to the dimensionality of the word vectors (so, 100-dimensional word vectors will be embedded in a 100-dimensional vector space). In this vector space, semantic similarity between words will be expressed by spatial proximity of the vectors representing these words. This principle is illustrated in figure 4 below.

```
# Display word embeddings in two-dimensional space
display_tsne_reduction(word_embeddings, 'carbon_dioxide')
```

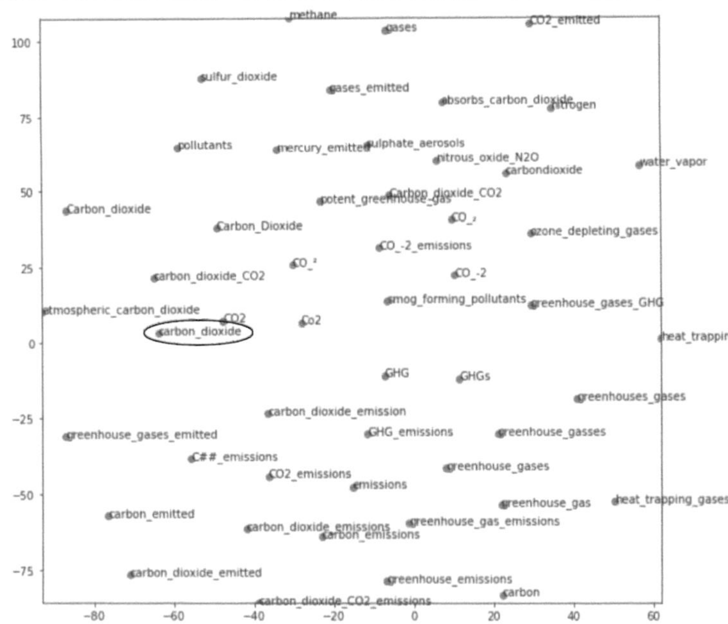

Figure 4: 2-dimensional vector space depicting the 50 words which exhibit the closest semantic similarity to the word *carbon dioxide*

Figure 4 shows the 50 words which exhibit the closest semantic similarity to the word *carbon dioxide*, represented in a 2-dimensional vector space. In order to allow for such 2-dimensional visualisations, the original high-dimensional (here, 100-dimensional) vector space was reduced to 2 dimensions using *t-SNE* (*t-distributed Stochastic Neighbour Embedding*, van der Maaten & Hinton, 2008), a specific technique for dimensionality reduction. As can be seen in figure 4, based on the underlying word embedding model, *carbon dioxide* exhibits close spatial proximity (and hence sematic similarity) to related concepts such as *pollutants*, *emissions*, *greenhouse gases*, etc.

When comparing the CO_2 frame depicted in figure 1 with the carbon dioxide vector space depicted in figure 4, it could be claimed that, while capturing semantic similarity between words, word embedding spaces exhibit less internal and external structure than frames. Word embedding spaces could therefore be broadly equated with concept *fields*,[6] whereas frames resemble more tightly structured concept *systems*,[7] where the nature of the relations between the individual frame concepts (such as the *origin* relation between CO_2 and *burning of fossil fuels*) are made more explicit.

As discussed above, natural-langue words are first converted into word embeddings and then fed into an NMT system for further processing. These original embeddings are decontextualised word embeddings, where one word form only has one vector representation regardless of how many meanings this word form may actually encode. For example, for the sentence *They arrived at the river bank and proceeded to rob the bank*, the word *bank* would have only one decontextualised word embedding. Within the NMT system, these decontextualised word embeddings are then processed by various self-attention layers, which establish the relations between the individual words of the input sequence (= source sentence) (represented by their decontextualised word embeddings) and compute a contextualised representation of the input sequence consisting of contextualised word embeddings. This process is depicted in figure 5 below.

6 According to ISO 1087 (2019: 4, italics removed), a concept field is an "unstructured set of concepts belonging to the same domain or subject."

7 According to ISO 1087 (2019: 6, italics removed), a concept system is a "set of concepts structured in one or more related domains according to the concept relations among its concepts."

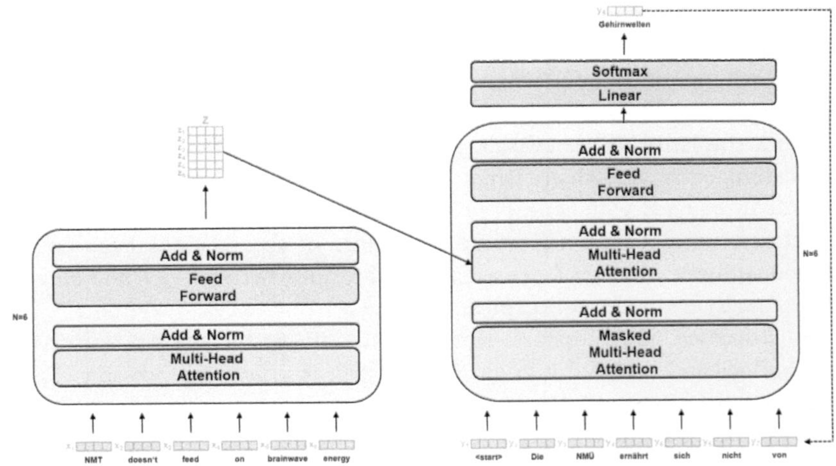

Figure 5: Going from decontextualised to contextualised word embeddings in a transformer-based NMT architecture (figure taken from Krüger, 2021b, 319)

Figure 5 shows the encoder-decoder architecture of a standard transformer-based NMT system. The encoder on the left side receives the decontextualised word embeddings x_1 to x_6 representing the input sequence *NMT doesn't feed on brainwave energy*. These embeddings are passed through six self-attention layers (called multi-head-attention in figure 5), which compute the contextualised word embeddings z_1 to z_6 constituting a contextualised representation of the input sequence. With regard to the example discussed above, the polysemous word *bank* would have one (decontextualised) vector representation at the beginning of the encoder's self-attention process and two (contextualised) vector representations after this process is finished. The contextualised representation z_1 to z_6 of the input sequence is then presented to the decoder (right side of figure 5), which, based on this representation, produces the output sequence (= target sentence) y_1 to y_n, one word at a time. At each decoding step, the decoder can look at the full contextualised representation of the input sequence and at the representation of the output words produced so far.[8] In other words, standard NMT systems have at their disposal a limited but very fine-grained discourse

8 For a more detailed popularised discussion of the working principle of modern transformer-based NMT systems, see, for example, Alammar (2018), van Genabith (2020) and Krüger (2021b).

context in the form of a full representation of the input sequence and a partial representation of the output sequence. This fine-grained discourse context is one of the reasons for the qualitative improvements of NMT over its predecessor architectures RBMT and PBSMT.

4. Contextual Meaning in Neural Machine Translation

Having established the principles by which NMT systems process linguistic meaning and the extent to which standard transformer-based NMT systems can draw on contextual information when producing a translation, the paper will now discuss the actual performance of NMT with regard to encoding contextually available meaning in its translation output. The first part of this discussion is largely based on Krüger (2020), who conducted a qualitative and (to a lesser extent) quantitative analysis of the capacity of the generic NMT system DeepL to perform explicitation shifts when translating a research report (about 7,000 words) on carbon dioxide capture and storage from English into German. Explicitation is understood here as an indicator of text-context interaction in translation (Krüger, 2015). The DeepL translation was analysed for instances of explicitation and compared to a high-quality human translation of the same text performed by a competent human translator. The quantitative analysis showed that DeepL only performed 70 explicitation shifts while the human translator performed 222 explicitation shifts (Krüger, 2020: 204). This rather pronounced difference points to a limited capacity of DeepL (and standard NMT systems in general) to draw on contextually inferable information and to explicitate this information in translation. Looking at specific instances where DeepL performed explicitation shifts or failed to perform such shifts when a human translator did so, specific patterns with regard to the contextual performance of standard NMT systems emerge. In the following example, DeepL performed a cohesive explicitation shift by inserting the pronominal adverb *damit* into the German target text, thereby establishing an explicit anaphoric reference to the previous sentence and raising the cohesive explicitness of the target text:

Source Text (ST): Due to the associated CO_2 emissions, the net amount of CO_2 captured is approximately 80–90 %.

DeepL: Aufgrund der *damit* verbundenen CO_2-Emissionen liegt die Nettomenge des abgetrennten CO_2 bei ca. 80–90 %.

Back-translated DeepL output: Due to the CO_2 emissions associated *with this*, the net amount of CO_2 captured is approximately 80–90 %.

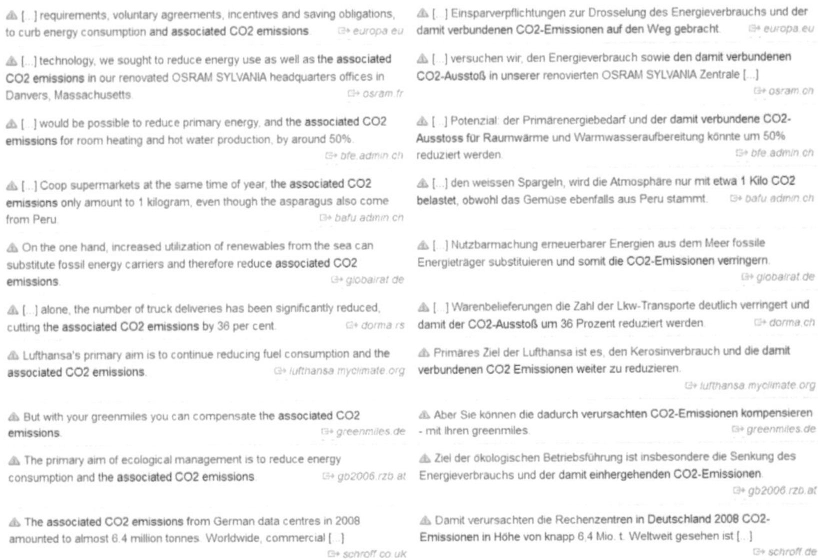

Figure 6: German translation equivalents of the string *associated* CO_2 *emissions* in the Linguee corpus

As discussed in more detail in Becher (2011: 156) and Krüger (2020: 205–206), the German lexicon has a much larger inventory than the English lexicon of pronominal adverbs (such as *damit*, *dabei*, *dadurch*, *hierbei*, *somit*, *wodurch*, etc.), which may be used to establish anaphoric reference and hence textual cohesion. This large inventory of pronominal adverbs may result in a certain communicative pressure to actually use these cohesive markers in German discourse (Becher, 2011: 157). This lexicon-induced discourse convention of German in contrast to English register becomes obvious when looking at figure 6 below, which shows the first 10 occurrences of the English string *associated* CO_2 *emissions* and its German translation equivalents in the Linguee corpus – which forms the principal training corpus for DeepL (Schwan & Lipski, 2017).

As can be seen, in 8 of 10 cases the German translation of the source sentence containing the string *associated* CO_2 *emissions* uses a pronominal adverb such as *damit*, *somit* or *dadurch*, with *damit* being the most frequent solution. If a pattern emerges in the training data where (part of) the target side of a translation unit was regularly rendered in a more explicit way than (part of) the source side of this translation unit (as is the case here), the NMT system will likely learn this specific pattern *less explicit source side of string x → more explicit target side of string x* and apply it when encountering the exact string in a text which it is asked to translate (as probably happened in the example discussed above). However, the system would not learn a high-level pragmatic principle such as *German discourse (in register/genre xyz) tends to exhibit a higher level of cohesive explicitness than English discourse (in register/genre xyz)*[9] and therefore would not learn to add cohesive markers in instances where the individual shift is not manifest as a pattern in the system's training data.

Looking at an example where DeepL failed to perform an explicitation shift in an instance where the human translator of the same text justifiably did so reveals more on the shortcomings of NMT systems in accessing and explicitating contextually available information in translation. This example was taken from an automotive corpus (sub-domain: piston technology) containing English source texts and their professional German translations, which was analysed for instances of explicitation and implicitation in Krüger (2015):

> **ST:** It was interesting to compare the *visual observation* with the temperature and gravimetric data used in our correlation.
> **Human Translation (HT):** Es war interessant, einen Vergleich zwischen den *durch Sichtprüfung festgestellten Ablagerungen* und den in unserer Korrelation eingesetzten Temperaturwerten und gravimetrischen Daten durchzuführen.
> **Back-translated HT:** It was interesting to make a comparison between the *deposits detected by visual inspection* and the temperature values and gravimetric data used in our correlation.
> **DeepL:** Es war interessant, die *visuelle Beobachtung* mit den Temperatur- und gravimetrischen Daten zu vergleichen, die in unserer Korrelation verwendet wurden.
> **Back-translated DeepL output:** It was interesting to compare the *visual observation* with the temperature and gravimetric data used in our correlation.

The wider discourse context of this example is concerned with deposit formation on pistons in internal combustion engines. The corpus analysis in Krüger (2015) yielded a high-level pattern which suggests that, if a comparison is made, German technical register requires parameters of comparison of a similar kind, while English technical register licenses comparing parameters of a dissimilar kind. The English source sentence in the present example compares a specific set of data (temperature and gravimetric data) with a process (visual observation), which will yield another set of data (the degree of deposits on the pistons). The German

9 Empirical evidence of this difference in cohesive explicitness in English vs. German register is presented, for example, in Krein-Kühle (2002) and Becher (2011).

translator rendered the ST string *visual observation* (= process) in a more explicit way in German by expanding it into the prepositional phrase *durch Sichtprüfung festgestellten Ablagerungen* (= specific set of data resulting from the process of visual observation). In the translation, this set of data is then compared with another set of data (*Temperaturwerte und gravimetrische Daten*), thus fulfilling the German register requirements concerning parameters of comparison of a similar kind. As can be seen, DeepL failed to perform this explicitation shift by opting for the literal translation *visual observation → visuelle Beobachtung*.

Compared to the string *associated CO_2 emissions* discussed above, the string *visual observation* is much more abstract in that the object of this observation is not encoded. Also, visual observations can be performed in a wide variety of contexts (hence applying to different objects of observation) and there is no lexicalised convention in German to always specify the object of a visual observation. This makes it highly unlikely that a shift such as *visual observation → durch Sichtprüfung festgestellte Ablagerungen* will be present in the NMT system's training data, let alone be present frequently (and at the same time exclusively) enough for it to constitute a stable translation pattern that the system could learn (a search for *visual observation* in the English-German Linguee corpus will confirm this for DeepL).[10] Of course, the concepts *visual observation* and *(piston) deposits* may exhibit a high degree of sematic similarity in the NMT system's embedding space. However, due to the relatively impoverished internal structure of this embedding space, the NMT system will not know explicitly how the two concepts are related (see the discussion in section 3 above). Hence, it will lack information on how to prioritise one concept (*[piston] deposits*) over another (such as *abrasive wear*) when both are spatially close (and hence semantically related) to the concept *visual observation* in the embedding space. And even if the NMT system were able to capture the nature of the relations between semantically related concepts in the embedding space and to identify that, in

10 The problem discussed here may be more pronounced in generic MT systems such as DeepL or Google Translate, which are trained with data from many different domains, and less prevalent in domain-adapted MT systems, which are trained with data pertaining to one specific domain (for an extensive discussion of domain adaptation for NMT, see Saunders, 2021). But even for an NMT system adapted to the automotive domain (where the range of contexts in which the string *visual observation* could appear would be restricted), it is questionable whether a) the object of this observation is verbalised frequently enough on the target side of the training data and b) whether this object, if verbalised explicitly, varies to such a low degree that the stable, learnable translation pattern *visual observation → durch Sichtprüfung festgestellte Ablagerungen* would emerge.

the present context, the concept of choice would be *(piston) deposits*, it would still lack the pragmatic awareness of a higher-level communicative principle (here: German technical register requires parameters of comparison of a similar kind) which would require explicitating this concept in the German translation.

The lower explicitness of German NMT output compared to human translations as established in Krüger (2020) and in the present discussion could be conceptualised as a specific manifestation of *machine-translationese*, which Loock (2020: 159–160) defines as "the fact that the translated data used to train the MT systems might show certain translationese features that get reproduced in the MT output." However, in the present case, machine-translationese does not arise from learned translationese patterns present in the system's training data, but from the *lack of pragmatic awareness* of NMT systems concerning higher-level communicative principles, which may not manifest themselves as stable translation patterns present in the training data that could be learned by the NMT system.

5. Contextual Extensions of Neural Machine Translation

Current NMT research is geared towards extending the degree of context that NMT systems can take into account when translating. As the previous discussion has shown, standard NMT systems only have access to a fine-grained discourse context of limited size, i.e. a fully contextualised representation of the source sentence as well as the words of the target sentence produced by the decoder up until a given decoding step. Beyond this limited discourse context, standard NMT systems have to rely on learned translation patterns with a more explicit target side if they are to produce a translation where contextually available meaning is rendered in a more explicit way than in the source text (see the discussion in section 4 above). The two major strands of research concerned with raising the 'contextual awareness' of NMT are *document-level NMT* and *multimodal NMT*, which will be discussed in the following sections.

5.1. Document-level NMT

The discourse context available to standard NMT systems only extends to the boundary of the sentence currently being translated. This sentence focus of standard NMT systems is called the "sentence independence assumption" (Lopes et al., 2020: 226), which makes it difficult for standard NMT systems to deal with transphrastic discourse features such as cohesion and coherence, pronouns, connectives, deixis, or ellipsis (Maruf et al., 2021: 8). NMT research aiming to go beyond the sentence independence assumption is concerned with *document-level NMT*, where "each sentence is translated by conditioning on the current sentence as well as other sentence pairs (source and target) in the same document" (Lopes et al., 2020: 226).[11] Within document-level NMT, a broad distinction can be made between approaches taking *only the source context* (i.e., several source sentences or the full source document) into account and those that focus on *both source and target contexts* (several source and target sentences or the full source and target documents). Another distinction can be made between *local* and *global* approaches to document-level NMT. In a local approach, a given translation decision of the MT system is conditioned only on a given number of source sentences or source and target sentences in the vicinity of the sentence currently being translated. In a global approach, on the other hand, a given translation decision is conditioned on the full source document or on the full source and target documents. Overall, this yields four basic document-level NMT architectures: 1) local source-only architectures, 2) local source and target architectures, 3) global source-only architectures, and 4) global source and target architectures (Maruf et al., 2021: 11).[12] Document-level NMT has left the research stage and is currently being implemented in production NMT systems. A commercial NMT system which already includes document-level context is *Language Studio©* by *Omniscien Technologies* (Koehn & Wiggins, 2021). Among popular public MT systems, DeepL also seems to have incorporated document-context features, as the quick test depicted in figure 7 below indicates.

Figure 7: DeepL opting for the female gender when provided with document-level context

11 A comprehensive overview of the various approaches to document-level NMT can be found in Maruf et al. (2021). Table 2 in Maruf et al. (2021: 11) provides a very concise overview of these approaches. The authors also discuss in detail various methods for actually integrating document-level context into NMT systems.

12 Currently, there are no document-level NMT architectures which incorporate only the target context, "as it is natural to leverage the existing source-side context" (Maruf et al., 2021: 10).

When presented with the isolated sentence *The doctor was happy*, DeepL outputs the male rendering *Der Arzt*, which could be interpreted as an instance of *gender bias* (Saunders & Byrne, 2020). However, when DeepL is provided with document-level context in the form of the following source sentence, containing the female pronoun *she*, the translation suggestion changes to the female rendering *Die Ärztin*, indicating that DeepL is able to incorporate document-level information (at least, a local source context). Google Translate, on the other hand, still seems to operate on the sentence independence assumption, as can be seen in figure 8 below.

Figure 8: Goole Translate opting for the wrong gender even when provided with document-level context

When presented with the isolated sentence *The doctor was very happy*, Google Translate betrays the same gender bias as DeepL, opting for the male rendering *Der Arzt*. However, contrary to DeepL, Google Translate preserves the male gender even when presented with document-level information indicating that a female rendering of *doctor* is required in German. Overall, Maruf et al. (2021: 28) point out that, despite encouraging progress made so far in document-level NMT, "there is still a lot that needs to be done, not only in terms of better modelling of the context." According to Maruf et al. (2020: 28–29), one particular challenge beyond architecture development for document-level NMT pertains to the compilation of training datasets which are aligned at document level and thus preserve document-internal sentence order. This sentence order is lost in most traditional MT datasets which are aligned at the sentence and not at the document level (on this point see also Koehn & Wiggins, 2021).

5.2. Multimodal NMT (with particular focus on image-guided NMT)

Another current research strand which aims to extend the context available to NMT systems beyond discourse/document-level context is concerned with *multimodal NMT*. Multimodal NMT "involves drawing information from more than one modality, based on the assumption that the additional modalities will contain useful alternative views of the input data" (Sulubacak et al., 2020: 97). The most prominent areas of research on multimodal NMT are spoken language translation, image-guided translation and video-guided translation (Sulubacak et al., 2020: 97).[13] By providing extra-textual auditory and/or visual information to an NMT system, multimodal approaches aim to extend the degree of situational context NMT systems can take into account, thus going beyond standard approaches "which often disregard many other characteristics of communication [beyond textual representations] such as non-verbal auditory cues, facial expressions and hand gestures" (Sulubacak et al., 2020: 97). Research on image-guided machine translation, for example, aims to "enhance the translation of … documents by leveraging their semantic correspondence to … images" (Sulubacak et al., 2020: 100). A standard approach here is to use image features extracted by convolutional neural networks (CNN) optimised for computer vision tasks,[14] which can be either *feature maps consisting of spatial features extracted from specific convolutional layers or pooled feature vectors*, which are spatially unaware, compact vector representations (Sulubacak et al., 2020: 114). When working with feature maps, an image-guided NMT system would have to combine the traditional language attention with a visual attention over the spatial features of the image's feature map, with most systems integrating this visual attention on the decoder side (Sulubacak et al., 2020: 116–117). A pooled feature vector on the other hand could be added, for example, to the beginning or the end of a source embedding sequence, letting the system's attention mechanism "attend to a mixed-modality source representation instead of a purely textual one" (Sulubacak et al., 2020: 115).

Coming back to the piston deposit example discussed in section 4, an image-guided NMT system could, in principle, attend to an accompanying image of a piston showing deposit formation and hence acquire from this image (which describes a part of the situational context of the text) the information that those piston deposits are the object of the visual observation. However, in contrast to document-level NMT, image-guided NMT has not yet left the research stage and is still confronted with basic problems. Most importantly, it could not yet be established whether providing image information to an NMT system actually

13 Sulubacak et al. (2020) provide an extensive overview of architectures, training datasets and evaluation methods for multimodal NMT.

14 Specifically CNNs trained for the *ImageNet* (Deng et al., 2009) image classification task (Sulubacak et al., 2020: 114).

enhances system performance (Sulubacak et al., 2020: 132). Sulubacak et al. (2020: 132) describe instances where image-guided NMT systems "were not guided by the image that the source language sentence describes, instead they are guided by a randomly selected image." Zhao et al. (2020: 111–112) stress that, if the attention mechanism of their image-guided NMT system focused on a wrong semantic image region, the system's translation performance was negatively impacted. Finally, Cho (2020), points to a phenomenon where, when attending to modalities beyond the text, the attention mechanism of a multimodal NMT system will tend to focus on that information in the external modality which is already present in the text to translate. In other words, the information already present in the text will be amplified and not enriched by new information discernible from the external modality that the NMT system attends to.

6. Conclusion

This paper has discussed the extent to which neural machine translation is able to incorporate contextual meaning in translation. As was shown, standard NMT systems only have at their disposal a limited (although fine-grained) discourse context ending at the boundary of the sentence currently being translated. At the same time, the vector space containing the vector representations of the natural-language words to be processed by NMT systems serves to indicate semantic (dis)similarity of concepts to the NMT system using spatial proximity. However, due to the relatively impoverished internal structure of this vector space, the exact nature of the relations holding between the concepts represented in this vector space are not made explicit to the NMT system (contrary to highly structured frames, which were assumed to represent and organise knowledge in human translation). Also, it was shown that NMT systems can only learn to explicitate contextually inferable information in translation when the exact explicitation shift is present frequently enough in the system's training data to be recognised and learned as a translation pattern by the system.[15] What NMT systems are yet unable to do is to learn high-level communicative principles from such individual shifts, which would lead them to perform similar shifts not represented in their training data. Contextual extensions to standard NMT systems are document-level NMT, which expands the discourse context available to NMT systems, and multimodal NMT, which expands the situational

15 Of course, the same would hold for specific *implication* shifts that an NMT system learns from its training data.

context (in the form of spoken language, images, and videos) these systems can principally draw on in translation. As was discussed with a view to image-guided NMT, this NMT architecture still suffers from basic problems so that it remains to be seen whether the potential of these systems to incorporate a rich subset of a text's situational context in translation can actually be fulfilled.

With regard to the current debate on the performance of NMT as compared to professional human translation, the paper has hopefully shown that there are still important systemic limitations which prevent NMT from attaining the same level of contextual awareness as human translators. Given that the ability to access, evaluate and, if required, integrate contextually inferable information in translation is an indispensable element of professional translation competence, claims that NMT has achieved (super)human performance should be met with a high degree of scepticism.

References

Alammar, J. (2018). *The illustrated transformer. Visualizing Machine Learning One Concept at a Time Blog.* http://jalammar.github.io/illustrated-transformer/

Aschenberg, H. (1999). 'Zum Kontextbegriff in der Übersetzungsforschung.' In N. Greiner, J. Kornelius & G. Rovere (Eds.), *Texte und Kontexte in Sprachen und Kulturen. Festschrift für Jörn Albrecht* (7–33). WVT.

Becher, V. (2011). *Explicitation and implicitation in translation. A corpus-based study of English-German and German-English translations of business texts.* [doctoral dissertation, Department of Applied Linguistics, University of Hamburg].

Busse, D. (2009). *Semantik.* Fink.

Busse, D. (2012). *Frame-Semantik. Ein Kompendium.* De Gruyter.

Carl, M. (2020). 'Translation, artificial intelligence and cognition.' In F. Alves & A. L. Jakobsen (Eds.), *The Routledge Handbook of Translation and Cognition* (500–516). Routledge.

Catford, J. C. (1965). *A linguistic theory of translation. An essay in applied linguistics.* Oxford University Press.

Cho, K. (2020). The future of translation. Interview at the Lilt Ascend 2020 conference. https://resources.lilt.com/ascend-2020-on-demand

Clark, H. H. (1996). *Using language.* Cambridge University Press.

Deng, J., Dong, W., Socher, R., Li, L.-J., Li, K., & Fei-Fei, L. (2009). 'ImageNet: a large-scale hierarchical image database.' *Proceedings of the 2009 IEEE conference on computer vision and pattern recognition* (248–255). IEEE. https://ieeexplore.ieee.org/document/5206848

ELIS. (2021). *European Language Industry Survey 2021*. https://ec.europa.eu/info/sites/default/files/about_the_european_commission/service_standards_and_principles/documents/elis_2021_european_language_industry_survey.pdf

Evans, V., & Green, M. (2006). *Cognitive linguistics. An introduction*. Edinburgh University Press.

Fillmore, C. J. (1982). 'Frame semantics.' In The Linguistic Society of Korea (Eds.), *Linguistics in the morning calm* (111–137). Hanshin.

Freitag, M., Foster, G., Grangier, D., Ratnakar, V., Tan, Q., & Macherey, W. (2021). 'Experts, errors, and context: a large-scale study of human evaluation for machine translation.' *arXiv*. https://arxiv.org/abs/2104.14478

Hahn, W. v. (1998). 'Das Postulat der Explizitheit für den Fachsprachengebrauch.' In L. Hoffmann, H. Kalverkämper & H. E. Wiegand (Eds.), *Fachsprachen. Ein internationales Handbuch zur Fachsprachenforschung und Terminologiewissenschaft. Volume 1* (383–389). de Gruyter.

Halliday, M. A. K. (1985). *Spoken and written language*. Oxford University Press.

Hassan, H., Aue, A., Chen, C., Chowdhary, V., Clark, J., Federmann, C., Huang, X., Junczys-Dowmunt, M., Lewis, W., Li, M., Liu, S., Liu, T.-Y., Luo, R., Menezes, A., Qin, T., Seide, F., Tan, X., Tian, F., Wu, L., Wu, S., Xia, Y., Zhang, D., Zhang, Z., & Zhou, M. (2018). 'Achieving human parity on automatic Chinese to English news translation.' *arXiv*. https://arxiv.org/abs/1803.05567

ISO 1087. (2019). *Terminology work and terminology science – vocabulary*. International Organization for Standardization.

Jia, Y, Carl, M., & Wang, X. (2019). 'How does the post-editing of neural machine translation compare with from-scratch translation? A product and process study.' *Journal of Specialised Translation, 31*, 60–86. https://www.jostrans.org/issue31/art_jia.pdf

Koehn, P., & Wiggins, D. (2021). *Everything that you need to know about customizing a great machine translation engine*. Omniscien Technologies NMT Webinars. https://omniscien.com/webinars/everything-that-you-need-to-know-about-customizing-a-great-machine-translation-engine/

Krein-Kühle, M. (2002). 'Cohesion and coherence in technical translation: the case of demonstrative reference'. In L. Van Vaerenbergh (Ed.), *Linguistics and translation studies. Translation studies and linguistics (Linguistica Antverpiensia)* (41–53). Hoger Instituut voor Vertalers en Tolken.

Krüger, R. (2015). *The interface between scientific and technical translation studies and cognitive linguistics. With particular emphasis on explicitation and implicitation as indicators of translational text-context interaction*. Frank & Timme.

Krüger, R. (2016). 'Situated LSP translation from a cognitive translational perspective.' *Lebende Sprachen, 61*(2), 297–332. https://doi.org/10.1515/les-2016-0014

Krüger, R. (2020). 'Explicitation in neural machine translation.' *Across Languages and Cultures, 21*(2), 195–216. https://doi.org/10.1556/084.2020.0001.

Krüger, R. (2021a). Understanding word embeddings for neural machine translation – fundamentals. Jupyter Notebook. https://colab.research.google.com/drive/1UUteTlvULD8mSh94Hd6pmL5OudP8l9bc?usp=sharing

Krüger, R. (2021b). 'Die Transformer-Architektur für Systeme zur neuronalen maschinellen Übersetzung – eine popularisierende Darstellung.' *trans-kom, 14*(2), 278–324. https://www.trans-kom.eu/bd14nr02/trans-kom_14_02_05_Krueger_NMUe.20211202.pdf

Langacker, R. W. (1987). *Foundations of cognitive grammar I: theoretical prerequisites*. Stanford University Press.

Langacker, R. W. (2008). *Cognitive grammar. A basic introduction*. Oxford University Press.

Läubli, S., Sennrich, R., & Volk, M. (2018). 'Has machine translation achieved human parity? A case for document-level evaluation.' In E. Riloff, D. Chiang, J. Hockenmaier, & J. Tsujii (Eds.), *Proceedings of the 2018 conference on Empirical Methods in Natural Language Processing* (4791–4796). Association for Computational Linguistics. https://aclanthology.org/D18-1512/

Läubli, S., Castilho, S., Neubig, G., Sennrich, R., Shen, Q., & Toral, A. (2020). 'A set of recommendations for assessing human-machine parity in language translation.' *Journal of Artificial Intelligence Research, 67*, 653–672. https://doi.org/10.1613/jair.1.11371

Loock, R. (2020). 'No more rage against the machine: how the corpus-based identification of machine-translationese can lead to student empowerment.' *The Journal of Specialised Translation, 34*, 150–170. https://jostrans.org/issue34/art_loock.pdf

Lopes, A. V., Farajian, M. A., Bawden, R., Zhang, M., & Martins, A. F. T. (2020). 'Document-level neural MT: a systematic comparison.' In A. Martins, H. Moniz, S. Fumega, B. Martins, F. Batista, L. Coheur, C. Parra, I. Trancoso, M. Turchi, A. Bisazza, J. Moorkens, A. Guerberof, M. Nurminen, L. Marg & M. L. Forcada (Eds.): *Proceedings of the 22nd annual conference of the European Association for Machine Translation* (225–234). European Association for Machine Translation. https://aclanthology.org/2020.eamt-1.24/

Marmaridou, S. (2000). *Pragmatic meaning and cognition*. Benjamins.

Maruf, S., Saleh, F., & Haffari, G. (2021). 'A survey on document-level neural machine translation: methods and evaluation.' *ACM Computing Surveys, 54*(2), 1–36. https://doi.org/10.1145/3441691

Mikolov, T., Chen, K, Corrado, G., & Dean, J. (2013). Efficient estimation of word representations in vector space. *arXiv*. https://arxiv.org/abs/1301.3781

Park, S., Bak, J., & Oh, A. (2017). 'Rotated word vector representations and their interpretability.' In M. Palmer, R. Hwa & S. Riedel (Eds.), *Proceedings of the 2017 Conference on Empirical Methods in Natural Language Processing* (401–411). Association for Computational Linguistics. https://www.aclweb.org/anthology/D17-1041/

Pinkal, M. (1985). *Logik und Lexikon. Die Semantik des Unbestimmten.* de Gruyter.

Popel, M., Tomkova, M., Tomek, J., Kaiser, Ł., Uszkoreit, J., Bojar, O., & Žabokrtský, Z. (2020). 'Transforming machine translation: a deep learning system reaches news translation quality comparable to human professionals.' *Nature Communications, 11*, 1–15. https://www.nature.com/articles/s41467-020-18073-9

Řehůřek, R. (2021). Gensim. Topic modelling for humans. https://radimrehurek.com/gensim/index.html

Risku, H. (2004). *Translationsmanagement. Interkulturelle Fachkommunikation im Kommunikationszeitalter*. Narr.

Saunders, D., & Byrne, B. (2020). 'Reducing gender bias in neural machine translation as a domain adaptation problem.' In D. Jurafsky, J. Chai, N. Schluter, & J. Tetreault (Eds.), *Proceedings of the 58th annual meeting of the Association for Computational Linguistics* (7724–7736). Association for Computational Linguistics. https://aclanthology.org/2020.acl-main.690/

Saunders, D. (2021). *Domain adaptation for neural machine translation.* [doctoral dissertation, University of Cambridge]. https://www.repository.cam.ac.uk/bitstream/handle/1810/319335/thesis.pdf?sequence=1.

Schwan, B., & Lipski, S. (2017). 'Google kann uns nicht überholen.' *MIT Technology Review*. https://www.heise.de/hintergrund/Google-kann-uns-nicht-ueberholen-3836524.html.

Sulubacak, U., Caglayan, O., Grönroos, S.-A., Rouhe, A., Elliott, D., Specia, L., & Tiedemann, J. (2020). 'Multimodal machine translation through visuals and speech.' *Machine Translation, 34*(2–3), 97–147. https://link.springer.com/article/10.1007/s10590-020-09250-0.

Taylor, J. R. (2002). *Cognitive grammar*. Oxford University Press.

Toral, A, Castilho, S., Hu, K., & Way, A. (2018). 'Attaining the unattainable? Reassessing claims of human parity in neural machine translation.' In O. Bojar, Chatterjee, C. Federmann, M. Fishel, Y. Graham, B. Haddow, M. Huck, A. Jimeno Yepes, P. Koehn, C. Monz, M. Negri, A. Névéol, M. Neves, M. Post, L. Specia, M. Turchi, & K. Verspoor (Eds.), *Proceedings of the Third*

Conference on Machine Translation: research papers (113–123). http://dx.doi.org/10.18653/v1/W18-6312.

van der Maaten, L., & Hinton, G. (2008). 'Visualizing high-dimensional data using t-SNE.' *Journal of Machine Learning Research, 9,* 2579–2605. https://lvdmaaten.github.io/publications/papers/JMLR_2008.pdf

van Genabith, J. (2020). 'Neural machine translation.' In J. Porsiel (Ed.), *Maschinelle Übersetzung für Übersetzungsprofis* (59–115). BDÜ Fachverlag.

Vashee, K. (2021). 'The human-in-the-loop driving MT progress.' *eMpTy Pages.* http://kv-emptypages.blogspot.com/2021/11/the-human-in-loop-driving-mt-progress.html

Vaswani, A., Shazeer, N., Parmar, N., Uszkoreit, J., Jones, L., Gomez, A. N., Kaiser, L., & Polosukhin, I. (2017). 'Attention is all you need.' In I. Guyon, U. von Luxburg, S. Bengio, H. M. Wallach, R. Fergus, S. V. N. Vishwanathan, & R. Garnett (Eds.), *Advances in Neural Information Processing Systems 30 (NIPS 2017)* (1–11). https://proceedings.neurips.cc/paper/2017/hash/3f5ee243547dee91fbd053c1c4a845aa-Abstract.html

Zhao, Y., Komachi, M., Kajiwara, T., & Chu, C. (2020). 'Double attention-based multimodal neural machine translation with semantic image regions.' In A. Martins, H. Moniz, S. Fumega, B. Martins, F. Batista, L. Coheur, C. Parra, I. Trancoso, M. Turchi, A. Bisazza, J. Moorkens, A. Guerberof, M. Nurminen, L. Marg, & M. L. Forcada (Eds.), *Proceedings of the 22nd annual conference of the European Association for Machine Translation* (105–114). European Association for Machine Translation https://aclanthology.org/2020.eamt-1.12/

Dominik Kudła

University of Warsaw

The "Blind Localisation" of Video Games: A Decontextualised Translation

Abstract: Despite the constantly increasing attention and financial resources directed at video game localisation, the language versions of many video games tailored for diverse target markets are not entirely flawless. A phenomenon which causes some of the translation errors present in the localised video game versions is sometimes referred to in the industry as "blind localisation." It is a set of circumstances inherent for the localisation process which deprive the translator of contextual information needed for making correct translation choices. Its primary source is the segmented nature of the translated text, often consisting of several- or one-word translation units. The units are sometimes not organised in a linear or chronological manner as a result of the structure of source code which they need to be extracted from and incorporated back into. Moreover, video game localisers are rarely provided with descriptive and extensive information on the contextual use of certain translation segments. The present paper demonstrates several reasons for such a situation to exist, as well as the types of errors it originates in video games of various genres and developed by both wealthy and independent companies, localised from English into Polish. The use of inappropriate lexical, stylistic, terminological, grammatical, and pragmatic equivalents of the original words and phrases is discussed. Such errors distort the coherence and plausibility of the in-game world and may sometimes hinder or prevent completing the game.

Keywords: video game localisation, translation errors, decontextualised translation, context in translation, video game translation

Introduction

Creating numerous language versions of video games significantly increases the revenues of the developing and publishing companies, as well as enables them to establish global user communities. This process, referred to both in the industry, user community and academia as video game localisation, involves a wide spectrum of activities aimed at adapting a certain game to the needs of a specific target market when it comes to linguistic, cultural, technical, and legal aspects (cf. Bernal-Merino 2015: 35). The scope of material which is modified within the last two categories of adjustment may involve the visual appearance of the game characters, some of the game control mechanics, changing or replacing some elements of the soundtrack and plot of the game or considerably altering its marketing campaign (cf. O'Hagan & Mangiron 2013: 19; Bernal-Merino 2015: 48). The complexity of this process stems also from the fact that it not only shares multiple similarities with other translation genres, such as literary translation, specialised translation, audiovisual translation or software localisation, but also combines them within one translation project and poses some unique challenges to the translator.

The gamer is not only a passive recipient of the video game content but participates actively in revolving the plot. As a consequence, the primary function of both the original and translated game is to evoke the most intense feeling of immersion (temporarily forgetting that the game world is not real, cf. Adams 2014: 641) possible. Consequently, the fidelity of the translation to the original text as well as its formal equivalence are subordinated to creating a coherent and believable in-game world. Some of the original elements need to be replaced with ones created anew, which underlines also the role of translator creativity in this process (O'Hagan & Mangiron 2013: 198; Bernal-Merino 2015: 244).

While the localisation process has so much impact on the player's experience it should take into account the vast variety of video games. Traditionally, nine video game genres are distinguished: adventure, puzzle, racing, role-playing, simulation, sports, strategy, and action games (the broadest category where vast subcategories could also be found: arcade, shooter, fighting, stealth, action-adventure games). The genre set provided is adapted from the largest online video game database, MobyGames (n.d.), although numerous subgenres could be distinguished and, in some regions, there are genres almost non-existent in other parts of the world (for more detailed descriptions of the genres cf. Wolf 2001). Every genre sets different goals for the user and requires specific approach from the localiser.

Video games are also commonly divided with respect to the company which developed or published a particular title. Titles referred to as AAA games are developed and published by global companies who are able to spend millions of dollars on creating a game and organise teams consisting of thousands of professionals for that purpose. Such games are commonly juxtaposed with independent (or indie) games, which are developed by minor companies or start-ups with limited financial resources and sometimes involving even less than ten employees. Games of this type often utilise topics or mechanics uncommon for the majority of titles. In general, the latter developers are believed to consider localisation of their games as less important than other companies.

However, even the greatest effort of the translators cannot overcome some of the issues interwoven into localisation. One of such challenges arises from the structure of the translated material, which is extracted from the game code and deprives the translator of at least some contextual information.

The article consists of three sections. The first one is focused on the issue of "blind localisation." The second one introduces the classification of errors in translation products. The third one describes the errors resulting from the lack of contextual details provided with the translated in-game material, as well as the possible reasons for their occurrence and ways of preventing them.

1. "Blind localisation"

One of the issues that a translator comes across while creating the new language version of a particular game is the decontextualisation of the translated text. It is worth noting that this situation stems from the very structure of the video game localisation process.

As pieces of software, video games are governed by a set of algorithms which are involved in the source code of the game. Some authors (e.g. Honeywood et al. 2012: 9; Bernal-Merino 2015: 80) point out that localisers in the vast majority of cases have no access to the source code due to its sensitive nature. Even adding or deleting a space or punctuation mark in one place may cause the game software to misinterpret a particular fragment and stop working correctly. For that reason, the translator is usually provided with the text elements of the game which have been extracted from the source code by the developers in a form of a spreadsheet file or a CAT tool format. Similarly to utility software localisation, the video game text provided to the translator in game localisation is divided into short, sometimes one-word, segments which are processed separately by the game mechanics (O'Hagan & Mangiron 2013: 96; Czech 2013: 17, Bernal-Merino 2015: 142). Although such a solution provides no obstacle in utility software localisation where the text is usually concise and stylistically neutral, it poses an additional challenge for game localisers who work with a wide range of text types from menu options and interface buttons, to dialogue lines or fragments of in-game books or newspapers.

Various authors (e.g. Czech 2013: 17; Drab 2014: 105; Bernal-Merino 2015: 144) underline that the structure of the game's source code also impacts the translation in video game localisation. Most video games are not linear, as there are usually several game endings possible with even more possible ways of reaching them. Thus, the translated text would also often have no linear or chronological structure. Mrzigod (2021: 57) as an example provides dialogues in role-playing or adventure games. The player is usually provided with a choice of several alternative answers which may have different consequences for the game plot. This is another reason why the linguistic elements of the game need to be divided into separate segments which the game algorithms would be able to use when the game plot started to develop in a particular direction. However, O'Hagan & Mangiron (2013: 96) underline that the short translation segments could be accidentally ordered alphabetically rather than chronologically or according to the speaking character. Thus, the decontextualisation of the translated content is interwoven into the structure of video game localisation process.

This issue could be overcome if the game developer supplements the in-game text segments with additional contextual details, e.g. the description of a particular situation, setting it in the game plot, or even samples of the original language version with visual and audio material. Nonetheless, such solutions are usually exceptions rather than norm in the market practice (cf. Dietz 2006: 125–126; O'Hagan & Mangiron 2013: 97; Czech 2013: 15; Bernal-Merino 2015: 141–145). Mrzigod (2021: 57) mentions that recently he encountered a detailed description of the dialogue lines while working on the Polish version of *Horizon: Zero Dawn* (Guerilla Games, 2017). Each line there was provided with the details on the person speaking, the manner of speech as well as the circumstances in which the words were pronounced. However, he also states that this was one of the several cases in his career (since 1993 he had participated in localising more than 350 video games into Polish) where so much contextual information was provided.

A single word or phrase can be interpreted in various manners depending on the communicative, cultural, or plot-related contexts of its use. For that reason if no or insufficient contextual information is provided, the translator is to make random decisions regarding the choice of a certain target-language equivalent with a much more limited semantic scope than the polysemous word or phrase used in the original version of a game. Mrzigod (2021: 57) ironically notices that in the case of such polysemous English words as "box" or "gun" identifying the correct meaning or part of speech in a particular context is just a lucky coincidence. Therefore, such a situation in video game localisation is referred to as "blind localisation" by many translators (cf. Dietz 2006: 2007).

In some such cases, the knowledge of the game setting, the specificity of a particular game series or genre may enable the translator to exclude all the inappropriate translation equivalents. However, as some of the examples from section 3. of the present text show, the translator's intuition sometimes is not sufficient for that purpose. Consequently, the translation in such circumstances requires the translator to assess the risk related to choosing a certain translation equivalent over other possibilities. This would allow them to use the solution preventing or minimising the possible issues arising from the translation error (cf. Pym 2005: 68; O'Hagan & Mangiron 2013: 119). Undoubtedly, the erroneous translation solutions resulting from this situation affect the main objective of video game localisation – providing the user with a believable and absorbing gaming experience, e.g. by distorting the coherence of the in-game world or providing them with misleading guidance. Bernal-Merino (2015: 145) points out that, apart from increasing the probability of translation errors, translating decontextualised translation segments can also be time-consuming and frustrating.

Moreover, some of the translation segments include variables, i.e. elements which can take one of several values assigned by the source code depending on the in-game circumstances. In fact, these values could be not only numbers but also other translation segments including nouns, adjectives or verbs. The process of supplementing particular values in variables is called concatenation (O'Hagan & Mangiron 2013: 132; Bernal-Merino 2015: 147–150). Often the translator is not informed which segments could replace the variable within the game, although the variable names may also refer e.g. to object categories. For inflected languages, such as Polish, the fact that in many cases it is not possible to edit the rules of concatenation forces the translator to use nouns of only one grammatical gender, so that they will match the adjectives and numeral forms chosen (cf. Mrzigod 2021: 79). Otherwise, the resulting phrases could be grammatically or stylistically incorrect.

Moreover, it should be noted that nowadays video games are frequently released simultaneously around the world. Due to this model referred to in the industry as "sim-ship" (or "simultaneous shipment"), the localisation process needs to be carried out parallel with the game development (cf. Bernal-Merino 2015: 172) and some faults may not be detected in the testing process, which is the final stage of localisation.

To the best of the author's knowledge no studies devoted exclusively to the phenomenon of "blind localisation" have been conducted, especially when it comes to the English-Polish video game localisation. The errors occurring due to the decontextualised original text were discussed in several works among other issues (e.g. O'Hagan & Mangiron 2013; Tarquini 2014: 165–169; Bernal-Merino 2015; Mrzigod 2021). However, they were not the central focus of these analyses.

2. Translation error typology

While analysing translation evaluation models used by translation companies, O'Brien (2012) notices that the majority of them is based on error analysis. Pedersen (2017) supports this claim with reference to theoretical models and states that many translation assessment models use such a basis in order to minimise the subjectivity of the assessor (cf. Pedersen 2017: 215).

There is a vast variety of approaches and classifications to the issue of errors within translation studies (Hansen, 2010, briefly discusses the commonly utilised ones). In the present work, the error distinction proposed by Dzierżanowska (1988), developed by Hejwowski (2001) and Kozłowska (2001), and adapted for video game localisation by Kudła (2020: 186–194) will be utilised. Dzierżanowska (1988) divides errors occurring in translation into linguistic and translation ones. The former ones are instances when the norms of the target language (spelling, grammatical, morphological, syntactic, etc.) are violated, while the latter ones (called "translation errors sensu stricto" by Kozłowska 2001: 139) could be detected while comparing the translation with the source text.

Translation errors are subdivided by Hejwowski (2001: 158) into: 1) interpretation errors, 2) superficial translation, 3) erroneous assessment of the translation recipient's knowledge, and 4) metatranslational errors. The first category was described by Hejwowski (2001) as situations when the translator misunderstands the meaning of the source text due to their insufficient command of the source language or insufficient general knowledge which is hindering the full interpretation of the information conveyed through all the communication channels used in the source text. A similar category is discussed by Karczewska (2001: 130–133), who calls such instances "errors in the expression plan." She subdivides it into lexical faults (the use of an inappropriate semantic or terminological equivalent of the original word or neglecting the case of a "false friend" in translation), stylistic faults (the use of linguistic measures belonging to an inappropriate language register, which is visibly different from the one used in the source text), and the erroneous reconstruction of the meaning of the whole structure (clause or sentence) based on the wrong choice of the target-language equivalent of several words or phrases used in the source text (called "errors in the linear plane" by Karczewska 2001: 131).

According to Hejwowski (2001: 158), "superficial translation" is the unjustified use of lexical, phraseological, or syntactic calques from the source language.

Thirdly, the translator misinterprets the recipient's knowledge when the translation includes insufficient or excessive explanation of the references of the source text to other texts (intertextuality) or a particular culture (usually, but not necessarily the culture of the author of the source text).

Metatranslational errors distinguished by Hejwowski (2001: 158) involve the wrong choice of translation procedures (in the sense advocated by Vinay & Darbelnet 1954/1995) by the translator (the ones most commonly utilised in video game localisation were discussed in Kudła 2020: 172–186), or gaps in translation caused by omitting words, phrases, or rarely full sentences, which are semantically relevant to the source text.

Due to the character of the translation setting of video game blind localisation, only some of the abovementioned errors could be caused by this phenomenon. The insufficient contextual description supplementing the translated text in some localisation patterns may cause morphological, lexico-semantic, terminological, and metatranslational errors (usually when it comes to adaptation, foreignisation, transcreation, compensation, cf. Kudła 2020: 176–186), as well as superficial translation. All the other faults discussed above are not based on the assessment of the contextual framework in which a particular word or phrase is situated.

3. "Blind localisation" in Polish language versions of video games

The present section demonstrates some instances of "blind localisation" occurring in video games localised from English into Polish. First, the data collected to illustrate this phenomenon are described accompanied by the method of their analysis. In the next section, the instances of decontextualised localisation from English into Polish are grouped according to the reason of their occurrence as well as the consequences to which they lead.

3.1. Materials and methods

The corpus of the study was based on the responses collected in a survey conducted in 2018 among Polish dedicated gamers participating in several Facebook gamer groups (407 responses, described in Kudła 2021) and a survey conducted by the author among students of the applied linguistics study program at the University of Warsaw who defined themselves as dedicated gamers (87 participants, selected according to the criteria listed by Adams 2014: 96–98) in October 2021. In both cases, the study corpus was compiled of the responses provided to one of the open-ended questions, which regarded the erroneous localisation of video games into Polish (the question in both surveys read "Which games were according to you translated incorrectly? Why?," both surveys were conducted in Polish).

The views of the dedicated gamers on errors in video game localisation were utilised in order to inspect the perspective of the end users of the localisation process. Additionally, this category of gamers is perceived as the most knowledgeable about and observant to details of video games, including errors (cf. Adams 2014: 97), so the corpus was hoped to include a considerable variety of video game titles, genres, and localisation errors.

The results obtained in the 2018 survey were supplemented with the ones from the 2021 survey in order to achieve a more recent insight into the issue. The more recent subcorpus was collected with the aim to compile a subcorpus of comparable length. Consequently, the full corpus analysed for this paper comprised 7,838 words/ 50,084 characters (with 3,862 words/ 24,673 characters in the 2018 subcorpus, and 3,976 words/ 25,411 characters in the 2021 subcorpus).

The responses comprising the corpus were later examined for any faults that could potentially be attributed to cases of blind localisation. Subsequently, the instances described by the participants were found in both the original (English) and localised (Polish) language versions of the games and thoroughly compared with one another, while taking into account the translation error classification described in section 2.

Ten localisation issues which could have been caused by "blind localisation" from seven games were found in the corpus. The number might have been higher if the question had been worded differently. Not every participant described particular instances of errors, but sometimes just provided the titles of games or used general notions referring to a particular problem. Moreover, as a more detailed description of the 2018 survey showed (Kudła 2021, the 2021 results are similar in that respect), the respondents notice mostly the issues concerning voice acting, stylistics of proper names, subtitle readability and unprocessed machine translation use, neither of which is caused by "blind localisation." The examples come from games of various genres, types of developers as well as platforms used to run a particular title (however, many of the described instances occurred within a particular game regardless of the platform used). To show the situation against the background of the Polish video game market, exclusively localisation from English into Polish were chosen. Furthermore, it is worth noting that, in most cases, errors caused by "blind localisation" are occasional, especially in AAA titles, and are corrected after being spotted and discussed by the game users online.

The instances of translation errors in video game localisation probably related to insufficient contextual information have been divided into several categories according to the most probable reason for their occurrence. Each example has been thoroughly analysed and all the possible causes were enumerated. The claims in this section are based on the author's knowledge of the video game localisation process as both a gamer and a localiser. Wherever a statement is not the opinion of the author, a relevant source is referenced.

3.2. Examples of decontextualised localisation into Polish

The analysis of the corpus evidenced ten situations referred to by the respondents as "translation errors," which could be caused by "blind localisation". After juxtaposing the described instances in the English and Polish language versions of the mentioned games, eight of them were classified as interpretation errors, one as metatranslational error, and one as misinterpretation as an error, which is, however, illustrative of how the translator could be blamed for errors made by the developer.

3.2.1. Interpretation errors

In the Polish market, translation errors emerging from "blind localisation" seem to be more common in video games by independent developers. In his book, Mrzigod (2021: 65–66) proves that such mistakes are usually more common in indie, browser, and mobile games than in the ones by renowned and wealthy developers. This perhaps stems from the limited budgets of such companies and thus reducing localisation costs, e.g. by not conducting localisation tests. Consequently, inappropriate translations not taking into account the polysemy of words, phrases or names used in the original language version of a particular game may occur even in the main elements of a particular game. This could be exemplified by two instances from *Terraria* (Re-Logic, 2012), a platform game with elements of crafting set in an imaginary fantasy world. The game is also available for gaming consoles where in order to type the character's name a screen keyboard is necessary (cf. Figure 1).

Figure 1: Decontextualised translation of the word "Space" in the Polish version of Terraria (Re-Logic, 2012, Xbox 360 version)

Accidentally, one of the keys, "Space" referring to the spacebar, has been translated as "Kosmos," which refers to the cosmological meaning of the original word. This lexical fault is more probable to stem from the lack of any description accompanying the one-word translation segment than from the carelessness of the translator. Even a short note that the translated fragment is an element of the interface would have helped the localiser to make the correct decision (which would be the Polish noun "spacja").

Another instance of ignoring polysemy from the very same game occurs in the overlay describing the weather in the game world at a particular moment (cf. Figure 2).

Figure: 2. Verb imperative form instead of adverb describing weather in Terraria (Re-Logic 2012)

One of the possible values that this overlay may take is "Clear." This adjective was translated into Polish as "Wyczyść," a verb in the second person singular imperative form. Apparently, the translation segment was interpreted as one referring to a command which the player use, e.g. while filling in a text field (the correct equivalent would be, e.g. using the word "pogodnie" – in Polish adverbs seem to be more common to describe the weather). This lexical error also stems from the lack of sufficient contextual information, which led the translator to make an assumption about the function of the translated element. In fact, the participant describing this game stated that several dozen similar errors occurred in its Polish version, which provides some insight into the scale of the phenomenon in the majority of indie games.

As the following examples are supposed to show, not only the lack of additional details could lead to decontextualised translation in video games. In some cases, the information provided could be insufficient for the translator to make the right decision.

Doodle Champion Island Games (Google, 2021) is a browser game that accompanied the Tokyo 2020 Olympic Games held in July and August 2021. It was developed by Google, which cooperated with an animation group *Studio*

4°C, and published it as an add-on to its search engine. The game features an arcade mechanics and refers to the Japanese traditions of 16-bit-computer games. The player helps Lucky (translated into Polish as "Szczęściara"), a female cat, to become a champion in seven different disciplines corresponding with some of the Olympic competitions. Additionally, the main character may talk to the inhabitants of the island and try to solve some of their problems. Each conversation in such a case allows the player to decide whether to help the local or apologise and refuse (cf. Figure 3).

Figure 3. Wrong equivalent of the English word "Help" in the Polish version of Doodle Champion Island Games (Google, 2021)

In the original version of the game, the user chooses between the options "Help" and "Sorry," which then turn into more elaborate answers by Lucky. However, the former in the Polish version reads "Pomocy." Although this word is the Polish equivalent of the English word as an exclamation asking for help, it does not fit the context in which the translated segment is used. Here the imperative verb form "Pomóż" should have been used. Although this case could be a lexical error (it has been classified by one respondent as an oversight of the original word's polysemy), there is a chance that unprocessed machine translation was utilised here. Alternatively, at least some contextual information might have been provided, as the word was translated into a from typical for conversation and not e.g. into a noun.

It should be noted that the issue of "blind localisation" is not limited to indie or browser games and can occur despite the evolution and developments in the video game localisation industry. This is exemplified by the latest instalment in the AAA multi-platform action role-playing video game series by Ubisoft – *Assassin's Creed: Valhalla* (Ubisoft, 2020). The user plays Eivor, a Viking warrior and clan chieftain (it is possible to choose the gender of the character), during the period of Viking raids of the British Isles in 9th century. One of the skills of the playable character is to call Sýnin, a partly domesticated raven, which may help to conduct reconnaissance. The screen view of such a sequence with all the subtitles and overlays in Polish is shown in Figure 4.

Figure 4: The wrong equivalent of the word "boost" in the Polish language version of Assassin's Creed: Valhalla (Ubisoft, 2020, Xbox Series X version)

Regardless of the platform version of the game, the player is provided with hints referring to the controls which could be used at the particular moment to take various actions. In this case the overlays read "Place Marker," "Remove All Markers," "Stationary Mode," and "Boost." Almost all of them were initially translated correctly into Polish (cf. Figure 4). However, the last overlay, which refers to increasing the flight speed, was translated into Polish as "Premia." This noun refers to another meaning of the original word – something used to encourage or gratify somebody. Consequently, this element misinformed the player, while providing an incorrect hint. The rationale behind this decision could be the fact that in action role-playing games, especially ones involving a fast-paced plot filled with fighting scenes, the mechanics often provides the player with additional experience points for performing particular actions or sequences of attacks. This situation could also be referred to as “boost” in English. Most probably, in this particular case the only element of the game which the localisation team had contact with was the in-game text in a segmented form, which led to its misinterpretation. The game was widely advertised and highly anticipated by the community, hence the access to the game material was possibly limited for the translator.

The previous example was not just an isolated case of lexical error in this particular title. The game enables the user to customise the playable character, e.g. by adding tattoos. Another instance of misinterpreting the polysemy of a particular word described by the survey participant occurred in the tattoo shop menu (cf. Figure 5).

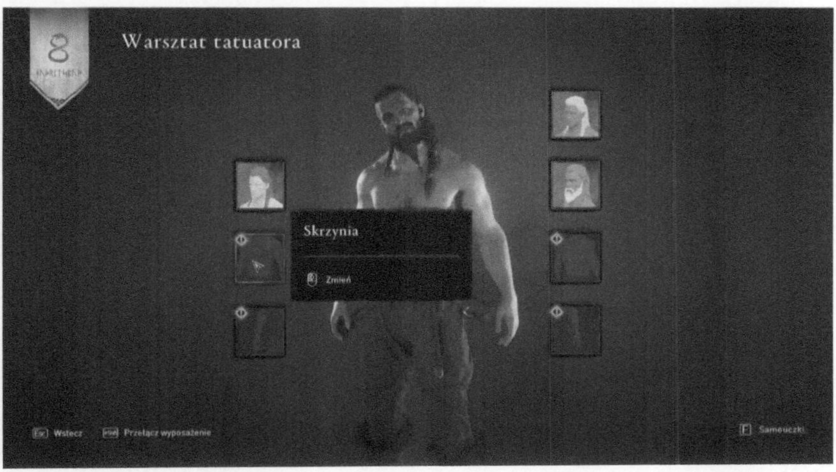

Figure 5: The wrong equivalent of the word “chest” in the Polish language version of Assassin’s Creed: Valhalla (Ubisoft, 2020, the PC version)

A tattoo could be done on several body parts of the character: the face, the arms, the back, and the chest. The last of the listed options is highlighted in Figure 5 (the screenshot comes from the PC version of the game but the error occurred in all its versions). The word “chest” was translated as “skrzynia,” a noun referring to a meaning of the original noun inappropriate in this context – a large box used for storing goods. This situation also shows a probable lack of contextual description accompanying the translation segment. In a game set during the ninth-century Viking raids on Britain, both meanings of the word “chest” were probable to occur. The games within the *Assassin’s Creed* series involve both exploring the world in search for materials and valuable goods, some of which could be pieces of armour which could be worn on the chest, and various possibilities to change the playable character's appearance. Consequently, if not provided with sufficient contextual information, the translator should have consulted the game developers on the use of this particular translation segment in the game.

Both errors described above were also debated by users soon after the game release in numerous online forums. As the game was constantly updated using patches, both inaccurate translations have already been changed into the correct Polish equivalents of the discussed words, "przyspieszenie" ("acceleration") and "tułów" (a functional equivalent of the word "chest," meaning "trunk/ torso") respectively. The most common Polish equivalent of the word "chest," "klatka piersiowa," was probably not used due to translation segment length limitations.

Lexical errors may occur not only in the overlays or subtitles in a particular game, but also in the voice-acting, although such instances are rarer. *Rise of the Tomb Raider* (Crystal Dynamics, 2016) is an action-adventure game which was published by one of the most successful video game companies in Japan – Square Enix (which set it in the AAA category). It has been fully localised into Polish (i.e. the in-game text, subtitles and voice-acting recordings were translated). In one of the scenes the main character, Lara Croft (a British archaeologist and adventuress), while aiming a gun at a thief who wants to steal her father's diary, shouts "Stop!" The Polish version of this scene is shown in Figure 6.

Figure 6: Using the wrong Polish equivalent of the exclamation "Stop!" in Rise of the Tomb Raider (Crystal Dynamics, 2016)

The exclamation was translated into Polish as "Przestań!." This verb is used in the second person singular imperative form and may urge somebody to stop doing something rather than to stand still and not to move. This form is present in both the dialogue subtitle and the dialogue recording (which has also been noted by the survey participant). An appropriate solution in this case could have been the Polish verb in the imperative "Stój!," which would have been better from the translation chosen also due to voice acting considerations. When Lara starts pronouncing the word, there is a close-up on her face, so the lip movements are clearly visible. The English version includes a one-syllable word, while the Polish version a two-syllable one. For that reason the suggested translation (which is also a one-syllable word) would enable a more accurate lip synchronisation of the recorded dialogue line. The described situation shows that there is a high probability that not only the translators but also the actors who voiced the dialogues in the Polish version of this game could have no access to any visual materials. Undoubtedly, being able to see the scene would allow the translation suggested by the localisation team to be modified also during the dialogue recording process.

In fact, this is not the only error in the Polish version of this game caused by the lack of sufficient contextual information in the study corpus. A lexico-morphological error in a dialogue between Lara Croft and her friend, Jonah Maiava, who are climbing an ice-covered wall in Siberian mountains, was noted by another participant. The dialogue in English and Polish language versions is shown in Table 1.

Table 1: A fragment of the dialogue between Lara Croft and Jonah Maiava in Rise of the Tomb Raider (Crystal Dynamics, 2016)

English (original) dialogue	**Polish translation**
Jonah: Whoa! There's lots of loose ice up here.	**Jonah:** Łooł! Pełno tu poluzowanych lodowych odłamków.
Lara: Let's take it slow and steady. Just stay with me.	**Lara:** Powoli i spokojnie, trzymajcie się mnie.

The verb form used in the Polish translation of Lara's answer (meaning "hold on to me") is used in the second person plural form, which suggests that she has more than one companions in this scene. However, only the two characters are taking part in this scene. Consequently, the Polish player might be confused by these words (occurring in both the subtitles and the voice-acting recording). Even if they cause no disinformation (the player can use the visual information channel to know that there are no more characters present), they disturb the user's feeling of immersion due to a discrepancy between the wording of the dialogue and the in-game world reality.

The structure of both mistranslated segments allowed the translator to guess that they come from dialogues. Two of them include an exclamation mark and two of them consist of more than one sentence as well as some colloquial language. However, most probably no description on who is talking to whom and in what circumstances was provided, which led to the misinterpretation of the fragment. Grammatically, the English phrase used in the described dialogue could be pronounced both to one person and to several people.

As one of the participants stated, apart from these mistakes the game also involved some other translation errors, such as variance between the wording in the Polish subtitles and voice acting recordings. In those cases, although the meaning of both the visible and audible text was the same or highly comparable, the words used to express it were different. All the described issues evidence that the Polish version of this game lacked appropriate localisation testing which would be able to detect such flaws. Alternatively, even if the errors were spotted, they could have been left unchanged due to the costs of re-recording the voice-acting lines. In fact, various authors (e.g. O'Hagan & Mangiron 2013: 111; Bernal-Merino 2015: 172; Mrzigod 2021: 52) state that voice acting is usually the most expensive element of a full localisation process.

A participant of the 2021 survey mentioned an example of a terminological error potentially caused by blind video game localisation in *Valiant Hearts: The Great War* (Ubisoft, 2014). This adventure, 2D game with action and puzzle elements describes stories of several people whose lives were completely changed by the Great War. The playable characters escape Ypres together by car. However, on their way south they are attacked by German aviation. In the cutscene introducing this scene, the narrator says: "But while approaching Vimy, a German squadron spotted them." The Polish translation of this phrase is shown in Figure 7.

Figure 7: Discrepancy between the subtitles and game visuals caused by "blind localisation" in the Polish version of Valiant Hearts: The Great War (Ubisoft, 2014)

The English word "squadron" which can refer to an air-force, naval, or, historically, cavalry unit (Britannica 2017), was translated into Polish as "szwadron." The Polish word changes the original meaning and confuses the gamer. The visuals clearly show aircraft, while the word used refers exclusively to a cavalry unit.

Although Mrzigod (2021: 103, 275) states that in this particular case the immediate use of the most similar Polish equivalent was the reason for this error to occur (which is highly probable), there is also one more explanation possible. The translator in this case knew that the game is set in a Word War One context. However, without access to the game graphics or a description of the following scene (where the user's task is to avoid bombs dropped by the airplanes), the translator still might be uncertain whether to use the word "eskadra," which refers to an air-force unit in Polish, or "szwadron." This stems from the fact that cavalry was also used during World War One, but to a lesser extent than before (cf. Britannica 2013). Undoubtedly, more thorough research by the translator or more detailed communication between the localisation and development team would have prevented the described error.

3.2.2. *Metatranslational errors*

Although most of the translation errors in video game localisation caused by the phenomenon of "blind localisation" result in slight confusion or discontentment of the player, in some cases the consequences of such a fault could be far more serious. This type of situation (mentioned in the 2018 subcorpus) occurred in *Syberia 3* (Microïds, 2017) which is the third instalment in the renowned series of graphic adventure games set in an imaginary steam-punk republic somewhere in Siberia. The player helps the main character, an American lawyer Kate Walker, to solve various puzzles in order to aid the nomadic Youkol people in their traditional journey. One of the puzzles the user comes across involves a steamship model and the accompanying description next to it. The English and Polish language version of the information plate are presented in Figure 8.

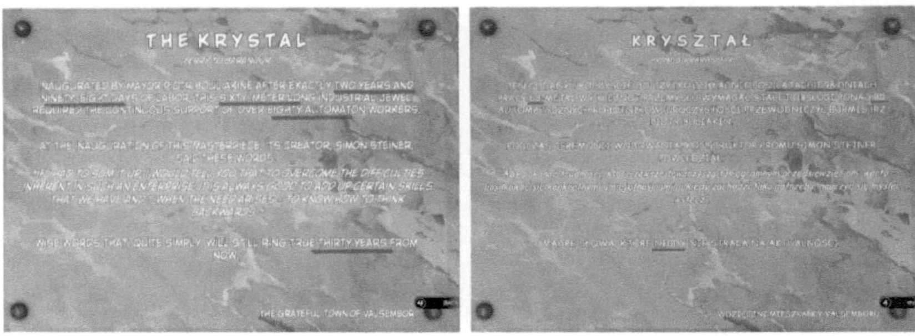

Figure 8: The steamship description from Syberia 3 (Microïds, 2017) in English and Polish. The numbers are not originally underlined in the game

The original description in English involves five numbers which have been underlined by the author in Figure 8. The Polish translation involves four of them, apart from the one present in the last sentence of the text. While the original sentence reads “Wise words that, quite simply, will still ring true thirty years from now,” in the Polish version is shorter and could be back-translated as “Wise words, which will never lose their relevance.” Although the translation seems to be reflecting the general meaning of the original sentence, the missing detail transpires to be crucial for solving the puzzle.

After thoroughly inspecting the model, the player could notice that one of the paddle wheels of the model is in fact a dial. In order to open the model and find a key, which would be necessary for completing the game, the player needs to dial the five numbers in the order in which they appear in the description (2, 98, 60, 80, 30). Consequently, the Polish users were misinformed and due to the lack of the last number in the Polish text (present in the game regardless of the choice to play with the English or Polish voice-acting) they were unable to solve the puzzle. In the months following the game’s release, online gaming forums were filled with discussions where users were asking for aid in solving the puzzle. The game provides a possibility to quickly change the language in the settings menu, so users soon found the difference between the Polish and the full English version of the game. However, the error described strongly affected the players immersion in the in-game world which in this fragment lost some of its coherence.

In this particular case, the use of the equivalence procedure (Vinay & Darbelnet 1954/ 1995) in the Polish translation also most probably stemmed from the lack of contextual knowledge provided to the localising team. Unaware of the importance of the number 30, the translator decided to change it to a semantically similar and shorter sentence. This example underlines the importance of careful communication between the localisation and development teams. A more thorough testing process might have exposed such an issue.

3.2.3. Issues in the original language version

In some cases, however, the translator is not to be blamed for a situation which seems to be a result of a “blind localisation.” Sometimes inaccuracies in the original language version of a game are the reason. A comparison of the Polish localisation and the English original has verified a claim by one of the respondents on that matter in *Forge of Empires* (InnoGames, 2012). In this browser, free-to-play, strategy game, the user is tasked with developing a city through various eras, since prehistorical times to distant future. Before the success of this game the studio could have been described as independent. One of the elements which the player is supposed to supervise is building and commanding the army. The error which was recognised by a participant of the 2021 survey as a mistake made by the translator, caused either by an oversight or insufficient contextual information, is shown in Figure 9.

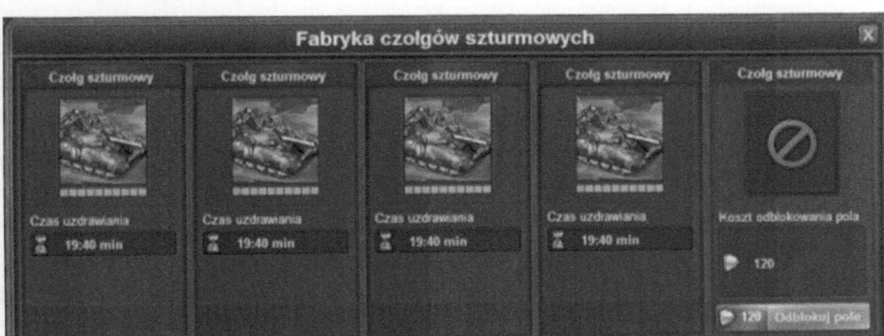

Figure 9: Erroneous label in the Polish version of Forge of Empires (InnoGames, 2012)

The table shown is displayed when the player opens the battle tank factory menu. One of various statistics of each unit is "czas uzdrawiania" (in English "healing time"), although all the units shown are battle tanks. One may think that this could be a case of a misplaced translation segment in the game code (an error which is not frequent but occurs rather regularly) or a translation error. However, within the settings of this factory the original feature in English is also called "healing time." Hence, in this particular case the informative mistake in the Polish version was caused by the erroneous original language version. Obviously, the original text segment should read "repair time" and the Polish translation should be "czas naprawy." The game is not always historically accurate (cf. Radetich & Jakubowicz 2015: 19) which may explain the occurrence of the described error. Consequently, this example shows the importance of communication between the localisation team and the developers, as sometimes an issue in the original language version may be noticed by the users of the localised version.

Conclusions

As the examples provided show, "blind localisation" is a phenomenon occurring in video games regardless of their genre, platform, and the type of the developing or publishing company. This stems from the fact that providing translators with insufficient contextual details due to the presence of short separated translation segments is an inherent part of video game localisation. Often deprived of even samples of the game graphic and audio materials, written scene descriptions or labels indicating the type of in-game asset a particular translation segment represents, the localiser is forced to make intuitive and guessing-based translation decisions. This phenomenon is not absent in video games localised into Polish.

Such a situation is a source of various errors in the localised video game versions. They could be based on the polysemy of some words, their ability to be used as different parts of speech and potential situational ambiguity. Furthermore, the amount of contextual information provided could be insufficient for the translator to choose the correct equivalent of the original wording. The word forms, grammatical structures or idioms utilised in such circumstances may be stylistically, lexically, terminologically, or grammatically inappropriate in the localised version. This negatively impacts the coherence and naturalness of the in-game world which is perceived by the gamer also through the utilised language means. As a result, the user's engagement (immersion) in the game may be blunted. Finally, the use of modified meaning of the original text may provide the user with incomplete message or misleading guidance. Thus, the localised content may become an obstacle hindering or even preventing the user to successfully finish the game.

The most effective solution to prevent "blind localisation" is supplementing the localised text with as much contextual information as possible. If the game is still being developed, the visual and audio material could be substituted with written explanations which apart from the game world would refer to the alternative versions of the plot, rules of the source code and organisation of the material undergoing localisation.

It is also worth noting that not all situations resembling the results of "blind localisation" are the effect of translator's decisions. Instead, they stem from factual errors and inconsistencies occurring in the original version of the game.

The issue may seem marginal, as there were only nine instances found in the study corpus. However, the corpus most probably does not reflect the real scale of the phenomenon, as the answers were provided by end users, who usually focus more on other (often technical) aspects of video game localisation. Consequently, blind localisation should not be neglected, as it may occur even in AAA games and can have potentially considerable impact on the player experience. This applies especially to the instances of unaware misinforming the player by either failing to provide the information essential for completing a particular task or providing them with a wrong detail which may totally misguide them.

For that reason "blind localisation" is a potential subject of diverse further research. In order to obtain a more in-depth perspective of this phenomenon in the Polish market, a more representative survey study of translators, localisation providers or gamers on that matter is recommended.

References

Adams, E. (2014). *Fundamentals of Game Design* (3rd ed.). New Riders.

Bernal-Merino, M. Á. (2015). *Translation and Localisation in Video Games. Making Entertainment Software Global*. Routledge.

Britannica, T. Editors of Encyclopaedia (2013, August 22). 'Cavalry.' In *Encyclopedia Britannica*. https://www.britannica.com/topic/cavalry

Britannica, T. Editors of Encyclopaedia (2017, May 17). 'Squadron.' In *Encyclopedia Britannica*. https://www.britannica.com/topic/squadron

Czech, D. (2013). 'Challenges in video game localization: An integrated perspective.' *Explorations: A Journal of Language and Literature*, *1*, 3–25.

Dietz, F. (2006). 'Issues in Localizing Computer Games.' In K. J. Dunne (Ed.), *Perspectives in Localization* (121–134). John Benjamins.

Dietz, F. (2007). 'How Difficult Can That Be? The Work of Computer and Video Game Localization.' *Revista Tradumatica, 5* (La localitzacio de videojocs). http://www.fti.uab.es/tradumatica/revista/num5/articles/04/04art.htm

Drab, E. (2014). 'Gry wideo a przekład: nowe pole badań w obrębie tłumaczenia audiowizualnego.' *Rocznik Przekładoznawczy. Studia nad teorią, praktyką i dydaktyką przekładu, 9*(1), 101–114.

Hejwowski, K. (2001), 'Źródła błędów w tłumaczeniu na język ojczysty.' In A. Kopczyński, & U. Zaliwska-Okrutna (Eds.), *Język rodzimy a język obcy. Komunikacja, przekład, dydaktyka* (149–159), Wydawnictwo Uniwersytetu Warszawskiego.

Honeywood, R., Fung, J., Bonfils, S., Campbell, D., Dellepiane, A., Edwards, K., d'Engelbronner, E., Klischewski, R., Alonso Lion, V., Lopez, E., Luppino, T., Minazzi, F., Petrarca, V., Santambrogio, A., Schmidt, M., Slattery, T., Solbiati, D., & Williams, S. (2012). *Best practices for game localization.* IGDA Localization SIG. http://englobe.com/wp-content/uploads/2012/05/Best-Practices-for-Game-Localization-v21.pdf

Kozłowska, Z. (2001), 'O błędach w językowych w tekstach polskich przekładów.' In A. Kopczyński/ U. Zaliwska-Okrutna (Eds.), *Język rodzimy a język obcy. Komunikacja, przekład, dydaktyka,* Warszawa: Wydawnictwo Uniwersytetu Warszawskiego, 137–147.

Kudła, D. (2020). *Ocena odbioru lokalizacji językowej gier komputerowych na podstawie danych okulograficznych.* Wydawnictwo Naukowe Instytutu Komunikacji Specjalistycznej i Interkulturowej, Uniwersytet Warszawski. http://sn.iksi.uw.edu.pl/wp-content/uploads/sites/306/2020/09/SN-50-Dominik-Kudła-Lokalizacja-językowa.pdf

Kudła, D. (2021). 'The Views of Dedicated Polish Gamers on the Localization of Video Games into Polish – Online Survey Results.' *Kwartalnik Neofilologiczny, LXVIII*(4), 530–549. https://doi.org/10.24425/kn.2021.139558

Moby Games (n.d.) *Game Browser.* Moby Games, https://www.mobygames.com/browse/games

Mrzigod, J. (2021). *Meandry lokalizacji gier.* Helion.

O'Brien, S. (2012). 'Towards a dynamic quality evaluation model for translation.' *Journal of Specialized Translation, 17*, 55–77.

O'Hagan, M., & Mangiron, C. (2013). *Game Localization: Translating for the Global Digital Entertainment Industry*. John Benjamins.

Pedersen, J. (2017). 'The FAR model: assessing quality in interlingual subtitling.' *The Journal of Specialised Translation, 28*, 210–229.

Radetich, L., & Jakubowicz, E. (2015). 'Using Video Games for Teaching History. Experiences and Challenges.' *Athens Journal of History*, *1*(1), 9–22. https://doi.org/10.30958/ajhis.1-1-1 doi=10.30958/ajhis.1-1-1

Tarquini, G. (2014). 'Translating the Onscreen Text Blindfolded: Possibilities and Impossibilities.' In C. Mangiron, M. O'Hagan, & P. Orero (Eds.), *Fun for All: Translation and Accessibility Practices in Video Games* (149–173). Peter Lang.

Vinay, J. P., & Darbelnet, J. (1995). *Comparative stylistics of French and English: A methodology for translation,* John Benjamins. (Original work published 1954).

Wolf, M. J. P. (2001). 'Genre and the Video Game.' In M. J. P. Wolf (Ed.), *The Medium of the Video Game* (113–133). University of Texas Press.

This publication was edited by prof. Władysław Witalisz.

List of video games referred to in the text
Game name (Developed by/Published by/Release year)

Assassin's Creed: Valhalla (Ubisoft/Ubisoft/November 10, 2020).

Doodle Champion Island Games (Google, Studio 4°C/Google/July 23, 2021).

Forge of Empires (InnoGames/InnoGames/April 17, 2012).

Horizon: Zero Dawn (Guerilla Games/Sony Interactive Entertainment/February 28, 2017).

Rise of the Tomb Raider (Crystal Dynamics, Inc./Square Enix/January 28, 2016).

Syberia 3 (Microïds/Microïds/April 20, 2017).

Terraria (Re-Logic/Re-Logic/May 16, 2012).

Valiant Hearts: The Great War (Ubisoft Montpellier/Ubisoft/June 26, 2014).

Martyn Gray

University of Nottingham

Translation under Review: Placing the Increased Visibility of Translation in British Reviews into Its Wider Societal Context

Abstract: In *The Translator's Invisibility* (1995), Lawrence Venuti claims that reviewers contribute to the notion of 'invisibility' of the translator by rarely addressing the 'fact of translation' at all. He asserts that, on the rare occasions that translations are addressed, reviewers' comments tend to focus on its style and in particular fluency, neglecting other relevant considerations. This paper will take Venuti's brief investigation as its inspiration and provide a comprehensive update on the current position of translation in reviews in the United Kingdom. In order to do this, it will present the findings from an analysis of more than 2000 reviews of translated works in 2015, taken from three distinct types of 'platform:' a popular platform open for comments from the public (amazon.co.uk); mainstream newspapers/supplements (*The Times Literary Supplement* & *The Guardian*); and specialised literary magazines (*London Review of Books* & *Literary Review*). The paper will aim to answer the following questions: how frequently is translation acknowledged in the first place? Do reviewers tend to comment upon the translations at hand? If so, by what criteria is the quality of the translation being assessed? The paper will demonstrate that the situation of the translator in the United Kingdom has evolved in several significant ways over the past twenty or thirty years and that translators are no longer as invisible as previously imagined, at least within reviews of translated works. The paper will subsequently examine the status of translation in wider society and draw upon the work of various translation associations and organisations to determine whether the increased invisibility of translation within the reviews is also indicative of, or indeed inherently connected to, an increased visibility of translation in the United Kingdom more broadly.

Keywords: Venuti, invisibility, quality assessment, reviews, activism

~

1. Introduction – Lawrence Venuti and *The Translator's Invisibility* (1995)

Back in 1995, Lawrence Venuti published his seminal work, *The Translator's Invisibility: A History of Translation*, in which he argued for an understanding of translation as an 'invisible' art. He uses the term 'invisibility' to refer to two sides of the same coin. On the one hand, translators themselves manipulate the language into which they are translating in order to produce an "illusionistic effect of discourse" (Venuti, 1995: 1), thus masking their own work. On the other hand, publishers, readers and reviewers judge a translation to be acceptable when it "reads fluently, when the absence of any linguistic or stylistic peculiarities makes it seem transparent … – the appearance, in other words, that the translation is not in fact a translation, but the 'original'" (Venuti, 1995: 1). These two phenomena in combination, Venuti claims, result in a situation in which we have two rather significant problems. Firstly, translators suffer from what Venuti terms 'cultural marginality' and 'economic exploitation,' their status being "seldom recognized, poorly paid writers" (Venuti, 1995: 13). Secondly, our literary cultures in the United Kingdom and the United States have developed in such a manner that they are "aggressively monolingual, unreceptive to foreign literatures [and] accustomed to fluent translations," meaning that readers of translated works have a certain "narcissistic experience of recognising their own culture in a cultural other" (Venuti, 1995: 12).

With a view to backing up this latter assertion, Venuti examines a sample of reviews of translated literature from a range of British and American periodicals across a 60-year period, asking, amongst other questions, by what criteria reviewers assess the quality of a translation. He discovers that "over the past sixty years the comments have grown amazingly consistent in praising fluency while damning deviations from it, even when the most diverse range of foreign texts is considered" (Venuti, 1995: 2). In other words, if the translator has concealed their own presence in the text, making themselves 'invisible' and producing a natural and fluent translation for the target reader, reviewers virtually always evaluate this positively. Words such as 'wooden,' 'clumsy' and 'unidiomatic' are used by reviewers to damn translations which are not immediately intelligible. However, it is rather difficult to draw any definitive conclusions from Venuti's study: after all, reviewing practices are not the focus of *The Translator's Invisibility*, and it therefore remains unclear how many reviews are included in the study and how Venuti chose the specific reviews which he draws upon. Despite this slight scepticism, it must be said that the brief study gave rise to a number of further studies of reviewing practices, particularly in the British context, in the late 1990s and 2000s. This increased interest in the field since Venuti's publication provided the inspiration for this paper, which has three very specific aims: to examine the findings of subsequent studies of reviewing practices in the British context in the ten or so years after *The Translator's Invisibility* was published; to provide an update on reviewing practices in the 2010s; and to situate the findings of this latter study in their wider societal context – in other words, to determine the extent to which translators and their work have become more universally visible.

2. Subsequent studies of reviewing practices in the British context

Three years after the publication of *The Translator's Invisibility*, Jeremy Munday (1998) investigated the way in which the translations of Gabriel García Márquez's novels were acknowledged and assessed by British reviewers. Of the seven reviews that Munday includes in his study, only three of them mention the translator alongside the author in the credits. In addition to this, Munday discovers that the only references in the reviews to the process of translation are "a passing comment by Gott [in *The Guardian*], 'the collection (translated beautifully as ever by Edith Grossman),' and Turner Hospital's simultaneous attack [in *The Independent*] on both the translator and the 'leaden prose' of García Márquez's *Strange Pilgrims*" (Munday, 1998: 141). This resonates particularly well with what Venuti had previously asserted: both that translators are very rarely acknowledged in the first place and that, if a reviewer comments upon the translation, they are overwhelmingly negative towards 'wooden' prose – or in this case, 'leaden' prose. Munday therefore concludes that reading the reviews seems to suggest that García Márquez's prose "has not only been *translated* into English – in the eyes of many reviewers it *is* English" (Munday, 1998: 143), echoing precisely what Venuti says about the 'appearance' of a translation not as a translation, but rather as the original text.

Venuti's discoveries are further corroborated by the publication of Peter Fawcett's paper. Fawcett's body of reviews was collected over a seven-year period (1992–1999) from the British broadsheets, mainly *The Observer*. Fawcett found that in those seven years from 1992, 11 translations of novels, short stories, poetry and biographies came up for review; however, it should be stated here that Fawcett only included those reviews which wrote 'explicitly' about translation. Despite the small number of reviews included in Fawcett's study, it does provide a crucial contribution to our understanding of the field, since it reveals certain critical criteria by which translations tend to be assessed by British reviewers. The four main features that Fawcett observes are "a preference for transparent translation; strong dislike of source-oriented modes of translation; paucity of evidence to back up criticism; [and] a tendency to offer no analysis to justify a criticism" (Fawcett, 2000: 296). Much like the findings of Munday, Fawcett's study adds weight to Venuti's assertion that translations which are fluent – or Fawcett's word, 'transparent' – are universally praised. Fawcett concludes that the reviews under study "constitute an exercise in institutionalised irresponsibility: an unexplained authority to use a limited physical space to brand a translation and a translator as poor in relation to a criterion assumed to be universal and unassailable" (Fawcett, 2000: 305).

Peter Bush takes a slightly different approach to the issue of reviewing practices; his paper rather analyses the quantity of reviews published by British publications compared to their French and Spanish counterparts. Bush therefore examines reviews from a two-month period in 2004 and claims that "if one criterion for book-buyers working for the book chains is the column space devoted to reviews, then translations don't [sic] get much of a fillip from that direction" (Bush, 2004: 31). This contention is fully justified by the statistics that he provides: in the two-month period at hand, *The London Review of Books* published just four reviews, *The Guardian* slightly more with thirteen, and *The Times Literary Supplement* managed thirty-one. In isolation, these figures perhaps do not tell us a great deal; however, it is the comparison with the number of reviews published by French and Spanish outlets which make his assertion more convincing. For example, *Le Monde* in France and *Babelia* (the literary supplement of *El País*) in Spain published eighty and eighty-one reviews of translation respectively during the same period. Although Bush does acknowledge that his study only provides a "somewhat arbitrary, impressionistic state of play" (Bush, 2004: 30), he ultimately arrives at a very strong conclusion: given that "the review pages of national newspapers … reflect and shape particular national traditions in relation to elsewhere in the world" and that the "present Anglo-American political climate … prefers bombs to words and holds most things foreign as objects of suspicion" (Bush, 2004: 43–44), it is perhaps not all that surprising that the number of British reviews published is significantly lower than that of France and Spain.

Penny Johnson's paper on reviews of translations into English of Pablo Neruda's *Canto general* is the most recent piece to be written in this field of Translation Studies. Johnson (2005) discovers that the fact of translation tends not to be acknowledged; however, this is not something with which she necessarily takes issue. She argues that, if a translated work is not marketed or reviewed as such, then it "might be a way to enter the target culture; a way for the readers to acquire a taste for foreign literature; and a way for the author to reach a wider audience" (Johnson, 2005: 139). In other words, a lack of visibility for translation in the first instance may lead to more readers actually engaging with translated literature in the long run. However, from an ethical point of view, she concedes that "the fact of translation needs to be acknowledged, to make the translator accountable for the quality (whether good or bad) of the translation and to allow readers to have a right to know that a text originated in another culture" (Johnson, 2005: 140). Johnson's paper also has the self-proclaimed aim of 'testing' and 'developing' the claims made by analysts of translated literature reviews; with this in mind, she examines whether fluency continues to be the main criterion by which translations are assessed. Johnson discovers that, whilst fluency remains prevalent within the reviews, the preference for "a readable or an accurate translation depends on the reviewer" and that a monolingual reviewer "may be more likely to prefer a readable translation since s/he does not have the capability to evaluate the accuracy of the translation" (Johnson, 2005: 137). By assessing the background of the reviewer and whether they could speak the language of the original text, Johnson was the first scholar in the British context to bring the notion of language proficiency into her study, thus introducing a new angle to the field.

By the mid-2000s, then, we have a clear picture of the way in which translations are reviewed in the United Kingdom. The four scholars discussed in this section have been able to provide further evidence to Venuti's overarching assertion – that the invisibility of translation and translators is encouraged by reviewing practices. Not only did the scholars discover that translators are still frequently unacknowledged by reviewers, but they also found that fluency and transparency generally continue to be the main tenets by which translations are assessed. However, it is also important to point out that, whilst these previous studies have made valuable contributions to the field, they also have a few shared issues. Firstly, the scope of the studies has been limited, by which I mean that they include a relatively small number of reviews (in the case of Fawcett and Bush) or that they focus only on reviews of translations of a singular author (in the case of Munday and Johnson). Secondly, the focus of these studies has been rather restrictive, almost always examining reviews taken exclusively from the broadsheets. This has provided us with an in-depth knowledge of how translated works are reviewed by this kind of press; however, broadsheets only form a small part of the network of reviewing and it would therefore be unfair to claim that translators are invisible in *all* reviews of their work. After all, each platform has "particular restrictions, characteristics and intended readership" and therefore the "content or the methodology of the review is likely to be different" (Johnson, 2005: 130). In addition to these shared issues, there have been no extensive studies in this field since the mid-2000s. This leads us to pose the question of whether the situation has changed for translators – are they now more visible in reviews of translated literature? The paper will now present the discoveries of an extensive study into reviewing practices in the mid-2010s in an attempt to provide answers to this very question.

3. The current study

The current study draws upon a corpus of reviews collected in the year 2015. To address the criticisms aimed at previous studies, the reviews were collected from a wide range of platforms:

- One popular platform, *amazon.co.uk*. The justification for including a popular platform is two-fold. Firstly, a Pew Research study shows that "more than 50 % of people now obtain news and information – including book reviews – on digital platforms" which are not traditional mainstream media (Fay, 2012); such platforms thus now wield a greater influence than ever before. Secondly, including reviews written by non-specialised, generally unpaid reviewers provides us with different insights into how translated works are reviewed.
- Two broadsheets/cultural supplements, *The Times Literary Supplement* and *The Guardian*, broadly comparable to those included in previous studies.
- Two literary magazines, *Literary Review* and *London Review of Books*. The justification for including more specialised publications in the study is to provide a 'counter-balance' to the popular platform: the reviewers for these publications are specifically trained and experienced in writing reviews about literature.

This collection methodology gave rise a corpus size of 2363 reviews: 1985 taken from *amazon.co.uk*;[1] 299 published in the broadsheets (211 in *The Times Literary Supplement* and 88 in *The Guardian*); and 79 published in the literary magazines (54 in *Literary Review* and 25 in *London Review of Books*). This ensures that the current corpus is the most extensive to date, in terms of both the raw number of reviews and the platforms from which the reviews have been collected. The conclusions that may be drawn from the study will therefore be more definitive than what has previously been found in this field.

In order to assess the claims and assertions made by Venuti and subsequent scholars about the visibility of translation in reviews, it is important for this paper to analyse the content of the reviews. Each of the reviews is therefore examined with four research questions in mind:

(1) Is the translation or translator acknowledged?
(2) If the translation or translator *is* acknowledged, is a comment made upon the translation?

1 All books for which a review had been published in *The Times Literary Supplement* or *The Guardian* in 2015 were searched for on Amazon. All reviews for that book published in 2015 were then included in the corpus.

(3) If a comment is made, what type of comment is it? Is the comment related to transparency?
(4) If a comment is made, does the reviewer provide analysis and/or examples?

There are two main reasons for using this set of questions. On the one hand, these questions broadly relate to those that Fawcett investigated, and Fawcett's study is the most comparable to the present study. On the other hand, these questions will allow us insights into different levels of visibility – in other words, are we simply talking about a passing reference to the fact that the work has been translated, or is the reviewer engaging with the work of the translator on a more meaningful level? This paper shall now look at each of these questions in turn and present the discoveries from this vast corpus of reviews.

4. Reviewing practices in 2015 – discoveries

(1) Is the translation or translator acknowledged?

Given the assertions of previous scholars, the reviews collected in this study present us with somewhat surprising findings: more than 85 % of reviews of translated works published in the four broadsheets and literary magazines in 2015 acknowledge the fact of translation or mention the translator (see Appendix 1 for a full breakdown). *The Times Literary Supplement* acknowledges the fact of translation without fail, whereas *London Review of Books* omit an acknowledgement of the fact of translation in just one case and *Literary Review* only fails to mention the translator in two instances, though the reasons behind these omissions remain unclear. 12 out of 88 reviews (or 13.6 %) published in *The Guardian* do not make any reference to the fact that it is a translation which is being reviewed. The reason for reviews in *The Guardian* not being as consistent as *The Times Literary Supplement* or the two literary magazines may be the prominence of the location of such a mention within the review. Whilst *The Times Literary Supplement*, *Literary Review* and *London Review of Books* almost systematically mention the name of the translator immediately after the title of the book and the author of the source text, and therefore achieve much greater consistency in this regard, the first mention of the translation or translator generally comes within the main body of the text of the review in *The Guardian*.

The only platform included in this corpus which acknowledges translation in less than 85 % of reviews – and by some distance – is *amazon.co.uk* (just 14.1 % of reviews). Nonetheless, this does not come as much of a surprise, since Amazon reviews are also written to provide feedback on delivery times and costs, the condition of the book, the recipient of the book, and, although reviewers do not have a limited number of characters for reviews on this platform, the majority of them will in reality have a limited amount of time to write reviews. In addition to this, the name of the translator is often mentioned in the product description elsewhere on the Amazon product page, and perhaps therefore reviewers do not feel the need to repeat the information.

(2) If the translation or translator *is* acknowledged, is a comment made upon the translation?

Of those reviews which acknowledge or mention the translation in the first place, an average of 58.4 % of these reviews comment upon the translation (see Appendix 2 for a full breakdown). Perhaps surprisingly, it is the specialised publications which do this least frequently: fewer than half of the reviews which acknowledge the fact of translation in *Literary Review* and *London Review of Books* comment upon the translation (39.6 % and 48 % respectively). *The Times Literary Supplement* is the most consistent publication at providing comments upon the work of the translator, with almost 4 out of 5 reviews published in 2015 doing so. Amazon is perhaps the biggest surprise here: 71 % of reviewers who acknowledged that they were reviewing a translated work also made a comment upon the quality of the translation. These reviewers are generally unpaid, non-professional readers who are engaging with translation in a more detailed manner than ever before; perhaps, then, this is indicative of a wider growing awareness of the role and work of the translator in the process of transferring a text from one language to another.

Admittedly, a great deal of the reviews which comment upon the translation quality do so with a brief blanket judgement, usually in the form of a single adjective or adverb. This could be regarded in one of two ways. Either we consider this to be problematic and question the purpose of such judgements, much like Isabelle Vanderschelden (2000: 285): “it could be argued that this type of commentary on a translation is of little value and has limited impact; if anything, it reinforces the general attitude of casualness towards the work of the translator.” Or we could take the opposing view, appreciating that the reviewer has at least attempted to engage with the work of the translator; this is precisely what translator Tess Lewis does when she declares that she will “readily acknowledge the satisfaction even a single adjective … can bring. I’m [sic] happy to take the reviewer’s judgement on face value, without expecting any examples or justifications” (Lewis, 2011). Regardless of whether we agree with Vanderschelden or Lewis on this matter, the fact that reviewers now attempt to comment upon the work of the translator is a far cry from what previous scholars had discovered.

(3) If a comment is made, what type of comment is it? Is the comment related to transparency?

Previous studies indicated that transparency – which encompasses various notions such as clarity, fluency, lucidity and readability – was the main tenet by which translations are assessed and reviewed. The most frequent adjectives used in this corpus of reviews to assess the quality of a translation by this criterion were 'clear,' 'flowing,' 'fluent,' 'lucid' and 'readable.' However, these adjectives only appear 47 times in total in the 2363 reviews collected from all five platforms, with 'fluent' being the most common (used 12 times). More than two-thirds of the reviews which use any of these transparency-related adjectives come either from *amazon.co.uk* or *The Times Literary Supplement*, perhaps not surprising given that we discovered that reviewers for these platforms are more likely to comment upon the quality of a translation than reviewers for the other publications. As we may have expected, these words are always used positively to praise the work of the translator. For example, Wright, in a review of the translation of *Leon Blum: Prime Minister, Socialist, Zionist* in *The Times Literary Supplement*, praises the translator, Arthur Goldhammer, who is "responsible, as with many other recent French histories, for a clear and fluent translation" (Wright, 2015), whilst an Amazon reviewer of the translation of *Why the World Does Not Exist* believes the translator has done a 'wonderful' job in achieving 'lucidity:' "It was written in German, but the translator Gregory Moss has done a wonderful job because the text is rendered so lucid for such a difficult subject" (Anonymous Amazon reviewer, 2015).

Whilst transparency has always seemed to be viewed positively by translation reviewers, previous studies have also demonstrated that reviewers tend to have, in the words of Fawcett, "a strong dislike of source-oriented modes of translation" (Fawcett, 2000: 305). The words used to test this claim are 'accurate,' 'faithful,' 'precise,' 'preserving' and 'sensitive.' These words appear 24 times in total in the 2363 reviews, with 'preserving' (or its verb 'preserves') cropping up most frequently, in eleven reviews – just once less than the word 'fluent.' Despite the relative lack of these words by reviewers compared to the words related to transparency above, they are almost always used positively to refer to the work of the translator – an indication that reviewers are now not simply focussing on how well the translation reads in the target language. In a review of the translation of *Conversations: Volume 2* in *Literary Review*, for example, reviewer Graham-Yooll praises translator Tom Boll for translating 'ably' and 'faithfully,' "capturing many twists in the old man's Spanish and in his Argentine quirks" (Graham-Yooll, 2015). In yet another review, Tree, examining the translation of *Dark Vales* in

The Times Literary Supplement, claims that the translator Yates deserves 'high praise,' as he has "managed to preserve the tone of the original Catalan without having recourse to potentially awkward archaisms. He does this by combining contemporary vocabulary with words that were used two or three generations ago" (Tree, 2015). Only one review, published on *amazon.co.uk* and discussing the translation of *The Three-Body Problem*, uses one of these words to comment negatively on the impact of the work of the translator: this reviewer accepts the "general consensus that his translation is accurate to the original," but finds that "such honesty rendered the people down to one-dimensional characters [who] were very difficult to warm to, or sympathise with, in many ways" (Anonymous Amazon reviewer, 2015). Overall, though, there is universal positivity shown towards translations which retain important qualities of the original text, perhaps backing up Johnson's point that the criteria by which translations are assessed ultimately depend on the individual reviewer.

The most frequent words used to comment upon translation in this corpus of reviews are 'well,' 'excellent' and 'beautiful,' which appear in 36, 28 and 16 reviews respectively. From a Translation Studies point of view, these words are what I would refer to as 'empty' adjectives, by which I mean that it is impossible to infer what aspect of the translator's work the reviewer is referring to with such a comment. Have they translated the work *well*, precisely because it reads fluently in the target language? Indeed, it may be possible that fluency is now engrained in the conscience of British reviewers to such an extent that it is taken for granted and not even considered to be worth commenting upon explicitly. Or is it an *excellent* translation, because it actually retains much of what is present in the original text? To make the situation even more complex, these words are overwhelmingly used by reviewers in isolation – in other words, they are never backed up with analysis of what the comment is actually referring to. Therefore, although these three words appear more frequently than any other in the reviews, it would be difficult to make a convincing argument that they clearly demonstrate that a reviewer prefers transparency or otherwise.

(4) If a comment is made, does the reviewer provide analysis and/or examples?

In his paper, Fawcett (2000: 297) claims that comments on translation are generally "supported by what, to an academic, is the flimsiest of proof (a few examples at most, and very often none at all)," and we can observe a similar trend from the reviews included in this corpus: just over a third of the reviews included in the corpus which comment upon the translation back up their comment with further engagement (see Appendix 3 for a full breakdown). Despite the fact that translations are only commented upon in less than half of the reviews which acknowledge the fact of translation in the *London Review of Books*, these comments are substantiated by further analysis or examples in 72.8 % of cases. This makes the *London Review of Books* the only publication in this study where the figure is greater than half; this may well be down to the editorial standards of the publication, or indeed preferences of the individual reviewers. By contrast, the other specialised literary magazine, *Literary Review*, provides further engagement with the translation in less than one in five reviews, and we can therefore not claim that what we discovered for the *London Review of Books* is indicative of a trend for the specialised publications. The broadsheet reviews which comment upon the translation analyse their comments and provide examples in roughly one third of cases (35.8 % and 33.3 % of reviews in *The Times Literary Supplement* and *The Guardian* respectively). Amazon, on which we saw 71 % of reviews which acknowledge the fact of translation also go on to comment upon the translation, is the least consistent platform in this regard: reviewers support their comments in just 15.1 % of the reviews. To a great extent, these results are not surprising as we would expect reviewers on the least specialised platform to provide the least analysis to support comments.

As far as the provision of analysis and examples is concerned, a very clear trend can be identified across the reviews in this corpus: reviews of translated poetry – with the exception of those published on *amazon.co.uk* – provide a relatively large amount of analysis and examples in comparison to reviews of translations from other genres. This is perhaps down to the fact that the translation of poetry is amongst the most contentious forms of translation and many different strategies may be adopted to retain certain elements of form, such as rhyme and rhythm, and content to different extents (see Holmes, 1968, for example). One review in particular stands out here – that of Michael Hofmann in *The Times Literary Supplement*, reviewing a translation of *New Selected Poems*. Almost two-thirds of the entire review are dedicated to analysing the translation. Hofmann initially provides an overarching comment on the translation – that it is 'torpid,' 'laboured' and 'stiff' – before adding a whole suite of examples to support the point he is making, such as the following: "their first quality is idleness: as in *translatio*, the word simply gets pushed across the page. 'Goldrichtig' is 'right as gold.' 'Schrotthaufen' is 'dump of scrap.' 'Plastron' is 'plastron.'" (Hofmann, 2015). It is perhaps noteworthy here that Hofmann is also a translator himself: this may well change the emphasis of the review, focussing more attention on the translation. Assessing whether the background and knowledge of the reviewer has an impact on how a review is written could, incidentally, form an interesting research project in the future.

To summarise, the discoveries of this study contribute rather significantly to, and perhaps even reshape, our understanding of the status of translation in reviews in the British context in several significant ways. Firstly, despite the results of Venuti's initial investigation and subsequent studies, the status of a book as a translated work is now very rarely overlooked; all of the broadsheets and specialised publications acknowledge the fact of translation in 85 % or more of their reviews. Only 14.1 % of reviewers do this on *amazon.co.uk*, but as previously discussed, this may well be down to the fact that the translator is already likely to be mentioned in the product details. Secondly, reviewers now seem more likely to engage with the work of the translator, albeit perhaps only in a superficial manner. Venuti and subsequent scholars in the early 2000s found that reviewers very rarely comment upon the translation and therefore contribute to the invisibility of the translator and their work to some extent. However, as we have seen, an average of 58.4 % of reviewers who acknowledge the fact of translation do go on to provide a comment on the translation. Thirdly, and perhaps even more importantly for the visibility of the translator's work, it seems that fluency is no longer the only criterion by which reviewers are assessing translations – this is a major development from what Venuti contended back in 1995. We seem, then, to have a situation in which translators are now more visible in reviews of translated work and their work is more appreciated. But why might this be the case? I would like to make the argument that this is due to the fact that translators now enjoy greater visibility than ever before in a wider societal context in the United Kingdom.

5. The wider societal context for translators since 2010

The societal context for translators has changed rather significantly, certainly since the publication of *The Translator's Invisibility* back in 1995, but also since the studies by Munday, Fawcett, Bush and Johnson were published. It is from roughly 2010 onwards that we see an important turning point for the visibility of translators. This was a time when celebrated translator Maureen Freely became the chairwoman of the board of the Translators' Association, which had previously not been doing a huge amount to promote the work of translators. Freely discusses what happens from 2010 onwards in a revealing interview with Chantal Wright. Upon Freely's appointment, the board came up with various ideas to promote translation: she went on to work with various people on the board of the Translators' Association in order to begin a 'revolution' in the way that translation is considered by the general public. These people included representatives from the British Centre for Literary Translation and Literature Across Frontiers and two renowned translators, Daniel Hahn and Ros Schwarz (Wright and Freely, 2017: 102). Freely goes on to outline how the board came up with various different ideas to promote translation – a literary translation centre at the London Book Fair, starting a mentoring system for young translators, using Arts Council funding, setting up translation weeks, and forging connections with various different organisations, like English PEN, the Foreign Fiction Prize and Boyd Donking (Wright and Freely, 2017: 103).

Many of the initiatives that were launched back in the early 2010s are still running today; a brief look at the report from the most recent Translators' Association AGM gives a good sense of the work that is still continuing in the promotion of translation (Society of Authors, 2020):

- Online events, most recently a panel, chaired by Daniel Hahn and with Arunava Sinha, a translator of Bengali literature
- Daniel Hahn receiving an OBE for services to literature
- Annual translation prizes administered by the Society of Authors, presented at a ceremony at the British library
- Sebald Lecture – in collaboration with the BCLT, British Centre for Literary Translation – given in 2020 by David Bellos, entitled *The Myths and Mysteries of Literary Translation* (this lecture received 1700 advance registrations from 85 different countries)
- BCLT Summer School, with more applications than ever in 2020.

A special mention here, however, must be reserved for the continuing work that goes into planning events for International Translation Day and The London Book Fair – two events which arguably have the greatest impact on the wider public understanding of what translation entails.

International Translation Day is, of course, precisely that, an *international* day: on 24th May 2017, the UN's General Assembly "adopted resolution 71/288 on the role of language professionals in connecting nations and fostering peace, understanding and development, and declared 30 September as International Translation Day" (United Nations, 2017). Long before the resolution had been adopted in 2017, however, British associations had been actively organising events as part of 'translation weeks,' events which have continued to take place to mark International Translation Day every year. For example, English PEN, in collaboration with the Translators' Association, has been hosting a "programme of talks, workshops and networking opportunities for literary translators," with the 2020 programme including talks/workshops on: diversifying translation;

translating regionally; translating internationally; and pitching to publishers (English PEN, 2020). Beyond English PEN, the Translators' Association highlights authors and their translators with various translation prizes (translators working with Swedish, German, French, Spanish and Arabic), and they also launched the campaign #CelebrateYourTranslation, aiming to "highlight the important relationship between author and translator and the vital work translators do in providing greater access to books and literature and engaging more readers across the world" (Society of Authors, 2020).

The London Book Fair has been another extremely important annual date in the diary for the promotion of translation in the United Kingdom since 2010. It welcomes 25,000 publishing professionals every year and considers itself to be the "global marketplace for rights negotiation and the sale and distribution of content across print, audio, TV, film and digital channels" (The London Book Fair, 2020). The entire publishing industry is represented: from the giant houses to the smallest independents, there are "publishers of blockbuster novels and academic texts, and the producers of children's books and graphic novels" (The London Book Fair, 2020). Importantly for the status and promotion of translation, in 2010, the London Book Fair inaugurated the Literary Translation Centre as "a feature area that would enable publishers and translators to come together, network and attend a variety of seminars on literary translation to further this art throughout the UK" (English PEN, 2011). The Centre is partnered with a whole host of supporting organisations: Arts Council England Literature Department, British Centre for Literary Translation, British Council Literature Department, The Calouste Gulbenkian Foundation, English PEN Writers in Translation Programme, Free Word, Literature Across Frontiers, the Translators' Association, Wales Literature Exchange, and Words without Borders. Each year, the Literary Translation Centre seminar programme covers a rich range of current subjects: "Discover international literary landscapes such as the Middle East, China and Japan; learn about children's literature in translation; get ideas about funding both in the UK and Europe; and find out how digital publishing may affect literary translation" (The London Book Fair, 2020). One of the Directors at the London Book Fair, Jack Thomas, believes that a core role of the fair is to champion the art of translation and it thus aims to create channels for dialogue between writers, publishers and the book industry. In his words, as a "vital lynchpin in any cross-cultural exchange, translation has never been more important" (The London Book Fair Hub, 2019).

Another reason which could explain why translation and translators seem to have an improved status in contemporary British society is that there now seems to be a wider understanding of what translation entails than perhaps there was when Venuti was writing *The Translator's Invisibility*: this became clear through the publication of other articles (beyond reviews) in some of the publications which were included in this study. *The Times Literary Supplement*, for example, has frequently published articles about translation focussing on the art of translation and the work that translators undertake. Discussion in a publication which is intended to be read by a general rather than specialised audience moves notions which are prevalent and widely debated in the field of Translation Studies into a more public domain; it contributes to the development of a wider understanding of what the translation process entails and moves us away from the common myth that translation is a simple transfer from source language to target language. As well as promoting the work of the translator through general articles, *The Times Literary Supplement* also sponsors prizes for translators within their wider goal of demonstrating that "there is plenty of excellent translated fiction available" to attempt to work against the fact that "it is rare, after all, to see a translated literary novel in the bestseller lists at all, let alone in the top five" (Tahourdin, 2015). The publication regularly reports on the winners of such prizes.

However, it is not only *The Times Literary Supplement* which contributes to promoting the work of translators; indeed, *The Guardian* has also been publishing a number of articles over the past ten years relating to the role of the translator and the importance of translated fiction. Daniel Hahn was commissioned to write a series of articles on various aspects of translation. One such article focusses very much on the need for visibility for translators. Hahn reflects on the fact that more than half of the books submitted for the prestigious TA first translation prize are debuts for their translators as well as English-language debuts for their authors, "showing that translators are in the vanguard of literary change" (Hahn, 2018). He hopes that such translation prizes will raise the status of translation by "make[ing] a statement about what should be valued, and what we need more of" (Hahn, 2018) and thus be appreciated by a wider range of readers. Another embodiment of the promotion of the work of the translator is an editorial piece, entitled *The Guardian view on translation: an interpretive and creative act*. The article considers the more than sixty prominent translations of Homer's *Odyssey* from various perspectives and asserts that "translation is always an interpretation: an act of creation that also, paradoxically, demands a fierce loyalty to the original text" (The Guardian Editorial, 2017). Again, this challenges the widespread notion that translation is a simple transfer from source language to target language and gets the reader to reflect on the role of the translator. This is further demonstrated in the conclusion of the article:

> We must cherish our translators for these shy acts of creation, these loyal betrayals … Translators are our guides into other times and territories. They encourage us to leave our own literary shores and to consider other ways of living, other ways of thinking. (The Guardian Editorial, 2017)

Another benchmark for the visibility and prominence of translation in general society is social media. A brief scout through social media sites, such as Twitter, demonstrates that translation is being discussed and debated by a much wider group of people than ever before. A clear demonstration of this is the development of campaigns and series which are accessible to a wider range of readers, particularly over the last ten years. One example is the #namethetranslator campaign on Twitter. This is a campaign which was started to "ensure that the contribution of translators is recognised" and "in response to a tendency amongst reviewers and marketers of translated works to omit the name of the translator" (Society of Authors 2018). However, it is not only restricted to Twitter: for example, a review of the translation of *One of Us* in *The Guardian* by Andrew Anthony (2015), which neglects to acknowledge the fact of translation or to mention the translator, is even criticised in the comments section by a person under the pseudonym of *TranslatorsAreCool*: "And who brought this powerful piece of writing to us from the Norwegian, please?" The campaign continues to run today and is advocated mainly by the Twitter account of Translated World (see Figure 1 below, for example).

Figure 1: A recent tweet published by the Twitter account of Translated World on 7th December 2021.

Overall, then, there has been a lot of work done since the early 2010s to promote the visibility of translation and translators – and this work continues more strongly now than ever. Perhaps it is little surprise, therefore, that translators are also more visible in reviews of their work than they were twenty or thirty years ago.

6. Conclusion

This paper has attempted to fulfil two important objectives. On the one hand, it has provided an essential update on the current position of translation in reviews in the United Kingdom. This update is both *temporal*, since the last major study of translation reviewing practices was published in the mid-2000s, and *extensive*, as it expands the scope of previous studies from just broadsheets – of course, an important part of the network of reviewing – to other more and less specialised publications or platforms. The discoveries in this regard have demonstrated that translation and translators are now more visible in reviews than they previously were. On the other hand, it has reshaped our understanding of how visible translation is in general society. From the late 1990s and 2000s, where not a great deal of work was being undertaken to promote the status of translation and translators, the 2010s saw a huge push for the work of translators to be acknowledged in a wider sense. This push has been supported by various groups of people, organisations and publications: from translation and literary associations with their myriad of initiatives, through general-reading publications such as *The Times Literary Supplement* and *The Guardian* with their articles on translation as a practice and an art, to social media with its engaging promotional campaigns.

It seems fair, therefore, to conclude that the increased visibility of the work of translators in British reviews is inherently connected to an increased visibility of translation in a broader societal context in the United Kingdom. Nonetheless, I must stress that this conclusion is based on reviews of translation and the various initiatives as discussed in the previous section of the paper alone. More research is required in this field to fully determine whether translators and translation are universally more visible than they were twenty years ago. This research could take the shape of the following: assessing (quantitatively) how many books are translated and sold, which works are chosen to be translated into which languages, and whether trends have varied over time; analysing translator's contracts and the legal status assigned to them; scrutinising what Martin de Haan (2011) refers to as the "cultural visibility" of the translator, for example, whether it is now general practice to invite translators to press conferences, book presentations, readings, discussions and talks; and determining the importance and success of public events organised around translation, i.e. do the public actually engage with these, or are they perhaps some kind of social media echo chamber? These are just some of the potential areas of research that scholars could pursue in the future, but there are of course many more. Only once we have a better understanding of such areas of research will we be able to gauge definitively what kind of status and visibility translators and translation really enjoy. But the signs as presented in this paper appear to be positive.

References

Anthony, A. (2015, March 8). 'One of us review – compelling account of Norway's lone-wolf killer.' *The Guardian*. https://www.theguardian.com/books/2015/mar/08/one-of-us-review-compelling-anders-breivik.

Bush, P. (2004). *Reviewing translation*. Brunel University.

De Haan, M. (2011, November 21). 'The translator's (in)visibility.' *Hofhaan*. https://www.hofhaan.nl/2011/martin-de-haan/the-translators-invisibility/

English PEN. (2011, March 3). 'Literary translation centre.' https://www.englishpen.org/posts/news/literary-translation-centre

English PEN. (2020, precise date unknown). International translation day. https://www.englishpen.org/international-translation-day.

Fawcett, P. (2000). 'Translation in the broadsheets.' *The Translator*, 6(2), 295–307. https://doi.org/10.1080/13556509.2000.10799070.

Fay, S. (2012, May 7). 'Could the internet save book reviews?' *The Atlantic*. https://www.theatlantic.com/entertainment/archive/2012/05/could-the-internet-save-book-reviews/256802.

Graham-Yooll, A. (2015, December 1). Versions of Borges. Conversations: Volume 2. *Literary Review*. https://literaryreview.co.uk/versions-of-borges

Guardian Editorial (2017, November 5). 'The Guardian view on translation: an interpretative and creative act.' *The Guardian*. https://www.theguardian.com/commentisfree/2017/nov/05/the-guardian-view-on-translation-an-interpretative-and-creative-act.

Hahn, D. (2018, March 1). 'Translators are the vanguard of literary change: We need better recognition.' *The Guardian*. https://www.theguardian.com/books/booksblog/2018/mar/01/translators-vanguard-literary-prize-ta-translation

Hofmann, M. (2015, November 9). 'Wings! Gills! Claws!' *The Times Literary Supplement*. http://www.the-tls.co.uk/tls/public/article1628363.ece

Holmes, J. (Ed.) (1968). *The nature of translation: essays on the theory and practice of literary translation*. Mouton.

Johnson, P. (2005). 'Capturing the spirit: Reviewing literary translation.' In I. Klitgård (Ed.), *Angles on the English-speaking world volume 6: Literary translation, world literature or 'worlding' literature*? (129–144). Museum Tusculanum Press.

Lewis, T. (2011, March 28). On reviewing translations: Tess Lewis. *Words without Borders*. http://www.wordswithoutborders.org/dispatches/article/on-reviewing-translations-tess-lewis

London Book Fair. (2020, precise date unknown). About the London Book Fair. https://www.londonbookfair.co.uk/en-gb/about.html

London Book Fair Hub. (2019, October 22). Katy Derbyshire, esteemed German-English translator, to be LBF 2020's literary translator of the fair. https://hub.londonbookfair.co.uk/katy-derbyshire-esteemed-german-english-translator-to-be-lbf-2020s-literary-translator-of-the-fair/

Munday, J. (1998). 'The Caribbean conquers the world? An analysis of the reception of García Márquez in translation.' *Bulletin of Hispanic Studies*, *75*(1), 137–144. https://doi.org/10.1080/000749098760110684

Society of Authors. (2018, precise date unknown). Name the translator. https://www.societyofauthors.org/Where-We-Stand/Credit/Name-the-Translator

Society of Authors. (2020, November 10). Translators' Association AGM. https://www.societyofauthors.org/SOA/MediaLibrary/SOAWebsite/Action-buttons/AGM-Co-Chairs-report-2020.pdf

Tahourdin, A. (2015, September 7). 'Abroad in English.' *The Times Literary Supplement*. http://www.the-tls.co.uk/tls/public/article1523435.ece

Tree, M. (2015, November 9). 'Strumpet call.' *The Times Literary Supplement*. http://www.the-tls.co.uk/tls/public/article1648601.ece

United Nations. (2017, precise date unknown). International translation day: 30 September. https://www.un.org/en/observances/international-translation-day

Vanderschelden, I. (2000). 'Quality assessment and literary translation in France.' *The Translator*, *6*(2), 271–293. https://doi.org/10.1080/13556509.2000.10799069

Venuti, L. (1995). *The translator's invisibility: A history of translation* (1st ed.). Routledge. https://doi.org/10.4324/9780203360064.

Wright, J. (2015, September 7). 'A state Jew.' *The Times Literary Supplement*. http://www.the-tls.co.uk/tls/reviews/biography/article1604532.ece

Wright, C. and Freely, M. (2017). 'Translators are the jazz musicians of the literary world: translating Pamuk, literary translation networks and the changing face of the profession.' *The Translator*, *23*(1), 95–110. https://doi.org/10.1080/13556509.2016.1251097

Appendices

Appendix 1 – The percentage of reviews which acknowledge the translation or the translator

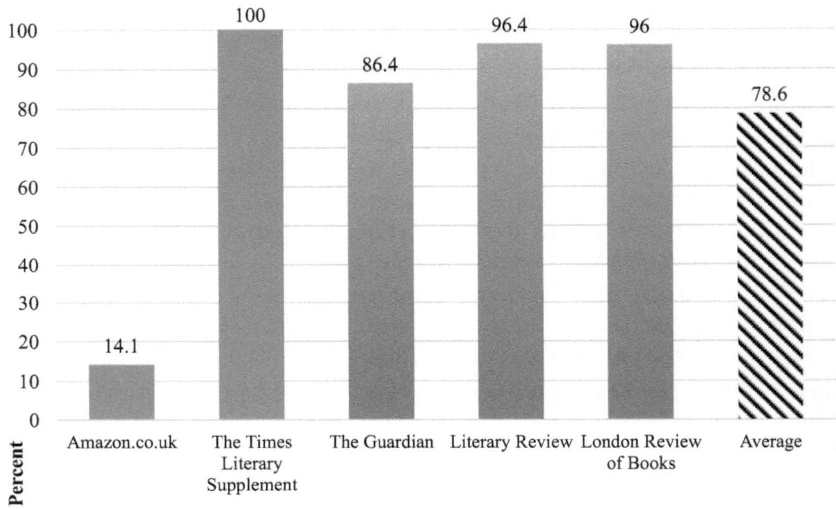

Appendix 2 – The percentage of reviews which, having acknowledged the fact of translation, also make a comment on the quality of the translation

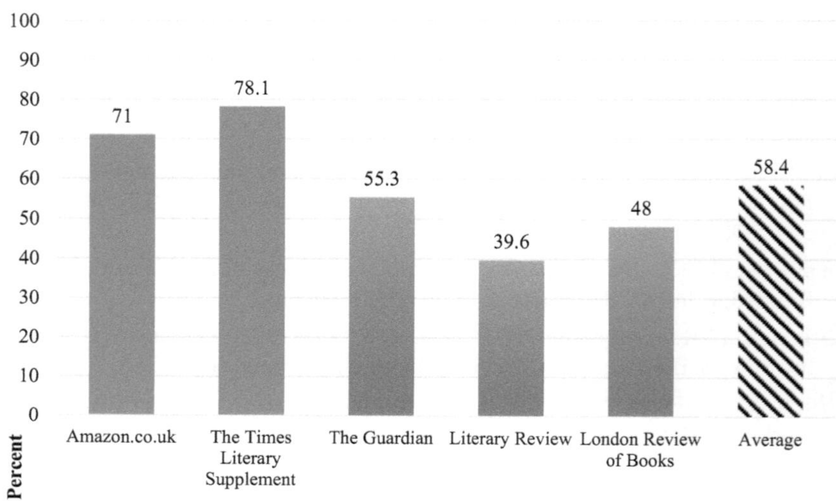

Appendix 3 – The percentage of reviews which, having commented on the quality of the translation, also support this with analysis and/or examples

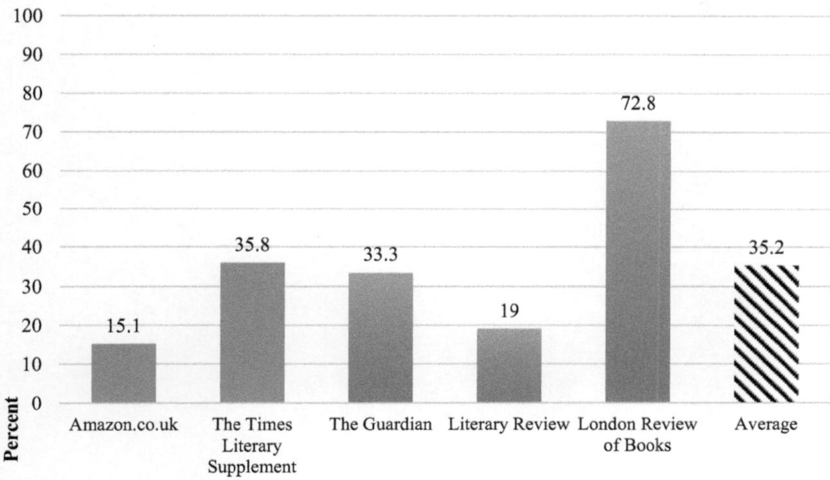

Mehmet Yildiz

Canakkale Onsekiz Mart University

Pseudo-Retranslation: A Novel Perspective on Translational Intertextuality

Abstract: Intertextuality is among the phenomena pivotal to the discussions on the originality/authenticity of translated texts. Undoubtedly, translation proper is an intertextual production that is built on an antedating text, typically written in a foreign language. The author of the present paper observed a new case of textual interdependence – i.e., pseudo-retranslation – where an academic author partially or completely uses another academic author's translation and presents it as a retranslation of a given source text. This paper avails of a corpus of 27 academic works (eleven master's theses, eight doctoral dissertations, five articles, two books and one conference paper), which were analysed to reveal the intertextual associations between them. These works from six different disciplines were purposively selected to include the Turkish (pseudo-re)translations of Milton Rokeach's five assumptions about the nature of human values in his seminal book *The Nature of Human Values*. Only the 27 works, purporting to have translated Rokeach's five assumptions from the original book, were included in the analyses. Intertextual similarity rates were operationalised as the primary parameter to reveal pseudo-retranslations and judge the degree of translational interdependence. R (Ver. 4.0.4), a statistical software program, was employed to generate the intertextual similarity rates and WCopyfind, a text comparison program, to produce the qualitative data. It was concluded from the results that the Turkish academic authors, particularly postgraduates, in the corpus chose to "pseudo-retranslate from" other Turkish academics' works rather than translate directly from the respective source text as they wrote in their native tongue.

Keywords: pseudo-retranslation, intertextuality, intertranslational similarity, academic works, retranslation

Introduction

The present paper presents a new perspective on translation intertextuality by problematising pseudo-retranslation as an indicator of textual interdependence between Turkish academic works. Pseudo-retranslation can be defined as an academic author's partial or complete exploitation of another academic author's translation and presenting it as a retranslation of the respective source text (Yildiz, 2021). Although this concept is similar to the act of plagiarising translated text, it is differentiated from this misconduct in several ways further elaborated on below.

Pseudo-retranslation as an intertextual phenomenon was discussed by analysing a corpus of 27 academic works (eleven master's theses, eight doctoral dissertations, five articles, two books and one conference paper), which include the Turkish (pseudo-re)translations of Milton Rokeach's five assumptions about the nature of human values in his seminal book *The Nature of Human Values*.

Before handling the relationship between pseudo-retranslation and intertextuality, the author attempts to account for how translation and retranslation occur as intertextual phenomena. After he conceptualises pseudo-retranslation by differentiating it from two translation-related misconducts, he presents a detailed account of the corpus. Then, he offers the results of the analyses performed with the statistical program R and the text-similarity program WCopyfind to reveal the intertextual ties between the academic works in the corpus. Finally, he provides the conclusions as to why pseudo-retranslation should be considered a new intertextual phenomenon and how it occurs as a distinctive intertextual phenomenon.

1. Translation and Intertextuality

De Beaugrande & Dressler (1981: 11) present intertextuality as one of the seven standards of textuality,[1] which assumably requires that a conglomeration of lexicographical elements attain this property to be perceived as a text. Listing this feature as a mainstay of textuality and claiming that every text is intertextual should not be misinterpreted that a text is simply a collage of previous or contemporary textual pieces. Therefore, an intertext should exhibit intratextual cohesive features that guarantee "the immanent integrity of the text" as it implicitly and explicitly establishes external links with other texts (Plett, 1991: 5). Otherwise, it could dissolve into its so-called internal components to result in a non-text. Thus, all intertexts can be presented as texts as long as they manage to preserve their internal connectedness between the constituent linguistic elements so that "at least one other text can be read" (Kristeva, 1980: 66). This is why it can be proposed that the properties of intertextuality and textuality are complementary; one would cease to exist without the other.

1 The seven standards of textuality: cohesion, coherence, intentionality, acceptability, informativity, situationality, and intertextuality (De Beaugrande & Dressler, 1981).

Translations are intertextual productions, primarily interlinguistic. Thus, intertextuality is inherent in, if not peculiar to, translation since a diachronic relationship is assumed between a translated text and an antecedent text created in a foreign language. Toury (2012) puts forth three postulates underlying this translational assumption. The first one is that "there is another text, in another culture/language, which has both chronological and logical priority over it." The second reads "the process whereby the assumed translation came into being involved the transfer from the assumed source text of certain features that the two now share." Lastly, "there are tangible relationships that tie [the assumed translation] to its assumed original" (2012: 29–30). These three postulates reveal the intertextual nature of a translation postdating an "assumed original," with which it shares "certain features" and to which it is tangibly related.

Venuti offers a broader perspective on translational intertextuality, which relies on "three sets of intertextual relations:" "those between the foreign text and other texts," "those between the foreign text and the translation," "those between the translation and other texts." Source text itself is derived from a set of intertextual connections, "established by and within the foreign text" and translators are expected to understand the intricate network of textual interrelations embedded in the original text (2009: 158). Translations can be considered intertexts owing to their ties with an antedating text and because, as texts produced in a target language, they are "recontextualised" within a new network of textual interrelations, a new intertextual system (Venuti, 2009: 162). Since translations are presented to a target culture to be read as a stand-alone, coherent text, the target readership expects translated texts to conform to the textual conventions they have grown familiar with because, as Neubert and Shreve (1992: 117) elaborate, "the reader has in mind a set of tacit expectations about what the text should be like," which originates from "intertextuality," denoting "the relationship between a given text and other relevant texts encountered in prior experience." This is why translational intertextuality does not result from a mechanical transfer of sense originally occurring in a pre-dating text but from a translation's capacity to form extratextual ties with the original text and its references and with other intellectual products – e.g., novels, articles, books, movies, songs – in the target culture.

The interrelation between an anterior and a posterior text suggests two types of intertextuality: retrospective intertextuality (establishing backward connections between a current text and a past one) and prospective intertextuality (establishing forward connections between a past text and a current one). Prospective intertextuality also connotes a current text's potential connection to a future text and its ability to guide and shape it. Fairclough (1992: 270) emphasises intertextuality's capability of exciting change in "existing conventions to generate new ones" and "anticipating and trying to shape subsequent texts." Thus, it can be concluded that intertextuality is not only concerned with the available interconnections between past and present texts but also incorporates potential ties with future texts. Pseudo-retranslation presents a similar form of retrospective and prospective intertextuality, which will be discussed below.

2. Retranslation and Intertextuality

Retranslations constitute a different mode of intertextuality by establishing a wider intertextual network because they come to interact not only with the source text but also with the initial target text and the other retranslations as well as with other non-translation texts in the source and target culture. This intricate network is evident from the rich variety of retranslation definitions, which address the phenomenon from different perspectives, particularly focused on the target language (into the same language or different languages?), the chronological standing (source text and/or (re)translations occurring simultaneously?) and the source text (from an original or a translated text?).

To elaborate, retranslation can be defined as "a new partial or complete translation of an already translated text into the same language" (Gambier, 1994: 413). It is also "situations where there is more than one translation, in the same target language, of a given source text" (Chesterman, 2017: 131). Koskinen & Paloposki (2010: 294) refer to retranslation as "second or later translation of a single source text into the same target language." These descriptions present that retranslations are derived from a single source text and rendered into the same language in which the first translation was produced. Şahin et al. (2019: 166) offer a different angle on target language by suggesting that "every translation after the first translation of the source text, regardless of the language it is translated into, is a retranslation." This definition connotes that every translation of a single source text into various languages is a retranslation. For Şahin et al. (2015: 194), retranslation also refers to "any repeated work of translation to the same target language, whether from the original or from the translated version," while Feng (2014: 70) is of the view that retranslations can be rendered by a different or the same translator. Focusing on the chronology of retranslations, Koskinen and Paloposki (2010, 294) claim that "simultaneous or near-simultaneous translations also exist, making it sometimes hard or impossible to classify one as a first translation and the other as a second translation." As stated above, these definitions lend a broader perspective to translation-related intertextuality. Do Amaral (2019: 254–255) provides a succinct explanation as to how prominent this perspective is in retranslational intertextuality. He states that previous interlinguistic renditions of a source text are not only prerequisites to the presence of retranslations but to their interaction with the other translations in a variety of languages as well. He asserts that, through retranslations, translators contribute to the incessant expansion of intertextuality originating from the source text and its translations in different languages.

It can be inferred from his foregoing remarks that retranslation comes into implicit or explicit contact with both its source text and other translations in the same language or different languages as well as with their accompanying textual interrelations. In a similar vein, the present study intends to reveal the intertextual relations between so-called retranslations, i.e. pseudo-retranslations, in the corpus by adopting a diachronic method of analysis and emphasising their potential "to contribute to the formation of a virtually ever-expanding intertextuality" (do Amaral, 2019: 255).

3. Pseudo-Retranslation and Intertextuality

Pseudo-retranslation can be defined as an academic author's partial or complete exploitation of another academic author's translation and presenting it as a retranslation of the respective source text (Yildiz, 2021). This new term is very similar to the misconduct whereby a translation is partially or completely plagiarised, yet it differs from it in the way it is conceptualised. The following are the reasons why the author of the present study preferred not to default to one of the definitions of this misconduct.

1. "There are … divergent views on how to define plagiarism" (Helgesson & Eriksson, 2015: 91). The same holds for "plagiarised translation" (Turell, 2004; Şahin et al., 2019; Şahin et al., 2015). Or should the author say "translational plagiarism" (Gürses, 2011)? Or translation plagiarism (Taş, 2019; Parlak, 2008; Leighton, 1994)? Maybe he should call it "plagiarism in translation (Şahin et al., 2015; Turell, 2004)," "plagiarism in retranslation" (Şahin et al., 2019), or "fake retranslation" (Şahin et al., 2015). All these terms commonly denote intertranslational appropriation in literary translation. Gürses (2011: 6) explains that translational plagiarism occurs when "a translation is published as an original work and the translator acts as the author" or "an old translation is published under a new translator name." Plagiarism in retranslation and plagiarism in translation are simultaneously used by Şahin et al. (2015: 197), with reference to Turell (2004), to refer to (a) the publication of translated text as an original work in another language and

(b) "the publication of an already translated text as a retranslation by another translator." They also use "fake retranslation" and "plagiarised translation" in their paper to address the same phenomenon. "Plagiarised translation" is also adopted by Venuti (2008: 267) and Fuertes (2015: 134) to discuss the same phenomenon in literary translation.

There are cases where translation can be associated with another misconduct where authors may appropriate others' textual or intellectual products via direct translation from the source text created in a foreign language and no credit is given to the author of the source text. Such an appropriation can also be performed through back-translation, where a piece of source text is translated into a foreign language from which the translation is rendered back into the same source language (Yildiz, 2021). This phenomenon is called cross-language plagiarism (Ezzikouri et al. 2019; Ferrero et al. 2017; Danilova 2013; Franco-Salvador et al. 2016; Potthast et al. 2011; Kent and Salim 2009) or translated plagiarism (Pataki 2012; Pataki and Marosi 2013; Gipp 2014).

Gipp et al. (2013: 1120) uses "plagiarised translation" synonymously with cross-language plagiarism. In the work by Şahin et al. (2019: 167), "plagiarism in retranslation" is operationalised as "the publication of an already translated text as a retranslation by another translator," which is referred to as translation plagiarism by Taş (2019), Parlak (2008) and Leighton (1994). However, for Kent and Salim (2009) and Dougherty (2019), translation plagiarism is synonymous with cross-language plagiarism.

The terminological discussion above leads to a profusion of confusing terms. Therefore, while multiple terms are adopted to denote the same or similar phenomenon, a single term may refer to two different translational phenomena. Any terminological confusion should be eliminated for a proper conceptualisation and discussion of a given subject since "terms give shape to concepts" (Berry, 2010: 21). However, the referential tie between a term and a concept may have broken over time because "terms can be manipulated and used to refer to an empty concept" (Berry, 2010: 22). "An intentionally or unintentionally modified or broken link between a term and its concept potentially leads to a confusing, misleading and/or errant conceptualization of an intended subject matter" (Yildiz, 2021: 257), which is applicable to the above terms pertaining to translation-related plagiarism. Thus, the author produced a new term – pseudo-retranslation – instead of resorting to the available terms not to compound the present terminological confusion; otherwise, the paper would fail to describe the intended intertextual phenomenon and readers could have difficulty appreciating how it was conceptually dealt with.

2. These terms were observed to foreground unethicality. Nonetheless, the present study does not intend to present the identified intertextual connections as unethical acts or to make any moral or legal accusations by using any of the above terms but to describe a new phenomenon of translational intertextuality, which occurs in academic papers, by presenting its evidence in a neutral way. Thus, the author is more concerned with "epistemic value" of the phenomenon, which is "conducive to truth" and "capable of furthering our knowledge" – of translational intertextuality as far as the paper is concerned – rather than its non-epistemic value,[2] which is ethicality here, (Dorato, 2004: 53).
3. The foregoing terminological discussion on a translation-related academic misconduct occurs in the context of literary translation; however, the present paper researches translational intertextuality across non-literary works, particularly academic papers.

Due to these three reasons, the author of this paper had recourse to a new nomenclature to refer to this phenomenon and called it "pseudo-retranslation," which can be defined as (1) an academic author's use of (a portion of) another's translation to present it as a (re)translation of a given source text and (2) the text resulting from this act. Thus, it can be used to describe the act, the process and the product. In this context, the author operationalised "to pseudo-retranslate (from)" as a verb to refer to the act and "pseudo-retranslation" as a noun to refer to the process and the product (Yildiz, 2021: 257–258).

Pseudo-retranslation is a blending of 'retranslation' and 'pseudo-translation;' neither can thoroughly account for the phenomenon in question, though. Still, pseudo-retranslation shares conceptual similarities with the two. To be specific, the above discussion shows that retranslation means any act of retranslating into the same or a different language and the product of this act, which postdates a supposedly initial translation or occurs simultaneously or near-simultaneously with it. Pseudo-retranslations too postdate the source translation, but it does not originate from a translational transfer process, rather from a verbatim or an almost verbatim representation of a previous (pseudo-re)translation in an academic text (Yildiz, 2021). Further, in contrast to an actual translation process, pseudotranslation as the second constituent is not derived from a source text, so it can be called 'false' translation considering that the morpheme "pseudo"

2 Dorato (2004: 53) uses "nonepistemic [values] to refer essentially to values that are ideological, economical, or political (like feminism, sexism, Marxism, fascism, capitalism, and racism), or ethical, environmental, esthetical, or religious."

comes from *pseudés*, which means "false" in Greek (Rambelli, 2011: 208). Pseudotranslations "resemble translations" (O'Sullivan, 2011: 123) and "may even mimic genuine translations" (Toury, 2012: 29). They are "presented as translations with no corresponding source texts in other languages ever having existed – hence no factual 'transfer operations' and translation relationships" (Toury, 1995: 40). A pseudotranslation "refers to a target-oriented practice of imitative composition which results in texts that are perceived as translations but which are not, as they usually lack an actual source text" (Rambelli, 2011: 208–209). Similarly, a pseudo-retranslation resembles a (re)translation and even mimics a genuine (re)translation. But it "can be eventually traced back to a source text" (Yildiz, 2021: 255).

The definition itself reveals pseudo-retranslation's intertextual characteristic. Specifically, a pseudo-retranslation in an academic work is already embedded in a pre-existing scholarly paper – or in more than one –, which creates an intertextual tie between them. The embedded textual segments examined in this study are marked by the in-text reference "Rokeach (1973)," which reminds Fairclough's (2003: 39) definition, "intertextuality is the presence of actual elements of other texts within a text – quotations." The current paper considers pseudo-retranslations to be the markers of "manifest intertextuality." Fairclough (1992: 271) elaborates on manifest intertextuality by saying, "individual other texts are explicitly present in the text under analysis they are 'manifestly' marked or cued by features on the surface of the text, such as quotation marks." Collet (2016: 74) highlights the notable role of "citations … in the social construction of knowledge" by emphasising their potential to generate an intertextual network connecting an author's text to those of others. "They are interconnected in networks that link current texts to prior texts and that anticipate, in addition, links to texts that have yet to be written" (Collet, 2016: 76). In this statement, Collet too emphasises that intertextuality does not only build ties between past and present works but also is likely to expand the textual network to include texts to be produced in the future.

In this sense, pseudo-retranslations contribute to the creation of three types of translational intertextuality: (1) their ties with the original text, namely Milton Rokeach's five assumptions about human values in his seminal book *The Nature of Human Values*, and (2) their connection(s) with source (re)translations. Drawing from Fairclough's and Collet's foregoing remarks on a past or current text's prospective interrelations with future texts and the findings concerning pseudo-retranslations' trajectory of dissemination, the author claims that (3) pseudo-retranslations tend to appear in future academic texts since academic authors will most probably continue turning to previous authors' translations as they write their scholarly works. The following titles attempt to evidence these three intertextual procedures.

4. Method

4.1. Corpus

The author created a corpus of 27 academic works to identify the initial translation(s) from which the detected pseudo-retranslations were taken. The corpus incorporates eleven master's theses, eight doctoral dissertations, four articles, two books and one conference paper from six different disciplines (Table 1), which means that five types of academic works were analysed, namely master's thesis (MT), doctoral dissertation (PD), articles (A), book (B) and conference paper (CP). The author used codes to identify the works in the corpus and anonymise the author(s). The codes consist of the author's last name's initial letter, publication year and the work's text type. For example, B2013MT is a master's thesis written by B in 2013.

These works were purposively selected to analyse the Turkish (pseudo-re) translations of Milton Rokeach's five assumptions about the nature of human values in his acclaimed book *The Nature of Human Values*. The following are Rokeach's (1973: 3) five assumptions of human values:

1. The total number of values that a person possesses is relatively small;
2. all men everywhere possess the same values to different degree;
3. values are organised into value systems;
4. the antecedents of human values can be traced to culture, society and its institutions, and personality;
5. the consequences of human values will be manifested in virtually all phenomena that social scientists might consider worth investigating and understanding.

Table 1: 27 works in the corpus

	Education Sciences	Business Administration	Psychology	Sociology	Theology	Communication Science
1.	AT1998CP	U2002MT	O2007MT	K1991A	M2006MT	OB2011PD
2.	S2004A	A2005B	A2005MT	M2014PD		
3.	SK2004A	CO2008A	A2011MT			
4.	Y2006PD	K2009MT	KO2014MT			
5.	S2011PD	C2011MT				
6.	B2013MT	F2012PD				
7.	K2014MT	KM2018PD				
8.	I2015A	T2019PD				
9.	K2019MT					
10.	Y2019PD					
11.	Y2021B					

Even though 52 works were identified to incorporate Rokeach's five assumptions, only the 27 academic works, purporting to have translated Rokeach's five assumptions directly from the original book, were included in the analyses. In other words, 25 works were excluded from the analyses because they either feature the Turkish translations of the five assumptions through secondary references or are non-academic texts. A collection of 27 works was observed to comprise eleven works from education sciences, eight from business administration, four from psychology, two from sociology, one from theology and one from communication science (Table 1).

4.2. Analysis

The author comparatively analysed the 27 Turkish (pseudo-re)translations of Rokeach's five assumptions of human values. Intertextual similarity rates were operationalised as the primary parameter to reveal pseudo-retranslations and judge the degree of translational interdependence. A text comparison software program, WCopyfind, was used to produce qualitative data and to examine the overlapping contents side-by-side. R, "a programming language" "for statistical analyses and creation of graphs" (Levshina, 2015: 21) was employed to generate the intertextual similarity rates. To benefit from R, "the user types and enters the commands from a script and the system interprets the commands" (Desagulier, 2017: 15). R is a free-of-charge tool, widely employed in corpus linguistics. Along with its great flexibility and capacity to generate a vast amount of useful information, it offers "a wealth of various functions and packages for specific tasks written by professional statisticians and specialists in different fields" (Levshina, 2015: 21).

The R package *quanteda* was used to produce the intertextual similarity rates. This package provides "a comprehensive workflow and toolkit for natural language processing tasks such as corpus management, tokenization, analysis, and visualization" (Benoit et al., 2018: 774). It incorporates "highly efficient methods for compiling document-[text] matrices and for manipulating these or using them in further quantitative analysis" (Benoit et al., 2018: 774). To process the works on R, they were first imported into the R environment, where the texts were transformed into a corpus and the tokenisation was performed. As Welbers et al. (2017) describe, tokenisation is "the process of splitting a text into tokens," "smaller, more specific text features, such as words or word combinations." This procedure is required for textual analysis on R "because full texts are too specific to perform any meaningful computations with." "Most often tokens are words [as in the present study] because these are the most common semantically meaningful components of texts" (Welbers et al., 2017: 6–7). The step is also needed to process texts as qualitative bodies for quantitative textual analysis. This transformation allowed the author to create the document-term matrix, "which is a common format for representing a bag-of-words type corpus" (Welbers et al., 2017: 2), by using the tokens and then to identify the term frequencies of the corpus. An efficient way to generate workable and interpretable data is "to compare the term frequencies of two corpora, or between two subsets of the same corpus" (Welbers et al., 2017: 15). This comparison eventually yields the rates of intertextual similarity. The similarity rates obtained in this study by using the *cosine* function as a measure of similarity (Levshina, 2015: 308), ranged between 0.00 and 1.00, referring to a lack of similarity and a perfect match, respectively. The textual interrelations were provided in groups corresponding to the similarity values of 1.00, 0.90–0.99, 0.80–0.89 and 0.70–0.79. The rates were presented in tables, which were further processed into graphs to visualise the intertextual ties between the analysed excerpts.

5. Results

This title presents the results as categorised into similarity-based groups. They were given in tables and figures. The first table and figure involve the highest rate of intertextual similarity (1.00), while the others feature the gradually lessening similarities (0.90–0.99, 0.80–0.89 and 0.70–0.79). This section also includes two tables offering the contents of three (pseudo-re)translations as juxtaposed by WCopyfind to reveal how two typical pseudo-retranslational procedures (namely, omission and addition) persisted for more than a decade. This part ends with an overview of the intertextual associations between the analysed works, which were established factoring in the similarity rates between 0.70 and 1.00.

5.1. Perfect matches at a similarity rate of 1.00

Table 2 reveals the similarities between nine works in the corpus at a rate of 1.00. This similarity value indicates a match rate of 100 %, in other words, a perfect match. These rates suggest that at least one of the authors in the table has pseudo-retranslated Rokeach's five assumptions from a previous work in Turkish instead of directly translating from the source text in English.

Table 2: Intertextual similarities at a rate of 1.00

	U 2002 MT	**O 2007 MT**	**K 2009 MT**	**C 2011 MT**	**A 2011 MT**	**S 2011 PD**	**B 2013 MT**	**K 2014 MT**	**I 2015 A**
U2002MT				1.00					1.00
O2007MT							1.00		
K2009MT					1.00	1.00		1.00	
C2011MT	1.00								1.00
A2011MT			1.00			1.00		1.00	
S2011PD			1.00		1.00			1.00	
B2013MT		1.00							
K2014MT			1.00		1.00	1.00			
I2015A	1.00			1.00					

Table 3 presents U2002MT and I2015A' juxtaposed contents and back-translations and the source text, namely Rokeach (1973). It can be observed that the master's thesis U2002MT and the article I2015A have the same content. Considering that the former is the earliest text and the latter is the most recent, it can be claimed that the translation decisions available in the former also occur in the latter to endure for 13 years. To exemplify, it is clear from the comparison of U2002MT and I2015A's Item 5 with the respective source item in English that this Turkish item includes lexical elements different from the English source. The prominent ones are "önem (importance)," "sosyal bilimler (social sciences)," and "ortaya çıkarmak (revealing)" to replace "consequences," "social scientists," and "investigating," respectively.

Table 3: Side-by-side view of perfectly overlapping U2004MT and I2015A

Similarity Rate: 1.00 (100 %)				
	U2002MT	**I2015A**	**BACK-TRANSLATION**	**ROKEACH (1973)**
1	Bir insanın sahip olduğu değerlerin toplam sayısı göreceli olarak küçüktür.	Bir insanın sahip olduğu değerlerin toplam sayısı göreceli olarak küçüktür.	The total number of values that a person possesses is relatively small.	The total number of values that a person possesses is relatively small;
2	Herkes aynı değere farklı derecelerde sahiptir.	Herkes aynı değere farklı derecelerde sahiptir.	All men possess the same value to different degrees.	All men everywhere possess the same values to different degree;
3	Değerler değer sistemleri içinde organize olmuştur.	Değerler değer sistemleri içinde organize olmuştur.	Values are organised in value systems.	Values are organised into value systems;
4	İnsanın sahip olduğu değerler kültürün toplumun, kurumların ve bireylerin kişiliğinin bir ürünüdür.	İnsanın sahip olduğu değerler kültürün toplumun kurumların ve bireylerin kişiliğinin bir ürünüdür.	Values that a person possesses are the products of culture, society, institutions, and individuals' personalities.	The antecedents of human values can be traced to culture, society and its institutions, and personality;
5	Değerlerin önemi sosyal bilimlerin ortaya çıkarmak ve anlamak üzere ilgilendikleri hemen hemen bütün olgularda açıkça gözlenmektedir.	Değerlerin önemi sosyal bilimlerin ortaya çıkarmak ve anlamak üzere ilgilendikleri hemen hemen bütün olgularda açıkça gözlenmektedir.	The importance of values is manifestly observed in virtually all phenomena that social sciences are interested in revealing and understanding.	The consequences of human values will be manifested in virtually all phenomena that social scientists might consider worth investigating and understanding.

Figure 1 offers a more vivid picture of the intertextual relations between the studied academic works. The figure shows that B2013MT must have pseudo-retranslated the five assumptions from O2007MT, while I2015A from either C2011MT or U2002MT and C2011MT from U2002MT. It can be observed in the cluster of four works that K2009MT is the source translation and A2011MT, S2011PD and K2014MT are its pseudo-retranslations.

The set of four works incorporates two works in education sciences (S2011PD and K2014MT), one in psychology (A2011MT) and one in business administration (K2009MT). In the cluster of three, U2002MT and C2011MT are the works in business administration and I2015A is a paper of education sciences. Besides, O2007MT and B2013MT have been created in psychology and education sciences, respectively. This indicates that pseudo-retranslations can occur across disciplines. To the author's best knowledge, this interdisciplinary property is less likely to occur in the realm of literary (re)translation, and this paper is the first to document this interdisciplinary textual interdependence.

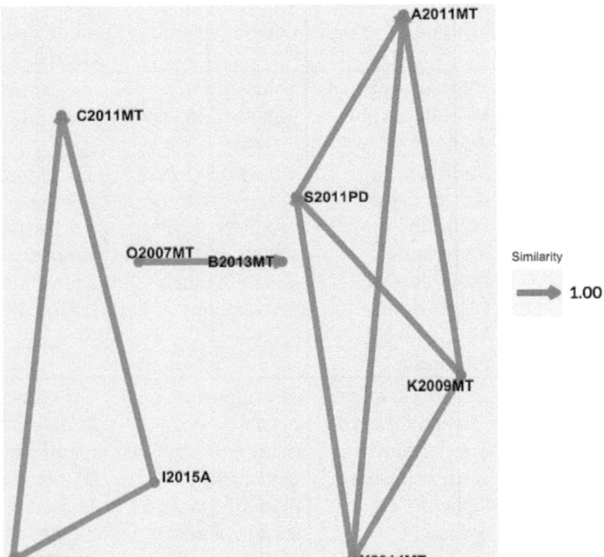

Figure 1: Intertextual similarities at a rate of 1.00

It is clear that seven of the works in Table 2 and Figure 1 are master's theses (MT) and one is a doctoral dissertation (PD). This finding suggests that postgraduate students tend to pseudo-retranslate a relevant piece of translation verbatim, including errors, rather than translate from the source text. Therefore, postgraduates should be informed about the possible risks of citing from secondary sources and encouraged to use primary sources. It goes without saying that they should also be encouraged to translate from the source text (segment) and give proper credit to the author(s) of the source, be it primary or secondary.

Besides, their supervisors should ideally make sure that their students have observed proper referencing rules. The following part offers a deeper insight into the intertextual connections within the corpus because it shows that the network of intertextuality based on the perfect overlaps is expanded considering the values of strong similarity, i.e., 0.90–0.99 and 0.80–0.89.

5.2. Strong intertextual ties: Similarity rates of 0.90–0.99 and 0.80–0.89

Table 4 presents the results from the similarity analysis conducted within a range of 0.90–0.99. The analysis yielded textual associations between 11 works at similarity rates occurring between 0.90 and 0.98. O2007MT, K2009MT, A2011MT, S2011PD, B2013MT and K2014MT (italicised), whose intertextual relations were already identified above, can be realised to establish new intertextual ties in Table 4 and Figure 2.

Table 4. Intertextual similarity rates between 0.90 and 0.99

	SK 2004 A	**Y 2006 PD**	***O 2007 MT***	**CO 2008 A**	***K 2009 MT***	***A 2011 MT***	***S 2011 PD***	**F 2012 PD**	***B 2013 MT***	***K 2014 MT***	**Y 2021 B**
SK2004A		0.94			0.98	0.98	0.98			0.98	0.90
Y2006PD	0.94				0.96	0.96	0.96			0.96	0.95
O2007MT				0.98				0.98			
CO2008A			0.98					0.96	0.98		
K2009MT	0.98	0.96									0.91
A2011MT	0.98	0.96									0.91
S2011PD	0.98	0.96									0.91
F2012PD			0.98	0.96					0.98		
B2013MT				0.98				0.98			
K2014MT	0.98	0.96									0.91
Y2021B	0.90	0.95			0.91	0.91	0.91			0.91	

It was stated that O2007MT and K2009MT are the source translations in Table 2 and Figure 1. It can be observed in Table 4 and Figure 2 that O2007MT is prospectively associated with CO2008A (0.98) and F2012PD (0.98). Because B2013MT is O2007MT's exact pseudo-retranslation, it has the same textual interrelations. Moreover, K2009MT can be seen to have its roots in SK2004A (0.98) and Y2006PD (0.96) and happens to appear in a later study, Y2021B (0.91). Since A2011MT, S2011PD and K2014MT are the verbatim pseudo-retranslations of K2009MT (Table 2 and Figure 1), they exhibit the same intertextual connections. Therefore, it can be concluded that SK2004A is the source translation of the pseudo-retranslations Y2006PD, K2009MT, A2011MT, S2011PD, K2014MT and Y2021B and that CO2008A, F2012PD and B2013MT seem to have been derived from O2007MT (Figure 2).

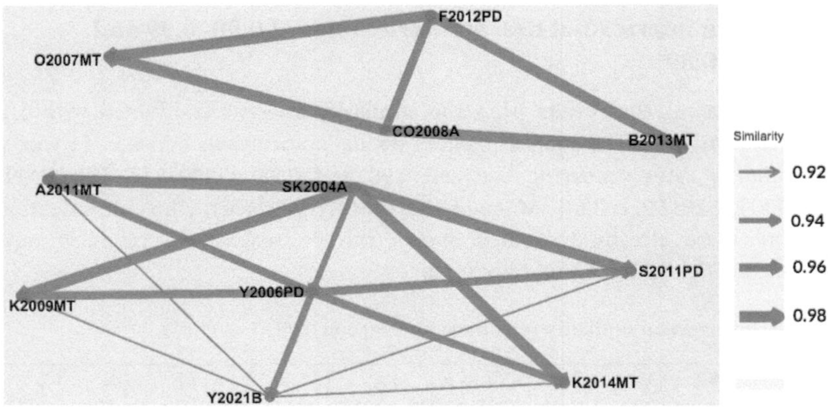

Figure 2: Intertextual similarity rates between 0.90 and 0.99

It is noteworthy that the doctoral dissertation Y2006PD and the book Y2021B (which is not the published Y2006PD) were authored by the same researcher, who is presently a full professor, and the rate of the similarity between these two works corresponds to 0.95. This finding suggests that Turkish authors may continue pseudo-retranslating in their future works if they have not been informed about the risks of this act, i.e., dissemination of inaccurate information, which would eventually lead to flawed scientific knowledge. Besides, another risk could be such academic authors' passing this behaviour on to young academics.

Table 5 provides the source translation in SK2004A, which introduces a new Item 1 and excludes Item 5 in Rokeach (1973). These text production decisions persistently occur in SK2004A's six pseudo-retranslations, including the most recent Y2021B (similarity rate: 0.90). This means that the errors have endured for 17 years, and it is highly probable that they will do so for the years to come given that the most recent work has been produced in 2021, i.e., Y2021B. This is indicative of pseudo-retranslations' potential to generate prospective intertextual ties with upcoming texts. The speed at which pseudo-retranslations spread across academic works and the greater likelihood of them appearing in later academic works can be two of their characteristics differentiating them from the act of plagiarising translations of literary works.

Table 5: Recurring addition and omission (N/A: Not available)

Similarity rate: 0.90					
ROKEACH (1973)	**SK2004A**		**ROKEACH (1973)**	**Y2021B**	
N/A	1	[*added*] her birey bir değere ve değerler sistemine sahiptir	3	1	değerler değer sistemleri içinde örgütlenmiştir
1	2	bir inanın sahip olduğu değerlerin toplam sayısı görece ufaktır	N/A	2	[*added*]her kişi bir değere ve değer sistemine sahiptir
2	3	herkes aynı değere farklı derecelerde sahiptir	1	3	bir insanın sahip olduğu değerlerin toplam sayısı görece azdır
3	4	değerler değer sistemleri içinde organize olmuştur	2	4	herkes aynı değere farklı derecelerde sahiptir
4	5	insanın sahip olduğu değerler kültürün, toplumun, kurumların ve bireylerin kişiliğinin bir ürünüdür	4	5	insanın sahip olduğu değerler kültürün toplumun kurumların ve kişilerin kişiliğinin bir ürünüdür
5	N/A	[*omitted*][the consequences of human values will be manifested in virtually all phenomena that social scientists might consider worth investigating and understanding].	5	N/A	[*omitted*][the consequences of human values will be manifested in virtually all phenomena that social scientists might consider worth investigating and understanding].

The similarity-based cluster of 0.80–0.89 is the smallest set of intertextuality, containing only two works, namely A2005B and M2006MT (Table 6). The former is a book on business administration, while the latter is a theological work. Their intertextual similarity rate corresponds to 0.88. In the following part featuring the intertextual similarity rates between 0.70 and 0.79, they can be seen to have further intertextual ties with three other works, namely U2002MT, C2011MT and I2015A.

Table 6: Intertextual similarity rates between 0.80 and 0.89

	A2005B	**M2006MT**
A2005B		0.88
M2006MT	0.88	

5.3. Intertextual similarity rates between 0.70 and 0.79

Table 7 shows the intertextual similarity values of 0.70–0.79. It can be understood from the table that 12 works in the corpus are interrelated at rates ranging between 0.70 and 0.78. U2002MT, SK2004A, A2005B, M2006MT, Y2006PD, O2007MT, CO2008A, K2009MT, C2011MT, A2011MT, S2011PD, F2012PD, B2013MT, K2014MT, I2015A and Y2021B were already shown to have strong similarities with the respective works in this list. Table 6 and Figure 3 indicate that U2002MT, SK2004A, A2005B, M2006MT, Y2006PD, K2009MT, A2011MT, C2011MT, S2011PD, K2014MT, I2015A and Y2021B bear further textual relationships; not so strong as the similarities in Tables 2, 4 and 6, though.

Table 7: Intertextual similarity rates between 0.70 and 0.79

	U 2002 MT	**SK 2004 A**	**A 2005 B**	**M 2006 MT**	**Y 2006 PD**	**K 2009 MT**	**A 2011 MT**	**C 2011 MT**	**S 2011 PD**	**K 2014 MT**	**I 2015 A**	**Y 2021 B**
U2002MT		0.76	0.70	0.73	0.75	0.78	0.78		0.78	0.78		0.73
SK2004A	0.76							0.76			0.76	
A2005B	0.70							0.70			0.70	
M2006MT	0.73							0.73			0.73	
Y2006PD	0.75							0.75			0.75	
K2009MT	0.78							0.78			0.78	
A2011MT	0.78							0.78			0.78	
C2011MT		0.76	0.70	0.73	0.75	0.78	0.78		0.78	0.78		0.73
S2011PD	0.78							0.78			0.78	
K2014MT	0.78							0.78			0.78	
I2015A		0.76	0.70	0.73	0.75	0.78	0.78		0.78	0.78		0.73
Y2021B	0.73							0.73			0.73	

Table 7 shows that there are three main sources of pseudo-retranslations – i.e., U2002MT, C2011MT and I2015A. The table reveals that these three segments exhibit similarities at rates ranging between 0.70 and 0.78 with the works but not with each other because they perfectly overlap at a rate of 1.00 (Table 2 and Figure 1). This table is significant because it demonstrates that the seemingly unrelated source translations U2002MT, SK2004A and A2005B (except for O2007MT) in the previous tables and figures are interrelated. The table indicates that U2002MT's rates of similarity with SK2004A and A2005B amount to 0.76 and 0.70, respectively. This suggests that U2002MT can be the source translations of SK2004A and A2005B.

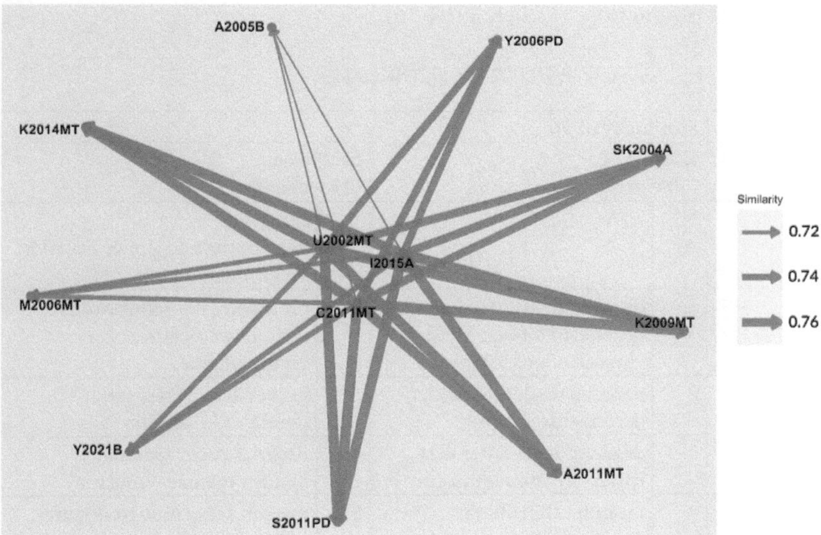

Figure 3: Intertextual similarity rates between 0.70 and 0.79

Table 8 presents a very striking finding as to how pseudo-retranslations facilitate the dissemination of flawed academic knowledge. The table was created from the overlapping contents of U2002MT and SK2004A as juxtaposed by WCopyfind. The similarity between them corresponds to 0.76. The table shows that Item 5 in Rokeach (1973) is available in U2002MT but *omitted* in SK2004. Besides, SK2004A *added* Item 1 to the list, which does not occur in the original work Rokeach (1973). These two textual procedures, which have been reported to be typical of pseudo-retranslations (Yildiz, 2020), were also observed in SK2004A's six pseudo-retranslations, namely Y2006PD, K2009MT, A2011MT, S2011PD, K2014MT and Y2021B. The table reveals that U2002MT is the source translation of SK2004A and its six pseudo-retranslations. This must be why U2002MT is at the intersection in Figure 3. The R analyses resulted in intertextual similarity rates of over 0.70 between 16 out of 27 works in the corpus (Figure 3). Moreover, it should be noted that 11 of the 16 interrelated works, including Y2021B, can be traced back to U2002MT, which means that the prospective influence of U2002MT extended as far as Y2021B to endure for 19 years. This particular case of manifest intertextuality epitomises pseudo-retranslations' potential to contribute to textual "historicity" because each work in this line of texts from 2002 to 2021 corresponds to "a link in the historical chain of text production" (Collet, 2016: 76).

Table 8: Side-by-side view of U2002MT and SK2004A

	Similarity: 0.76			
ROKEACH (1973)	**U2002MT (50 words)**		**SK2004A (41 words)**	
N/A	N/A	N/A	1	[*added*] her birey bir değere ve değerler sistemine sahiptir
1	1	bir insanın sahip olduğu değerlerin toplam sayısı göreceli olarak küçüktür	2	bir inanın[sic] sahip olduğu değerlerin toplam sayısı görece ufaktır
2	2	herkes aynı değere farklı derecelerde sahiptir	3	herkes aynı değere farklı derecelerde sahiptir
3	3	değerler değer sistemleri içinde organize olmuştur	4	değerler değer sistemleri içinde organize olmuştur
4	4	insanın sahip olduğu değerler kültürün toplumun kurumların ve bireylerin kişiliğinin bir ürünüdür	5	insanın sahip olduğu değerler kültürün, toplumun, kurumların ve bireylerin kişiliğinin bir ürünüdür
5	5	değerlerin önemi sosyal bilimlerin ortaya çıkarmak ve anlamak üzere ilgilendikleri hemen hemen bütün olgularda açıkça gözlenmektedir	N/A	[*omitted*][the consequences of human values will be manifested in virtually all phenomena that social scientists might consider worth investigating and understanding].

Until this part of the paper, the works were analysed as categorised into similarity-based groups to present an in-depth insight into the manifest intertextuality between individual works. In doing so, the intertextual ties were presented as ordered from the strongest similarity to the least. The subsequent title features an overview of the analyses based on the similarity rates of over 0.70.

5.4. An overall intertextual picture: Similarity rates of over 0.70

Figure 4 shows the identified associations between 16 out of the 27 works. It is understandable from the figure that there are two intertextual clusters. The small set includes O2007MT, CO2008A, F2012PD and B2013MT, whereas the larger group consists of U2002MT, SK2004A, A2005B, M2006MT, Y2006PD, K2009MT, S2011PD, C2011MT, A2011MT, K2014MT, I2015A and Y2021B. This duality suggests two source translations, from which the pseudo-retranslations were derived. Based on the available data, a diachronic examination reveals that U2002MT and O2007MT are the initial translations of the larger and smaller cluster, respectively. The figure also shows that M2006MT and A2005B are closely associated yet weakly with the other ten works, which are apparently more interrelated.

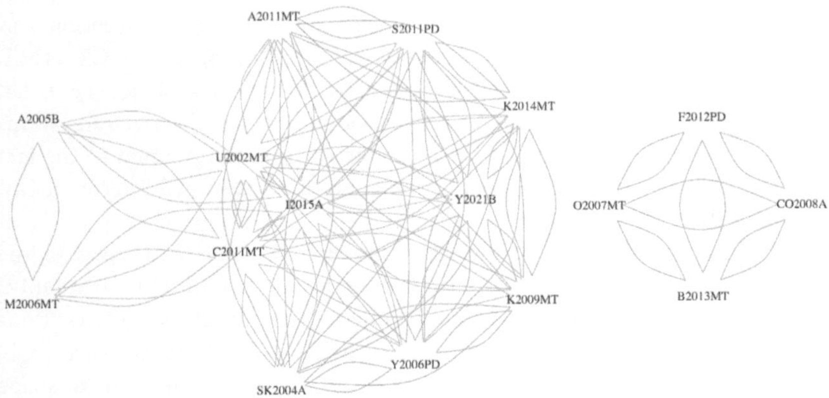

Figure 4: Intertextual associations based on similarity rates of over 0.70

The figure supports the view that pseudo-retranslations generate intertextual networks "that link current texts to prior texts and that anticipate, in addition, links to texts that have yet to be written" (Collet, 2016: 76). Considering the historicity of pseudo-retranslations from 2002 to 2021 in the present corpus, pseudo-retranslation will potentially continue to appear in future works to "contribute to the formation of a virtually ever-expanding intertextuality" (do Amaral, 2019: 255).

6. Conclusion

This paper attempted to present a new case of translational intertextuality that is established by pseudo-retranslations, a phenomenon first documented by Yildiz (2021). Pseudo-retranslation can be referred to as an academic author's partial or complete use of another academic author's translation and presenting it as a (re) translation of a given source text. To show how pseudo-retranslations establish intertextuality, the author analysed a corpus of 27 academic works, consisting of 11 master's theses, eight doctoral dissertations, five articles, two books and one conference paper by using R (Ver. 4.0.4), a statistical program, and WCopyfind, a textual similarity program. The analysis was built on "manifest intertextuality" (Fairclough, 1992: 271), where "individual other texts are explicitly present in the text under analysis they are 'manifestly' marked or cued by features on the surface of the text, such as quotation marks." Thus, the author diachronically analysed the assumed initial Turkish translations and Turkish pseudo-retranslations of Rokeach's (1973) five assumptions of human values.

The analyses yielded two sets of intertextuality networks. The first consists of 12 works and the second of four. It was found in the examination of the 12-work cluster that the translation U2002MT is the assumed source translation and that SK2004A, A2005B, M2006MT, Y2006PD, K2009MT, S2011PD, C2011MT, A2011MT, K2014MT, I2015A and Y2021B are its pseudo-retranslations. Further, O2007MT was found to be the source translation of the pseudo-retranslations CO2008A, F2012PD and B2013MT. These intertextual ties pointed to the fact that pseudo-retranslation is a new phenomenon of translational intertextuality, observable in academic works.

The analyses indicated that pseudo-retranslations lend themselves to the formation of textual interrelations, which are typical of "manifest intertextuality." These peculiar characteristics are (i) citation-based textual connections (Fairclough, 2003), (ii) "manifestly marked or cued" surface features (Fairclough, 1992), (iii) intertextual "historicity" (Collet, 2016), (iv) the potential "to shape subsequent texts" (Fairclough, 1992) and (v) the likelihood to "contribute to the formation of a virtually ever-expanding intertextuality made by the original and its translations in different languages" (do Amaral, 2019).

Because pseudo-retranslators "do not typically question the authenticity and accuracy of the source translations" (Yildiz, 2021: 275), the intertextual historicity of pseudo-retranslations poses a risk of corrupting the existing body of scholarly knowledge and producing flawed scientific knowledge, which is evident in SK2004A's omission of Item 5 in its source translation U2002MT and insertion of a new Item 1 unavailable in the respective source translation. This trait of SK2004A was observed in its six pseudo-retranslations. It can be claimed that the predominance of postgraduate works – 11 of 16 intertextually associated works – aggravates these detrimental effects of pseudo-retranslations since it seems that they tend to use secondary sources rather than have recourse to the original work. Postgraduate students may persistently exhibit this behaviour in their future works if they have not been taught about the merits of using primary sources and giving proper credit to original works. This behaviour was identified in the doctoral dissertation Y2006PD and the book Y2021B, which were written by the same author and in which the pseudo-retranslations of Rokeach's five assumptions are strongly associated (0.95).

Moreover, the analyses suggest that pseudo-retranslations potentially establish intertextual networks across disciplines and text types. The interrelated 16 works were observed to have been produced in four different fields (education sciences, business administration, psychology and theology) and four text types (master's theses, doctoral dissertations, articles and books). The author believes that such diverse interactions are less likely to occur across literary works.

References

Berry, R. (2010). *Terminology in English language teaching: Nature and use.* Peter Lang.

Benoit, K., Watanabe, K., Wang, H., Nulty, P., Obeng, A., Müller, S., & Matsuo, A. (2018). 'quanteda: An R package for the quantitative analysis of textual data.' *Journal of Open Source Software*, 3(30), 774. https://doi.org/10.21105/joss.00774

Chesterman, A. (2017). *Reflections on Translation Theory: Selected papers 1993–2014.* John Benjamins.

Collet, T. (2016). 'Intertextuality in specialised translation: Citations as semantic markers in social science.' *Journal of Specialised Translation*, (26), 72–95.

Danilova, V. (2013). 'Cross-language plagiarism detection methods.' In I. Temnikova, I. Nikolova, & N. Konstantinova (Eds.), *Proceedings of the Student Research Workshop Associated with RANLP 2013* (51–57). INCOMA.

De Beaugrande, R., & Dressler, W. U. (1981). *Introduction to text linguistics.* Longman.

Desagulier, G. (2017). *Corpus Linguistics and Statistics with R: Introduction to Quantitative Methods in Linguistics*. Springer International Publishing. https://doi.org/10.1007/978-3-319-64572-8

do Amaral, V. A. (2019). 'Broadening the notion of retranslation.' *Cadernos de Traduçao,* 39(1), 239–259. https://dialnet.unirioja.es/servlet/articulo?codigo=6765656

Dorato, M. (2004). 'Epistemic and nonepistemic values in science.' In P. K. Machamer & G. Wolters (Eds.), *Science, Values, and Objectivity* (52–77). University of Pittsburgh Press.

Dougherty, M. V. (2019). 'The corruption of philosophical communication by translation plagiarism.' *Theoria*, (85), 219–246. https://doi.org/10.1111/theo.12188

Ezzikouri, H., Oukessou, M., Erritali, M., & Madani, Y. (2019). 'Fuzzy cross language plagiarism detection approach based on semantic similarity and Hadoop MapReduce.' In S. Melliani & O. Castillo (Eds.), *Recent Advances in Intuitionistic Fuzzy Logic Systems: Theoretical Aspects and Applications* (181–190). Springer. https://doi.org/10.1007/978-3-030-02155-9_15

Fairclough, N. (2003). *Analysing Discourse: Textual Analysis for Social Research*. Routledge.

Fairclough, N. (1992). 'Intertextuality in critical discourse analysis.' *Linguistics and Education*, 4(3–4), 269–293. https://doi.org/10.1016/0898-5898(92)90004-G

Feng, L. (2014). 'Retranslation hypotheses revisited: A case study of two English translations of *Sanguo Yanyi* – the first Chinese novel.' *Stellenbosch Papers in Linguistics Plus*, 43, 69–86. https://doi.org/10.5842/43-0-209

Ferrero, J., Besacier, L., Schwab, D., & Agnes, F. (2017, August 3). 'Deep Investigation of Cross-Language Plagiarism Detection Methods.' *The Tenth Workshop on Building and Using Comparable Corpora, Vancouver, Canada* (6–15). https://doi.org/10.18653/v1/W17-2502

Franco-Salvador, M., Rosso, P., & Montes-y-Gómez, M. (2016). 'A systematic study of knowledge graph analysis for cross-language plagiarism detection.' *Information Processing and Management, 52*(4), 550–570. https://doi.org/10.1016/j.ipm.2015.12.004

Fuertes, A. (2015). 'The Echoes of the translator's voice: Plagiarism as a translation strategy in English-Spanish narrative translations.' In A. Fuertes & E. Torres (Eds), *And Translation Changed the World (and the World Changed Translation)* (132–140). Cambridge Scholars.

Gambier, Y. (1994). 'La retraduction, retour et détour.' *Meta: Journal Des Traducteurs*, 39(3), 413–417. https://doi.org/10.7202/002799ar

Gipp, B. (2014). *Citation-based plagiarism detection: Detecting disguised and cross-language plagiarism using citation pattern analysis*. Springer Vieweg.

Gipp, B., Meuschke, N., Breitinger, C., Lipinski, M., & Nürnberger, A. (2013, July 28 – August 1). 'Demonstration of citation pattern analysis for plagiarism detection.' *SIGIR '13: Proceedings of the 36th international ACM SIGIR conference on Research and development in information retrieval, Dublin, Ireland* (1119–1120). https://doi.org/10.1145/2484028.2484214

Gürses, S. (2011). 'Translational plagiarism: National History Global Prospects.' *Çeviribilim*, (4), 6–7.

Helgesson, G., & Eriksson, S. (2015). 'Plagiarism in research.' *Medicine, Health Care and Philosophy*, 18(1), 91–101. https://doi.org/10.1007/s11019-014-9583-8

Kent, C. K., & Salim, N. (2009). 'Web based cross language plagiarism detection.' *Journal of Computing*, 1(1), 39–43.

Koskinen, K., & Paloposki, O. (2010). 'Retranslation.' In Y. Gambier, & L. van Doorslaer (Eds.), *Handbook of Translation Studies*, Vol. 1 (294–298). John Benjamins.

Kristeva, J. (1941/1980). 'Word, Dialogue and Novel.' In L. S. Roudiez (Ed.), *Desire in Language: A Semiotic Approach to Literature and Art* (T. Gora, A. Jardine, & L. S. Roudiez, Trans., 64–91). Columbia University Press.

Leighton, L. G. (1994). 'Translation and plagiarism: Puškin and D. M. Thomas.' *The Slavic and East European Journal*, 38(1), 69–83. https://doi.org/10.2307/308547

Levshina, N. (2015). *How to do Linguistics with R: Data exploration and statistical analysis*. John Benjamins. https://doi.org/10.1075/z.195

Neubert, A. & Shreve, G. M. 1992. *Translation as text*. Kent State University Press.

O'Sullivan, C. (2011). 'Pseudotranslation.' In Y. Gambier & L. van Doorslaer (Eds.), *Handbook of translation studies*, Vol. 2 (123–125). John Benjamins.

Parlak, B. (2008). 'Çeviri intihalleri bağlamında *İlahi Komedi*' [*The Divine Comedy* in terms of Translation Plagiarism]. In B. Parlak (Ed.), *Çeviri Etiği Toplantısı: Çeviri ve Çevirmenliğin Etik Sorunları* (147–159). Istanbul University Press.

Pataki, M. (2012, July 16–18). 'A new approach for searching translated plagiarism.' [Presentation]. *The 5th international plagiarism conference, Newcastle, UK.*

Pataki, M., & Marosi, A. C. (2013). 'Searching for translated plagiarism with the help of desktop grids.' *Journal of Grid Computing, 11*(1), 149–166. https://doi.org/10.1007/s10723-012-9224-5

Plett, H. F. (1991). 'Intertextuality.' In H. F. Plett (Ed.), *Intertextuality* (3–29). de Gruyter.

Potthast, M., Barrón-Cedeño, A., Stein, B., & Rosso, P. (2011). 'Cross-language plagiarism detection.' *Language Resources and Evaluation, 45*(1), 45–62. https://doi.org/10.1007/s10579-009-9114-z

Rambelli, P. (2011). 'Pseudotranslation.' In M. Baker, & G. Saldanha (Eds.), *Routledge Encyclopedia of Translation Studies* (208–211). Routledge.

Rokeach, M. (1973). *The Nature of Human Values*. Free Press.

Şahin, M., Duman, D., & Gürses, S. (2015). 'Big business of plagiarism under the guise of (re)translation.' *Babel. Revue Internationale de La Traduction / International Journal of Translation*, *61*(2), 193–218. https://doi.org/10.1075/babel.61.2.03sah.

Şahin, M., Duman, D., Gürses, S., Kaleş, D. & Woolls, D. (2019). 'Toward an empirical methodology for identifying plagiarism in retranslation.' In Ö. B. Albachten, & Ş. T. Gürçağlar (Eds). *Perspectives on retranslation: Ideology, paratexts, methods* (166–191). Routledge.

Taş, S. (2019). 'Çeviri İntihalini Açığa Çıkarmak: Türkçede Sultan II. Abdülhamid'in Hayatı Üzerine Bir Çalışma' [Uncovering Translation Plagiarism: A Case Study on the Life of Abdul Hamid II in Turkish]. *Turkish Studies*, *14*(1), 695–712. https://doi.org/10.7827/TurkishStudies.14891

Toury, G. (1995). *Descriptive translation studies and beyond*. John Benjamins.

Toury, G. (2012). *Descriptive translation studies – and beyond* (Revised edition). John Benjamins.

Turell, M. T. (2004). 'Textual kidnapping revisited: The case of plagiarism in literary translation.' *International Journal of Speech, Language and the Law*, *11*(1), 1–26. https://doi.org/10.1558/ijsll.v11i1.1

Welbers, K., Van Atteveldt, W., & Benoit, K. (2017). 'Text Analysis in R.' *Communication Methods and Measures*, *11*(4), 245–265. https://doi.org/10.1080/19312458.2017.1387238

Venuti, L. (2008). *The translator's invisibility: A history of translation*. Routledge.

Venuti, L. (2009). 'Translation, intertextuality, interpretation.' *Romance Studies*, *27*(3), 157–173. https://doi.org/10.1179/174581509X455169

Yildiz, M. (2020). 'Identification of Morphological, Lexical, and Syntactical Obfuscating Elements in Pseudo-Retranslations.' *Amasya Üniversitesi Sosyal Bilimler Dergisi (ASOBİD), Translation Studies Special Issue*, 131–161.

Yildiz, M. (2021). 'In Search of Patient Zero: Pseudo-Retranslation in Turkish Academic Works.' *Journal of Academic Ethics*, *19*(2), 253–278. https://doi.org/10.1007/s10805-020-09371-4

Karolina Siwek

Jan Dlugosz University in Czestochowa

Non-Textual Aspects of a Literary Translator's Work in the Nineteenth Century

Abstract: The literary translator is not independent because of various factors which determine his/her work. The aim of this paper is to present non-textual aspects of a literary translator's work in nineteenth century Poland and to attempt to investigate their influence. Three factors will be discussed: sociological, cultural, and political. I will also attempt to answer the question of their translation identity i.e., whether they saw themselves as literary translators and how society saw them as well. The issue will be presented on the example of selected silhouettes of English- and German-speaking literary translators in the nineteenth century in Poland – Kazimierz Brodziński, Ignacy Hołowiński and Józef Paszkowski. These translators were chosen because of their vast impact on the development of translation as a profession at that time. Kazimierz Brodziński was famous for being the first translator of Goethe's works in Poland. Ignacy Hołowiński was the first person who translated Shakespeare's works into Polish and used original English texts for it. Finally, Józef Paszkowski who was appreciated for the translations of both Shakespeare and Goethe works. Furthermore, it is worth mentioning that Paszkowski worked on the original English and German sources. On the basis of biographical backgrounds, the presentation will be concluded with a discussion of how the non-textual aspects moulded their work and translation choices. It is assumed that one's sociological background had a large impact on having access to this profession. In the case of historical and political factors, it can be supposed that they had an influence on the choice of texts for translation and the source language. In conclusion, only people from higher social strata had access to this profession because of the opportunity of learning foreign languages and using original source texts. In addition, their work and translation choices were often determined by historical and political circumstances. The texts of Shakespeare and Goethe were gladly chosen because of the social unrest in nineteenth century Poland. Moreover, the expectations of the publishing market at that time as far as censorship is concerned were also significant and influential.

Keywords: literary translator, Paszkowski, Brodziński, Hołowiński, nineteenth-century Poland

Introduction

A literary translator is not independent during translation work and this fact was known and investigated by researchers trying to develop the sociology of translation. Research on the translator as a full agent in the translation process is not a new phenomenon and has been noticed since the 1980s. The first time the translator was focused on and made the main object of study was in 1995, when Lawrence Venuti observed that a translator was visible in the translated text. For Venuti, however, this discovery was an inconvenient truth as, in his view, the translator should try to remain invisible (Venuti, 1995). Nevertheless, translators were no longer hidden, because researchers began to look increasingly closely at them.

At this point, it is worthwhile to mention Anthony Pym, who noted that a translator should be visible in the targeted text, and negated Lawrence Venuti's call for translators to stay invisible in the texts translated by them. Pym called for the humanisation of the translation process (Pym 2009: 23–45). Susan Bassnett and Andre Lefevere went one step further and proposed to set translators in the culture and investigate how that can influence the translation process, translators' choices and decisions (Bassnett and Lefevere, 1998). As a result of further research, Bassnett concluded that a translator is/should be an intercultural mediator (Bassnett, 2011). A subsequent researcher, Michaela Wolf, decided to study the translator in the context of not only in the culture but also in society. Looking at the translator from the sociological context gave new opportunities and new perspectives for Translator Studies, which caused a so-called *social turn* (Wolf, 2007). Finally, Andrew Chesterman decided to separate Translator Studies from Translation Studies and to formally situate the translator in research (Chesterman, 2017).

Sociologists of translation reached for the field theory developed by the French sociologist Pierre Bourdieu to place a literary translator more precisely in society. According to this theory, individuals or groups with similar aims, competing with each other, operate in a single *field* that functions according to specific and central assumptions and objectives. It provides a useful tool in exploring the sociological aspects of the translator's profession i.e. to reconstruct the place of literary translators in society and in the analysis of the networks therein.

The use of biographical data, which made it possible to compile translators' biographies, proved to be insightful in reconstructing the situation of translators. Renata Makarska is a pioneer in providing useful guidelines for the creation of translator biographies, and she has identified four segments of information that such a biography should contain (Makarska, 2016). A translator's biography is understood as a biography of the translator which also includes their extra-translational activities. A translator's biography is not only a biography that contains the most important information about the translator's life, but also a collection of information about the situation in which they learned a foreign language – a topobiography i.e. information about where they lived, worked, moved, who they met and what kind of relations they had, and the fourth segment which deals with other activities that the translator was involved in (Makarska, 2016). The inclusion of the same four segments allows for collecting key information in the context of being a translator and, most importantly, comparing several translators to each other.

The most recent research of translation sociologists concern for the exploitation of the information obtained through biographical research. Nowadays, a translation biography is not a goal in itself, but a means of comparing several biographies and drawing wider conclusions about the situation of a literary translator working, for example, in a certain time period or a certain place. Moreover, it has also become possible to analyse the issue of a translator's identity which concerns the translator's self-perception, but also the perception of the society in which he lives and works (Eberharter, 2021).

All of the above outcomes provide tools to investigate the situation and work context of literary translators in nineteenth century Poland. This paper will consider three non-textual aspects: sociological, cultural, and political. The research was conducted based on the works of three translators: Kazimierz Brodziński, Ignacy Hołowiński and Józef Paszkowski. The common thread is the time and place of their translating activity. All of them worked in nineteenth century Poland and were engaged in translation of Shakespeare's or Goethe's texts. Poland at that time did not exist on the maps of Europe and the Polish nation was divided into three partitions. This act further impacted the culture, traditions, language and also the translators' activities. This paper will examine how these three non-textual aspects influenced the translation activities of the mentioned translators and their socio-cultural situation. Moreover, an attempt to answer the question of their translational identity will be made i.e. whether they saw themselves as literary translators and how society saw them.

In order for the analysis to be authoritative, and able to reconstruct the situation of a literary translator working in the nineteenth century, the representatives had to be thoughtfully selected. Therefore, the choice of translators was dictated by the fact that they started with original English or German texts, which was not so obvious at that time, and that they worked in the nineteenth century, but with a slight shift to each of them which give opportunity to present the perspective of contexts broadly. Each of the three translators had to have translated Shakespeare or Goethe, whose texts were already considered literary classics in the nineteenth century and were widely commented on by literary critics; providing a variety of opinions on the translators themselves. Brief biographical details will be given to show the background of the translators, and place them in the translation *field* and analyse the paths which led them to translation activity. This will also enable broader conclusions to be drawn about the situation of nineteenth-century translators in Poland and their translational identity.

Translator Profiles

Kazimierz Józef Brodziński was born in 1791 in Królówka, a village located in today's Nowy Wiśnicz Gmina approximately 40 km southeast of Kraków. His family was impoverished nobility. Kazimierz's parents were Jacek Brodziński, who came from a poor noble family, and Franciszka, born Radzikowska, also of noble birth (Encyklopedia PWN, 2021). The young Brodziński stayed in Królówka for the first few years of his childhood until 1794 when Kazimierz's mother died. This fact influenced the rest of his life and future poetic works. Throughout his life, he felt the absence of his mother; he constantly idealised her image and brought her to his thoughts so much that she appears in his dreams. The word mother was sacred to him. After his wife's death, Jacek Brodzinski moved with his children to Lipnica Dolna, where he independently leased the Lipnica district. It was in Lipnica (until 1805), that the personality of the young Kazimierz Brodziński was formed. Jacek Brodziński's second wife was a certain Anna Fichhauzern, a modest and humble person at first, as Kazimierz's stepson writes about her, but soon she became a cruel stepmother. No wonder little Kazimierz, finding no tenderness at home, only fear and humiliation, ran away from home wandering around the countryside. He was happy to stay at country farms, where he found an understanding and kind environment.

Between 1797–1800, Kazimierz Brodziński attended an elementary school in Lipnica, and his older brother Andrzej also studied there. The school was closed after the First Partition of Poland in 1772, but was reopened in 1794 thanks to the efforts of Jacek Brodzinski, Kazimierz's father. Unfortunately, for the future poet, the Lipnica school almost exclusively provided bad memories. He did not like school because of the social stratification of the time, which was also visible among children. Most of the pupils were the children of the Lipnica bourgeoisie, who emphasised their superiority over the rest of the children, the village children, and who also expressed their dislike of the noble origin of the Brodzińskis. Despite the poor education he received at Lipnica's school, he became famous years later as a poet and author of literary treatises. Kazimierz Brodziński spent 10 years in Lipnica. On December 21, 1804, while studying in Krakow at a gymnasium, his father died and was buried in the Lipnica cemetery. Kazimierz interrupted his studies and returned to Lipnica (Anioł, 2016).

The next step on the trail of Kazimierz Brodziński is Rajbrot. Jacek Brodzinski was able to lease the Lipnica manor farm for life, so his wife was forced to leave it. In Rajbrot, a village neighbouring Lipnica, she took on the lease of the Rajbrot vicarage. Deprived of his father's means of subsistence on his death, Kazimierz was at the mercy of his stepmother, staying with her for nine months at the turn of 1804/5. An important part of his education and the formation of his personality during his stay in Rajbrot were his favourite excursions to the picturesque group of rocks situated on the Paprotna Hill between Lipnica Górna and Rajbrot. Brodzinski was not a diligent student and did not read books. His adventure with literature began in 1805 in Rajbrot, when he returned to his family home and found writings from the time of the Great Sejm and some poems and texts by Naruszewicz and Trembecki. Thus began Brodziński's adventure with literature. His hunger for liturgy and the need to express his thoughts through poetry were aroused (Grzybowski, online). Books lent to him by the Rajbrot parish organist helped him with this. He also used the melodies of local songs heard at village weddings and composed his own words to them.

On graduating from grammar school in Tarnów in 1809, Kazimierz Brodzinski also broke physical ties with his hometown. He had learned German at school, and it was there that he first became interested in the literature of Schiller and Goethe. Brodziński himself admitted that in 1807/8 he became particularly interested in the German literature of Uz, Kleist, Hagedron and Wieland. A great contribution to this was made by his professor Schmidt. Brodziński's favourite, however, was Goethe (Ciechanowska, 1928).Through his career as a soldier of Prince Józef Poniatowski (1809–1813), he reached the heights of Polish literature in his manhood (Anioł, 2016).

He begun his career in the army of the Duchy of Warsaw and in 1812 he was promoted to lieutenant. He was sentenced to Prussian prison after the Battle of the Nations at Leipzig (Witkowska, 1968). After returning from the army, he did not have many opportunities and his financial situation was beginning to become worse, so he decided to bet on literature (Grzybowski, online). In 1814, he came back to Warsaw and started working as a clerk. Then he worked as a Polish literature teacher. Finally, he received his doctor's degree in philosophy and became a Professor at Warsaw University (Witkowska, 1968). In 1826 he married Wiktoria, born Holly. They had one daughter, Karolina(Grzybowski, online). He frequently travelled to health resorts, while also becoming acquainted with Czech researchers of Slavic and Slavonic folklore. During the November Uprising, Brodziński worked as an editor of *Kurier Polski* and *Nowa Polska*. He is considered a poet who had a huge impact on Polish Romanticism. Brodziński is also a recognisable historian, a critic and theorist of literature, and a literary translator. He died in Dresden on October 10, 1835 at the age of 44 on his way back from treatment in Carlsbad (Witkowska, 1968).

Kazimierz Brodziński was the first translator of Goethe in Poland whose poetry he translated as early as 1819. The conflict between the Classicists and Romantics at the beginning of the nineteenth century did not make it easier for Goethe's work to find its way to Poland. However, Brodziński rid himself of the prejudice against Goethe's oeuvre propagated by the Classics, and slowly began to convince people that Goethe was worthwhile, even if he broke the established classical literary patterns. Brodziński's personal tastes were also evident in his texts and commentaries promoting Goethe's works. Unfortunately, there is no information as to which of Goethe's works he was acquainted with. Brodziński is regarded as the first propagator of Goethe in Poland. He also became a promoter of pre-romanticism (Ciechanowska, 1928).

Brodziński's translations were written according to what appealed to him at the time. They were not planned or arranged in a deliberate series. Brodziński translated poems like *Płocha, Nawrócona, Pasterz, Różyczka,* which were well received due to the preservation of Goethe's melodiousness, simplicity, and style. It should be remembered that in his youth spent in the countryside, Brodziński had plenty of opportunity and passion for listening to folk songs, which is the reason why he rendered them with such naturalness in translation. Brodziński's translations were received positively. They were appreciated for their diligence and naturalness which resulted from his personal fondness for the translating texts. Kazimierz Brodziński translated not only Goethe, but also Schiller and Herder; however, it was Goethe that he brought to Poland and made famous first. Clearly, the translator's passion, which is evident in his works, only made it easier to attract new readers.

Ignacy Hołowiński, working under the nicknames Zegota Kostrowiec or Ignacy Kefaliński, was born in 1807 in Owrucz (now in the Ukraine) in an impoverished noble family. He was the seventh of eight children of Peter, the village administrator, and Dominika, born Łęska. He was christened in the parish of the Basilian Fathers on September 25 of that year, and that day is generally considered to have been his birthday. In the years 1819–1825 he attended a Piarist grammar school in Międzyrzecze Koreckie, where his uncle – Dominik Szybiński was rector and a translator. After that Hołowiński entered the Theological Seminary in Łuck. From January 1827, he continued his theological and philosophical studies at the Main Seminary in Vilnius, where he obtained his master's degree in June 1830. He was distinguished by his great talents and high erudition. He learned foreign languages, read Latin classics, and studied German philosophers (Wodzianowska, 2017).

After his ordination to the priesthood on September 25, 1830, in Luck by the Bishop of Luck and Zhytomyr Michal Piwnicki (1771–1845), he worked as a catechist in the nobility school in Zhytomyr. Appointed cathedral canon in 1834, he was also dean of the Zhytomyr cathedral from 1835. From February 1837 to June 1842 he taught theology at St. Vladimir's Kyiv University and was chaplain of the academic church. After the Kiev university was closed in 1839, he made a six-month journey to the Holy Land, and published his impressions in *Pilgrimage to the Holy Land*. In the early 1840s, together with Michał Grabowski (1804–1863), Józef Ignacy Kraszewski (1812–1887) and Józef Emanuel Przecławski (1799–1879), he belonged to the so-called Petersburg coterie, a conservative literary and social group established on the initiative of Henryk Rzewuski (1791–1866). Gathered around the *Tygodnik Petersburski*, published in 1803 by Przecławski in St. Petersburg, the writers were characterised by a conciliatory attitude to the tsarist authorities, at the same time fighting the pro-independence and patriotic aspirations of the Poles. Membership of the coterie won Hołowiński the favour of the then Governor-General of Kiev, Dmitry G. Bibikov (1792–1870), who became one of his patrons when he was appointed Rector of the Roman Catholic Theological Academy in St Petersburg. As a conservative in social matters, Hołowiński simultaneously enjoyed the confidence of the Russian government (ibid.).

In June 1842, Hołowiński became the first rector of the Roman Catholic Theological Academy in St Petersburg after its transfer from Vilnius to the Russian capital of Moscow. In 1848 Hołowiński became coadjutor bishop, and in 1851 archbishop of Mogilev, and thereby head of the Catholic churches in Russia. He held his office during a difficult period of the church's dependence on the tsarist regime. His actions are described in extremely contradictory testimonies, and he himself is seen as either an opportunist or a heroic defender of independence. He died on October 19,1855 in St. Petersburg as a famous clergyman, writer, and translator. Hołowiński was the author of numerous theological and literary publications. He translated Francesco Petrarch (1304–1374) and William Shakespeare (1564–1616), and printed his poems and short stories under the pseudonyms Kefaliński and Żegota Kostrowiec in *Tygodnik Petersburski* (ibid.).

Ignacy Hołowiński was the first to undertake a translation of Shakespeare's works into Polish, using the English source text. Until then, Shakespeare's texts had appeared in Poland only as adaptations from German-language texts which significantly affected their quality. In 1828 Hołowiński and two other seminarians[1] petitioned the Seminary Council for additional English lessons. He

1 One of them was Placid Jankowski, who later himself translated Shakespeare.

motivated his request by the wealth of English literature (Cetera-Włodarczyk and Kosim, 2019). He probably also explored the works of Shakespeare during these lessons.

Hołowiński knew Józef Korzeniowski and together they decided to undertake the translation of all Shakespeare works. They were to be in volumes, one volume per year. The translators shared the texts and already in the first year there was a split and Korzeniowski accused Hołowiński that his Shakespeare was 'not like that' (ibid.) and too faithful. Despite the break in cooperation, the first volume of Hołowiński's translations was published in Vilnius in 1839, containing *Hamlet*, *Romeo and Juliet*, *A Dream on St John's Eve*. The second volume appeared in 1841 and included *Macbeth*, *King Lear* and *The Tempest*. The publication was richly illustrated and expensive. The books won the interest and admiration of readers. They even found their way to Siberia and Paris. However, the translations were not equal in quality, and the order in which they were produced is also unknown, so it is not known whether this affected the quality. It is known, though, that Hołowiński read a lot about these texts in other languages – German, French, English before he started his translations. Hołowiński mastered his translator craft and tried to be faithful to the original. The problem was that he was working under immense pressure of time, literary criticism, and the responsibilities of being a clergyman. Being a clergyman did not make it easy for him to translate broad and erotic passages, and his superiors insisted that he should not deal with literature. Juliusz Słowacki mocked it for its restraint, while others took issue with the language being indecent (ibid.).

In any case, Holowiński's works were a source of polemic for supporters and opponents alike. The fact that readers were familiar with Shakespeare from German adaptations did not help. They found Hołowiński's Shakespeare quite different and sometimes unacceptable. However, Józef Ignacy Kraszewski received the works very favourably and analysed the translation in detail in the *Tygodnik Petersburski*. In the end, it became apparent that the publication of Hołowiński's translations was a literary event. And even if he was not a great talent and followed the original too faithfully, he was nevertheless the first who did such an immense undertaking and produced translations based on English source texts (ibid.).

Józef Edmund Paszkowski spent all his life in Warsaw. He was born on January 3,1817 and died in 1861. Paszkowski came from a military family – his father, Dominik Paszkowski was an officer in the staff of Prince Józef Poniatowski, was administrator of the Poniatowski estate in Jabłonna, and took part in the November Uprising. His mother was Anna, born Niemojewska.

Józef Paszkowski was educated at home first and that gave him good knowledge of foreign languages (English, German, and French) and then he graduated from the Piarists School in Warsaw. In the then Kingdom of Poland, he did not have the opportunity to continue his education at university, so he supplemented his knowledge as a self-taught person. After that he worked as a clerk and then as a teacher. He started his apprenticeship at the Government Commission for Internal and Spiritual Affairs, and in 1834 he joined the Department of Religious Denominations and Public Enlightenment. In 1836 he became member of the Examination Board of the Warsaw Scientific District, and in 1848 the Secretary of the Pedagogical Courses and Examination Committee. In 1843 Paszkowski married Kazimiera Seweryna, born Stompf. They had three children: Leon, Franciszka and Laura (ibid.).

During his twenty-five years of work in education administration, he rose to the rank of collegiate assessor. Parallel to his clerical work, he developed his literary creativity. The knowledge he acquired at school later supported by his own thorough and systematic study of French, German and, in particular, English literature – in addition to his literary talents and passions – made him an excellent translator. He debuted in 1840 with a translation of a fragment of V. Hugo's drama *Hernani*. Paszkowski tried to create his own poems, but his works were criticised causing him to finally resign from this activity and devoted himself to translating. At the end of his life his health condition was poor, and the translation work became the main source of income for him.

He died on April 17,1861 in Warsaw after six years of suffering from tuberculosis and was buried at the Powązki Cemetery in Warsaw. He translated mostly tragedies and became famous as a translator of Shakespeare works, in which he also worked out the most canonical solutions. Paszkowski also translated *Faust* by Goethe using the German source text. Interestingly, he included a lot of information about his translation strategies. On this basis, it can be assumed that he approached his translation activities professionally and not just artistically. Unfortunately, the publishing of the translated *Faust* was withheld by censors and was finally published in 1881, after the translator's death (ibid.). Compared to other translators in the nineteenth century, Paszkowski seems to be the most focused and committed to his translation activity.

Non-textual aspects

As non-textual aspects of a translator's activity, sociological, cultural, and political issues can be considered. These are wide-ranging aspects which interlink, complement, and permeate each other, thereby making it difficult to draw clear boundaries between them. In addition, it is worth mentioning that in the social aspect, linguistic and cultural issues are also possible to include which are inevitable in society. Social issues often interweave with political issues, especially in the case of nineteenth century Polish lands, because society was divided into three partitions, being a political issue with a strong impact on the nation/society, as well as on its language and culture.

Looking at the authors chosen by the translators, it is clear that they were interested in literary notables: Shakespeare, Goethe, Schiller, and Hugo. These decisions were often based on personal taste, but also on the conviction that lowbrow literature was a waste of time. This was a conviction that had been passed on to translators-people of letters, who chose literary masterpieces to learn how to write. However, the most important factor in choosing specific works was the socio-political situation prevailing at the time in the Polish territories under partition. The lands were divided, but the nation was trying with all its might to unite. There was an atmosphere of sadness and mourning after the loss of independence, but at the same time motivation and enthusiasm to fight. This time of unrest was a great foundation for Romanticism, which with its restless spirit broke classical conventions. Shakespeare and Goethe broke convention in a similar way, so reading and translating their texts was the highest literary trend. Nor should their theatrical adaptations be forgotten, which remained on the stage throughout the nineteenth century. Shakespeare was the model for developing Romantic drama. Goethe, as a promoter of Romanticism, wrote his life's work, *Faust*, which before its official publication became a literary masterpiece and a translation challenge for centuries.

First, regarding the profiles, it can be noticed that all three translators came from noble families or families connected with the army. It gave them wealthy upbringing, or as was the case of Hołowiński – connections. Moreover, such families were conscious that education is very important and worth investing in. Even the short profiles given above are able to present the significance of culture in the lives of the mentioned translators. They had access to literature, foreign languages and people who could introduce them into the cultural or literary life. Faced with the political situation which influenced formal education, Paszkowski's parents provided him with home schooling which gave him profound knowledge including foreign languages. Brodziński's parents were able to send him to school. It is not without significance that he grew up in the vicinity of one of the largest cultural centres – Kraków. Hołowiński was supported by his uncle, headmaster of the school where Hołowiński was educated. Moreover, this uncle also translated, which allows the conclusion that perhaps he was the first person who introduced Hołowiński to translation. As seen, a proper family background was a great base for further personal development of the translators. Their parents possessed money, connections or even sometimes literary novelties in private libraries which were not available in official publishing circulation because of censorship but were very important in the development of literary tastes as far as future translation choices are concerned.

Partitioning states controlled the publishing market and hence exerted appropriate pressure on the unwanted Polish culture. In such a situation, access to the works of Shakespeare, already considered as a classic of literature at that time, was very difficult. The only source was very often private family or acquaintance collections. Even access to Goethe's works was problematic. They were novelties which suited the climate of the time very well. Poles could have had the impression that Goethe spoke directly to Polish rebellious souls, so all of his new literary works (published in limited quantities) disappeared in the blink of an eye. Brodziński, Hołowiński and Paszkowski chose to translate Shakespeare's and Goethe's works because even then Shakespeare was treated as representative of classic literature. Goethe's texts aspired to enter the canon of literature. Literary translators of the nineteenth century mainly chose classics, which was also a way to find inspiration to create own texts, or to exercise in foreign languages (what should be also done with a proper language base).

The Polish language was displaced by the process of Germanisation and Russification which strongly limited the development of Polish culture especially literature and finally banned teaching Polish at schools. As a result, translation into Polish was sometimes an exercise to learn native Polish. Only wealthy families were able to provide a private tutor for their children who could teach them Polish and supply knowledge free from censorship. This gave a better orientation of the political situation as well. At this point it becomes clear that the translator activity was available only for people with an upper-class family background. This issue can be also observed in the case of Brodziński, Hołowiński, and Paszkowski.

By observing the profiles, it is evident that Brodziński, Hołowiński, and Paszkowski can be considered as representative of the intelligentsia. This view can be based on two methods of classification proposed by sociologists studying Polish society: the origins of the nineteenth century Polish intelligentsia from impoverished nobility and their performed professions. The first aspect was already presented – all three translators have similar family origin. In case of professions, they worked as clerks (Paszkowski, Hołowiński) or teachers – all of them. Being a priest, as it was in case of Hołowiński, classified him also as a representative of the intelligentsia.

In the nineteenth century, literary translation was not considered a profession. It was treated like an additional activity, hobby, or language exercise, especially for people connected in some way with literature e.g. the authors themselves. Although contemporary biographies refer to Brodziński, Paszkowski, and Hołowiński as translators, none of them were likely to identify with this. It is evident from their obituaries alone that their contemporaries saw them rather as 'meritorious to literature' (Brodziński), 'an official' (Paszkowski), 'an archbishop' (Hołowiński) (Minakowski, 2021). They themselves, especially Brodziński and Hołowiński, treated translation as an additional activity. One can assume that the situation was somewhat different in the case of Paszkowski, for whom translations eventually became his only occupation and only source of income, which was a quite rare phenomenon. As a rule, those involved in translation in the nineteenth century saw it as a hobby, or possibly an additional source of income.

Nevertheless, the nineteenth century is a time of breakthrough, when the situation of literary translators in Poland began to change. In previous centuries, only poets or writers were treated as adequate specialists who were able to cope with translating. However, the second part of the nineteenth century is the first moment when this point of view started to change. The situation of a literary translator in Poland can be divided into the period before the January Uprising (1863–1864), and after the January Uprising, which means that the year 1864 can be marked as a border of significant change. Kazimierz Brodziński and Ignacy Hołowiński were famous for their literary works. Brodziński was quite good at it and recognisable especially in the case of texts concerning literary criticism. Hołowiński concentrated on tales and poems with religious elements, what is not a surprise in the face of being a priest. But Józef Paszkowski, who died in 1861, can be treated as the pioneer of the first changes. He was not good at creating his own texts but surprisingly his translations were appreciated, published, and used even today as proof of being more popular in translation than Brodziński and Hołowiński, who were poets and writers. Being a good translator is no longer synonymous with being a poet. As late as the beginning of the nineteenth century, the translator was considered equal to the poet and these two roles were treated almost synonymously. Thus, translation was not considered a separate creative activity.

There were no book publications except for one, *Dzieła dramatyczne Williama Shekespeara* edited by J.I. Kraszewski and published in 1875. The translations were published mainly in magazines divided into fragments. In the case of these slender publications, mainly translators decided which texts would be chosen for translation. They could also sometimes count on some payment for their work.

Translation work was the source of income for Paszkowski towards the end of his life when he was ill and unable to work as a teacher. His translations were also used on the stage, but there was no evidence that he received payment for his services. Brodziński and Hołowiński were in better financial situations and there was no need for them to look for extra income to survive. Nevertheless, literary translations were not common and frequent enough to be a main source of income or a stable occupation. They were treated as an additional activity or additional source of income while being a teacher, a professor, or a clerk.

During the period around the November Uprising (1830–1831), poets and writers who worked on translations were criticised by representatives, mainly, of the intelligentsia, who were deeply involved in national liberation activities. In their opinion, translation was a waste of time, and poets and writers should have created to nourish Polish hearts in hope of regaining independence soon, if only through the November Uprising. This issue was investigated by Wacław Sadkowski in his publication, *Odpowiednie dać słowu słowo: zarys dziejów przekładu literackiego w Polsce* (Sadkowski, 2002). Nevertheless, literary translators as well-educated people were oriented in the political situation and very often involved in the national liberation activities. In the first half on the nineteenth century, Kazimierz Brodziński worked as an editor in insurgent magazines. After the fall of the November Uprising, he did not emigrate for long and settled in Warsaw. Ignacy Hołowiński was associated with Żytomierz (today's Zhytomyr) during the November Uprising. He was not involved in it. He concentrated on his clerical career. Although he was accused that he had the opportunity to pursue this career only because he obeyed the tsar. During the November Uprising, Paszkowski was too young to participate in it. Nevertheless, as a result of the repression after the uprising, he was unable to study at university.

Conclusion

To conclude, non-textual aspects can have a great impact on translators' activities and paths of their translation development. After analysis of the family backgrounds of Brodziński, Hołowiński and Paszkowski, it appeared that they came from the same translation *field* – they were representatives of the Polish intelligentsia which provided them with a similar *habitus*, understood as a set of skills, competences, and opportunities. In this case, it was an opportunity to educate, and have access to literature and people who were able to support their personal development. Germanisation and Russification caused translation to become a way of improving the native language, and the best sources of texts became classic literature. The November Uprising and the whole political situation had an influence on translators' lives. They were sentenced to prisons, wrote patriotic texts like Brodziński, simply avoided being involved in the unfavourable situation like Hołowiński, or lost access to university studies as Paszkowski. The nineteenth century was not a time when they were ready to call themselves *literary translators*. As can be seen from their necrologies, their contemporaries did not perceive them through the prism of their translating activities either, even in the case of Paszkowski, who had considerable achievements in the field of translation. It was definitely too early, but without a doubt, each of them was a literary translator by contemporary standards. This kind of work was not a profession but only additional activity, which gradually began to generate additional income for them. All three individuals were fully influenced by the society, culture and political influences which can be sometimes stimulating for work and translators' development or quite the contrary – hindering and suppressing. These aspects led to the selection of specific works for translation, to selected specific foreign languages from which they translated and, above all, made decisions to deal with translation. It is worth mentioning that for each of the discussed individuals, this last decision was supposed to be the natural turn of events. Each of them learned languages and became interested in literature. As a result, the initial grammar exercises were transformed into the improvement of their writing skills, the drawing of inspiration for their work and, finally, into the preparation of standard full-fledged translations. As the above examples have shown, despite the difficult situation in a country without independence, literary translations finally got a chance to be practiced and developed. The difficult national situation triggered changes in literature, which were driven by the works of, for example, Shakespeare and Goethe, who provided literary role models for the Romantics. This, in turn, motivated the creation of translations. Nevertheless, the change in perception of literary translators and translation issue is a long-term process, but the first premises for a change appeared in Poland in the nineteenth century.

References

Anioł, C.. (n.d.) 'Lipnickie biografie – Kazimierz Brodziński (1) – W Królówce.' https://www.lipniczanin.pl/lipnickie-biografie-kazimierz-brodzinski-1-krolowce/

Anioł, C. (2016) 'Lipnickie biografie – Kazimierz Brodziński (2) W Lipnicy Dolnej i Murowanej.' https://www.lipniczanin.pl/lipnickie-biografie-kazimierz-brodzinski-2-lipnicy-dolnej-murowanej/

Anioł, C. (2016.) 'Lipnickie biografie – Kazimierz Brodziński Część III – w Rajbrocie.' https://www.lipniczanin.pl/biografie-lipnickie-kazimierz-brodzinski-czesc-iii-rajbrocie/

Bassnett, S., & Lefevere, A. (Eds.). (1998). *Constructing cultures: Essays on literary translation*. Multilingual Matters.

Bassnett, S.. (2011). 'The translator as cross-cultural mediator.' In K. Malmkjær, & K. Windle (Eds.), *The Oxford Handbook of Translation Studies* (77–85). Oxford University Press.

Bittner, I. (1981). *Brodziński – historiozof*. Zakład Narodowy im. Ossolińskich.

Chesterman, A. (2009). 'The Name and Nature of Translator Studies.' *Hermes S – Journal of Language and Communication in Business, 42*, 13–22.

Cetera-Włodarczyk, A., & Kosim, A. (2019). *Polskie przekłady Shakespear'a w XIX wieku. Część I. Zasoby, strategie, recep.cja*. Wydawnictwa Uniwersytetu Warszawskiego.

Ciechanowska, Zofia. (1928). 'Kazimierz Brodziński jako pierwszy tłumacz Goethego w Polsce.' *Pamiętnik Literacki: czasopismo kwartalne poświęcone historii i krytyce literatury polskiej, 25/1/4*, 205–237.

Eberharter, M. (2013). 'Der Übersetzer als Akteur im Literaturbetrieb.' *Między Oryginałem a Przekładem, 19/20*, 189–205.

Eberharter, M.. (2014). 'Socjologiczne spojrzenie na rolę tłumaczy literatury. Na przykładzie Wandy Kragen i recepcji literatur niemieckojęzycznych w Polsce po 1945r.' *Rocznik Przekładoznawczy, IX*, 115–128.

Eberharter, M. (2021). 'Translator biographies as a contribution to Translator Studies. Case studies from nineteenth-century Galicia.' In K. Kaindl, W. Kolb, & D. Schlager (Eds.), *Literary translator studies* (73–88). John Benjamins, .

Fast, P., & Kozak, A. (2002). *Biograficzne konteksty przekładu*. Wydawnictwo Naukowe Śląsk.

Encyklopedia PWN (2021). Hołowiński. https://encyklopedia.pwn.pl/haslo/Holowinski-Ignacy;3912447.html

'Ignacy Hołowiński.' (n.d.) http://polskiszekspir.uw.edu.pl/ignacy-holowinski-tlumacz

Minakowski, M. J. (2021). Wielka genealogia Minakowskiego (Wielcy.pl), online resource. Available from: http://www.sejm-wielki.pl/b/2.320.13. Accessed: 6 August 2021

'Józef Paszkowski.' (n.d.) http://polskiszekspir.uw.edu.pl/jozef-paszkowski-tlumacz

'Józef Paszkowski.' (n.d.) http://www.chronologia.pl/biogram-pajo18170103w0.html

'Józef Edmund Paszkowski.' <https://www.ipsb.nina.gov.pl/a/biografia/jozef-edmund-paszkowski> (Accessed: 6 August 2021).

'Józef Paszkowski. Jeden z najwybitniejszych tłumaczy Szekspira.' (n.d.) https://www.polskieradio.pl/39/156/Artykul/2651397,Jozef-Paszkowski-Jeden-z-najwybitniejszych-tlumaczy-Szekspira

'Kazimierz Brodziński.'(n.d.) http://www.chronologia.pl/biogram-brka17910308k0.html

'Kazimierz Brodziński.' (n.d.) https://encyklopedia.pwn.pl/haslo/Brodzinski-Kazimierz;3880840.html

'Kazimierz Cibor-Brodziński z Brodzynia (ID: 2.320.13).' (n.d.) http://www.sejm-wielki.pl/b/2.320.13

Makarska, R. (2016). 'Translationsbiographische Forschung. Am Beispiel von Siegfried Lipiner (1856–1911) und Grete Reiner (1892–1944).' In A. F. Kelletat, A. Tashinsky, & J. Boguna (Eds.), *Übersetzerforschung. Neue Beiträge zur Literatur- und Kulturgeschichte des Übersetzens* (215–232). Frank & Timme.

Oleksowicz, B. (n.d.) 'Kazimierz Brodziński.' https://literat.ug.edu.pl/autors/brodzin.html>

Pym, A. (2009). 'Humanizing Translation History.' *Hermes – Journal of Language and Communication Studies, 32*, 23–45.

Pym, A. (2006). 'On the social and cultural in translation studies.' *Sociocultural Aspects of Translating and Interpreting* 67, 2006: 1–25.

Sadkowski, W. (2002). *Odpowiednie dać słowo słowu. Zarys dziejów przekładu literackiego w Polsce*. Warszawa: Prószyński i S-ka.

Witkowska, A. (1968). *Kazimierz Brodziński*. Państwowy Instytut Wydawniczy.

Wolf, M. (2007). 'Introduction: The emergence of a sociology of translation.' In Michaela Wolf, & A. Fukari (Eds.), *Constructing a Sociology of Translation* (1–36). John Benjamins.

Wodzianowska, I. (2017) 'Hołowiński Ignacy.' http://www.polskipetersburg.pl/hasla/holowinski-ignacy

Venuti, L. (1995). *The Translator's Invisibility: A History of Translation*. Routledge.

Judyta Mężyk

University of Silesia in Katowice, Paris-East Créteil University in Paris

Simultaneous Interpreting in Evangelical Churches in Poland as an Example of a Non-Professional Practice

Abstract: This paper examines the interpreting work environment in Evangelical churches in Poland, focusing on simultaneous interpreting practice. Interpreting, a crucial communication skill that facilitates communication between people who do not share a language, has always been important in the church. However, it was not the subject of much academic interest for a long time. Only with the growing interest in non-professional interpreting and translation (NPIT) in the last decade have papers on church interpreting started slowly appearing (e.g. Hokkanen, 2017, Peremota, 2017), but few of them have dealt with the Polish context. The aim of the present paper is twofold: to examine what exactly about Polish church interpreting can be considered non-professional (the interpreters themselves and/or their work conditions) and verify whether there are any differences as to how the interpreting is conducted depending on a denomination. To achieve that, nine churches from different Evangelical denominations were interviewed about their interpreting equipment, setting, and the competencies of interpreters, among other issues. The results point to the non-professional nature of church interpreting, both in terms of who performs the interpreting and the work environment, but also show some peculiarities, such as the use of the interpreting booth by the non-professional interpreters. The paper starts with an explanation of the context of Evangelical Christianity, especially in Poland, and elaborates on the role of interpreting in Evangelical churches, discussing the topic of NPIT. Then the methods used to conduct the study are presented, along with the results. The paper ends with conclusions and a brief discussion of the possibilities of further research connected to the topic of church interpreting.

Keywords: interpreting, simultaneous interpreting, non-professional interpreting, church interpreting, Polish-English simultaneous interpreting

1. Introduction

Interpreting is a communication event that facilitates the cross-cultural communication of two (or more) interlocutors who speak different languages (Odhiambo, et al., 2013) and often come from different cultural backgrounds

(Qian, 1994). In this communication process, the interpreter is the transmitter of the message sent by the sender and directed to the receiver. Well-done interpreting is such that it conveys the meaning of the original message in the target language, with the focus on grammatical meaning, lexical meaning, and rhetorical meaning (Hatim & Mason, 1990).

One of the environments where meaning is absolutely crucial is the church setting. This paper will focus particularly on Evangelical churches, and the word "church" will be used to refer to this type of Christian faith in short. To describe what will be meant by "Evangelicalism" in this paper, the more general notions need to be explained first. While there is no consensus on a definition of a Christian, three main traditions can be enumerated, that is, the Catholic, the Orthodox and the Protestant (Raszewska, 2016). Within Protestantism, there are a number of different typologies, and some of them divide Protestant churches into liberal, moderate, and conservative, while others distinguish charismatic and non-charismatic churches, among other divisions; in general, one cannot say that there are any universal factors according to which one could classify Protestant churches.[1] However, it is certain that Evangelical churches are a part of Protestantism, no matter which definition one adapts. In English, there is one term[2] that is often treated as being synonymous with 'Evangelical,' namely 'Born-Again' (Coleman, 1980: 133).[3] Raszewska (2016: 20) suggests a broad definition of Evangelical churches, claiming they are "the ones that proclaim the Gospel (Good News) about Jesus and His redemptive death on the cross," and in a narrower sense, "those churches which emphasize the necessity of personal

1 Source: Divisions within Protestant Christianity: http://www.religioustolerance.org/chr_divi3.htm. (Accessed: 26 November 2021).

2 In some dictionaries, the term 'Evangelic' is also present as a British English word used to describe something in connection with the Gospel; however, taking into the account its frequency over time, it seems to be outdated (e.g. Collins Online English Dictionary: https://www.collinsdictionary.com/dictionary/english/evangelic. (Accessed: 26 November 2021)).

3 In Polish, there are even more terms similar to each other, i.e., 'ewangelicki,' 'ewangeliczny,' and 'ewangelikalny:' the first describes churches originating from the 16th and 18th century reformations (that is, the Lutheran church, the German reformed churches and the Methodist church), while the other two can be considered synonymous and describe churches of so-called "second reformation" which started at the beginning of the 20th century and which can be particularly distinguished from the other one by the fact that these churches practice adult baptism (source: Ewangelikalna Wyższa Szkoła Teologiczna: https://ewst.pl/centrum-edukacyjne/ewangelikalizm/. (Accessed: 26 November 2021)).

conversion, often associated with adult water baptism and the role of the Bible, which is the true Word of God inspired by Holy Spirit." The personal conversion, the act of believing in Jesus and changing one's ways, is what leads Evangelical Christians to consider themselves "born again" (Erickson, 2001). In this paper, 'Evangelical churches' will be understood as in the narrower definition suggested by Raszewska (2016), and the term 'Born-Again' will be used alternately.

In Poland, there are between 50 000 and 100 000 Evangelical Christians, which constitutes around 0,2 % of the population. Despite the fact that there are over a dozen denominations, each having a few thousand members, it is one of the lowest percentages of Evangelical Christians in any national population.[4] Since many Evangelical denominations were born outside Poland (for instance, the Pentecostal church originated in the United States[5]), many churches have been planted in Poland by foreign missionaries since the beginning of the Born-Again movement. This leads to a conclusion that interpreting must have been present since the very beginning of the Evangelical church in Poland, and is also necessary today, when country borders are no longer so difficult to be crossed, and the number of people living outside of their homelands is rising rapidly. Furthermore, Downie (2014) observes that interpreting has been a vital part of the whole Christian church practice (it is not a topic exclusive to modern Poland); however, it has not been the subject of academic research until recently. In fact, the present paper may be one of the few research studies on simultaneous interpreting in an Evangelical church setting, and definitely one of the first to study it in the Polish context. In Section 2, interpreting in Evangelical churches will be covered in more detail, and in Section 3, the study conducted in nine Evangelical churches in Poland will be presented, along with the methods used and its results. Finally, in Section 4, the study will be concluded and discussed with a focus on future research possibilities.

2. Interpreting in Evangelical churches

Today's world is becoming more and more multicultural and multilingual, and so are churches. That is true for every part of the world, and it constitutes a challenge for church leaders who may be now faced with new people wanting to join their church but who speak a different language. Interpreting is a way to

4 Source: Ewangeliczna Polska: https://ewangeliczna.pl/czym-jest-ewangeliczna-polska/ (Accessed: 16 August 2021).

5 Source: Encyclopedia Britannica Online: https://www.britannica.com/topic/Pentecostalism (Accessed: 26 November 2021).

overcome this challenge and allow people living abroad to find a church, practice their faith, and meet other believers. According to Peremota (2017: 73), church interpreting can be defined as "any translational activity enabling immediate interlingual and intercultural communication in church settings."

To understand the importance of interpreting in Evangelical churches, it is necessary to understand the importance of the message that is preached there (for the history of church interpreting see Peremota, 2015). For Evangelical Christians, the most important meeting is the Sunday service,[6] but this does not include only a sermon that is supposed to shape the morals of the believers. The full service with all its parts (prayers and songs as well as the main sermon[7]) is a spiritual experience, a way to encounter God, with the sermon being "intended to induce and reinforce the experience of being a Christian" (Odhiambo et al., 2013: 192). Therefore, the interpreter's role is not only social but also spiritual, and this should lead them to make interpreting strategy decisions with regards to the possible effects of the sermon on the believers (Downie, 2014). Downie (2014), who focuses on homiletics with regards to interpreting, argues that one should not ignore the complexity of sermon interpreting by viewing it simply as conveying a message in a different language and/or questioning its meaning for the congregation. According to him, the role of the church interpreter is, in fact, similar to that of the preachers themselves and should be understood as such. Downie (2014: 65) suggests that thanks to the "single performance hypothesis," the idea that the preacher and the interpreter are in partnership to create a single "sermon performance," multilingual preaching can become more effective. That is why preachers should also treat their interpreters as partners in their work, not as "conduits through which the sermon gets mysteriously transferred into

6 This paper focuses on interpreting of the Sunday church service; however, it has to be stressed that church interpreting is a topic that goes beyond the Sunday service, as interpreting is needed also in other church settings such as ordinary conversations between people, small groups, conferences of any type, Sunday School classes, leadership training meetings, bishopric meetings, and missionary discussions, among others (source: https://www.churchofjesuschrist.org/bc/content/shared/content/english/pdf/callings/interpreter/interpretation-instructions-for-priesthood-leaders-eng.pdf. Accessed: 26 November 2021).

7 It is impossible to generalise about the structure of an Evangelical service because all churches function independently and there is no one universal structure they have to follow; however, it can be assumed that prayers, songs, and a sermon are present in every church service. Other parts may include announcements, the offering, Sunday school introduction, and occasional events such as a baptism, marriage, communion, and blessing of children.

another language" (Downie, 2014: 65).[8] Meanwhile, Owen (2014) stresses the importance of other parts of the service, saying that it is necessary to make sure that foreigners who do not know the language will also feel a part of everything that happens during the church service, for instance, by supplying in advance a translation of the lyrics of the songs that are scheduled to be sung.

The role of the interpreter in an Evangelical church requires certain competencies. In order to interpret the message properly, they have to be familiar with the language of 'Born-Again' Christianity. Raszewska (2016) notes that there are significant differences between the language used by Evangelicals and that of Non-Evangelicals, as the vocabulary and grammar used in Evangelical circles are visibly influenced by the Bible and their system of beliefs. She adds that Protestant speeches are often shaped in a way that imitates Biblical speeches. Furthermore, to understand some terminology (and therefore interpret it well), a knowledge and understanding of the Bible and its doctrines are necessary.

However, although church interpreters need to have particular competencies, they are usually non-professionals (Raszewska, 2016). Non-professionalism, when used to refer to work of any kind, translation and interpreting included, does not have good connotations. It is often used to refer to people who are not trained and thus produce bad quality products. For instance, Pérez-González and Susam-Saraeva (2012: 151) define non-professional translators and interpreters as "individuals not only without formal training in linguistic mediation but also working for free" which certainly does not evoke positive associations. Nonetheless, Hokkanen (2017: 196) opposes the negative connotations of non-professional translation and interpreting (NPIT), saying that "[t]hese connotations are hardly justifiable in most cases of real-life nonprofessional translation and interpreting practices, which, despite being ubiquitous, have not received much scholarly attention until recently." She adopts a different definition of non-professional translation and interpreting, which states that it a practice that one is not paid for (as in Harris, 2012; 2010; 2009). While it is still vastly understudied, over the last decade there has been a growing research interest in NPIT, and it seems clear now that 'non-professional' does not necessarily mean that the product quality is insufficient or that the translator or interpreter

8 Due to space limitations of this paper, it is not possible to elaborate on how such a partnership should be conducted; however, a few of Downie's ideas on it are: spending time with interpreters to understand the cognitive and performative challenges of interpreting, and describing the synopsis of the sermon, among others (Downie, 2014: 65).

skills are not adequate.[9] Pym (2000) notes that non-professional translators and interpreters have been important throughout history, including in the religious realm. However, while church interpreting is a major case of NPIT, it cannot constitute a general example for all non-professional settings. Owen (2014) stresses the differences between church interpreting and interpreting conducted in secular settings. First of all, as has been mentioned earlier in this section, the goal of the interpreter is not only to convey the message but also to let the listeners achieve spiritual edification. Then, it is not advisable for the church interpreter to be neutral or invisible; it is rather preferable that they be Christians with similar beliefs and even members of the church where they volunteer. Scholars such as Raszewska (2016) and Hokkanen (2017) mention that for church interpreters, their work is a calling (Raszewska, 2016: 23), or a service to God and the church (Hokannen, 2017: 207), and therefore it constitutes something more than a secular act of volunteering, that is, an act of gratitude for God's love and a "result of personalized gifts or skills that God has provided for each individual" (Hokkanen, 2017: 207). Furthermore, Peremota's (2017) study on the ideal church interpreter proves that the spirituality of the interpreter is an important factor also to the interpreting recipients.

The fact that the professional background in interpreting does not seem to be the main requirement in order to become a church interpreter, is one of the reasons why usually, the people who are church interpreters are not trained in the field (Raszewska, 2016). However, one may ask whether the work environment of church interpreting is as non-professional as often are the interpreters. The present study seeks to answer this question, focusing on the Polish context. Furthermore, this paper also aims to verify whether there are any differences as to how the interpreting is conducted in churches according to the Evangelical denomination they represent.

3. The analysis of simultaneous interpreting conducted in different Evangelical churches in Poland

3.1. Methods

In order to examine the setting of simultaneous interpreting in Evangelical churches in Poland, nine interpreters and one pastor were interviewed.

9 Source: 2nd International Conference on Non-Professional Interpreting and Translation: https://ikk.fb06.uni-mainz.de/tagungen/2nd-international-conference-on-non-professional-interpreting-and-translation-npit2/ (Accessed: 26 November 2021).

The churches were carefully selected to represent various denominations of Evangelical Christianity with the hope of answering the question of possible differences (and/or similarities) in how the interpreting is conducted depending on the denomination. In all, the participants represented ten different churches: five of Kościół Zielonoświątkowy w RP (the Pentecostal Church in Poland), three of Społeczność Chrześcijańska (Christian Fellowship), one of Kościół Boży w Chrystusie (Church of God in Christ[10]) and one of Kościół Chrześcijan Baptystów w RP (Baptist Union of Poland).

The churches are located in different parts of Poland, so that they can be compared based on geographical location as well. However, all of them are situated in big cities, with 8 out of 10 being the capitals of voivodships. The reason why smaller cities were excluded from the study is that in Poland, there are around 700 towns (not to mention villages) where there are no Evangelical churches;[11] so only big cities could be taken into consideration.

The interviews were conducted in Polish. Participants were asked seven questions about the general interpreting environment in their churches:

1) What languages do you interpret to?
2) How many interpreters are there in your church? Who are they (that is, are they professional interpreters, native speakers, etc.)?
3) Where is the interpreting conducted (does the church have an interpreting booth, or does the interpreter sit in a particular place in the church)?
4) What kind of interpreting equipment do you use? How many people can you serve with the equipment you have?
5) Which parts of the service are interpreted?
6) Does the interpreter have the opportunity to prepare themselves beforehand?
7) What is the demand for interpreting in your church (how many foreigners usually attend the church)?

Once the participants had been interviewed, one church had to be excluded from the study because the interpreting conducted therein proved to be consecutive and therefore inappropriate for further examination and comparison with other churches that focused on simultaneous interpreting.

10 While the translation of the name of this Polish denomination may be associated with the American Church of God in Christ denomination, the two should be considered separate.

11 Based on the data provided by 700miast church planting ministry: https://700miast.pl/ (Accessed: 26 November 2021).

3.2. Results

The Table 1 presents the summary of the answers provided in the interviews:

Table 1: The summary of the interview

Church	Q1	Q2	Q3	Q4	Q5	Q6
I	English (ENG), Russian (RU)	20	Booth	27	All (without songs)	Yes
II	ENG	10	Booth	60	All (without songs)	Yes
III	ENG	3	Booth	70	All (without songs)	Yes
IV	ENG	4	Back of the chapel	10	All (lyrics of the songs displayed)	Bible verses prepared
V	ENG	3	-	12	All (without songs)	No
VI	ENG	4	-	6	All (lyrics of the songs displayed)	Sometimes
VII	ENG	6	Technician's studio	10	All (without songs)	Bible verses prepared
VIII	RU	1	Next to technicians	50	All (without songs)	No
IX	RU	5	Booth	Stream only	All	Yes

The main languages that the service is interpreted to are English and Russian.[12] That is not a surprise, as a large number of foreigners in Poland do speak English, and the greatest numbers of foreigners living in are Ukrainians (over 244 000 as of 2021), with a large immigration wave noted after the Russian invasion of Ukraine in 2014, and Belarussians (over 28 000 as of 2021),[13] who have continued to come to Poland in large numbers after the presidential election in Belarus in 2020. Both of these groups are Russian-speaking. The last question in the interview was about the actual demand for interpreting in English and Russian.

12 Three churches also added that they are able to provide interpretation to other languages such as German or French if such a need is signalised in advance (i.e., it is not a regular practice).

13 Source: https://www.gov.pl/web/udsc/cudzoziemcy-w-polsce-po-2020-r (Accessed: 26 November 2021).

However, the answers to it are not presented in Table 1 as this question did not prove to be easily summarised. Every participant of the study responded that the exact number of foreigners attending their church is difficult to estimate as it is not constant and may change weekly. The highest number of English-speaking foreigners attending the church can be found in the Church number 4 and totals between ten and thirty, while the Church number 7 has the lowest number with only one English-speaking foreigner attending the church on a regular basis. Moreover, the number of foreigners who need interpreting to Russian is even vaguer, as in all three churches providing Russian interpreting, participants admitted that these foreigners quickly cease needing an interpreter because most of them learn Polish and think that participating in a church service without interpreting will help them learn faster, or that their Polish level is good enough to understand most of the service on their own.

The second major question concerned the interpreters. In number, they are most numerous in the Church number 1 and least numerous in the Church number 8, where only one person is responsible for interpreting. Furthermore, the Church number 2 is the only one that has a division between interpreters who handle consecutive (two people) and simultaneous (eight people) interpreting. Meanwhile, Figure 1 presents the background of the interpreters (either professional or personal) on the basis of which they were thought to be competent and chosen for the interpreting service:

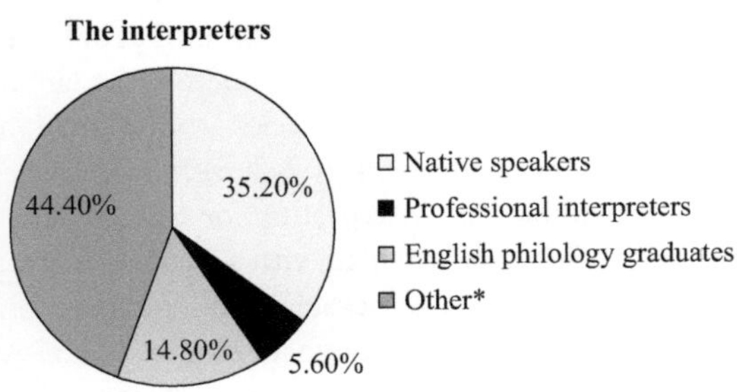

Figure 1: The professional or personal background of the interpreters considered important for choosing (or allowing) them to interpret in the church

The results show that the vast majority of interpreters are non-professionals. Out of 54[14] interpreters, only three are interpreters in their professional life. Eight

14 The overall number of interpreters was 56 (see: Table 1); however, the two people who only handle consecutive interpreting in the Church number 2 were excluded from further investigation as the focus of this paper is on simultaneous interpreting.

others are English philology graduates (14,8 %), while 19 people (35,2 %) are native speakers who have been living in Poland for many years and have learned Polish well enough to interpret. The largest group, called "other" (see: Figure 1) for the purpose of this study, consists of 24 people (44,4 %). These are people who either are married to native speakers, are graduates of philology (other than English or Russian), use English (or Russian) regularly in their professional life (e.g. in international corporations), or simply determine their foreign language level to be good enough to interpret the service. It should also be noted that no matter the language background of the interpreters, all of them are believers and interpret in their churches as volunteers.

In terms of work environment, interpreting booths are present in four out of the nine churches. In three others, the interpreters have a different, particular spot where they are seated, and in two of these, it is connected to the place where technicians are located. In two churches interpreters do not have a regular place to sit and may choose for themselves.

As for equipment provided for the foreigners in need of interpreting, the majority of the churches interviewed for this study (eight out of nine) use what is used in professional simultaneous interpreting, that is, sets consisting of pocket receivers and headphones. The number of these sets is sufficient to provide interpreting for every foreigner attending the church regularly (except for the Church number 4, where there are from ten to 30 English-speakers weekly and only ten sets), and in many cases, it even exceeds the usual need: for instance, in Church number 3 there are 70 sets, but the weekly number of English-speakers in need of interpreting is only six. This can be explained by the fact that Evangelical churches often host large groups of missionaries from abroad, and sometimes they also organise conferences attended by believers from other churches, so they should be prepared to provide interpreting for more people in these cases. In every church, the interpreter is provided with a wireless microphone. But the Church number 9 is an unusual case because the interpretation is held solely online, and the listeners can access it through an online stream. As became clear in the interview, this has caused some inconvenience because if a person wanted to attend the church in person and get the interpreting from the stream, the delay between what is being said live in the church and on the online stream would be bothersome. So as of the time of conducting this research, this church was working on a different way of providing interpreting.

It remains to examine the material that is subject to simultaneous interpreting in the interviewed churches. In all cases, not just the sermon, but the whole service is interpreted, with all its parts discussed briefly in Section 2 of this paper. Nevertheless, interpreting/translation of songs seems to be a problem for the majority of churches, as in six out of nine they are left in the source language, i.e., Polish. Only two churches display English translations of the lyrics of the songs being sung in real-time, along with the lyrics in Polish on a large screen for all believers to follow. In contrast, the Church number 9 approaches it differently, with the interpreter briefly summarising what the song is about. Moreover, the topic of what is interpreted is connected to whether the interpreters can prepare themselves before the service. One could say that interpreters may expect what is coming, because the parts of the service usually do not change from week to week. However, sermons are not the same every week. Therefore, in four churches interpreters are given the synopsis of the sermon in advance, which allows them to get familiar with the topic. In two more churches, the interpreters are handed Bible verses that will be used in the sermon, so that they do not have to browse through their Bibles in a hurry while interpreting, while in two other churches, the interpreters are left with no chance for prior preparation.

4. Discussion

In Section 2, interpreting done in churches was presented as an example of a non-professional practice. The study conducted for the purposes of this paper allows to elaborate on the exact details due to which church interpreting can be considered non-professional.

First, the study showed that not only are the people involved in church interpreting in the majority non-professional, but so too is the environment they work in. Most of the interviewed churches did not have an interpreting booth for the interpreter to work in without interruption in quiet conditions; in the majority of them, the interpreter was also left without any summary or synopsis of what will be said in the sermon. This seems to confirm the statement that church interpreters must be familiar with the teachings of the Bible as usually they must rely on their own knowledge, not glossaries prepared beforehand. However, prior communication between the preacher and the interpreter might prove to be useful and more fruitful, as Downie (2014) suggests.

Nevertheless, in terms of the work environment, it might seem surprising that booths were present at all, since only 5,6 % of the interpreters were professionals. It suggests that all of these non-professional interpreters had to learn how to work in and with a booth and adjust to these, to them unfamiliar, conditions. It may put into question whether, after some time, they should still be considered non-professionals, because they certainly become aware of professional working conditions and are specialised in a particular type of language, and as Raszewska (2016: 68) notes, "professionalism is associated with the proper, special training that helps to develop some additional skills to cope with the problems that one may encounter."

In only three churches were songs interpreted or translated. Despite the fact that many scholars agree that all parts of the Sunday service are important for the faith-growing experience (see: Section 2), it may appear that explaining songs to foreigners in the church is neglected. There may be several reasons why this is so, e.g., technical difficulties, such as the problem of displaying lyrics simultaneously in two languages when there is not enough space on the screen, and the interpreters not wanting to interrupt the music by explaining the meaning of the song (an experience Poles know all too well from watching musicals on television with voice-over translation). However, it is definitely a matter that should be improved in these churches so as to allow all the people present at the service to participate in the entire 'Praise and Worship' experience (Raszewska, 2016).

What is interesting is that there were no visible differences between the interpreting environment and the denomination a given church represented. All of the churches use the same equipment (with slight variations to the reception mode); there are also no significant differences in what is interpreted or who the interpreters are. Therefore, one can conclude that these denominations are similar to each other, at least in terms of such technicalities as interpreting, and can be further studied together.

Finally, the fact that the second largest group of interpreters (35,2 %) was that of native speakers might attest to the importance of missionaries in Evangelical churches, but also to the possibility that the number of foreigners who decide to stay in Poland, live here and learn the language, is growing. That said, it is difficult to estimate the scale of the need for interpreting in Evangelical churches. All the churches stated that they would provide interpreting even if a single person needing it attended; however, the situation is changing dynamically. Therefore the church seems to be a good place to observe the situation of foreigners in Poland: some are students who visit the church and go back to their respective countries after a few months, some are people who are sent to Poland for a multi-year work contract, while others have had to leave their country due to the political situation (e.g., Belarussians in the Church number 9). One can also remark on the language situation of these foreigners, as those who stay longer tend no longer to seek interpretation services because they want to try to understand Polish themselves.

The present study explored interpreting conditions in Evangelical churches in Poland. The author hopes that the results of the study will inspire and help church interpreters and people responsible for interpreting work environment in church settings (e.g. pastors, technicians) to improve. Furthermore, the author's hope is that thanks to this paper, the topic of church interpreting will become popularised among those who had not been familiar with it before. While several things have been discovered, there is still a lot to be done. As mentioned before (see: Section 2), the topic of NPIT is relatively recent in academia, and in that, church interpreting appears to be a niche, especially in Poland. Nonetheless, the reason behind the low academic interest in Polish Evangelical churches does not seem to be the lack of importance, but the fact that the general awareness even of the existence of Evangelical churches is low. A few questions to be answered in future studies may address the quality of interpreting and its results, the differences between church interpreting and interpreting in professional settings, and different types of interpreting beyond the simultaneous interpreting studied in this paper.

References

Coleman, L. (1980). 'The Language of "Born-Again" Christianity.' *Proceedings of the Sixth Annual Meeting of the Berkeley Linguistics Society* (133–42). Berkeley Linguistics Society.

Collins Online English Dictionary (n.d.). 'Evangelic.' https://www.collinsdictionary.com/dictionary/english/evangelic

Downie, J. (2014). 'Towards a Homiletic of Sermon Interpreting.' *Journal of the Evangelical Homiletics Society*, *14*(2), 62–69.

Erickson, M. J. (2001). *Christian Theology*. 2nd ed. Baker Books.

Ewangeliczna Polska (n.d.). *Czym jest Ewangeliczna Polska?* https://ewangeliczna.pl/czym-jest-ewangeliczna-polska/

Ewangelikalna Wyższa Szkoła Teologiczna (n.d.). *Ewangelikalizm*. https://ewst.pl/centrum-edukacyjne/ewangelikalizm/

Harris, B. (2009, July 13). *Essential definitions*. Unprofessional translation. https://unprofessionaltranslation.blogspot.com/2009/07/essential-definitions.html

Harris, B. (2010, November 12). *From Natural to Expert Translator, With Essential Definitions*. Unprofessional translation. https://unprofessionaltranslation.blogspot.com/2010/11/from-natural-to-expert-translator.html

Harris, B. (2012). *Unprofessional Translation: A Blog-Based Overview*. Keynote speech presented at The First International Conference on Non-Professional Interpreting and Translation, Forlì, May, 2012.

Hatim, B., & Mason, I. (1990). *Discourse and the Translator*. Longman.

Hokkanen, S. (2017). 'Simultaneous interpreting and religious experience. Volunteer interpreting in a Finnish Pentecostal church.' In R. Antonini, L.

Cirillo, L. Rossato, & I. Toressi (Eds.) *Non-professional Interpreting and Translation: State of the art and future of an emerging field of research* (195–212). John Benjamins.

Johannes Gutenberg Universität (n.d.). *2nd International Conference on Non-Professional Interpreting and Translation (NPIT2)*. https://ikk.fb06.uni-mainz.de/tagungen/2nd-international-conference-on-non-professional-interpreting-and-translation-npit2/

Melton, J. G. (2014, August 31). 'Pentecostalism.' *Encyclopedia Britannica*. https://www.britannica.com/topic/Pentecostalism

Owen, A. (2014). *One Among a Thousand. Interpreting in Christian Settings*. The Wakeman Trust-Kindle edition.

Peremota, I. (2015). *Pilot Survey on Church Interpreting in Evangelical Churches with Russian-language Services*. [Bachelor Paper]. The University College of Economics and Culture, Riga. https://www.academia.edu/21959209/Pilot_Survey_on_Church_Interpreting_in_Evangelical_Churches_with_Russian-language_Services.

Peremota, Irina (2017) *Church Interpreting in Evangelical Churches with Russian-Language Services*. [Master's thesis, University of Latvia, Riga].

Pérez-González, L., Susam-Saraeva, S. (2012). 'Non-professionals Translating and Interpreting.' *The Translato*r, *18*(2), 149–165.

Projekt zakładania Kościołów 700miast (2021, December 3). https://700miast.pl/

Pym, A. (2000). *Negotiating the Frontiers: Translators and Intercultures in Hispanic History,* St. Jerome.

Qian, H. (1994). 'Looking at Interpretation from a Communicative Perspective.' *Babel, 40*(4), 214–221.

Raszewska, A. (2016). *Non-Professional Consecutive Interpretation Used in Evangelical Churches*. [M.A. thesis Tischner European University, Kraków].

Robinson, B. A. (2009). *Divisions within Protestant Christianity*. Ontario Consultants on Religious Tolerance. http://www.religioustolerance.org/chr_divi3.htm

Siwak, K. (2021, October 28). *Cudzoziemcy w Polsce po 2020 r.* Urząd do spraw cudzoziemców. https://www.gov.pl/web/udsc/cudzoziemcy-w-polsce-po-2020-r

The Church of Jesus Christ of Latter-day Saints (n.d.). *Interpretation: Instructions for Priesthood Leaders*. https://www.churchofjesuschrist.org/bc/content/shared/content/english/pdf/callings/interpreter/interpretation-instructions-for-priesthood-leaders-eng.pdf

ŁÓDŹ STUDIES IN LANGUAGE

Edited by
Barbara Lewandowska-Tomaszczyk and Łukasz Bogucki

Vol. 1 Barbara Lewandowska-Tomaszczyk / Patrick James Melia (eds.): PALC'99: Practical Applications in Language Corpora. Papers from the International Conference at the University of Łódź, 15-18 April 1999. 2000.

Vol. 2 Lou Burnard / Tony McEnery (eds.): Rethinking Language Pedagogy from a Corpus Perspective. Papers from the Third International Conference on Teaching and Language Corpora. 2000.

Vol. 3 Barbara Lewandowska-Tomaszczyk / John Osborne / Frits Schulte: Foreign Language Teaching and Information and Communication Technology. 2001.

Vol. 4 Piotr Cap: Explorations in Political Discourse. Methodological and Critical Perspectives. 2002.

Vol. 5 Ewa Waniek-Klimczak / Patrick James Melia (eds.): Accents and Speech in Teaching English Phonetics and Phonology. EFL perspective. 2002.

Vol. 6 Barbara Lewandowska-Tomaszczyk / Kamila Turewicz (eds.): Cognitive Linguistics Today. 2002.

Vol. 7 Barbara Lewandowska-Tomaszczyk (ed.): PALC 2001: Practical Applications in Language Corpora. 2003.

Vol. 8 Corpus Linguistics by the Lune. A Festschrift for Geoffrey Leech. Edited by Andrew Wilson, Paul Rayson and Tony McEnery. 2003.

Vol. 9 Barbara Lewandowska-Tomaszczyk (ed.): Practical Applications in Language and Computers. PALC 2003. 2004.

Vol. 10 Imagery in Language. Festschrift in Honour of Professor Ronald W. Langacker. Edited by Barbara Lewandowska-Tomaszczyk and Alina Kwiatkowska. 2004.

Vol. 11 Seana Coulson / Barbara Lewandowska-Tomaszczyk (eds.): The Literal and Nonliteral in Language and Thought. 2005.

Vol. 12 Piotr Cap (ed.): Pragmatics Today. 2005.

Vol. 13 Jacek Waliński / Krzysztof Kredens / Stanisław Goźdź-Roszkowski (eds.): Corpora and ICT in Language Studies. PALC 2005. 2007.

Vol. 14 Krzysztof Kosecki (ed.): Perspectives on Metonymy. Proceedings of the International Conference "Perspectives on Metonymy", held in Łódź, Poland, May 6-7, 2005. 2007.

Vol. 15 Barbara Lewandowska-Tomaszczyk / Tomasz Płudowski / Dolores Valencia Tanno (eds.): The Media and International Communication. 2007.

Vol. 16 Krzysztof Kredens / Stanisław Goźdź-Roszkowski (eds.): Language and the Law: International Outlooks. 2007.

Vol. 17 Barbara Lewandowska-Tomaszczyk (ed.): Corpus Linguistics, Computer Tools, and Applications – State of the Art. PALC 2007. 2008.

Vol. 18 Barbara Lewandowska-Tomaszczyk / Katarzyna Dziwirek (eds.): Studies in Cognitive Corpus Linguistics. 2009.

Vol. 19 Barbara Lewandowska-Tomaszczyk / Marcel Thelen (eds.): Meaning in Translation. 2010.

Vol. 20 Łukasz Bogucki / Krzysztof Kredens (eds.): Perspectives on Audiovisual Translation. 2010.

Vol. 21 Piotr Stalmaszczyk (ed.): Turning Points in the Philosophy of Language and Linguistics. 2011.

Vol. 22 Stanisław Goźdź-Roszkowski: Patterns of Linguistic Variation in American Legal English. A Corpus-Based Study. 2011.

Vol. 23 Kamila Ciepiela (ed.): Identity through a Language Lens. 2011.

Vol. 24 Stanisław Goźdź-Roszkowski (ed.): Explorations across Languages and Corpora. PALC 2009. 2011.

Vol. 25 Krzysztof Kosecki / Janusz Badio (eds.): Cognitive Processes in Language. 2012.

Vol. 26 Alina Kwiatkowska (ed.): Texts and Minds. Papers in Cognitive Poetics and Rhetoric. 2012.

Vol. 27 Paul A. Wilson (ed.): Dynamicity in Emotion Concepts. 2012.

Vol. 28 Piotr Pęzik (ed.): Corpus Data across Languages and Disciplines. 2012.

Vol. 29 Mikołaj Deckert: Meaning in Subtitling. Toward a Contrastive Cognitive Semantic Model. 2013.

Vol. 30 Łukasz Bogucki: Areas and Methods of Audiovisual Translation Research. 3rd Revised Edition. 2019.

Vol. 31 Janusz Badio / Kamila Ciepiela (eds.): Language, Action, Interaction. 2013.

Vol. 32 Barbara Lewandowska-Tomaszczyk / Krzysztof Kosecki (eds.): Time and Temporality in Language and Human Experience. 2014.

Vol. 33 Iwona Witczak-Plisiecka (ed.): Cognitive and Pragmatic Aspects of Speech Actions. 2014.

Vol. 34 Małgorzata Anna Kamińska: A History of the *Concise Oxford Dictionary*. 2014.

Vol. 35 Łukasz Bogucki / Mikołaj Deckert (eds.): Accessing Audiovisual Translation. 2015.

Vol. 36 Joanna Jabłońska-Hood: A Conceptual Blending Theory of Humour. Selected British Comedy Productions in Focus. 2015.

Vol. 37 Krzysztof Kosecki / Janusz Badio (eds.): Empirical Methods in Language Studies. 2015.

Vol. 38 Katarzyna Stadnik: Chaucer's Choices. Through the looking-glass of medieval imagery. 2015.

Vol. 39 Paulina Pietrzak / Mikołaj Deckert (eds.): Constructing Translation Competence. 2015.

Vol. 40 Małgorzata Fabiszak / Karolina Krawczak / Katarzyna Rokoszewska (eds.): Categorization in Discourse and Grammar. 2016.

Vol. 41 Marcel Thelen / Gys-Walt van Egdom / Dirk Verbeeck / Łukasz Bogucki / Barbara Lewandowska-Tomaszczyk (eds.): Translation and Meaning. New Series, Vol. 1. 2016.

Vol. 42 Łukasz Bogucki / Barbara Lewandowska-Tomaszczyk / Marcel Thelen (eds.): Translation and Meaning. New Series, Vol. 2, Pt. 1. 2016.

Vol. 43 Łukasz Bogucki / Barbara Lewandowska-Tomaszczyk / Marcel Thelen (eds.): Translation and Meaning. New Series, Vol. 2, Pt. 2. 2016.

Vol. 44 Przemysław Łozowski / Katarzyna Stadnik (eds.): Visions and Revisions. Studies in Theoretical and Applied Linguistics. 2016.

Vol. 45 Marek Kuźniak / Bożena Rozwadowska / Michał Szawerna (eds.): From Motion to Emotion. Aspects of Physical and Cultural Embodiment in Language. 2016.

Vol. 46 Anna Rędzioch-Korkuz: Opera Surtitling as a Special Case of Audiovisual Translation. Towards a Semiotic and Translation Based Framework for Opera Surtitling. 2016.

Vol. 47 Mateusz Sajna: Video Game Translation and Cognitive Semantics. 2016.

Vol. 48 Kamila Ciepiela (ed.): Identity in Communicative Contexts. 2016.

Vol. 49 Mikołaj Nkollo: The Entrenchment of the 'unus alterum' Pattern. Four Essays on Latin and Old Romance Reciprocal Constructions. 2016.

Vol. 50 Paweł Rydzewski: Backness Distinction in Phonology. A Polish Perspective on the Phonemic Status of *y*. 2016.

Vol. 51 Piotr Pęzik / Jacek Tadeusz Waliński (eds.): Language, Corpora and Cognition. 2017.

Vol. 52 Janusz Badio (ed.): Events and Narratives in Language. 2016.

Vol. 53 Mikołaj Deckert (ed.): Audiovisual Translation – Research and Use. 2017. 2nd Expanded Edition 2019.

Vol. 54 Michał Szawerna: Metaphoricity of Conventionalized Diegetic Images in Comics. A Study in Multimodal Cognitive Linguistics. 2017.

Vol. 55 Artur Gałkowski / Monika Kopytowska (eds.): Current Perspectives in Semiotics. Signs, Signification, and Communication. 2018.

Vol. 56 Artur Gałkowski / Monika Kopytowska (eds.): Current Perspectives in Semiotics. Text, Genres, and Representations. 2018.

Vol. 57 Łukasz Bogucki / Piotr Cap (eds.): Exploration in Language and Linguistics. For Professor Piotr Stalmaszczyk on the Occasion of His 60th Birthday. 2018.

Vol. 58 Michał Kornacki: Computer-assisted Translation (CAT) Tools in the Translator Training Process. 2018.

Vol. 59 Marcin Walczyński / Piotr Czajka / Michał Szawerna (eds.): On the Verge between Language and Translation. 2018.

Vol. 60 Łukasz Bogucki / Paulina Pietrzak / Michał Kornacki (eds.): Understanding Translator Education. 2018.

Vol. 61 Marcin Walczy ski: Psycho-Affective Factors in Consecutive Interpreting. 2019.

Vol. 62 Kamila Ciepiela (ed.): Language, Identity and Community. 2019.

Vol. 63 Olga Łabendowicz: Audiovisual Translation in Poland. Changing Audiences. 2019.

Vol. 64 Enrique Bernárdez / Joanna Jabłońska-Hood / Katarzyna Stadnik (eds.): Cognition in context. New insights into language, culture and the mind. 2019.

Vol. 65 Montse Corrius / Eva Espasa / Patrick Zabalbeascoa (eds.): Translating Audiovisuals in a Kaleidoscope of Languages. 2019.

Vol. 66 Barbara Lewandowska-Tomaszczyk / Valeria Monello / Marco Venuti (eds.): Language, Heart, and Mind. Studies at the intersection of emotion and cognition. 2020.

Vol. 67 Marta Chodkiewicz: Understanding the Development of Translation Competence. 2020.

Vol. 68 Urszula Paradowska: Developing Information Competence in Translator-Training. 2021.

Vol. 69 Luca Valleriani: Upper-class English in Natural and Audiovisual Dialogue. 2021.

Vol. 70 Michał Kornacki and Gary Massey (eds.): Contextuality in Translation and Interpreting. Selected Papers from the Łódź-ZHAW Duo Colloquium on Translation and Meaning 2020–2021. 2022.

www.peterlang.com

www.ingramcontent.com/pod-product-compliance
Ingram Content Group UK Ltd.
Pitfield, Milton Keynes, MK11 3LW, UK
UKHW041825100926
8556IPUK00002B/34

9 783631 869215